OLUKEMI OGUNYEMI

Brown Girl in the Ring

Memoirs of a brown girl living in Scotland

Published by New Generation Publishing in 2021

First Edition

Paperback ISBN: 978-1-80031-066-7
Hardback ISBN: 978-1-80031-065-0
Ebook ISBN: 978-1-80031-064-3

www.newgeneration-publishing.com

New Generation Publishing

I dedicate this book to Auntie.

Not a day goes by without you in my thoughts. Thank you for your presence in my childhood, for teaching me how it feels to receive unconditional love and for showing understanding when I felt I had none. Your presence built a foundation inside me which I believe has helped keep me alive. Anyone who had the pleasure of knowing you, or even just meeting you, will know the presence I'm talking about.

You never met my children, but just like you taught me, you are very much part of them; as I am part of you. I never felt like I was part of my family - never accepted - but you accepted me and I accepted you.

I sometimes wonder how my life would have played out had my parents shown me that same acceptance - I believe I would be a very different person to the one I am today. But I am very grateful for their lack of understanding of my needs, because our times spent together and the life lessons you taught me in those times, would not have been so meaningful and influential.

So, if I had been given a choice - for things to have been different - I would have declined, as I would always choose you.

Thank you, Auntie, for showing me the way. My eternal love will be with you, always.

Contents

PART THREE

Introduction

My name is Olukemi Helen Adebowale Ferguson-Ogunyemi. I'm known as Kemi[1]. I am a 49-year-old, mixed-race, Scottish-Nigerian woman who has lived in Scotland for the last 40 years. I'm a body therapist - oh, and by the way, I'm dyslexic.

I want to ask: did you ever experience that feeling? You know, the one where you reach a tipping-point; a cliff-edge; the point of no return. That happened to me last year. I didn't see it coming; I couldn't have planned for it and it hit me like a train. It signalled a dramatic and completely unforeseen change in my life.

The events of early summer 2020 opened an old wound. Like most white people, I was not ready to talk about racism. However, *Black Lives Matter* changed all that.

The particular day that sent me 'over the edge' was of enormous significance to my family. It was the day of an event that, to us specifically, was a celebration of a long, hard, but very special journey. It wouldn't have been important to most people, even many black people would have had no interest, but to us it was huge.

As the weeks wore on and news of the peaceful protests was no longer being reported in the mainstream media, I got to the point of waking up every morning in tears of despair.

Why was no one saying anything about it anymore? Why had the news reports stopped? Why had none of my friends asked if I was okay? Why? Because they still couldn't hear.

I want to be clear about this: this is a choice. I believe we can all choose to be aware of our attitudes and beliefs. In addition, we can choose to be responsible for those attitudes and beliefs and learn from the mistakes our ancestors made. By doing this, we can end racism. However, choosing not to listen to this, is a conscious choice not to change, which makes a person a part of racism in our society.

I have a lot of friends and clients who hadn't realised just how big a 'pandemic' racism actually is – yes, that's how I would describe it: a pandemic that has been in our midst for centuries.

In the times when I have felt safe enough to share, or it has been public knowledge about my family's, or my experiences of racism, I have been deeply touched by people's display of genuine shock and empathy and their responses of: "What can I do to help as a white person?" This has been a new experience for me; to discover there are responsible, white people who want to try to do something about racism when they are aware of it, and how

---

[1] Pronounced: *Keh-me*.

important it is for me to be able to share my experiences, as this can help me heal. This gives me hope. I have learned how important it is for me to be heard and validated.

Sharing my experiences of racism has been very new for me, because as a child I didn't have a place of safety. I had parents who didn't understand how important it was to validate a child's experiences, especially a child of colour. I was raised by a white mother, who was an unconscious racist with a clear, unconscious, racial bias in favour of white people. As a child, this instilled in me that I was a lesser being than white people and that nobody cared; this was how most people in my life behaved. People who do not experience racism don't know how deeply embedded it is in our society. This is why I've decided to share my story. I believe awareness is the first step; once we are aware, we have the choice to change it.

We need to stop coming from a place of defence. If we are defensive, we won't hear each other - and we *must* hear one another. We need to listen and adjust our language so we can be heard. We live by the beliefs of our ancestors, not *our* beliefs, and I believe we now want to come from a clearer, more authentic place. It will be very uncomfortable, but I believe we can overcome that by starting the real, meaningful conversation. We need each other's voices. We need people of colour to share their experiences with white people, just as we need white people's voices to speak up for us; with us. Together we need to find the language we all understand.

My personal experience is in Scotland, but this is all through our society. Our laws on racism - on paper at least - are among some of the best in the world. However, the problem is lack of understanding and from my personal experience, the individuals who up-hold and enforce these laws are, at the very least, unconsciously racially biased; at worst, racist; and at best, politely 'colour-blind'.

I want to take a moment to explain the importance of awareness. Describing my experiences will bring more awareness to the choices you make. Until very recently I didn't know what white privilege meant. Until a couple of years ago I didn't even know that there was such a thing as unconscious, racial bias. These two things have been embedded in my life and I didn't even know it. I was unaware.

Most people who choose to be colour-blind are doing so thinking that it is a good thing. Colour-blindness is a consciously taken approach, but not necessarily one taken with negative intentions. Colour-blindness, (or 'colour evasiveness' as more accurately labelled by Subini Ancy Annamma, Associate Professor at the *Graduate School of Education, Stanford University*), is when a white person acknowledges you as an equal: "I don't think of you as black"; "I don't see you as being of colour"; or "I see us as all the same". Whilst this sounds a positive approach, it isn't. Even if the sentiment is sincere, there is an underlying ignorance. I am black. To choose not to see me this way is choosing to ignore my existence as a black woman.

That takes away my experience as a woman of colour in our society. Furthermore, choosing not to see my race insinuates that to acknowledge it would bring issues.[2]

I feel that we have all lived in a time of colour-blindness and this has been very damaging to people of colour. This blindness means that people who don't experience racism cannot see it. They witness it, but they can't see it. If they cannot see it, how can they understand it?

The foundations of our society are built on unconscious, racial bias and racism. If we could display society as a piece of tapestry, racism would be our core pattern. It affects every one of us, black and white. It is woven so intricately into our lives, we don't even realise it's there.

The exposure of the horrific and brutal murder of George Floyd brought everything into focus. It made the whole world see how people of colour are still being treated today. It has escalated the need to look at this in every part of our society. This has started to instil hope in me; awareness is one of the first steps. I can see this in parts of my own life, in the small glimpses of my experiences when I have felt safe enough to share.

I believe that change can occur. However, in order for change to occur, we have to start with awareness. Then, and only then, when we all know what we are looking at as a society, can we begin to change attitudes on racism.

One thing that the *Black Lives Matter* protests have taught me is that I still have a gaping wound that needs to heal. Over the years, I have been kidding myself that it had healed up long ago. I had, in fact, successfully put a big plaster over it and ignored it; but it wasn't really healed, merely scabbed over. The events of summer 2020 ripped off the scab and I started to bleed all over again. Now I need to do something about it. I know that I have the power within me to make a change and to help other people do the same by inviting them to come with me on this journey.

I've no axe to grind; no blame to apportion; the anger has gone. I still believe in human beings. Please join me in friendship and understanding. Let's do this together.

Some names in this book have been changed in order to protect the identities of those people.

---

[2] Source: information taken from an article by Subini Ancy Annamma in the journal Race, published on-line, 11th November, 2016.

Prologue

Saturday 27th June, 2020.

As I sat in bed having my first coffee of the morning, I sent Sola[3] a message:

Morning Solie, so excited for today!! Such a huge moment for Joy!! Remember to send pictures and videos! Remember the Covid rules! Have a happy day! Life is good! Love you, Mum. Xxx.

Hi Mum. So excited!! On my way to meet Andrew and then another couple of friends. Of course I'll send pics and vids and of course I'll be careful. Rules: be safe, do not remove my face mask and of course I'll leave before any 'craziness' starts!

As the day wore on my excitement grew. I received the pictures and videos from Sola. I was so proud of him, taking the opportunity to represent us all.

That night I sat down with my husband, filled with excitement and anticipation, to watch the *ITV News*. I was desperate to see the coverage of today's momentous, peaceful protest. I thought I was going to burst with pride. The iconic Big Ben 'bongs' at the beginning of the programme rang out with each headline story being announced.

Nothing. Absolutely nothing.

My heart sank, while desperation filled every cell of my body.

"I can't believe this. How can there be no reporting on the *ITV News* about something as big as the *Black Trans Lives Matter* protest?" I said upset and frustrated.

"Kem, try not to get upset, let's just watch. It's probably a smaller story without a headline."

Our hopes of coverage were being ever-deflated with each news story reported. By the end of the news - or rather lack of it - I was completely flattened.

# # #

Monday, 29th June, 2020.

I'm being driven by a feeling of despair. We are now over a month into the *Black Lives Matter* protests in the UK and nothing has changed. On

---

[3] Pronounced: *Shaw-lah*. This is a Nigerian name and with there being no letter 'h' in the Nigerian language, 's' sounds 'sh'.

Saturday, *Black Lives Matter* dedicated its protest to *Black Trans Lives Matter*; a fact that was not reported on the mainstream news anywhere. However, that event was an historic moment, not just for my family, but for every single black, transgender person. I was devastated. Somehow, it didn't matter. No one was listening. Not the politicians, the influencers, nor anyone else in authority. Why? Because most of them were white.

As I prayed for strength and guidance to help me deal with this great pain, the same answer returned, again and again: *write to everyone Kemi. Allow them to read your story in the safety and comfort of their own homes, so that they can hear your voice.*

I started to write.

Part one

London

The first seven years of my life were spent in London and I loved it there. I was blissfully unaware that I had been born into a racist world. I lived in a multi-cultural society with lots of black and white people which mirrored my home life. My mum is blue-eyed and blonde-haired; the palest of white women you could ever imagine. My dad is Nigerian. He is so black you would call him blue-black.

All of my mum's family lived in Scotland and I adored going there for holidays to visit my grandparents and cousins. I would even sometimes go to the local school with my cousins, Tracey and Lee, when I went to visit. I had such a good time back then.

My mum had some real, set ideas. When pregnant with me, she travelled to Scotland from London two weeks before her due date, so that I was born Scottish and not English. No way was I going to be English as well as mixed-race! In my experience a lot of Scottish people feel this way. I was also brought up as a Catholic, which made life very confusing - what with being half-Nigerian, with a voodoo-practising, medicine-woman grandmother! I spent a lot of time in Nigeria when I was younger, so I was fed very well from both cultures.

We lived in a place called Thamesmead, which at the time was a new, up-and-coming development. I went to a Catholic school, St. John Fisher, run by nuns. This was the happiest time of my life as a child.

One of my most memorable times there was in 1979. My teenage uncles, Bruce and Simon - my mum's younger brothers - came down from Scotland with my grandparents to stay with us. One Friday evening we went on the Number 79 bus to see the film *Grease* at the cinema. I had never experienced anything like that before in my life! I was mesmerised. I remember going back to school and playing *Grease* with my friends - even the nuns joined in, singing along and shaking their hips to the dance routines of the movie.

Even at this young age of my life, I had a deep faith in God. I was nurtured gently in my younger years by the mystical stories from both of my cultures. My belief in God, as a child, always made me feel safe and protected. Although I was at a school run entirely by priests and nuns, it never felt anything other than wonderful. I even wanted to be a nun!

There was a lot in my family life that was, let's say, not exactly a healthy environment for a child; in fact, it was decidedly unhealthy for a young, impressionable person. Luckily for me, my mum's younger sister, Auntie Joan, had relocated to London, as she couldn't bear to remain so far away from us in Scotland. She was my favourite auntie and also my godmother. Mum and Dad's marriage wasn't good and Auntie Joan made up for a lot that was wrong in my life at that time.

My brother, Tunde[4] lived with us. He was four years older than me and had a different mother. In addition, I had a younger brother, Tayo[5], who was born in 1976, in London.

Around this time Tunde disappeared out of my life. Whenever I asked where Tunde had gone, I was told he was on holiday in Nigeria. The truth was that he had been sent to live with an aunt and uncle in Nigeria, as my mum didn't want to look after him.

My dad's business meant he was away for varying periods of time. He would frequently be here and then gone again, back and forth to Nigeria. I had no concept of time back then; it was just normal that he was either at home, or away working. So, I don't remember the exact date when he actually left us; somewhere around 1977-78.

I was beginning to realise that my dad had not been home for longer than normal when my mum started bringing boyfriends to the house. With these other gentlemen in my house, I began to question her:

"Where is my dad and when is he coming home?"

"On holiday in Nigeria with Tunde," was the only reply I ever received.

#

In late 1979, we moved to Scotland. My grandparents and two of my Scottish uncles came down to London to help us move. I adored these people and got to travel up to Scotland with them in the lorry that carried our furniture – but not without a fight. I did not want to go on the train with my mother, brother and gran. I remembered previous train trips with my mum. I must have been five or six years old when she made me walk through the entire train, by myself, to heat up my baby brother's bottle. I remembered the feeling of being too weak to open the doors and how small I felt next to all the strangers. It was a very scary experience that I knew she would make me repeat.

"You can't possibly let her travel up to Scotland in that lorry. There's not even anywhere for her to sit, Daisy!" my gran said defiantly to my mum.

"Mum just leave it," my mum requested, in a familiar tone.

I recognised this tone from whenever she was trying to pass me onto my grandparents so that she didn't have to put up with me.

"She'll be fine."

"But Gran, I want to go," I added. "I want to be with Grandad!"

"Kemi, do you know how long it will take in a lorry? They will be smoking and smelly. Little girls don't do things like this," my gran explained, hoping the content of her list would be enough to persuade me not to go.

---

[4] Pronounced: *Toon-day*.
[5] Pronounced: *Tie-oh*.

"Gran, please, please, please," I replied with my biggest smile, hoping to counteract her list.

"She's coming and that's the end of it," my grandad concluded.

He had spoken, so that was that. I was going!

My gran was right. I can still recall the smell inside that tiny, cramped cabin. A thick, hot smog of fags mixed in with the smell of men; sweat and 'pumps', as my gran would teach me - the 'ladies' way' of saying 'farts'.

I remember observing that Scottish people used different words to those I was familiar with in London. Slang words, or even just simple words said in the Scottish accent really tickled me. I would love to practice these words, such as 'aye' for 'yes', 'naw' meaning 'no' and my grandad's favourite, 'airse' meaning 'arse'. And I loved the word 'fart'. I would playfully drop these words into conversation with my gran for the sheer pleasure of her reaction, which was always a lesson in the 'ladies' way' of speaking.

"Gran, you're not going to believe this," I announced as I arrived in Scotland in the lorry, "but men fart all the time!"

I delighted in my use of the word 'fart' and relished the emphasis in my cheeky delivery. In truth I had been dying to share this intelligence with my gran. I had always been taught that a lady didn't 'pump' in public. I didn't even get to ask her why it was okay for men to behave like this in public before she interrupted:

"Who told you that word?" she said, switching swiftly into interrogation mode. "Were they saying it on that lorry?

Bluey . . . ?"

My grandad was known as Bluey. I'd never thought before to ask why, but I'm sure it must have been because of his 'colourful' language.

"Kemi, young ladies don't use that word. We use the word 'pump'!"

Looking back at that whole episode, I can vividly remember falling asleep in the lorry, lying across my two uncles' laps, thinking that my mum looked happier with my decision to travel in the lorry. She had been glad to get rid of me. I had been glad to go, despite the smell and smog. It was still better than being with her. I was just so happy to be going to Scotland. It had always seemed a very welcoming place and I was excited about living there. I had no idea what lay ahead of me.

Scotland

I remember my first few weeks in Scotland. My grandad was so happy to have us. He would sing *Boney M's, Brown Girl in the Ring* to me. This song originates from an old Caribbean nursery rhyme written to give confidence to little brown girls. A dance is performed to the song, with a circle of girls forming a ring around a dancing girl, copying her dance moves: "Show me your motion." The girl in the centre, the 'sugar', then swaps places with a girl from the ring, the 'plum', and the song repeats. This song and dance is an expression of freedom within your body and your inner-self and breeds confidence. My grandad would constantly sing it to me, even inserting my name.

"Kemi's my brown girl in the ring, tra la la la la!"

This was my cue to dance for him and we would have so much fun in those early days of arriving in Scotland. It only took a couple of weeks of this before I would recoil in fear at the sound of those lyrics.

We lived with my grandparents and two of their teenage sons, my uncles Bruce and Simon, for some time until we got our own house. This was in a small, rural village called Caldercruix, halfway between Glasgow and Edinburgh. We were the first mixed-race family to live there and I don't think there has been one since! At this time, there were next to no black or mixed-race people in the suburbs of Scotland and very few in the city. And here I was, with my little brother and our white mum. It took very little time before I was taught that I was black and beneath white people. Being mixed-race was hard enough for the people of the village to accept, but I also had a very strong English accent. It wouldn't be long before I would be teaching myself to speak in a Scottish accent. I couldn't do anything about looking like everyone else, but I could try to sound like them.

As my Uncle Simon and I entered the convenience store, I remember feeling very excited. I had a whole ten pence to spend on myself! *What will I buy?* The possibilities were endless. *Fizzy cola bottles? Strawberry laces? No, strawberry bonbons . . . definitely strawberry bonbons!*

"Uncle Simon, do they sell strawberry bonbons here?" my eager, English, questioning voice rang out across the store.

"I want strawberry bonbons. I'm going to get bonbons from the sweet shop next door if they don't," I continued excitedly as my taste buds tingled in anticipation.

"Wee man! Oi, wee man!" the shop owner barked as he approached us from out of nowhere and addressed my uncle.

I remember feeling scared and nervous. Butterflies tumbled around in my stomach. I was not used to an adult, a grown man no less, speaking in this tone.

"You can't have that in here."

"What?" Uncle Simon replied looking confused.

"That! Her! You!" the shop owner animated, pointing towards me.

His fixed stare was filled with disgust. He walked closer to me, all the time looking right at me, right into my eyes. My legs felt like they were made of jelly.

"You! You need to wait outside," he commanded.

I could feel my eyes welling up as I turned and looked at my uncle for clarity on what was happening and for protective reassurance. With fear and shock on his face he motioned with a nod of his head, directing me to wait outside.

I remember my overwhelming confusion. I was racking my brains, trying to understand what I had done wrong. Shame filled my eight-year-old body. This was the beginning of me coming to realise that my only crime was my brown existence; that's what I had done wrong.

When my uncle came out of the shop, he was so angry that he hit me immediately upon sight.

"You're so embarrassing," he uttered. "I'm never taking you anywhere ever again."

I couldn't speak. I was so confused. He had always shown great love towards me whenever he visited me in London. I was drowning in feelings of guilt and shame and felt unbearably dirty.

As I became older, I would slowly come to understand how much my white family had been affected by the racism that was directed at me and my brother. I now have total understanding of how hard it would have been for a white teenager trying to survive in a racist society and not be condemned for his black relations. I now understand he had to turn on me publicly for his own preservation.

When we got home to my gran's, Uncle Simon told everyone what had happened with the shopkeeper. Bang! I jumped as my grandad's fist thumped the table. With great sadness on his face, he stood up and left the room without saying a single word. Despite his absence, the same sadness remained in the room, only now it featured on my gran's silent face.

My mum was extremely angry and grabbed me by the upper arms: "You have to behave! Do you hear me?"

I could hear her, but the mixture of shock, shame, guilt, fear and confusion made it impossible for me to reply. I remember thinking I was going to choke on all those feelings building up behind my throat.

"Do you hear me?" she shouted again.

Now I couldn't even breathe, let alone speak. I felt as if my entire body was filling with warm tears.

"We have to fit in here," she continued. "I don't fucking believe this! What did she do?" she screamed at my uncle.

Silence filled the room. As she let go of my tiny arms, I watched her indented handprints slowly fade away.

I never did get my strawberry bonbons.

Looking back, I can see that it must have been hell for my mum; having to return to the village where she had achieved so much before out-growing it and moving to the 'big city' of London with her exotic husband, completely unaware of the racism she would be subjected to coming back. Now she would be punished, through her children, for marrying outside of her race.

When I think about how it was for my mum having little brown children in London, it didn't seem to be a problem. We were her little accessories that she loved to show off. I was even modelling at four years old! She liked being different and having the prettiest children. Unfortunately, she didn't know just how racist Scotland was; nor her family; nor herself.

I remember being terribly upset, not to mention very badly affected, by the absence of my dad and brother and being continuously told they were on holiday. At school, it was just as bad. I remember being that little girl who had lost her dad and along with that, the link to explain her appearance. The only person of colour in her family had disappeared and the only comfort she got, from all the adults around her, was to learn from them to stop talking about it. So, she did just that, and in doing so, she internalised her abandonment.

My first year of school in Scotland was a quick, steep learning curve to realising that I was not the same as white people - not a full human being. The 'good Catholic' people of the village would not let their children play with me. They taught them that I was dirty and smelly and that my dad ate people!

I remember the first time a man spat on me. After doing so he instructed his son to go and hit 'it' to see if 'it' cried. I did. I remember being so scared that the boy wouldn't stop, so I just ran. I have been running ever since. Everything that ever happened to me had a theme. A theme that was being downloaded and installed: that I was not as good as white people.

In my first year existing in Scotland, I was to make my First Communion. This was a very big deal. Tracey was also making her First Communion and gran was making the white dresses. My Scottish gran was an amazing dressmaker, which made me, my cousins Tracey and Lee, and my brother, Tayo, the best dressed children in the village. She would make beautiful clothes for us all, hand-crafted from the richest of materials. I had to be fitted many times and I loved it!

I stood like a real-life mannequin on her special stool next to her *Singer* sewing machine, tucked away behind the sofa in her living room - in her dressmaking 'fitting area' - wearing a paper pattern.

I loved her fitting area. Her state of the art, top of the range sewing machine was just so mesmerising. It sat on its own magical table and when you pressed a button, it would disappear, leaving you with just a table and no machine in sight. Ta dah! The area felt like a den; it was filled with an array of fantastic offcuts of materials, all different colours and textures.

I was not allowed to enter her 'fitting area' without her being present. Nobody was. However, unknown to her, whenever she was out, my grandad would let me play there with my *Cindy* dolls, using the offcuts as their clothes. It was a comforting, snug-of-a-place, securely tucked away out of sight and all enclosed.

"Kemi, pull your bumbum in. Stand up straight," my gran gently instructed, with concentration etched across her face.

My grandad laughed from somewhere behind the other side of the sofa.

"Don't be ridiculous Nelly, how can she pull her bumbum in? She's got a brown girl's bumbum!"

This was an interesting conversation to witness, one filled with love and playfulness. I remember innocently pondering how brown girls' bumbums could be different from white girls' bumbums.

"Oh Bluey, just be quiet. I'm only thinking out loud," my gran quipped whilst extending the measuring tape and taking notes.

"What do you mean? You're only making a frock, Nelly!" my grandad's perky voice boomed.

"No Bluey, I need to cut this dress so that it looks right. Her wee African bum sticks out so much it makes her waist lower at the front," my gran said defiantly having taken his bait, trying to both explain and justify her thoughts and methods.

"Well she's the luckiest girl in the world to have a gran like you who can tailor-make all her beautiful dresses then, isn't she," my grandad concluded, raising his head over the sofa to share a wink with me.

My gran just continued to pin the beautiful white silk to her adjusted pattern without as much as making eye contact with him. I couldn't hear the muttered response under her breath, as I was still giggling from my grandad's teasing.

# # #

Catholicism to me, at eight-years-old, was becoming more serious. The responsibility of my First Confession and First Communion weighed heavy on my heart. I loved God. I had always been encouraged to talk to God. I had often spoken to Him for reassurance, whenever I felt sad or worried.

However, with my First Confession looming, I was being told that I now answered to God.

My biggest stress came from the confessional prayer. In performing the prayer, I was basically making a promise to God that I would never sin again. However, I was constantly being taught by Catholicism that I would always sin; we are all sinners. In my mind, I was torn; how could I possibly go in and confess my sins to God and then lie by saying I would never sin again? A lie was a lie. I knew the difference between right and wrong. I just couldn't get my head round this. So, in my looking for understanding, I went to speak to the priest. He was someone I had felt safe with. He had always been open to my conversations and questions that I needed to be answered. Then, at the point when I most needed reassurance, his door was closed to me. I could not visit him anymore and my gran was the one to 'educate' me as to why.

"Kemi come into the kitchen," she summoned as I entered the house.

"Coming," I replied making my way through, all the while racking my brains as to what I could possibly be in trouble for this time.

"Yes, Gran?" I enquired in as innocent a tone as I could muster.

"What have you been saying to the priest?" she bluntly questioned. She wasn't stern; just clear.

"What? About confession?" I responded, with my tone now switching to a rather unconvincing clueless.

"Yes, you know fine what I am talking about," my gran surmised, seeing straight through my intended ignorance.

"But Gran, I don't understand. I don't want to be saying that part of the prayer. I don't want to lie."

"Oh, you will be saying that prayer young lady," she concluded with conviction.

"But Gran . . . ," I began.

"Kemi," she interrupted, with a calmness that told me what she was about to say was to be heard and adhered to, "good Catholic girls do not ask these sorts of questions. You're thinking too much about it. Anyway, you will not be going back to visit with the priest. Do you understand?"

"Yes, Gran," I reluctantly conceded with a defeated tone.

By the end of our conversation, reality began to sink in. I had lost my holy friend.

Nevertheless, I continued to spend a lot of my time in the woods of the chapel grounds as it was peaceful and I felt safe. Lee, his friends and I would frequently play in the ruins of the church grounds. There, we would get chalk from abandoned offcuts of plaster board and once, even tried to smoke a rolled-up newspaper!

# # #

16

My Uncle Simon used to babysit us when my mum had to work at night. He used to beat me in front of his friends to prove he didn't like me. When I told my mum, she would beat me too, saying I deserved it and this behaviour was making her life harder and I should appreciate that she had let me be part of her family.

My grandparents never showed that I was any different and tried to get Mum to see that she couldn't treat me so harshly, but I guess she was in so much pain herself she couldn't see what was happening to me. She didn't have any experience of racism. I remember believing that maybe she didn't know I was black and dirty. So maybe as long as I didn't tell her everything that went on, she wouldn't find out and I would be safe. However, she did know and experienced a lot of pain herself, which meant I became a problem for her.

# # #

I spent a lot of time with my two cousins, Tracey and Lee. They were more like siblings to me. Tracey was six months older than me and her brother, Lee, six months my junior. However, Tracey hated me. She didn't want to be around me. She would frequently beat me up and call me racist names to remain socially accepted. She would tell me she wished I had never come to Scotland and that her life was bad because of me. Lee was much more accepting - I was even allowed to play with him *and* his friends . . . sometimes. He wouldn't let anyone call me names and would beat up anybody who tried, no matter how big they were. Most of my friendships were found with the boys. They seemed to be more accepting of me and if I could pass their scary dares, then I could play.

I did have a special friend called Archie that I made after we moved into our own house in the village. He had firecracker, red hair and freckles and there was something special about him too. He was an outcast. Looking back, I'm not quite sure whether or not there was something wrong with him. He always seemed like a fragile child. I would later find out that he died after I left the village, aged only 14. He was my first true best friend. Together, we had many adventures in all the places we were not allowed.

# # #

Auntie Joan was still a prominent figure in my life during this time. She would later tell me that she knew I was a good girl, but that I would always be blamed if anything bad ever happened. She told me I had to learn how to protect myself, to always think before I spoke and to stop talking so openly, as anything I said would be used against me. So, I did.

17

My magic white dress

My First Communion was such a big day for me. For two weeks I had the unbearable experience of being able to see my dress hanging on the coat stand in the fitting area, without being allowed to touch it. Its cellophane surround acted as a poorly designed transparent wrapping paper, teasing me with: *look, but don't touch!* Every day, for two weeks, I had longingly stared at it tormenting me. Finally, the day came when I was going to be able to wear it.

I still remember how soft the embossed silk felt against my skin. It had a beautiful cuffed-neck, with a single row of two-pearl buttons which mirrored the matching pearl arrangement at the short-cuffed sleeves. This handmade, tailored dress was made with so much love and attention to detail, just for me.

"Daisy, she will not be having a netted underskirt. It's the middle of June! Mass could last two hours . . . do you know how uncomfortable and itchy that would be for her to sit through? A good dressmaker can make the skirt puff naturally without the need for an underskirt!"

"You tell her Nelly!" my grandad chuckled.

And she had been right. It was cut beautifully for my small, African frame, with the skirt of the dress subtly kicking out with no need for an underskirt. I remember my gran telling my mum this part of the dress was her proudest feature. By the time I'd put on my white tights, finished off with a pair of white sandals with a little block heal, I felt like a real-life princess!

Auntie Joan came up from London and I was so happy to see her. She brought with her two nine-carat gold necklaces with bamboo crucifix pendants for Tracey and me. I felt so special and complete when she placed it around my neck after my gran had put on my veil.

When we were just about to leave the house to go to chapel, Tracey and I were outside at the front step waiting for the adults to come out, when my gran stepped out of the door holding two velvet capes - one royal blue and one emerald green - with long flowing velvet tiers.

"Surprise girls! Look at these beautiful capes for my beautiful girls!" she announced.

As I watched her tie the royal blue one around Tracey's shoulders I began bouncing with excitement! The cape felt weighty on my shoulders. Not heavy, more reassuring, as if I had been shrouded in comfort and love. The silk lining was soft and gentle against the bare skin of my arms, soothingly caressing me. I just loved it. Tracey was delighted we had different colours. She hated anything that made us the same and always showed distain anytime our mothers or gran made us matching colour clothes. I had always felt safer, more acceptable to the white world wearing matching clothes with my white cousin. However, today, for the first time, I was delighted with the different coloured cape. I already had my white dress, so I was just the same as all the other white girls anyway.

When we were ready, Tracey, Lee and I made our way to the chapel with both of our mums and our grandparents. We had to meet with the rest of the children making their First Communions in preparation for our 'parade of twos' into the chapel to take up our positions in the front seats. Before we arrived, my grandad whispered to me: "Remember and hold your head up high, Kemi." This was something my grandparents had tried to instil in me and my brother. Hold your head high. Look out to the world with pride. Even if you didn't feel that way, it was important to present yourself as if you did.

I had been nervous and full of anxiety leading up to this part of the day. I was dreading having to walk through the chapel in front of all the other attendees, some of whom had already shown racism and discrimination towards me. However, now, in my empowering dress, I remember I felt better about it. Braver. Plus, the 'good Catholics' were always 'nicer' on a chapel day! I continued to feel this way, emitting confidence and happiness, until half-way down the aisle where I saw the man who'd spat on me. The flutters returned in the pit of my stomach. However, by the time I took my seat and laid my tiny hands on my lap, the soft touch and warmth of the embossed silk instantly started to soothe my nasty memory of the man. I truly had a magical dress.

After the service finished and after what felt like hour after hour of photographs by the professional photographer, we finally made our way to Tracey and Lee's house for the big celebration. Here, Tracey and I were showered with gifts, cards, Rosary Beads and money - boy did we make some money!

When it was time for the two of us to go and change out of our outfits, I tried to argue my case, but was quickly told that I especially out of the two of us, would not be keeping it on. Reluctantly conceding and with the aid of my Auntie Maxine, I got changed out of my dress of invincibility.

I wore my dress for the second time to Sunday Mass the following morning, before watching my gran pack it away that afternoon.

"When will I get to wear it again, Gran?"

"Only on special occasions," she replied.

"But that's not until Christmas, seeing as my birthday's passed already!" I argued in vain as she banished my dress to the cupboard, before closing the door.

# # #

During the summer holidays there was to be a children's disco held in the local village community centre. This would be the third time I'd get to wear my white Communion dress - minus the veil - and I'd also get to wear my special underwear from *Marks & Spencer*: a white cotton vest with small laced detail at the neck and pants with a small lace waistband. They were both part of a three-pack set. I was also allowed to wear my white, deep laced frill, cotton ankle socks. As I lay in bed the night before the disco, I remember feeling like it was Christmas Eve. All my best clothes, that were to be worn the next day, were laid out on the chest at the foot of my bed. My socks and the last pair of the three-pack *M&S* pants and vest were all neatly arranged. My dress, which I could see from my bed, was hanging up on the outside of my cupboard door, being aired. I remembered, as I fell asleep, how the dress had made me feel clean and fresh. I was desperate to put that dress on again to feel its magic once more.

I awoke to a beautiful morning and the first thing I saw when I opened my eyes was my dress. Its intoxicating, healing presence had begun its charm at first sight. My excitement had already started to build and I wasn't even out of bed yet! Before the disco however, and more importantly, before I could wear my dress, I had to go to dance class, well two classes actually, lasting three hours in total. When I got home, I would still have to have a bath, as my gran insisted that I always bathed after dancing. I didn't really see why I had to have one - I'd already had one the night before! Eventually, when it was time to get ready for the disco, I remember taking my time getting dressed and going into my gran's room to look at myself in her full-length mirror. As I stroked down the front of my dress, I remembered the familiar feelings of cleanliness, purity, contentment and happiness.

I left my gran's house for the disco early that Saturday evening. I skipped up the hill with eagerness and through an area leading to the back of the shops, where some houses overlooked. It was a very short distance to the community centre and I would be there before I knew it. I was already predicting the songs that would be played and the dances that I could do in my magical dress when, out of nowhere - *whack* - I was hit on the side of my head and taken by two men, one young and one older, to be raped.

It's all quite blurry. I can just see their faces laughing and the older man instructing the younger man on what to do to me. I was in and out of consciousness. I don't remember the journey, but I can remember arriving back home at my gran's house with my beautiful white dress destroyed, covered in a combination of dirt and cow shit. One of the sleeves was ripped and only one of the pearl buttons remained. The pearl buttons were lost from the neckline, part of the zip was ripped at the seam and the lace was torn from the waist band of my pants. What a sight I must have been. Can you imagine a child in this state, walking into your house? I must have had visible, physical injuries too, yet, they were only added to by my mother's rage for having destroyed my dress. She beat me that night and sent me straight to bed. How could my mother - or any decent mother for that matter - when faced with the sight of a young girl in ripped clothing complaining of pain and confused at not knowing how she ended up in the state she was in, not investigate any further? It still sends chills up and down my spine that my mum didn't once question how my pants managed to get ruined. Only my dress. I truly believe that my mum, amongst others, knew what had happened to me that day, but it was not important, because I was not white.

I developed a terror after the attack - a deep fear that a white man in a white coat was coming to get me. In school, we used to watch an educational TV programme; I can't remember what the show was called but it had a character called *Wordy*, and in this programme, there was a 12-minute, continuing drama within each episode. This drama had an alien from outer space - a white man wearing a white coat with white powder all over his skin. As I had blocked out what had happened to me, my fear went onto the character from the TV programme causing me not to sleep at night. I totally believed the white, alien-man in his white coat was going to come and kill me. In the end, my mum and grandad had to go to the school to insist that I didn't watch it anymore.

Years later it transpired that the older man who raped me was the local baker; he was jailed for being a paedophile.

I was left with a phobia about anything to do with baking. It even got to the point that my gran, who loved to bake, wouldn't do so if I was in the house, because it caused me so much distress and upset. I remember when my gran broke her arm, the dry plaster of her cast reminded me of dry dough, so she would have to eat her dinner in the living room because I couldn't eat or function around it. I later understood that this was because of the rape.

Still to this day I cannot eat anything that's been made with dough. My children were not allowed to play with plasticine or *Play-Doh,* and I've been unable to bake with them throughout their childhoods. My husband had to take on that responsibility, as long as I wasn't in the house. That still remains the rule.

I will write no more about this year of my life, except to say that that was not the last time I was sexually violated at the tender age of eight years old.

I just want to be white

I learned very quickly to adapt to my new life. By the time we had our own house I would often sleep over at my Uncle John and Auntie Maxine's house - Tracey and Lee's parents - as my mum didn't trust her boyfriend around me when she wasn't there. We, as a family, spent a lot of time with them, if not all of our time, along with me being there every weekend. They were our extended family and made up for Tayo and I not having our dad. We went on holidays together, swimming, Christmases, birthdays and on a Saturday, Uncle John would drive me and Tracey to dance classes and anywhere else we had to be. He treated Tayo and me like his own children and he and my grandad were my father figures at that time. My auntie and uncle loved me - even if their daughter didn't. Tracey wouldn't even let me use her hairbrush, as my afro hair would "give her germs and smelled". She would also refuse to share her room with me so I would sleep in Lee's room. It was still better than being at home.

At school, if anything ever happened in the class, it was always my fault. So, I became quieter in class, like my Auntie Joan had advised. Sadly, I've had to pass this lesson onto my children. It still causes me pain to think about it.

Unfortunately, this is how unconscious, racial bias works. It is a part of society's historic tapestry that is still woven so deep, as are its effects. If an incident occurs in any kind of community, no matter how trivial or severe, where the majority of people are white, in both my experience and my children's experiences, the unconscious, racial bias favours whites over people of colour. Every time. Owing to my children's experiences, I have had to sit down with each of them and explain to them why this happens. I have watched all of my children struggle, trying to accept this fact, whilst feeling completely powerless to be able to do anything to change this. All I can do is try to help them accept and prepare for the times when this happens.

Despite being quiet at school, there was one thing I was amazing at: sports. I could beat anyone at running and as for netball, well what can I say? I was a star! Uncle Simon thought it was great and would get the other children from the village to race me around the block. He always seemed proud of me. In that moment, I had his kindness and I actually enjoyed racing and winning and making him proud. I remember the whole village would turn out for the school's sports day; it was a big event in the village, like a gala. There, they would see me run and win. This was a time when I could shine and succeed and have validation. When one of the parents complained that I was turning into a star, the teacher told her not to worry as, "that was all I was good for".

Looking back, my time with sports became obsessive. I remember when

I was ten years old, I had given myself a very bad ankle sprain – three weeks before sports day. I ended up on crutches. I can still remember the pain and not being able to walk. I had done it trying to do a scissor-kick, high-jump over a fence. I can still remember hearing the crunch.

My grandparents took me to the hospital to have an X-ray as my mum was working - and thankfully it wasn't broken. Sitting in the cubicle, having the tight bandage and support put on my leg and ankle, through tears I said to my grandad:

"What about sports day?"

"Don't think about that just now Kemi, you've just had a bad fall," my grandad said, trying to deflect my attention.

"But Grandad, it needs to be better for sports day," I explained with desperation in my voice.

"Well young lady, you're not going to be running in any sports day anytime soon," the nurse informed me, in a matter-of-fact tone.

Overwhelming panic filled my tiny body as I reached out to God in my thoughts. It has to be better; I can't miss this day. It's the only day when people are happy with me. God. Please, I'll do anything. Please, please, please!

As we drove home in my grandad's car, I could hear my gran talking to my grandad.

"Well Bluey, I think it's good that she's going to miss sports day."

"What do you mean Nelly? She needs sports day. That's her day." He knew how important this day was to me for my acceptance.

"Joe, look at her. This isn't right. This is making her ill," my gran said, looking over her shoulder from the front seat of the car.

Their voices seemed to tail off and I could no longer hear them over my inconsolable sobbing.

The next day I went to school on my crutches. My mum hadn't wanted me to go, but I'd denied the pain and nausea to her, and myself, so I could go to school. I was already planting the seed that I was perfectly fine. I was not running the risk of being told: "You're not fit enough for school, so you're not fit enough for sports day".

By the time I arrived at school I was late. As I got to the last step before entering the school doors, I met Tracey on her way out.

"Kemi, where have you been? I waited for you, but the bell went, so I've been waiting in the cloakroom for you. Kemi, please don't cry."

As she took my bag and led me into the cloakroom, I collapsed into a slumped heap on the floor. My arms and shoulders were throbbing from my weight being balanced on the crutches, my hands were bright red from gripping the handles so tight and I was covered in sweat and felt sick.

"Kemi, are you okay? Is it sore?" Tracey asked with genuine concern. I nodded, as she put her arm around me. "What do you want me to do? Should I get the teacher? Do you want to go home?"

"No Tracey, I just want to be better for sports day. And I hate this stupid leg," I said, with all my frustration contorting my little frame, like a toddler during a tantrum in a supermarket.

The sight of this made Tracey giggle unintentionally. She honestly didn't mean to, and she certainly didn't think my predicament was funny, but the action I'd made emphasising my annoyance must have looked rather foolish. Her giggles had been contagious and now we were both giggling, even though my giggles were filled with self-pity.

"Don't worry, I'll look after you," Tracey said, comforting me by gently stroking my back.

From then on, she would wait for me every morning on our way to school so she could carry my school bag and lunch box. She never told anyone how much pain I was really in - she kept my secret. She really did look after me; I was in pain and we were 'sisters'. She made that time so much easier for me. This, for once, wasn't about race, which looking back, she didn't know how to handle. How could she? I didn't know and it was me who was experiencing it!

Two weeks later and one week before sports day, I went with my mum back to the hospital to have my leg checked. By now I was well practised in praying every night before I went to sleep:

"Goodnight sweet Jesus, guard us in peace. Our homes and our bodies while we sleep. And please God, don't make my leg better. Please, I don't want to do sports day."

I remember getting my tight bandage taken off. From my calf to my foot, my right leg looked tiny in comparison to my left leg. It was still very bruised, with all the colours of a painter's pallet and it looked so weak and limp just lying there on the bed. My leg was mimicking how I felt inside.

"Well Kemi, there's definitely no sports day next week," the nurse concluded, again in her matter-of-fact tone. This time there would be no need for a tight bandage, but I had to keep on the tube support and continue to use the energy sapping crutches.

Overwhelming relief filled my whole body. My injured leg had allowed me to take some time out from the pressure of expectation the world demanded of me on sports day. When the day finally came, I decided to stay at home for the first time since I had hurt my leg. I remember feeling ashamed and disappointed for not wanting to be there. I got to spend the day with my gran, who, apart from that day in the car, hadn't said anything else upsetting regarding my state of being in front of me. However, I now knew what she'd meant in the car after the hospital. She could see the distress I was feeling, before I even knew it existed.

# # #

I also found pleasure and peace in dancing. I just loved it. My mum would never take me and the other mums there were horrible to me with their racist, stereotypical comments, but I still enjoyed going. I took dance classes between the ages of four and 15. Movement and being in my body were so important to me at that time.

It was at this time I learned of apartheid in South Africa. My neighbour, an older girl who would often beat me up, would come out of her house just to be racist to me whenever I went to the shop. I swear it was the highlight of her day. She once told me that if I lived in South Africa, I wouldn't be allowed to walk on the same side of the street as her and could even be killed for speaking to white people! That terrified me. What made it even more terrifying was her dad's opinion: "That's how it should be here in Scotland".

This was when I tried to cover myself with white *Scuff Kote*, the polish I used to brighten my white tap shoes. I was obsessed about being white and having long, blonde, straight hair instead of my short, tight, afro hair that made me feel like a boy. My mum didn't know what to do with it and she hated having to try to manage and maintain it, so she kept it very short for her convenience and tolerance.

It was a Saturday afternoon and I had been to my dance class. I remember this day had been particularly horrible, with all the white mums and their horrible comments and actions. Whenever I got home from dance, my routine was to clean my tap shoes straightaway, but that day I took my *Scuff Kote* polish out of my dance bag, where I kept it for emergency touch ups, and went out to the den that my grandad had built for Tayo and Lee, at the end of the garden. I remember sneaking out unnoticed while my grandad and Tayo were in the living room. Some annoying sports programme was droning on in the background, drawing all my grandad's attention, while Tayo played with some toys. Mum and Gran were not home.

Once safely out of sight in the den, I took the *Scuff Kote* and started applying it all over my legs. However, it was a hot day, and I was a combination of sweat from dancing, clammy from the tears I had been crying for what seemed like hours and sticky from the heat. As I began applying it, it rejected me, behaving like oil on water and began running down my leg like diluted white paint. I became even more distraught. I had genuinely and innocently believed that this was going to work; that this would be my answer to being like everyone else but just like the white people, the white polish was rejecting me. It would not co-operate with me.

"What are you doing, Kemkem?" Tayo curiously asked, startling me, as he came bouncing into the den. I hadn't heard him come in.

"Go away, Tay," I ordered.

He did, but it wasn't long before my grandad appeared. Our eyes locked. I was anticipating the consequences of my actions. However, he didn't tell me off. I don't even think he asked me what I was doing. He just crouched down to my level, placed his loving hand on my shoulder and said:

"Now lassie, that's no' going to work. I just canny[6] get my head around why you'd want to be like those peely-wallies[7]. Kemi, people like you have been kissed by the sun. That means you're special."

Crying freely, I explained: "But I don't want to be brown! I want to be white! I want to be like everyone else. Everyone hates me. I smell. I'm ugly. I'll never have long hair. I want long, lovely, blonde hair and I'll never have it!"

He took my little brown hand his giant-like, rough, white hand and said with a wink:

"Come on, let's go into the house. I've got something for you."

I didn't believe he could solve my predicament, but curiosity had intrigued me, so I willingly followed his lead. He sat me on the black-leather, high-sheened, silver-framed, kitchen chair. He went over to a drawer, my eyes absorbing his every move. He took out one of my gran's finest, bright golden-yellow tea towels. Next, he took one of Tracey's hair bobbles, with two pink beads at each end, from off the windowsill. With careful precision, he draped the tea towel over my head, gently but firmly pulling it across my forehead, just below my hairline, and then down behind my ears and bobbled it into a ponytail. That day, for the first time, I felt as if I had long, blonde, flowing hair!

"There you go Kem, you're a brown girl in the ring with blonde hair now," he said, looking me straight in the eyes after securing the bobble in place. I started to cry.

"What's wrong?" he asked, wiping my cheek.

"I don't like it when you sing that anymore," I confessed.

"What? Why? That's *our* song. We love our song," he tried to reassure.

Through my sobs I told him that the older boys would sing it to me outside the shop whenever I walked past, teasing me, so now instead of making me happy, it made me sad.

"I'm sorry that's happened to you, I will be speaking to those boys."

I begged him not to as it would make matters worse. To calm me down he made a promise not to.

When my mum and gran returned home and my gran noticed my 'hair': "Is that my good tea towel?" she quizzed.

"Nelly," my grandad quickly interrupted, "this is Kemi's new blonde hair . . . doesn't she look pretty?"

"No," my mum snappily answered with contempt. "She looks ridiculous. Kemi, take it off right now . . . or do you want everyone to laugh at you? Dad, why do you insist on feeding into her fantasies?"

"Well Kemi, I for one, think you look sensational," my gran chimed in.

---

[6] Scottish slang word meaning 'cannot'.
[7] Scottish saying meaning pale in colour, often used to describe someone who looks ill.

Afterwards my gran and grandad discussed who would go to the shop in the morning to buy me a set of my own bobbles for my new blonde hair. I remember being so happy playing in the garden, with Tayo and Lee both saying that my hair looked so pretty!

The next time my Auntie Joan came to visit from London she brought me a long, blonde wig with ringlets. I thought I looked wonderful, but it made people laugh at me even more. But I didn't care - I felt more like a white person because I had hair that moved in the wind! I wore that wig so often that my gran had to repair it several times!

By the time I was ten, I was very broken. No one seemed to notice except for my Auntie Joan and my grandparents, but there wasn't anything they could do to heal me other than tell me I was special *because* I was different. This didn't help, but it did show me that someone cared.

# # #

All of a sudden, my mum's boyfriend disappeared and I was being told my dad was coming to visit! My initial reaction was both relief and excitement, all rolled into one. *He'll save me – that's what dads do.*

"What? What do you mean? Forever? Is Tunde coming too? When? Where are they now?"

So many emotions were released inside of me. I had not been able to talk to anybody about my dad and brother for so long. I could feel the warm tears of happiness start to stream down my face.

"Kemi don't start! This is a good thing. This is something to be happy about. He'll be here on Saturday," my mum explained.

"But Mum . . . is Tunde coming too?"

"Do not mention Tunde again!" Anger now filled her voice.-"Your dad is coming to visit us. This is what you've always wanted, isn't it? So, let's just be happy. And remember, little girls don't ask about things that are none of their business."

I knew not to ask any more questions.

I remember Tayo was so excited as I don't think he could even remember our dad or even the fact that he was black. By the time I went to bed, I remember becoming more and more terrified and anxious. If my dad came home, it would make things worse: he was so black. They might even kill him - and me for that matter. My fear wouldn't let me sleep that Friday night. I was so terrified I was no longer wondering where he had been all this time. My only thoughts now were about trying to stay alive.

I learned a few years later what was actually going on: my dad was on weekend release from prison. After many visits from the priest, my mum had eventually decided to stop punishing him and let him visit us, hence no more boyfriend. I was warned by my mum not to mention her boyfriend. By now I knew not to speak out or question anything.

27

The return of my dad

I got up early that morning; I had a plan. I went out onto the street to play in my skates so that I was waiting and watching for him, to escort him indoors as quickly as possible, before any of the neighbours could see him. My plan however, had a flaw. We lived at the top end of the village. The bus stop was at the bottom end of the village. Everyone would definitely see him make his walk home. I can remember the moment he walked around the corner.

"There he is," I said to Tayo. Instantly, my brother ran towards him and into his arms, while I skated towards home in the opposite direction, too embarrassed to be seen with him. No one questioned why I ran.

During the time my dad had been away, my mum made it very clear that she wanted nothing to do with his side of the family; they were "black, rude and smelled". I heard her tell her family this on one of the occasions that my dad's sister had tried to come and visit Tayo and me. She did eventually come for a visit, soon after my dad was permanently home from prison.

I loved Auntie deeply. I felt more comfortable in public at the time of her visit, with both her and my dad. Everyone was mesmerized by her. She wore bright, colourful, traditional Nigerian dresses and brought clothes for me and Tayo. She spent a lot of time with my Scottish gran and had even attended my chapel with her. She lit up the room! Everybody seemed to be drawn to her warmth; they were all so in awe of her and happy to know this exotic woman. She wasn't meek or quiet, more often at the forefront with loving confidence. Everyone could feel her presence whenever she entered the room with her larger-than-life aura. Scotland gave her the same welcome that my brother and I had received previously, when we were visitors, before permanently living here.

I can still taste the food she made: hot beans, jollof rice, fried plantains and my favourite Nigerian stew! I can remember how my taste buds tingled and came alive, bringing back fond memories of previous times in London and Nigeria. I remember she plaited my hair with intricate cornrow designs, tight into my scalp; lots of detailed little spirals, all meeting at the crown of my head, in the tiniest, little afro puff ponytail. I felt amazing and proud every time I looked in the mirror. I was developing moments of feeling a little safer in my skin, in the privacy of my own bedroom and away from the outside world's judgement. She even gave my dad refresher lessons on how to twist and oil my hair. I felt so safe sitting there during these lessons, cross-legged with my back to her, resting in between her legs on the floor. I can still smell her sweet aroma.

My mum had always found Auntie very challenging. She was a tall, elegant and graceful woman; the strongest woman I have ever known and she would always suggest, very clearly, what Tayo and I needed to look after our skin and our hair. My mum, however, never took any of her suggestions on board. She just saw it as criticism and judgement, rather than recognising that her children had different needs.

During her visit, it was determined that I was now old enough to travel to Nigeria by myself. There was nothing my mum could say that would alter Auntie's determination.

I was in bed and could hear raised voices - not shouting, just louder than normal. I heard my name being discussed, so I sneaked out of bed and crept along the hall. I could see the living room door was closed over, but not tightly shut. I sat down quietly on the floor and listened intently.

"That's not happening! That is not going to happen! Kemi is too young to travel to Nigeria by herself!" were the first words I heard my mum say.

Panic struck! *What? Are they sending me to Nigeria?*

"Children travel back and forth from Nigeria to the UK daily, Daisy. That is why they have the minor service, to look after the children who are travelling alone. But I do not think that this is really what this is about, is it Daisy?" Auntie's voice was loud, with a beautifully calming, Nigerian lilt.

"What do you mean by that?" my mum began to question.

"Shh! Shh!" my dad interjected, trying to stop Auntie's line of questioning. "You are going to wake up the children, sister."

I held my breath, too frightened to run the risk of breathing too loudly and being discovered. *Can't be heard, need to know what they are talking about.*

"Samuel, we have already spoken about this," Auntie continued, undeterred.

"Sister!" my dad pleaded, still trying to hush his sister from talking any further.

"What have you two fucking spoken about? Have you discussed my children? When I'm not here? How dare you?" my mum screeched with anger. Although she was now angry, I could hear fear in her voice.

"No Daisy, it's . . . ," my dad began.

"Yes, we have, and you need to listen," Auntie directly confessed.

"Where have you two been all these fucking years when I've had to bring up these two children by myself, without any fucking help from any fucking Nigerian?" my mum bellowed.

I could now hear that she was out of breath and breathing heavily. What followed seemed like an eternity of silence.

"Daisy, I take nothing away from you. What you have had to endure through Samuel's choices and behaviour, and how you have managed with these small children is commendable. But the children are paying the price. They are well-behaved, well-presented and carry themselves in a manner that makes us all so very proud. But I have repeatedly contacted you, to try to visit these children. I am in the UK at least once a year and for over four years now, you have refused to let me see my niece and nephew. You have brought them to Scotland, which I totally understand; you need the support of your family, but let's face it, this is not London. There are no other black faces in this place and your children, especially your daughter, are carrying shame because they do not understand their identity."

"How dare you?" my mum accused, having now apparently regained her breath.

"No, how dare you!" Auntie rebounded. "Your pride and refusal to see that your daughter is mixed-race and suffering, is going to affect her for the rest of her life and I will not back down on this. Kemi will be travelling to Nigeria, to spend the whole summer with her Nigerian family - and most importantly, her brother Tunde. And Samuel agrees."

Silence filled the room once more. *Tunde? So, Tunde is in Nigeria after all!*

Out of the silence the living room door quickly swung open.

"Uh, uh, Kemkem, what are you doing down there?" Auntie asked, shaking her head.

"What? Is she up? She knows better than this. Kemi!" my mum's voice targeted me from inside the living room.

"I am putting her to bed," Auntie replied, taking my hand and escorting me back to my bedroom, before my mum could reach me. She motioned me into bed and tucked me in. Sitting on the edge of my bed, she began to sing my Nigerian birth song:

"Olukemi, Oh . . . "

"Do you know where Tunde is?" I butted in. I had to ask her. I was compelled to. I can still hear her sharp intake of breath from the shock of realising that I didn't know.

"Of course, Kemkem. Tunde lives with me."

"With you?" I asked, confused.

The relief of finally knowing exactly where my brother was made me cry inconsolably. She lay down on the bed beside me and began stroking my head.

"Don't cry Kemkem. You are going to see him soon and I will make sure that he continues to write to you, and you can write to him."

"Continues to write to me? What do you mean?" I asked bewildered.

I quickly realised that my brother had been writing to me and she realised that I had never received any of the letters. As I fell asleep listening to her sing my song, thoughts began swimming around in my mind, flooding me. *What will he look like? What did his letters say? He misses me. I'm going to see him.*

Auntie was leaving early the next morning to catch her flight back home to Nigeria. I awoke very sleepily to find her entering my room.

"Kemi, I have come to say good bye."

"Oh no, I forgot," I managed to respond.

I was still exhausted from all the tears of the night before and now warm, fresh tears filled my eyes once again. *Oh God, please don't let her go. My mum is going to kill me for listening in to their grown-up conversation.*

"Oh, do not cry Kemi. It is not going to be long. You are coming to Nigeria. We are all so excited. Tosin[8], Yemesi[9], Gran and Grandad. And especially Tunde! So, I need you to be a very brave and a very good girl and do as you are told. Then we will have the whole summer together in Nigeria. That is what you want, yes?"

"Yes Auntie," I willingly agreed.

"That is my African Princess," she said approvingly, as she leaned over and gave me one last kiss on my forehead.

I watched her leave from my bedroom window. *Why can't she be my mum?*

My mum never raised what had happened the night before.

# # #

My dad had two visits home from prison before he was released permanently. My mum fell pregnant with my youngest brother the first weekend visit home. I know this because the next time my dad came to visit, they told us he was coming back home for good and that she was going to have a baby. I was devastated! A black daddy at home all of the time and another black baby would only make me stand out even more.

Looking back, I believe this to have been deliberate on her part, as she had been in many relationships and never fallen pregnant. I think she did this to emphasise, as a constant reminder to my dad, that she had total control over her brown children; that because he left, we belonged to her.

Despite this, my dad managed to make time to instil some of his culture in me to try to repair the damage his absence had caused. I was starting to find a new place of safety in the hell I lived in. I remember my dad telling my mum that she must let my hair grow and now that he was home, he would take care of it. It was all I could think about; my hair could be like Diana Ross's! He did take control of my hair. He would spend hours on Fridays and Saturdays, oiling, greasing, plaiting; getting it ready for my new hair style for the forthcoming week. This made my hair grow very quickly, which made me so happy; at least now people couldn't call me a boy anymore.

On Saturday mornings, my dad would take me on the bus to Glasgow to go to a hair salon on Great Western Road, owned by someone we called 'Uncle Segun'. We would get the bus early and I would sit as far away from him as possible, thinking people wouldn't know we were together. Once we were a safe distance from home and those who knew me, about half-way

---

[8] Pronounced: *Toe-son.*

[9] Pronounced: *Yeah-meh-see.*

there at a place called Coatbridge, I would go and sit beside him and even hold his hand.

It was mainly black people in Uncle Segun's salon the first time I went and I got my hair plaited. It had gold thread and gold beads and I loved it! I finally had real, long hair! I looked like someone from the TV show *Fame* that I had started to watch.

I was obsessed at this time with Diana Ross and Michael Jackson. They were my first hope. They were black and beautiful and even white people loved them. I was on top of the world when my dad bought me the *Beat It* jacket and I even took a photo of me standing next to a Michael Jackson poster and told people I had met him!

When we got back on the bus after getting my *Fame* mane, I sat beside my dad until we got to Coatbridge. Then, for the rest of the journey, we sat apart. We never spoke about it.

In our special time together, he taught me about people; their fears and how it could influence their behaviour. He would tell me that people we were all equal and whenever someone was racist towards me, that was them showing me that they were beneath me, in which case, I should always walk away. He didn't teach me to be angry or hateful. I understood.

In the spring of 1983, my dad drove me to Edinburgh to arrange my passport for Nigeria. I was so excited. This was the first time I'd had a Nigerian passport. There were black people in Edinburgh which meant I could walk with him and hold his hand; it was amazing! We went to the embassy and then shopped for sandals. He bought me a pair similar to my First Communion shoes, only this pair was pink. It was the best day ever.

During these special, intimate and culturally educational moments - the travels to Glasgow and Edinburgh, the salon and him caring for my hair - my dad shared stories about Nigeria; traditions, family members and beliefs. I loved our 'story times' together. No one ever knew what we talked about. I made it our secret, between just him and I. It was a time I could be with him and be brown and enjoy it. My mum was never present during these special moments.

My dad told me that, after I returned from Nigeria and when Tunde's school term ended, my older brother would be coming to live in Scotland.

"For how long," I asked excitedly.

"Permanently," was his sole response.

I didn't know what that meant but by the look on his face I knew it meant forever. I would find out later that he had told my mum she had no choice.

Nigeria

Just as Auntie had promised, I received six letters in the six weeks leading up to my trip to Nigeria: two from Auntie, two from my cousin, Tosin and two, very gratefully received, from my brother, Tunde. From both Tunde's and Tosin's letters, I could tell that Auntie had shared much about what went on in my daily life. Tunde was very impressed that I could skate down the steep hill that my Scottish gran lived on - and on the road no less! He thought this was very brave of me. Auntie had told them I now had a Scottish accent and for some reason they thought I would sound like Audrey Hepburn's character from their favourite movie *My Fair Lady*, despite her playing a cockney. I guess they thought all western accents sounded the same!

I treasured those letters; I took them with me to school in my school bag, I slept with them under my pillow; they even travelled with me to Nigeria in my suitcase.

I remember flying as a minor, which, in those days, meant I would be looked after by an air hostess. The first leg of my trip was from Glasgow to London Heathrow, where I was collected by my Auntie Joan before spending the night at her house.

The next morning her husband, my Uncle Bill, drove me back to Heathrow to catch my connecting flight to Geneva, before flying to Lagos, Nigeria. When he dropped me off with the air hostess, he gave me £10 for a *Coke* in Geneva, telling me it would cost that much as it was very expensive there. The air hostess was very kind and I was actually in first class without realising it. I also got to look around the cockpit.

On arrival in Lagos, I was then handed over to Auntie. I was to stay with her and her husband and their two children: Yemesi, who was six years older and Tosin who was one year older than me. I remembered my cousins from my previous visits to Nigeria and they had also visited us in London. I was excited to see them and spend time with them. This was the family my brother Tunde had been living with since he left London and I was eager to know what his life had been like. I was bursting with excitement about seeing my brother again and it was a huge relief when Tunde and my cousin Tosin greeted me at the door with screams of surprise and cuddles. They were equally as excited to see me!

My trip was filled with my dad's huge number of siblings and cousins who I had not seen for many years. I remember Auntie's house-woman and house-man and their daughter. They lived in a separate house on Auntie's land and it was their job to upkeep the house with various chores and maintenance. Their daughter and I would often play together, having a lot of fun.

Tunde and Tosin were obsessed with Marvin Gaye, especially the song *Sexual Healing*, and as part of my welcoming celebration they entertained

33

me by performing their dance routine that they had been practising for weeks in preparation for my arrival. We would spend many hours in the evening dancing to many Marvin Gaye hits, with routines that I choreographed.

"Uh, uh, Tosin, No!" Tunde insisted, shaking his head in disagreement. "She cannot be in charge; she is the youngest!"

"But you don't know how to dance," I said, defending my claim to the role.

"No, no, no. Kemi has to be in charge, Tunde," Tosin urged with sincere belief, applying his logic and reasoning. "She is the dancer. No?"

"So . . . that does not mean a thing," Tunde surmised, avoiding facing the facts of his predicament.

"Okay, Kemi. How often do you go to dance class, hm?" Tosin began his line of questioning, sounding like a lawyer guiding his client.

"A Saturday and a Wednesday," I declared with conviction, whilst revealing a hint of annoyance and offense towards my older brother for denying me my rightful role.

"And you have been in lots of shows, and on a stage? No?"

"Yes," I replied, succinct and straight to the point.

"Ah, okay. Then she is teacher!" Tosin concluded. No further questions.

Tunde, now out of any logical argument, let out a huff, accepting his defeat.

# # #

We visited my grandparents nearly every day and I enjoyed my simple, sacred time with them. Granma spoke very little English, but my beautiful grandfather was well educated and spoke English perfectly. I was very special to them and I knew that they loved me dearly, as I loved them. It was in their village that I was fitted for traditional Nigerian clothes and my head wrap, which I wore on a Thursday over the treatment in my hair, in preparation for my hair being done on the Thursday evening. That's when all the black ladies would go to a local auntie's house where several aunties did hair. It was at this point I learned that in my Nigerian culture, girls' hair is sacred and it carries their wisdom. Something my white mother didn't want to know anything about. In this culture - my Nigerian culture - the thing that had caused me the most pain growing up, my afro hair, was celebrated! I loved having different patterns and colours plaited into my hair every week.

It was at this time that Auntie educated me on what real poverty was, because in Nigeria you are either very wealthy or very poor - no in-between. My family were wealthy, but at the end of their road were shanty towns, with no separation anywhere. It was devastating poverty and filth. At the age of 11, I remember feeling this overwhelming pain at the sight of the conditions people actually had to live in. Coming from the UK and seeing what I saw, I have no words that can explain that sense of sadness I remember feeling.

Auntie was a doctor and one day she took me to a township hospital. I followed her about like her little junior, thinking that this would be fun . . . until one particular consultation.

I was sitting across the table from a 12-year-old Nigerian girl, who had been raped, listening to discussions about a termination because she was pregnant. I was filled with shock, horror and fear. She was just a year older than me - how could she be pregnant? I could not understand how something like that could happen. However, somewhere deep within me, I did know. I remember just having an overwhelming compassion for this girl sitting across from me - whose pain was plain to see, from the torture and abuse that she must have gone through. I knew we had a common understanding; that people were capable of anything. That evening, when I spoke to my dad on the phone and told him I had been to the hospital with Auntie, he asked to speak to her.

"Why the hell would you take my daughter to a place like that?" he demanded.

"Your daughter is growing up in the UK and she must appreciate and respect the NHS," Auntie replied.

Auntie did a very good job of showing me the two very different sides of Nigeria, so that I would appreciate growing up in the UK. She told me that she understood, and could see, how difficult it was for me to be growing up in Scotland and told me that I had to believe that God never gives you more than you can handle; that you can always grow from your experiences, especially if you know who you are. She told me that I was half Nigerian and half Scottish and no matter what anybody said, nobody could take that away from me. I had a birth right to both.

Four weeks into my trip I became very sick from malaria. This made me feel very homesick. So, two weeks later, when I was well enough to travel, I returned home. I will never forget my last day in Nigeria. Auntie took me to spend the day with my grandparents. I remember Granma cried for most of the visit and I can still remember the love and the sadness that poured from my grandfather when we said our goodbyes. In that moment, I felt a physical pain that made me not want to leave early anymore, but I knew I had to. I would see my grandparents again, but it still didn't lessen the pain I felt leaving. It was very hard to say goodbye to Tunde, although I knew he would be following me within a couple of months. We had spent six weeks together, every day, reunited and bonding as brother and sister. Our goodbye was very emotional. Looking back now, I realise we never once spoke in Nigeria about the fact that he didn't live with me or that he had left. I wonder who told him not to talk about it. We still, to this day, have never discussed it.

Just as a side note, when I returned to Scotland everyone was interested to know what it was like in Nigeria, with some of the children asking if we really did eat people there!

#

By the time my trip to Nigeria was over, life was very different on my return. We had a new car and what seemed to me like lots of money. We were moving to a Victorian house in Coatbridge, the town we used to pass through on the way to Glasgow, where I would take my seat on the bus beside my dad. Coatbridge has been voted the worst town in Scotland in more recent years. The move terrified me; all I could think about was that a bigger town equalled more racism.

My dad continued looking after my hair and we continued to go to Uncle Segun's to have it plaited, which helped me feel less black. I didn't look less black, but at least my long plaits concealed my afro hair.

There was some relief in moving: leaving Caldercruix meant I would never be sexually violated again.

Tunde's return

Tunde returned to the UK in time to start secondary school. Unfortunately, before school resumed, we had to take a trip to Oxford for Auntie's eldest son Kayode's funeral. Kayode[10] had not been present during my most recent trip to Nigeria. This was the only time in all the visits, whether in London or Nigeria, that he had not been present. I still have a very strong memory of him.

I remember he was very tall with a lean yet muscular physique and a smile just as big. He was stunning. Kayode had been studying in America when he became ill. Looking back, I remember the period in between being told that he was sick and his death as being very short.

We travelled to Auntie Joan's house in London, then on to Oxford for the funeral, returning to Auntie Joan's for a few days before coming home.

I wanted to wear one of my Scottish gran's hand-made outfits, one that she had made for me to wear during my trip to Nigeria. It was a white rah-rah skirt that had three deep frills to my knees. They had been trimmed on the bottom edge with a multicoloured, thin band of pinks, greens, blues and yellows. It had a matching sleeveless, bolero top, with a deep frill all around the neckline. I remember being very excited, as this was one of my favourite outfits.

"Kemi, I'm not arguing with you today!" my mum said dismissively, whilst buttering what appeared to be rather burned toast.

"But why can't I wear it?" I dared to continue.

"Because we're going to your cousin's funeral and you don't wear white at a funeral, Kemi," she said in a patronising tone, before spreading some marmalade.

"People wear black, because they're mourning," she inferred with an air of superiority on the matter.

"No, you're wrong," I corrected. "You don't know anything. You always wear white to weddings and funerals in Nigeria. I'm going to ask Dad."

"Kemi, come back here. Don't be bothering your dad," she began, as I skipped hurriedly away to find him. "This is a big day for him – he's representing Auntie," was the last thing she said to me within ear shot.

Represent? What does that mean? "Dad? Dad, where are you?" my voice rang throughout my Auntie Joan's house.

I knew my mum was closely stalking me to shut me down so, I had to be quick. As I bundled into the room that my parents had been using as their bedroom I blurted out, in my no nonsense, matter-of-fact way:

"Dad, sure I'm allowed to wear white to the funeral? Sure that's the colour you're supposed to wear?" I directly quizzed looking for validation

---

[10] Pronounced: *Ky-oh-day.*

for my mum to witness. "Shh," was all he got to say before my mum tried to usher me out of the room.

"Kemi, what did I tell you? Leave your dad alone!"

I remember feeling more empowered since my trip to Nigeria. I was now more active in challenging my mum and took any opportunity given to prove to her that I knew more about my culture than she did. It had always been unimportant to her. However, on this occasion, there was definitely a softening. The same softening that I had noticed from my mum towards Auntie. Looking back, after I returned from Nigeria, my mum's attitude towards Auntie had changed. I think this was because of the loving time Auntie had given to me and to my brother Tunde. Something that my mum was unable to do. Maybe more importantly though, Auntie had given my mum validation that my dad had mistreated her with his illegal choices.

Before my mum could lead me away, my dad sat down on the edge of the bed and motioned me to come and sit beside him.

"Kemi, it is: "Isn't it correct that I am allowed?" not "sure I am allowed" yes?" he said nodding encouragingly, looking for agreement. I nodded compliantly.

"Now, I want to tell you what will be happening today. First of all, I want to remind you of how respectful you have to be," his Nigerian voice gently began.

"Death, in Nigeria, is a celebration. It is a celebration of life. In Yoruba[11] tradition, the body is presented for people to come and pay their respects and celebrate the person's life with family."

"What, like a Rosary?" I sincerely reasoned.

"Ha, ha, ha, ha," his deep African laugh chugged all the way from his stomach to his lips. "No, Kemkem. It is a big party in your village, that can last a week. There are lots of traditional foods and colourful clothes; not just white."

"I knew it. I told Mum that," I interrupted, vindicated.

"It is a time to be thankful," he reassured, smiling, causing his chiselled, bulbous cheekbones to rise as if they were floating.

"What? You're not sad? You don't greet[12]?" I asked rather baffled. Catholicism had only taught me death was a sad affair.

"No, Kemkem, you do not cry," he confirmed with warmth. "Well, not the way that you mean. People can still cry, but they are happy tears, because you are celebrating and honouring someone you love."

"So, is this what's going to be happening in Oxford? Are we having a

---

[11] The Yoruba is an ethnic group that inhabits western Africa. There are around 47 million Yoruba worldwide, with the vast majority being in Nigeria, where they make up 21% of the country's population. This makes them one of the largest ethnic groups in Africa. (Source: Wikipedia.)

[12] Scottish slang word meaning 'cry'.

street party - like Auntie Nika's[13] wedding in Lagos, when I was a flower girl?"

I had been a flower girl at the wedding of one of my dad's sisters when I was four years old. I still remember the itchy, white lace dress and gloves that I had to wear in the sweltering heat.

I had also witnessed, what seemed to me, a scene from a horror movie. At four years old, I obliviously entered the back garden at the exact moment the groom performed the traditional sacrificing of the goat in preparation for the wedding feast! I let out a scream, to which Auntie, who, out of the corner of her eye, had seen me make my way through the kitchen towards the back garden and had been in hot pursuit of me, quickly grabbed me by the hand and escorted me back into the house. In the chaos of all that was happening - wedding preparations, guests in and out, goats being sacrificed - she still found the time in a quiet space to explain to me what I had just witnessed. She educated me that Uncle had taken care of this goat since it had been born. That he loved it and it had been his friend. But now, the goat had wanted to give its life, as a sacrifice for the wedding, because of their friendship. I remember just accepting this as kids do, but I couldn't bring myself to eat the meat!

"No, Kemkem, no street party. This is England. This is a bit different. In our Nigerian culture, it is a great sadness if children die before their parents. Parents cannot celebrate if one of their children dies. So, Auntie and Uncle will not be coming with us to the service. They will have their sadness, in Oxford, but in private. But tradition says, all life must be celebrated. So, I will represent them at the service and we can all celebrate for them."

I also learned when I went to Oxford, that this was the second child of Auntie's that had died. Some years earlier, I'm not quite sure when, tragically, her two-year-old daughter died. Up until this point I had no idea of the sorrow that had been in Auntie's life; and still there was more to come.

It was a very sad day. I still remember the silence, which was very strange and eerie, as Nigerian's are normally happy, animated and definitely not quiet! I did spend time with Auntie and my cousins in Oxford. Even through her beautiful smile and behind her vibrant eyes, I could see her deep pain. When I think about that day, I still feel profound sadness.

After the funeral, when we went back to Auntie Joan's in London to stay for a few days, Tunde and I were sharing a room with bunkbeds. I was "obviously sleeping on the bottom bunk" - according to Tunde - as I was the youngest. When we were in bed at night and after he had been wholeheartedly practising his new Scottish accent, he surmised: "I might not need this." I wasn't sure if he was trying to convince me or himself.

"Of course you will need it!" I said, shocked at this ridiculous statement. "You sound Nigerian and English . . . do you want them to batter you?" I

---

[13] Pronounced: *Neh-kay.*

stressed.

"No," his voice concluded sounding vexed from the other side of my view of bed slats and mattress. I could tell there was more he wanted to say and after a lengthy inner debate with himself, he shared his next confession. "I have spoken to Auntie Joan about Mum," he disclosed.

I remember gasping a deep audible inhale. *Is he stupid?* Sitting upright now, with full attention, I could feel my heart racing.

"What? You are going to get into so much trouble."

He had broken the cardinal rule; you do not speak about her, to anyone. Ever. He had not experienced the consequences of this like I had and I was now gravely concerned, only this time, for him.

"What did you say?"

"I said the truth; that she hates me," Tunde stated both with integrity and naivety.

Tunde's mum was another white, Scottish woman that my dad had met before he knew my mum and they had separated before he and my mum got together. My mum hated the fact my dad had a child to someone else; someone other than her, so she told my dad that they could get married and raise Tunde together. She then began to actively encourage my dad to apply for custody of Tunde. At that point in time, Tunde, who was just two years old, had fallen from the veranda of his mum's flat and broken his arm.

However, my dad told my mum that he couldn't marry her straight away - partly because he wasn't professionally established enough yet, but partly because their relationship had happened very quickly. He still wanted to be a family, but she said she wouldn't take care of Tunde unless they were married. As a result, Tunde went into foster care in the town of Coatbridge for two years. Once he was in foster care, my mum fell pregnant with me. She did so knowing that her parents, being Catholic, would insist on her being married before I was born. So, they got married when she was three months pregnant, and Tunde eventually came to live with us in London after I was born.

"But Tunde . . . she hates me too! Auntie Joan will tell her. You do know that don't you?" The words poured out of my mouth, keeping pace with my ever-racing heartbeat.

"No she will not. She promised. She said I do not need to move to Coatbridge - that I could stay here," Tunde testified.

"Tunde, she *will* tell her," I warned, before a silence fell over the room; a silence which amplified the suddenly raised voices from downstairs.

"That little bastard!" we heard my mum roar.

Tunde quickly shuffled and by the sagging bulge in the mattress over my head, I could tell he too was now sitting bolt-upright.

"Who the fuck does he think he is?" were the last words we heard my mum shriek from downstairs, followed by her accelerating footsteps, thudding louder with each nearing step.

"Daisy, calm down. This is not the way to handle this," my Auntie Joan implored, following my mum upstairs.

"Quick, Tunde, pretend you're sleeping," I urged, pulling back my bed covers.

"Tunde! You little fucking bastard!" my mum erupted into the room.

"Daisy, you can't speak to him like that!" Auntie Joan ordered.

"Mum?" I began, trying to protect Tunde from the inevitable onslaught.

"Kemi, shut up," she stabbed with venom. *I hate her. I hate her. I hate her.*

"Daisy, come downstairs. We can sort this out in the morning," Auntie Joan encouraged.

"Joan, shut up!" my mum chastised. "I am his mother and he will not speak about me like this ever again!"

She turned her attention to Tunde: "Tunde. Downstairs. Right now."

I could feel Tunde's fear before I even saw it on his face, as he descended the ladder of the bunkbeds. I was filled with humiliation. I felt his humiliation; she could so easily make me feel this way when I was on the receiving end of what my brother was about to experience. In that moment, I really did hate her. Had my brother's life not been sad enough, without her inflicting her control and power over him too, and all in my dad's ever-silent presence? Fighting back my tears, I could hear her cursing all the way back downstairs accompanied by the slamming of a door. Then silence, only fractured by the pounding of my heartbeat. I had no idea what was being said, but I knew it wouldn't be good.

Auntie Joan tiptoed over to my bottom bunk and perched at the edge, wrapping one arm around me. No words were exchanged, but I could see in her face her compassion and empathy. However, I was still disappointed with her for telling my mum what Tunde had confided in her. Even at my young age, I knew what the consequences were of speaking out against my mum. Auntie Joan would have known too. I felt a little betrayed but took comfort from what looked like her deep regret. Not before long, she left to attend to my cousin who had been awoken by all the commotion.

When Tunde returned to the room, which seemed like hours later, and got into bed and lay down, I could tell he was crying.

"Tunde, are you okay?" I whispered, knowing that I was supposed to be asleep by now.

"I do not want to talk about it," he replied sheepishly.

As I lay there listening to his sobs, before we both finally fell asleep, I realised that my brother had now learned the cardinal rule: never to speak out against her.

I did not find out about Tunde's early life until I was older. At the time of his lambasting, I believed his reluctance to move to Coatbridge, Scotland, was solely aimed at my mum. I just thought he didn't want to live with this woman who'd been both directly and indirectly appalling to him, causing him so much pain. Today, with more knowledge of Tunde's early life-struggles, I question my own original beliefs as to why he was reluctant to move to Coatbridge. I now wonder if he remembered his time spent there in foster care; was that what was discussed downstairs that night at Auntie Joan's?

Tunde never spoke out against my mum again.

Coatbridge: big town of terror

Tayo and I were enrolled at *Saint Augustine's Primary School*. My first day was surprisingly good and continued to be so in the days that followed. My teacher, Mrs Kelly, liked me and treated me as equal to the other children. This was my first experience since leaving London of schooling where I felt both part of a class and accepted. I felt more acceptance in the seven months that I'd attended this school, than during my entire time of schooling in Caldercruix. People would still call me names at my new school, but not as many. It would be here that I learned to be part of a team in sports, as well as part of a collective. The class, being in its final year of journeying primary school, had an amazing bond. I had never experienced being accepted as part of any sort of group before, but this class accepted me completely. I still look back in wonder at how this little pocket of time in my life really did set me up for what society would sometimes expect of me.

Netball was my passion. I remember listening to my mum proudly telling my dad what she had been told at my parent's meeting:

""Mrs Ogunyemi," she said. Can you believe it? She pronounced it correctly first time," my mum began excitedly.

"Kemi's the class star of netball and running! She has been picked along with two other girls to train with the Scotland youth squad for netball, and if she's good enough, she could play for them in the forthcoming season," my mum revealed with awe.

"Olukemi, is this true?" my dad asked smiling, his delight consuming his whole being.

Until that moment, I hadn't fully appreciated how big a deal this was for both my school and my dad. I could feel the overwhelming pride he had for me. I remember feeling delighted on the one hand - my dad was proud of me - but on the other was resentment. Why was I expected to represent a country – Scotland - that had only ever shown utter contempt and hatred towards me? I learned I could be tolerated in some areas of my life, if I had something 'they' wanted.

Saint Augustine's had been a safe haven for the time being. I was learning what was expected from me in an environment where I felt I could fit in. This was partly down to the amazing Mrs Kelly; she recognised that my talents gave me value and acceptance. She also nurtured the class as a team; a collective who supported each other. That was the perfect place for me to be before the massive experience of moving onto high school.

Because of my running and netball skills, and being picked to represent Scotland in both sports, I'd gained some value at school, resulting in the racism I encountered mainly occurring outside of school. Furthermore, I'd caught a break when we moved into our new house, with my school now conveniently located at the bottom of the same street. This meant I could now travel in relative safety between my home and the school without coming into contact with too many people who were not from my school.

For the first time I had value to white people; they wanted to win and I always won. I didn't care at this time if people were pretending to like me; it felt better either way and at this point I would take any crumbs of value society was willing to give me.

My parents never attended any of my games or running events. This still makes me sad when I think about it, but I guess it was easier to be what society expected me to be without their expectations being present too, confusing me even more. Their absences would later come in handy when I was at high school. I could lie about having training sessions, knowing full well they wouldn't attend to check, allowing me instead to go out drinking with Joanna.

###

I didn't really have many friends outside of school until I met Joanna. She was Italian and my dad had given her dad a job. Joanna was the first person to tell me I was beautiful and I could tell she really liked me. We were best friends. She was already in her second year of high school while I was in my last year of primary school.

It was about this time when I first learned about the *NF* - the *National Front* - and skinheads. Our neighbours were friends with *NF* followers, so I had to be careful at home or I would be beaten up and spat on.

Tunde didn't go to school in Coatbridge, but instead went to school in the neighbouring town of Airdrie. When he returned to Scotland, we were still living in Caldercruix, just outside Airdrie, so he'd started high school there. My parents didn't want him changing schools when we moved to Coatbridge as he'd already settled, so not everyone in my town knew I had a big brother. One of his first experiences of racism in Coatbridge took place at our back gate, when about five or six skinheads tried to beat him up. Little did they know he was a martial arts champion and he whooped the lot of them. That was helpful. Word got around about my ninja brother, meaning from then on, only girls would have free rein on me. I wasn't a fighter, but I could run, so I didn't always get caught.

This was when I met Andy, the first mixed-race boy I knew who wasn't related to me. However, he would also tease me about being mixed-race; he was adopted by a white family, so he was just surviving.

As I got older and attended secondary school, it was always the girls who were the worst towards me. They hated me. They would spit on me and shout names at me: "black bastard", "nigger", and, "NF" to name a few. They would tell me to go back to Africa where I belonged. They would wait for me at the street corner where I lived, so I would have to go through my friend Ruth's garden, my Italian neighbour, so as not to get caught. Ruth was a year older than me.

In my first few days at secondary school someone ripped my skirt, splitting it right up to my bum. When the teacher asked how it had happened, they shouted their response in front of everyone: "She's a black slut". This treatment continued. It was hell.

This was the time when lots of the boys, mostly two years above me in school, wanted to go out with me because I was different. This made matters worse for me with the girls, as they didn't want any of the white boys going near me. They would say things like "she smells" and "how can you kiss *that*?" But boys liked me regardless. Boys would like me until I rejected their advances, or until other people criticised them for kissing a nigger. Then I would be dumped.

# # #

When settling into Coatbridge, I remember the conversation my dad had with me and Tunde about how we should behave and present ourselves to the world. He taught us how to react if we ever found ourselves in contact with the police, or any other authority with power. We had, always to be polite, honest and clear. We were never to show any aggression and certainly never argue at anything that may happen. He taught us to be *Uncle Toms*[14].

Education was everything to my dad as he, along with all of his siblings, had left Nigeria to attend university in the UK. This influence came from my Nigerian grandfather. He instilled in all of his children that education was everything and a way for black people to be accepted. Education also meant more choice. My dad instilled this in us, not realising society had already taught us that we would never be equal. I think Tunde's time in Nigeria had been very difficult in many ways, but he understood these concepts: behaviour and education. I, however, found it harder, as my mother had instilled the same values that society had taught me - that of never being enough. My dad had wanted us to go to private school for many reasons, one being that if you paid enough money the racism became more subtle, but my mum couldn't get her head around why it was so important. The result wasn't private school, but instead, plenty of extra tuition after most school days.

In all of this, I had a small, lucky break, which gave me some hope. My English tutor actually saw me for who I was and having noticed how my confidence and self-esteem had nose-dived between my first and third years, he got me to write a piece of work about my experiences of racism for the purpose of awareness.

---

[14] Uncle Tom is the title character of Harriet Beecher Stowe's 1852 novel, Uncle Tom's Cabin. He was an exceedingly subservient and non-resistant slave. (Source: Wikipedia.)

My dad had bought my mum her first shop, then another shop, before buying her a post office. Tunde and I would work weekends and school holidays without pay. My dad said that was our contribution to the family, seeing as we did travel a lot and never really wanted for anything. The main reason for this though, was so we could understand how other people lived and conducted themselves. The shops were in deprived areas of Airdrie and Coatbridge and I learned that people were basically all the same, no matter their background. This helped me to understand people's behaviours.

The teenager

By the time I'd turned 14 years old, my life was becoming increasingly difficult, especially in my relationship with my mum. It was around this time that I went looking for proof that she wasn't my real mum because I refused to believe a real mum would treat their own daughter so harshly. I was hoping to discover Diana Ross was actually my real mum. I searched my parent's bedroom one day while no one was in and found a suitcase under their bed, containing letters written by my dad to my mum . . . from prison. This was how I learned, during all the time that he was away from home in my younger years, he was actually serving a jail sentence. My Auntie Joan later filled in the blanks of the whys and wherefores. I'd asked my mum first, but that had only resulted in her normal reaction of slapping me about for asking questions on matters that were apparently none of my business!

This was when I developed my coping mechanism for the next 14 years of my life. I remember this as a time when my body had started to change and develop. African women tend to 'thicken', developing bigger bums and bigger thighs than white women. This really disturbed my mother; her daughter's perfect body was changing and this was not okay. I was never overweight, but I didn't look like anyone else. This caused my mother to start criticising me, calling me fat and ugly. My youngest brother made up a song: *'What's the Breadth of Kemi'* and my mum would even join in singing it to me. I think she thought it would change the way my body was developing, as if I had some kind control over it. By now, she had stopped all contact with my dad's black friends and we rarely saw any family from Nigeria, so she didn't understand that black girls grew differently from white girls.

It was at this time I learned of the sadness that was happening in Auntie's life. I remember the day my mum told Tunde and me that Auntie had breast cancer. I didn't really know what cancer meant, other than you could die from it. I didn't want to ask my parents about the severity of her illness, as I didn't want to hear them say she might die. I just stood there listening and asking no questions. I remember Tunde was trying to be so cool about this devastating news, externally at least. However, sharing a glance with him as I left the room, I could see the same fear and worry on his face that I felt inside of me. In that moment, I knew we shared the same thoughts: *she can't die; what about me? I can't live without her.*

Auntie was back in the UK for treatment and I remember being very brave. I would keep myself updated by listening in from the other side of the partly closed door, gathering snippets of intelligence disclosed by my parent's in their evening recaps of what Auntie was going through. I knew it wasn't okay to show how I really felt - that my mum would only tell me I didn't feel that way anyway - so I kept my feelings secret. Even when we went back to Oxford to visit Auntie during her treatment, the only person I can ever remember openly talking to about Auntie was her son, my cousin, Tosin. He had been coming to stay with us at least twice a year, as he was now at a boarding school in Oxford. I loved his visits so much, just as I loved him.

I remember that Auntie was really thin and her body looked so frail - not strong and safe like before - but she still greeted me with the same huge, loving smile. That always made me feel safe and understood.

"Ah, Kemkem!" she cried out with huge joy at seeing me. "Come, child. You are turning into a beautiful African princess. Tell me all about your new school and your friend, Ruth. Tosin tells me you are great friends."

I smiled, knowing Tosin hadn't told her just how great friends he and Ruth were, as I knew they had certainly exchanged kisses!

"Kemkem, I will not die. I am a doctor, remember?"

This did give me reassurance and, true to her word, Auntie went into remission shortly after.

Auntie's illness had definitely changed how my mum felt about her; there was now genuine worry and concern. I think my mum had been scared of my dad's sister from the beginning. I believe she thought Auntie would hold the same contempt for her that white people had shown to me and my siblings. This had made her come from a place of defence. Over time, my mum would come to see that this was not the case. Auntie carried no racism towards anyone.

However, my mum couldn't extend her tolerance of Auntie to Auntie's children. She hated having to host my cousin Tosin. She couldn't relate to him and always found it hard not to show her contempt for him. Auntie had given Tunde and me love and kindness, but my mum couldn't return the same to my cousins Yemisi and Tosin - two teenagers, living far away from their home in the UK. Why? Because they were black.

Looking back, I know that her lack of acceptance of my blackness didn't give me the solid foundation that I've given my children. She didn't see the damage that was taking place because she hadn't educated herself – she didn't see the importance of doing so. Her white privilege traumatised me deeply as a child.

My dad would never interfere in how she treated us. I don't think he allowed himself to fully see it, but even if he had, it wouldn't have made any difference. This is how white privilege affects black people; they don't feel equal enough to have a voice. He accepted we were hers and that she knew best. My dad is still obsessed with my mum and supports her in all her dysfunction.

#

By 14 years old, I'd discovered that alcohol 'helped' to numb my feelings.

I'd also started using laxatives to help me stay really thin and with no curves, seeing as my mum didn't accept my 'thickening' body. My mum loved this. She'd often tell me she'd always wanted me, her daughter, to be like the 'other white girls'. I thought this was helping me be accepted, but really it was about me disappearing and not being seen. I discovered that if you starve yourself, you don't feel. I had found the perfect solution: lack of food to numb the feelings and alcohol to drown them when the numbing didn't work. This was how I survived.

Joanna and I continued to be best friends - outside of school at least - as her friends at school didn't think it was cool to hang out with someone two years younger, which was fine as by now I'd figured out that if I hung out with the naughty children in school, I would be better protected. Out of the whole school, it was the girls in her year who hated me the most, but by then that wasn't so important to me anymore. Joanna and I would have sleepovers at her house at least three times a week, which made my life easier. I was still playing netball, dancing and running - the things that had always fed my soul so well - but by the time I was 15, everything that was getting in the way of drinking and boys, stopped.

# # #

When I was 15 years old, my mum and dad went on a trip to Puerto Rico followed by a dinner at the *St. Gregory Hotel*, San Francisco, hosted by the organisation, *Round Table*. Joanna and I were to travel there to meet them with my two younger brothers, Tayo and Wale[15], for a big trip travelling the coast of California. I was so excited and so was Joanna. However, just before the trip, Joanna left school and got her first job and wasn't allowed any time off, so now I would be escorting Tayo and Wale and doing the stupid trip alone. I no longer wanted to go. I spent all of my time with Joanna; we did everything together and couldn't imagine being on the other side of the world without her.

Once again, I was faced with being alone. At 15, I didn't understand that this is what happens when your best friend is two years older than you and at the start of her adult life. I felt abandoned by her and we never recovered from it.

The trip was a nightmare. I felt alone without Joanna and I had to spend all my time with my parents, or babysitting my younger brothers. Her absence also made it very difficult for me to hide my not-eating. My dad just would not accept that. It was hell. I had to eat at least one meal a day, every day. That was the agreement. So, for weeks, I had food in my system every day. This made my life unbearable. I could no longer control my emotions, nor prevent my buried, intolerable feelings from resurfacing,

---

[15] Pronounced: *Wah-lay*

sprouting throughout my body from my deep-rooted pain. Not eating always made me feel in control of something, but on this trip, I didn't have any.

My mum and dad collected me and my two brothers at the airport in their hired car. What was already a nightmare of a holiday suddenly turned into a horror show. Not long after leaving the airport, we got a flat tyre. While we waited for the hire company to send us recovery, the police pulled into the hard shoulder behind us and asked my dad to step out of the car. I was terrified. All I could do was watch their hands resting on their guns and hope that my dad wasn't going to be killed. I knew that black people got killed by the police in America. I just kept thinking I would be left with this white woman, who didn't understand me, or as I thought at that time, hated me. The police stayed with us until the recovery came and nothing happened, but my fear was heightened for the rest of my time in America.

# # #

When we arrived back in Scotland, I learned that Tunde, who had remained at home, had been having house-parties while we were gone. My now-popular, big brother, who everyone wanted to be friends with or date, was really making a name for himself. He was one of the first DJs to bring rap music to Scotland, which made him a lot of money and definitely helped him be more socially accepted. Rap music was so exciting at that time. It gave black people a voice and people were listening; we were apparently cool. His life was not easy by any stretch of the imagination, but he made it work for him, which in turn made a lot of people be more accepting of me.

# # #

Other things in my life were changing very quickly. My friend Ruth - the one whose garden I would take a short-cut to my garden through to avoid being beaten up - told me about a school holiday to Costa Brava, Spain. I asked my dad if I could go, as he would be the most likely one to say yes, and he did. Three weeks later I was travelling by bus to Newcastle with my friend Ruth, her two friends, Angela and Yvonne (who only really wanted to be friends with me because of Tunde), and my English teacher; the amazing after-school tutor, Mr. Brown. He was the one who would get me to talk to him about whatever was going on for me racially; he said it would help. I remember he always smelled of fags and coffee and how I would make him two cups during my lessons. I remember how relaxed the aroma made me feel, but with hindsight, it was actually him. This scruffy, unkempt, white man was probably the only person in my life at that time who understood how difficult life was for me.

We arrived in Spain in June 1987. I was to share a room with Lorraine and Karen, two girls that I actually liked from my year. They were cousins.

Whitney Houston had just exploded all over the globe with *I Wanna Dance With Somebody* and everywhere we went in Spain, men and boys would call me 'Whitney'. On our first night there, our room was broken into by three steaming-drunk, German men whilst we were in bed. Thankfully our teachers and hotel staff came to our rescue. I remember Mr. Brown telling us we were no longer allowed out without him as we were in danger. I thought it was because I was black and asked him this privately.

"No Kemi. You are different and 'exotic'. Men will always be interested in you because of this, but a lot of them will turn on you because they're not seeing you as a full person."

He was right about that. Up to that point I had only thought of the consequences of people hating me because of my skin. Now I was learning there were also consequences to people over-liking me because they saw only my colour and not me, the person.

We all had a ball that holiday and I met two lovely young men, a Spaniard and an Englishman. When I returned home, I continued to have a great summer with my five new girlfriends.

# # #

My family and I moved to another, posher part of Coatbridge, nearer to one of my new friends, Yvonne, and I met my first real boyfriend, Michael, in the autumn of that year. He had been at my school but had left by now and was working. He was 17 and lived a couple of towns away from me, nearer Glasgow. In the beginning he was lovely, even though his dad didn't really like me. However, as the darkness of winter drew in, he became very possessive and didn't want me to spend any time with my friends. The brightness I'd rediscovered in life during my happy summer had drastically dimmed. Life would be hard for a while.

# # #

I studied hard and sat my exams. By the time my exams arrived the following May, I had lost all contact with all of my friends. Michael had cheated on me numerous times and had become violent; but he was all that I had. I spiralled deeper and deeper down into the 'dark hole' once again. I remember being at Michael's friend's grandmother's 80th birthday party in Glasgow. Michael tried to go outside with another girl, so I followed him. We argued, then the next thing I knew the police had driven past and stopped. They got out and that's when it all becomes a bit of a blur. Things happened so quickly, but we were both beaten and taken to the cells at London Road Police Station in Glasgow around midnight. When we arrived there, I was submissive, just as my dad had instilled in me. I knew the police could be unfair to black people, I mean let's face it, I'd just been beaten up and arrested for it. We were both to be charged with police assault, seeing as Michael had tried to fight back, but my dad knew the procedure of dealing with the police – he'd dealt with them regularly, ever since Tunde had become a teenager and learned to drive - so I was released at 4am the next morning. My dad had scared them with his swishy, Edinburgh lawyer, as a result of them assaulting his 16-year-old daughter. Michael, however, remained in the cells for the whole weekend, before appearing in court on the Monday morning.

Within a few days, the local police from my town came to see me to apologise about what had happened to me in Glasgow and to assure me that I shouldn't be scared. It was far too late for that. I truly believed it would only be a matter of time before I would be killed because of the colour of my skin.

I didn't want to leave my house for a very long time after the police beating, only doing so to go to school and even then, my mum would drive me to and from. Meanwhile Michael's dad wouldn't let him see me anymore; I was no longer welcome at their house. It worked out fine – I didn't want to leave the house anyway, so Michael would just come to our house.

Aged 17

Auntie died when I was 16.

I can still feel the loss I felt then, as I tried to accept that she was no longer in my life. After a few years of remission from the breast cancer, it was discovered that she had ovarian cancer.

"She was riddled with it. How could she not have known? She was a doctor!"

My mum said this as if Auntie had had any control over it. It still angers me that she thought that of Auntie. Ovarian cancer is known as the silent killer, with no symptoms, until it's too late.

I felt defeated in life; what was the point? I had no one who truly 'got me'. Auntie had totally understood me and her presence in my life had made me feel free in my skin. By now, I had lost the connection with my dad that I'd had in the earlier years of his return. He no longer wanted me to be proud of my blackness; he wanted me to be whatever was acceptable to the whites, or more importantly, to my mum. That's what he did; he gave her all his power. In doing so, he relinquished to her his children's powers too.

By the time I turned 17, I had given all control of my life to my mum. I no longer outwardly rebelled against her. I think I accepted that her control kept me safe. My mum's love came in the form of control; she believed that if you love someone, then you control them. Control, to my mother, was love; so, if I surrendered then she would love me.

When I found out I was pregnant, Michael wanted me to have an abortion and I nearly did, but my overriding feeling was to keep the baby as this could be someone who had to love me. So, I went ahead with the pregnancy, while Michael's dad, in his bid to make Michael end the relationship with me, bought him a car. His mum was heartbroken as she didn't want to turn her back on the baby, but Michael and his dad didn't want a mixed-race baby with a 'microphone' head.

I remember thinking this baby was my way out. I wouldn't have to engage in life anymore. My mum was on board from the get-go, stating this baby would be her second chance, seeing as I'd been such a disappointment. The way she'd always treated me with immeasurable contempt left me feeling as if she utterly despised me. I felt like I could never be what she wanted me to be. I used to think that if I'd been white, then maybe she would have loved me.

While my parents started making plans for me and my baby, my dad refused to speak to me about the pregnancy. He told none of his friends or colleagues. He acted as if it wasn't happening. He couldn't cope with his shame and wanted to send me to Nigeria. I could see where he was coming from. He'd had to work hard to achieve success, making sacrifices to make a name for himself and here I was in 1989, bringing his reputation down into the gutter. I remember feeling the same shame from him that I'd felt from white people; not being good enough and being an overall disappointment. I felt the relationship that we'd built together since he had come back into my life no longer existed. The little connection I'd had with my dad, I'd lost. He would now only ever look at me with disappointment, condemning me to go deeper into my feelings of never being enough.

My parents began making plans about my future. One thing was very clear; my mum wasn't giving up any of her life to bring up this baby, so I was to have a nanny, paid for by them, to allow me to continue to study.

"No way . . . my child will not be raised by someone else."

So instead, I worked full-time in my mum's post office until my baby was born and for once I got paid. I did this comforted in the knowledge that I had a plan: I'd be moving out as soon as the baby was born. However, I was not telling my parents just yet; they were very controlling and me being pregnant had only strengthened their grip. For now, I had no choice. I needed them, so I submitted.

I wasn't happy that I was having to eat more, but I was too scared this little baby wouldn't have everything it needed to grow.

My mum threw me out of the house the week before Christmas.

"Mum I don't think I'll make it into work tomorrow," I said shakily entering her bedroom and feeling like I could collapse at any moment. "I don't think I'm well."

"What? Oh Kemi, stop being a drama queen!" she accused.

I was only a month away from giving birth. As I stood there, feeling like my body was about to burst with all the fluid it was retaining, I felt so exhausted and overwhelmed and began to cry.

"Oh, here we go again with 'The Kemi Show'. There's fuck-all wrong with you. You're just too fat. You've put on far too much weight. You actually wobble when you walk," she said, imitating how she thought I looked.

"Shut up. Don't say that," I sobbed.

"Well, it's true. You are fat and you're lazy and if you're not going to work tomorrow then you'd better find somewhere else to live," she blackmailed, feeling like she held all the cards.

"Fine then," I accepted, before leaving her room feeling disgusted at myself and even more self-conscious of my size.

"Oh, and where do you think you will go?" she smugly enquired.

"My gran's," I said, with a clear-cut tone.

"Oh no you fucking won't," she said, all hell-bent.

I was determined I was. They were my grandparents and she couldn't control how much they loved me. They'd always offered me shelter in times like this and she hated that. I called my grandad and asked him to come and pick me up with my mum still screaming in the background. She tried to grab at me, to get the phone off me, but for once, my ever-silent father stopped her before she made contact. As I left the house and climbed into my grandad's car, she was still screaming: "I will never take you back and you will never survive without me." As we drove away in the car, I remember believing both those statements.

I had only been living with my grandparents for a few days when I had an antenatal appointment. I decided, along with my cousin Tracey, who still lived in Caldercruix and who I had been spending a lot of time with, that it would be a good idea for us to go on the bus. We'd heard that this was a way of inducing labour – a way to relieve me of my terrible discomfort. Well, we did go on the bus and as a result I experienced the most horrific contraction pains and ended up being taken into hospital the day before Christmas Eve.

My mum came to my gran's house, as my gran had called her and took me to the hospital. I didn't argue when my gran told me my mum was on her way, even though I knew this would result in me going back home. I hadn't spoken to my mum since I left nearly a week earlier, but she had told my grandad that I would not be getting back home until I had apologised. I wasn't ready to; I was happy being with my grandparents and was enjoying a bit of 'fun time' with them and Tracey. However, I knew I couldn't go into hospital without her; she wouldn't have wanted anyone to know she had thrown out her eight-month-pregnant daughter.

"Well Kemkem," she began. I knew instantly she had let the fight go as I would have been called 'Kemi', not Kemkem.

"I have decided to forget about your behaviour," she proclaimed, expecting me to be grateful. I didn't even bother to look over at her, but instead continued to stare out of the window.

"We have our baby on the way," she announced with excitement.

This is when I surrendered my power as mother to my child over to her.

I was kept in hospital for a couple days with the doctors advising it was very important that I rest. I left hospital and went back to my parent's home on Christmas morning.

Around this time Michael's mum phoned me, confessing she was deeply sorry for abandoning me and that she could no longer support her husband and son's wishes; she wanted to be a part of my baby's life. I accepted but warned her she only had one chance; if she ever let my baby down it would be for the last time.

Shortly after, Michael called and we got back together. I remember my dad getting involved, telling me that I didn't need a man, that I could raise my baby by myself with *his* support. He also advised that *if* I was going to continue to see Michael and let him be part of the baby's life, that the baby had to have my name. He explained that black, mixed-race children needed to have a solid foundation and since I was the parent of colour, it was my job to lay that foundation. He warned that if I didn't insist on the name and this "man-boy" left again, that my baby would be left with a different surname to its mum. A white surname in a black family. So, I decided then that all my children would have my family name: Ogunyemi.

Michael and my mum were both at the birth, but my mum had to wait in the waiting room. After hours of labour and complications, owing to the fact that I have sickle cell trait, I had to have a caesarean section. My daughter was born on 25th January, 1990. I was 17 years old and had no clue what lay ahead for me.

The name

I only had up to three weeks after the birth to name and register my baby. At the time, Michael worked away from home and only returned every second weekend. In order for Michael to be named as the father on our daughter's birth certificate, he would have to be present at the registration office when the application was submitted. However, the office was only open on weekdays, meaning Michael and I would have to attend a weekend appointment with a Justice of the Peace. Michael would be witnessed as being the father, then an affidavit would be released to be used at the registration office in Michael's absence. I remember my father setting up the appointment with the Justice of the Peace, as they were acquaintances.

Michael collected me to go to our appointment on the Saturday. *Beep-beep*. He remained in his car while I gathered up 'Babygirl' - as I called her - and put her into her basket. The morning had been non-stop and I was already chasing my tail. Whilst trying to pack all the essentials into the baby's travel bag my dad approached me.

"Kemi," he said with a weighty tone. He looked me straight in the eyes, rendering my peripheral vision redundant. I had to look away; I felt the potency of his stare.

"Kemi. Look at me," he instructed.

Feeling uncomfortable, I met his deep, darkest-of-brown eyes, hoping I wasn't going to have another argument over the name of my baby. Michael had already been lecturing me on what the baby's name must be and I could do with avoiding 'round two' with my dad. *Beep-beep*.

"Yes Dad?" I replied, bracing myself for the oncoming lecture whilst juggling buttoning my coat, holding a baby basket in one hand and a travel bag in the other.

"Ogunyemi," he said. "She must have your name."

"Dad, I know this. I wouldn't ever call her anything else."

I was very clear about this; I would not be backing down. He must have been reading my thoughts. *Beep-beep*.

"Kemi, she is your daughter. Michael left you. He was missing during your whole pregnancy." He sounded so final and sure in his African tone.

"And . . . you also call her Yemisi."

I was not as sure. I'd wanted to call my daughter Yemisi throughout my entire pregnancy, but now I knew there would be a price to pay from Michael if I did. One 'black' name was going to be bad enough, let alone two. I had heard his anger building in his voice over the previous couple of weeks, whenever we had spoken on the phone.

"You idiot! Are you fucking mental?" he berated. "You don't know how lucky we've been; she doesn't even look black," he stated relieved. I was appalled at his 'lucky' revelation.

"What? Of course she looks black," I replied, gripping the phone tighter with frustration. "Do you mean because she doesn't have afro hair? You do know she has African features . . . she is black. You're the idiot!"

"Who the fuck are you calling an idiot? I'm not talking to you when you're behaving all black," he seethed, before slamming the phone down. I was always braver over the phone. I knew I'd pay for it later.

Finally, organised and running late, I opened the front door to reveal Michael impatiently waiting in his car.

"Okay Dad, I need to go. We're running late," I said, as I kissed him on the cheek and made my way to the car.

As I strapped the baby basket into the back seat and climbed into the front, I observed that Michael seemed more pleasant than he had been the night before. Irritated more than angry.

He had returned home the night before and had visited, resulting in us continuing the argument of 'the name'. I thought I was going to get my payback then for having been brave on the phone. He had been so angry, but he didn't hit me. He hadn't hit me since we got back together; but it had only been six weeks and I knew the signs.

For the majority of the journey, we sat in silence. When we eventually arrived outside the Justice of the Peace's house, Michael parked up:

"Kemi," he started.

I felt anxious. I was exhausted; I had been up since 6am, got myself and Babygirl washed and dressed; fed Babygirl twice; just about got her travel bag organised and all in between multiple nappy changes. There was always just so much to organise and I was always very conscious of taking too long getting myself and Babygirl ready, as I knew Michael hated being late. We now were - he'd been waiting for us in his car for 15 minutes.

"My dad has called to say we were running late," I began, anticipating another one of his lectures on time keeping. "The woman said it was fine," I said as quickly as possible, wanting to get it all out before he could complain.

He unclipped his seatbelt and turned to face me, still in silence. The tension grew.

"It's so hard Michael. I'm exhausted and it's not even one o'clock yet," I continued.

Further silence. The look of annoyance on his face made chills run up my spine, causing my neck to stiffen, contorted with spasm. That had become the natural, instinctive reaction whenever I saw that look. The words that came out of his mouth, however, didn't match.

"Listen," he finally voiced. "Let's just agree; I'll agree to Ogunyemi if you drop Yemisi for Michelle."

He sounded so calm, but I could see from his tense jaw and fixed stare that if I didn't agree, he would beat me. I knew that face. I swallowed my pride along with everything I believed in. I knew my daughter having a

Nigerian name was very import for her identity. My dad had insisted that I had a Nigerian name and my mum had had no choice. I felt sick with disappointment as I resigned myself to defeat.

"Okay, I'll name her Michelle."

We went in and as agreed my daughter was registered as Michelle. The Justice of the Peace concluded the paperwork and we left. I strapped the baby basket into the back seat and began to fasten my seatbelt. *Bang!* I felt a warm, thick liquid in my mouth. My lip tingled with pins and needles and numbness. I ran my tongue along the inside of my mouth and could feel the indentation where my tooth had embedded and punctured my lip. I felt my mouth fill with blood. Then I felt pain. A deep, throbbing pain. *That bastard has just hit me.* Next, I felt consumed with shame.

Don't speak . . . don't say a single word. Just keep your mouth shut. Kemi . . . you can do this . . . you've got to keep it together. Just get the baby home. I didn't speak one single word. In that silence, the five-minute journey home seemed to take forever. *Get it together Kemi. Come on. You need to be able to carry this baby inside. Stop shaking, stop shaking.* I don't know how I managed to lift Michelle out of the car.

"You and your family just want to make her black. She could pass as white with a tan. You do know that?" Michael rambled, trying to convince himself.

Having found a new strength in my anger, I slammed the car door and walked away.

I entered the house quickly and quietly so I could get upstairs, undetected. I needed to see my damage to figure out what excuse I could get away with this time. I didn't make it past the first set of stairs.

"Kemi where are you sneaking off to with my baby?"

Shit . . . Mum! I put the baby down, still with my back to her.

"I need to use the toil . . . "

I didn't get to finish. I could hear the distortion my swollen lip was causing to my speech. My mouth was struggling to complete the words I was trying to say.

"What the . . . ? Kemi turn around. Let me see you," my mum ordered with confusion in her tone.

My face was thumping, I was losing my strength and I felt incredibly vulnerable and weak.

"Kemi?" my mum said, as she pulled me around to face her. "What has he done to you?" she gasped.

"Nothing." I painfully sobbed.

"Samuel - get through here! That bastard has hit her and smashed up her mouth and she's going to try to defend him," my mum ranted.

As my dad entered the hall to inspect the situation, the shock on his face made me feel even more shame.

"Dad, Michael didn't do this . . . it was an accident, honest. It was a football, Dad." He just shook his head and sucked his teeth.

"Why would you let someone do this to you?" he snarled.

"But Dad . . . ," I tried.

"But Dad, nothing!" my mum interjected. "Where did he get the ball? Did the Justice of the Peace give it to him? You make me sick! Look at you. I mean, you're still so fat. How could that skinny bastard batter you? You could sit on him!"

"Daisy," my dad spoke sternly to my mum. "Kemi, go upstairs and get yourself cleaned up. I will look after Yemisi."

"Michelle," I corrected.

A look of disgust and disappointment shot across his face before he turned and walked away. I still, to this day, carry my own disappointment for the choice I made that day.

As I climbed the stairs to the bathroom, I could hear my mum ranting. She was in a frenzy. Spewing out as many hurtful words as her breathing would allow, followed by the vicious and vindictive singing of the same old song: "What's the breadth of Kemi? What's the breadth of Kemi?" As I closed the bathroom door, the feeling of regret choked me.

Looking in the mirror I could see my mouth was swollen, with even more swelling to the side of my face. My lip was so swollen you could see the blood pouring from the big gouge where the tooth had embedded, even though the puncture took place at the back of my lip.

I couldn't feel my nose, or that whole side of my face up to my eye for over a week. Yet, I continued to see Michael; I was too scared of the outside world and he was all I had.

# # #

Owing to my mum's regular pastime of tormenting me about my weight, I was introduced to self-loathing. Never mind the fact that I had just given birth, I was a size 12-14 at the time - which I think is about average for a lot of women - when my mum's rhetoric inspired me to stop eating again. Within three weeks I was an 'acceptable' size ten. This stopped the 'fat-bashing', but she further encouraged me to be even thinner; being rewarded with praise. Being thin helped me feel loved by my mother. Looking back, I can see that the thinner I was, the less resistant I was to my mum; and she needed that to retain her control. I was very broken.

# # #

I went to the local council when I turned 18 on 4th March, 1990 and had the offer of my own flat by early May. I finally told my parents I was moving out after the offer arrived. My mum was devastated. She had made it so difficult for me to see Michael - after he burst my lip, she refused to have him enter her house.

Michelle had not been well for the first four months of her tiny, little life. She would barely feed and anything she did take down came straight back up. She was in severe pain with colic and cried all day, every day. This resulted in very little growth in her first four months. We spent two separate occasions in hospital. She became so poorly I was too petrified to leave her side as I thought she might die. I believed God was punishing me for considering having an abortion earlier in my pregnancy. I would lie in my bed on the floor at night and speak to God, begging for help, over and over.

"Please God, don't let my baby die. Please make her better. I promise to be the best mum I can. Please, I can't live without her."

I slept on the floor on a pull-out bed and after about four days, Michael's dad, who had been at the hospital every day, finally convinced me it was safe to "leave Michelle and go and freshen up; maybe even try to eat a little food".

I did, and in doing so, started a routine where he would come daily to the hospital at 11am so I could go home for a quick shower and a change of clothes, before returning to the hospital. My mum was astonished that he had somehow convinced me to leave the hospital for once and was impressed that he was making such an effort. With Michael working away most of the time, if ever Michael's mum had to be at work, his dad would always step in.

My mum was so impressed she allowed Michael back into her house - we just wouldn't speak about the assault.

Michelle continued to reject milk and by her third admission to hospital was diagnosed as having a milk intolerance, and so was given soya milk to help her put on some weight. She was tiny until she was a year old. I was so young and naive and had thought I knew it all, but during that time I felt I was losing control of my daughter.

Before I moved out, my mum would come in from work to find her house spotless and the dinner made, as had been my role since the age of 14. The job of cooking the family's dinner was one that I liked to control because everybody ate at different times, so I could always say that I had already eaten and nobody would question it. She would take Michelle and say that I could have some time to myself. It didn't matter what I did for my little baby, my mum would always criticise me, adding that I was too young to be a good mother. This made me feel as if Michelle loved her more than me. However, after I had decided to keep my baby, I'd always known she'd be my way out of my family.

Once my mother had got her head around the fact I was moving out and accepted I wasn't going to change my mind, she had to support me. She and Dad did help me a great deal financially and by June, Michelle and I had moved out.

Michael hadn't seen the flat as he was working away, but when he came back, he moved in. As his work was based in Canary Wharf, London, he would only be at the flat one weekend in every three.

I had nice neighbours next door, but the racist, old man downstairs made his feelings known - "There shouldn't be any blacks living here" - and would frequently complain and lie about me to the Council, to try to have me removed. With my skin colour, I didn't have to do anything wrong; just breathing the same air as some people was an offence. So, I just tried to always be good - just as I had been taught – but by now, racism was totally embedded in my everyday existence.

Michael and I split up on New Year's Eve because he didn't want me to go out to celebrate. This wasn't something new – at times it didn't suit him to have a black girlfriend. I remember him laying into me in the hallway yet again, when from somewhere deep inside of me, I managed to find the courage to tell him to leave and not to come back. He spat in my face and called me a black bastard. I knew then I would never let him back. I also realised I had a line and he wouldn't cross it again.

I packed his stuff, as I had nothing else to do. Michelle was at my parent's house and my only friends were his. When I finished packing, I phoned his mum and asked her to come and pick it up. She agreed to collect it the next day.

I remember his dad waited in the car and how upset his mum was when she saw the state of my face. She told me I'd made the correct decision in making Michael leave, that I was only 18 and that Michelle and I deserved better. She also confessed that Michael's dad hit her and had only recently stopped since the birth of Michelle. Finally, she said she was sorry.

From this point on she would take Michelle once a week, with Michael having access to see her. He didn't really have the maturity to have her by himself, but he did pay money towards her needs every week. He did put the time in with her as she got older and was able to build his own strong connection. He is a good father. Our relationship grew to become respectful of each other, with him always being supportive of me as a mother.

Cool

At 19, with no boyfriend, I was on my own for the first time. With Michelle able to go to an adjoined nursery while I was in class, I'd started a course at the local high school. It was a class for mature students and it was where I met my friend, Lynne. She was older, 27, with long, blonde hair and beautiful, piercing blue eyes. She was so cool. She was divorced with two little boys, but had a great relationship with their dad. Their relationship appeared equal; something I hadn't really seen between a man and a woman before. It was good for me to see this other side of relationships. I got her a job working for my dad in his restaurant, where we would work together two nights a week and go out dancing after work at the weekends. We had great fun!

It was at this time in my life I was introduced to hash/cannabis - call it what you will - Bob Dylan and Tom Petty.

I'd been quite naive in regard to drug use up until this point, having been too busy being a teenage mum to have ever been in contact with any. The first time I had a smoke was at Lynne's friend's house. I'd arranged to join up with them one Saturday afternoon. Michelle was staying overnight at my parents' house, so I had until the Sunday evening before I was needed to be on-duty mum again. I was so scared.

"But won't I die?" I replied to Lynne's offer of having a smoke. I thought all drugs came in silver, tin foil and killed you.

"Kemi," she began through fits of laughter. "You can't possibly believe that . . . this isn't *Grange Hill.*"

"I know I won't," I replied, backtracking, trying not to sound inexperienced. "I was just joking," I added, feeling quite embarrassed. I knew she didn't believe me, but she cared enough not to point it out.

I can still remember the peace I felt with the second drag.

"Peacefully happy and no man to spoil it," was my first statement, which made the others laugh.

"Kemi, do you feel cool?" Lynne asked, dragging the word 'cool' out really long.

"You know, me think I do, no?" I said imitating my dad's thick, Nigerian accent.

"Kemi, you are one of the coolest chicks I know. I'm just so glad you finally feel it!"

She said it so matter of fact. *Cool? Am I cool? What a new concept, to think I might be cool.* I knew, for the first time ever, I certainly felt cool.

# # #

At this time, the closest person in my life was my brother, Tayo. He had graduated, by my estimates, at being a very cool teenager. We had always been close, but when I had Michelle, he became an even bigger part of my life. When I was still living with my parents, Tayo would come straight in from school and take Michelle off me so I could have a break. He was so good. He had grown into being our cousin Lee's best friend.

They did everything together; even things Tayo was too young to be taking part in! He was just so cool and chilled. Everyone loved to have him around and be in his company. He was affectionately infectious. Thinking back, I'm ashamed of how much I depended on him. Tayo must only have been 16-17 years old, but I often forgot that, as he was such a strength to me at the time. He would often babysit Michelle when I was working on a Thursday night and would always get me hash so no one would find out I smoked, especially Tunde.

Tunde, being the eldest, had always acted like he was the boss of me and would even warn boys off from dating me with the threat of beating them up! He was so annoying! When he eventually found out that I smoked, instead of his usual authoritarian attitude, he actually joined in with me and Tayo! From then on, we regularly smoked together, sitting around sharing our most recent racist experiences, all the while getting stoned. This made the conversation feel freer to share.

I was working in the family restaurant two nights a week and my mum or Tayo would come to my house to babysit Michelle, unless she was at her dad's. I didn't realise at the time, but my mum still had the same level of control over me after I'd moved out as she'd had when I lived with her at home.

My mum would use my wages to pay my bills and then give me whatever money was left over. She said I was no good with money. I accepted it because I didn't think I was good at anything, except for my not eating. She loved that I didn't eat as, to her, thin was beautiful. She thought I couldn't be beautiful without being thin, as the black thing wouldn't be accepted if I was fat. I don't think my dad was so aware; by this time, he was heavily into gambling. This had been his escape.

My godmother was still in my life and her volatile relationship with my mum meant that I found out a lot of details that had been missing from my early life. I used to love going to my Auntie Joan's house in Bromley. I loved Bromley. I nearly moved there, with my Auntie Joan's encouragement, which pissed off my mum. I felt I truly belonged there. I had always dreamed of returning to England; this dream made my time in

Scotland more bearable.

I would spend school holidays in Bromley, with Michelle, looking after my three younger cousins, to help my Auntie Joan and Uncle Bill with childcare while they worked. At the weekends, they in turn, would look after Michelle so I could have some social time with my friends. I'd made a couple of friends in Bromley - two sisters -and I had a London boyfriend, who I actually liked. I was planning to move there when, out of nowhere, I saw a different side to my Auntie Joan.

"Well Kemi, you need to see your mum's side of this too," she lectured, out of character.

Devil's advocate didn't suit her; she came across as being too biased, as if she was gaining pleasure from highlighting my dad's faults. I had never heard her defend my mum before.

"Your dad's been a complete bastard to your mum you know."

I felt like I had been stabbed in the chest. Her words felt vicious. *She's intentionally attacking me.* I was confused.

"What?" I managed to reply in my shock.

Nerves sparked off inside my stomach, releasing a thousand butterflies. As I sat on the pink velvet seats built into her beautiful Georgian fireplace, I suddenly felt emotionally ambushed.

"Do you know . . . before he left you in London . . . he sent flowers to your mum *and* his girlfriend? But he got the cards mixed up - that's how your mum found out. I've told you about him being in prison?"

I nodded. *You know fine well you've told me; how else would I know?* She was the one who had drip-fed me information about my dad; him being in prison and why he was there. I recognised that this was her waging an assault; using words that she knew would hurt. *Where is this conversation going? What the hell is going on? Why are you suddenly assassinating my dad?* I was in shock. I had never seen this side to her before. She took on that same tone and look that my mum did whenever I questioned her.

"Well . . . *I* had to go along to court with your mum and listen to all that man had done," she retold, for her own pleasure, emphasising her hardship.

How could my dad going to jail, all those years ago, be about her hardship? The gravity in her tone when she said 'all' that he had done, sounded like he had murdered someone. It was fraud; serious fraud nonetheless, but come on, he hadn't killed anyone.

By the time her self-indulgent lecture had concluded, I no longer recognised the lecturer. Our relationship changed that night and I no longer visited to babysit. I figured out that I had held my Auntie Joan up too high on a pedestal. She now showed a different side to her, one that she had hidden for many years and that now made me feel uncomfortable. The older I got, the more I realised that she had her own issues with both my parents.

After I returned to Scotland, having decided never to go back to Bromley, my mum found out that I'd intended to relocate there. I told her I was no longer thinking about it after seeing a different side to my Auntie Joan. My mum simply told me:

"Your Auntie Joan was only using you for free childcare. Kemi, she doesn't think that you're any different from the ghetto kids. You know she thinks blacks are beneath her, right?"

21 years old

This is when I met my first husband, Rab. He was a year older than me and had attended my school. He was one of those white guys who thought it would be 'cool' to be black and was always hanging around the raves that Tunde disc jockeyed.

I never really went to his raves. They were full of the racists who had made my life at school a living hell. I didn't like those kinds of people; they act as if you are so cool, then once they get drunk, they turn and call you a black bastard. Tunde, however, saw them as a market to make money from and combined that with his passion for rap music. I don't think Tunde would have wanted me there anyway; even the guys I knew wouldn't have been allowed to buy me a drink! I preferred to go to the clubs in Glasgow with real, black people who were genuinely pleased to see you. So, how I ended up with Rab still surprises me to this day.

When we first got together it wasn't a serious, long-term thing as I knew he was due to be heading out to Crete to work for the summer.

He would stay over at my flat a lot from the beginning. He didn't work, partied too much and had a drink problem and, unknown to me at the time, had been involved in a lot of drugs and violence. However, somehow, I fell into this relationship.

His best friend didn't like that we were together. Some of his friends had previously shouted 'nigger' at me and had only stopped now that I was seeing Rab. In the beginning, Rab always stood up for me whenever I was confronted with racism; something not many people had done. Little did I know he was just the same.

One day, a neighbour approached me to tell me they knew of somebody who was keen on my flat, and to ask if I would be interested in swapping it for a two-bedroom, council house with a huge, gable-end garden. I jumped at the chance and before even seeing the house, instantly agreed to the proposal. A garden for Michelle would be fantastic. She would love it.

When I went to view our new house with my mum, it was grim. The lady that was swapping with me had learning difficulties and sadly, it appeared she might have been struggling. The house was filthy, while the cooker had 'fur' growing on it.

"Oh mum, it's so dirty, but I love it! I can see me and Michelle here." I was already imagining how I would style this house and make it our own home. "I know, it has great potential."

Even my mum agreed. I was filled with excitement. The house felt so much bigger and fresher than my flat, even in its filth. The spaciousness felt welcoming. As we stepped out into the front garden, I saw a very tall, elderly man, loitering in the adjoining garden. He didn't come across as being nosey, more rather gentlemanly and well-mannered.

"Hello," he greeted us, with a huge and very welcoming smile.

"Hello, my name is Michelle," Michelle responded before I could say a word.

"Very pleased to meet you, Michelle. I am John," he announced, affording her all his attention before turning to me.

"I heard there was a young woman and her daughter coming to see the house. Are you going to take it?" He sounded genuinely excited at the prospect of us being his new neighbours.

"Yes. Definitely. I'm definitely going to take it. I'm Kemi, you've already met Michelle and this is my mum, Daisy." This was the first of many conversations I would come to have with dear John.

We continued our friendly conversation for a few minutes before making our way back to the car. What a pleasant surprise! My mum and I were both relieved and pleased with this nice new neighbour; he was nothing like my racist neighbour back at the flat.

"Kemi, me and your dad have been talking," she said opening the car door. *Oh no, what now?*

"Yes?" I replied with trepidation, as I sat down to fasten my seatbelt.

I was completely consumed with my future new home and friendly neighbour, John and I didn't want her dampening my excitement. She sat her bag on the back seat before turning to face me.

"Your dad and I are concerned about Rab. Kemi, he doesn't work. We hope you're not considering letting him move in with you and Michelle," she instructed. *No. He's going to work in Crete in the summer . . . but this is now June - he was supposed to leave in May.*

"What? No. God, no. Of course not," I responded trying to convince myself as well as my mum, while gazing out of the window onto my future happiness.

"But Kemi," she began, insistent on disrupting my besotted gaze to gain my full attention.

"Mum, please. Can we just think about the house right now?" I pleaded, trying to resuscitate my excitement back to life.

"Okay, Kemi," she said under her breath, with a hint of frustration and a touch of disappointment. I knew we would speak about it again.

That evening, after I'd put Michelle to bed, Rab began asking questions about the viewing I'd had earlier.

"Well? What was it like?" he said, sincerely interested.

"Yeah, it was good."

Shit! How do I bring this up? He has been living with me for months and he doesn't pay anything. We need to speak about money. My mum had already warned me that they would not be helping financially if Rab moved in while still not having a job.

"What's up? Do you not want to talk about it?" He sounded annoyed and I felt myself trying to make him feel better,

"No, of course I do. It's just, erm. Okay, I'll just say it. My mum said to me earlier, when she dropped me off, that if you move in, they won't help me with renovation costs and, well, I need their help." He looked very pissed off.

"It's because you don't have a job, but I know you're going away to Crete anyway . . . right? So, it's fine." I felt relieved. Finally, I'd asked. Now I could get a straight answer about when he would be going away.

"Well, actually," he began boldly, "I was going to say I wasn't going anymore. I'm just going to stay here, 'cos I want to be with you. But if you don't want me . . . "

"No, it's not that," I offered, surprised. "It's just that you hadn't said."

"Listen, I know the house is yours and Michelle's, but I would like to officially move in; I will get a job."

I was shocked. Before that moment, he'd always made out that he was leaving for Crete. Looking back, I see that was one of the ways he controlled me; by keeping me on edge, forever anticipating.

He did get a job at the local chicken factory and moved in. I was starting to lose all of the happiness and confidence that I had gained in my two years of being single. Lynne had also got a new boyfriend and we had drifted apart. The only person who remained a constant friend now, was my little brother, Tayo. This was not a bad thing; we both understood how the other worked and each other's needs. I have always been truly grateful for his friendship and the connection we share.

In our first month of being in the new house, I got to see how far Rab's binge drinking would go. He had invited some of his friends over for drinks. There were four of them and two of them brought their girlfriends. I didn't mind as they would always bring hash. His best friend, Billy, especially disliked me and made his feelings towards me very clear, for all to see. That is, unless my brother Tunde was present, in which case Billy became, as they say, an arse-licker! I didn't like him, but he was Rab's best friend.

"Ah, Rab," Billy began, "bet you didn't tell Kemi about that bird you shagged last week on our bender." Devastation overwhelmed me.

"What the fuck, Billy? Are you fucking stupid? Why the fuck would you say that?" Rab spat out, overly defensive, trying to silence his friend from saying anymore. I knew his friend wasn't lying.

"Yeah. Okay, okay. I'm just taking the piss, Kemi."

Arsehole. I smiled and raised my joint in a salute. *I hate you, you dick. You will not see me upset.* I supressed my fury towards Rab, waiting to question him without an audience.

By the time they had all left, I could not hide my anger any longer. I was going to find out exactly what Billy had been talking about. However, by the time Rab had closed and locked the front door, I could tell his whole demeanour had changed. The atmosphere was charged, its negative current palpable. Instantly I felt scared. I was no longer wanting to discuss Billy's revelations; I just wanted to get out of the room. As I stood up from the sofa, pretending to be oblivious to his anger in an attempt to avoid conflict, I caught a glimpse of his face. He was looking down his nose at me, with pure disgust; his cold, vacant eyes filling with venom, before releasing an explosive backhanded slap to my face, propelling me off my feet. My jaw cracked off the arm of the sofa as I fell to the floor, smearing the blood from my cheek all across its peach leather.

I instantly felt shame and humiliation replace the anger his friend had created. I lay there in shock and fear, my face reverberating, too petrified to move in case he hit me again. The pressure under my eye built instantly, the swelling fastening my eye lid firmly shut. I recognised this pain and knew its results - another black eye. I could smell the stale *Buckfast* on his breath as he knelt down beside me.

"Don't you ever think you can question me! I'm fucking stuck with your black arse, ain't I?" he growled in my face before standing up and leaving the house.

I don't remember how I got to bed that night.

He stayed away for three days, drinking non-stop on a bender. He phoned me blind drunk on the second night; slabbering that he was sorry and blabbering all the things a broken person like me needed to hear in order to grant a pardon.

And so, it began. This would be my pattern with Rab. He would continue to go on benders, every four to six weeks, if not more frequently and I would continue to be his punch bag. He would continue to tell me that he loved me - only when he was drunk - and that he was sorry; and I continued to forgive him. This became my life. I learned not to question or argue with him when he was on his drinking binges, as this would enrage him, making him aggressive and violent. His absences from home, due to his binging, became a relief.

He also developed an alliance with my mum. He would report back to her how much I was eating and what I did each day; everything and anything. If either of them wanted me to do something, they would approach me together and back each other up. They became a team; them against me. I never told my mum of Rab's assaults. She never asked. Whenever I had black eyes, she would unequivocally accept my story of how it happened. She never questioned once, because he was her source of information on me.

During this time, I would regularly dream of a little boy. I knew this would be my next child. Even before I became pregnant, I felt a connection to this little child and when I did become pregnant, in 1995, I was totally in love with the little boy I was carrying. I loved Michelle deeply and took care of her, but I'd never felt as if she was truly my daughter; she was my mum's. I wasn't going to let this happen again.

#

I went into labour just before midnight.

"Wake me up when you're ready to call your mum, eh?" Rab yawned.

"Okay," I replied, relieved not to have him wait with me.

"No point in us both losing sleep . . . and I don't really want to watch you in all that pain," he said wincing, leaving the room to go to bed.

Rab had continued his normal binge drinking every few weeks and there was never any doubt about him wasting precious sleep waiting for me to have our baby.

I had just enough time to finish watching *Four Weddings and a Funeral* before waking Rab to call my mum.

"Yes Daisy, she's fine. You know Kemi - she can take her pain," he chuckled. "Yeah, I've been with her holding her hand."

Fucking liar. You've been sleeping. I wasn't brave enough to say this out loud. He always had to have people think he was Mr Nice Guy.

My mum arrived soon after and drove us to the hospital and I delivered my beautiful son, Dayo[16], on 17th November, 1995. Rab left me with my mum after the birth and I didn't see him again until three days later, when I was leaving hospital to return home. His absence at the hospital was obvious, so we told visitors and staff that he was ill. He wasn't ill. He was drinking right up until the morning baby Dayo and I came home.

His absence suited me though; I got some special alone-time to bond and connect with my baby. I remember holding him and thinking I would never let anyone take him away or come between me and my little one.

Rab's mother was not happy about this new mixed-race grandchild and made it perfectly clear at the hospital.

"Oh God!" she said excitedly, sounding relieved. "He's not as dark as Michelle!" *You mean 'thank God'.*

"What?" my motherly instincts snapped back, protecting my baby.

"Oh no . . . I mean, he's quite fair," she said backtracking, "Considering how African his face looks."

The emphasis on the word 'African' combined with her distorted face, revealed her racist relief: thank God he's light *despite* his African features! *I can't believe this woman is my son's grandmother. How 'lucky' are we?*

I really disliked this woman. She would take every opportunity to use the word nigger whenever I was in earshot. Her lame excuse, every time, would be: "I'm talking about the colour 'nigger-brown'," delighting in getting to say it again - and to my face this time.

Before I even left hospital, I was on high alert. There was so much potential for damage to my children by the people who were supposed to love and protect them.

---

[16] Pronounced: *Die-oh*

I was losing more and more control of Michelle to my mum. My mum made me feel like such a failure as a mother. I hoped that if I could prove I was a good mum to Dayo, she would release her hold on Michelle and allow us to be a family. However, I was scared she would try and take control of this baby too. The day I left hospital with my tiny, five-pound baby and my tiny, sickly, size 10 body, I wondered where I would get the strength for this next part of my life.

#

I'd visited my family doctor a few years before I fell pregnant with Dayo. He was a black man and had been my doctor ever since I moved to Scotland. He was always a very kind man, so much so that I never minded getting sick as I would get to see him. He was aware just how hard life had been.

My motive for the visit was to convince him to prescribe me diuretics. I reported having water retention around the time of my period. I had constructed a great system where I could get two prescriptions in a month, which aided my ability to eat very little.

In the first week of being home with Dayo, I tried to order a repeat prescription over the telephone. I don't know what happened, but instead of getting the prescription, the doctor's receptionist called me to say he wanted to see me and my mum. When I put the phone down, I knew I had been found out, despite the receptionist insisting she didn't know what it was about. A part of me worried about what I was doing to my body, as I knew these tablets were not good for me; they could make me so weak at times I could hardly walk upstairs. When I was taking them, I was surviving in an extremely dehydrated body.

I knew what the appointment was about and I was scared as my mum didn't. I even thought I would go to jail for lying to get my diuretics. When we arrived at the doctor's surgery, he was so angry . . . with my mum. He told her she must have known that I had an eating disorder – "just like Princess Diana" - and that it was a miracle I was still alive and Dayo so healthy. He said it was a good job babies were parasites and took what they needed, but that I was risking my own life.

My mum denied any knowledge of it, and the next thing I knew I was being referred to a specialist team at the hospital to be assessed.

This was devastating news for me; I knew there was something wrong with why I didn't eat, but I didn't think I had an eating disorder; I didn't even feel worthy enough to have that label. I just thought that I didn't need to eat a lot to survive.

I received a letter a couple of days later – information and appointment times for my three-week assessment. I thought they'd realise they'd made a mistake and that I didn't have an eating disorder within the three weeks.

Marion

Dayo was three weeks old by the time of my first appointment. I met a counsellor called Marion who looked to be about the same age as my mum - somewhere in her forties - and a psychiatrist called Debby, who appeared much younger, maybe somewhere in her early thirties. They were the ladies who would conduct my three weeks of assessments. I really liked them. They were warm and kind; but I felt like a fraud. I thought that after the three weeks, they would tell me I was fine and that I just needed to eat more. The latter, in particular, terrified me. So, I attended twice or three times a week, for three weeks.

I remember believing that if it wasn't for my two children, I was ready to die. I'd had enough. I was losing all sense of myself and I didn't care. All I did, and wanted to do, was love my children. I didn't want to be part of a world that had taught me I was disgusting and repulsive. The hate consuming me was killing me and here were two women who could see it all.

At the end of the three weeks, I was confirmed as suffering from anorexia. I then had to continue to see Marion, twice a week, which I did. To begin with, I actually enjoyed attending my appointments, as there was never any pressure to eat. My parents would pay for me to get a taxi there and back, as I was too scared to take public transport anymore - I'd recently had racist abuse chanted at me by a group on the bus, with some of them stalking me once I got off.

Marion and Debby suggested that I attend a session along with my mum and Rab. I had disclosed my great anxiety regarding the forthcoming Christmas Day to be spent with my parents and how food would be the centre of the occasion. On top of this, Rab was pressuring me to leave the kids and travel with him to Blackburn, to celebrate New Year at his friend's house. I didn't even know his friend and regardless, I didn't want to be separated from my children, especially at a time like Hogmanay. Rab, however, was being persistent and my mum, as usual, supported him. There was no way I could think of leaving Dayo, at just six weeks old. Their pressuring was generating even more anxiety within me.

When I got home from my appointment, I told Rab about Marion's request.

"What the fuck does she want to see me for?" he asked defensively, giving me all his attention.

"It's about Christmas," I revealed nervously. "I don't want to go because you're all going to pressure me to eat." I braced myself for his reaction.

"Well Kemi," he said switching into Mr Nice Guy mode, "It's only because we care."

His façade never worked on me. Unlike the outside world, I knew what lay beneath it. *Your only care is keeping up your performance.* He was very calculated. I knew from that moment he would be on his best behaviour leading up to the meeting; he needed them to believe he was Mr Nice Guy.

"So, will you go?" I questioned, looking for a definitive confirmation.

"Of course I will," he said with a tone of certainty. "I'm going to do anything to support you in this." *You're going to do everything to make yourself look good.*

I was filled with panic. When Marion and Debby had initially suggested that Rab should attend my session, I had felt positive about it; it would facilitate the pressure being eased off. But now, I was filled with scepticism. If Rab was going to continue to act like Mr Nice Guy, there was a good chance he, with the supporting role of my mum, would manipulate Marion into thinking that he was the perfect husband and that I was so terrible. Together, they could turn everything around and put the blame on to me. *Now I've got to go and ask my mum. Why did I think this would be a good idea?* I picked up the phone with apprehension and dialled in the numbers, each digit gaining more reluctance. *Ring, ring. Ring, ring.*

"Hello?" my mum questioned. She didn't see the point in having caller ID.

"Hi, Mum," I replied, hiding my newly formed resistance.

"Oh, hi Kemkem, I was just thinking about you. How did it go today at Marion's? What did you talk about?" Her tone was direct. *You mean what did I say about you?* Straightaway I felt intruded.

"Yeah, it went fine, thanks. I can't really remember much of what was said," I lied, shutting down her line of questioning, "but Marion and Debby would like you and Rab to come in for a session," I invited, rerouting the direction of conversation.

"That's fantastic news Kemi. I think this wee woman really wants to help you. I mean, if she wants me and Rab involved, then she totally understands you can't survive without us." I felt my anxiety reaching its tipping point.

"Okay Mum," I swiftly exhaled, "so, you'll go then?" I pressed, now very eager to conclude the conversation and get off the phone as quickly as possible.

She agreed and as I put the phone down, feeling completely resigned to defeat, my imagination kept repeating different scenarios all with the same conclusion: *Marion and Debby are going to end up siding with Rab and my mum.*

I felt as if they would 'expose' me, whatever that meant. I wasn't sure what it was that I had to be exposed, but I just felt very vulnerable having them narrate their self-preserving version of my existence to Marion and Debby.

The night before the session, my mum turned up at my house with a beautiful, emerald green, velvet, double-breasted coat. I remember she was so eager for me to try it on. I hated the pressure that she put on me to try on clothes. Trying on new clothes was always a stressful chore that I dreaded, as it made me have to look at my body. As I buttoned up the coat, feeling like a self-conscious muse, I realised this had been bought for me as a bribe - to make her look good the next day.

My mum did a lot of talking at the beginning of the session. This was a mixture of both her nerves at potentially being judged by my counselling team and her desperation to quickly establish her 'concerned and supportive mother' role. She dominated the conversation early on, laying the foundations of her public persona. *She's getting in there first. Here we go.*

"I mean, I love my daughter, very much. There is nothing that I wouldn't do for her." I recognised her audition; not her finest, but it was up there.

"I mean she's my everything," she gushed, emphasising her commitment with a well-timed, arm around the shoulder.

I tensed. Her performance was growing in confidence. Her timing was on point. As she ended the scene, she placed her hand on my leg, causing my instinctive reflex to kick in; I flinched, pulling away. At seeing this, Marion instantly interrupted my mum's soliloquy.

"Daisy, can I just stop you there?" Her strapping Glaswegian accent was not seeking permission. "Can you just look at Kemi and her body language." All eyes turned towards me shrinking in my seat.

"Yeah, yeah. I know that she doesn't like being touched," she began to argue whilst squeezing her lingering arm tighter, "but she's my daughter and I'm not going to stop," she concluded with authority, before patronisingly patting my leg. I moved my small frame out of her clutch.

"Please Mum . . . don't." I quietly requested.

"But Kemkem, you're my girl," she asserted, insinuating that her 'ownership' of me superseded my request of no contact.

"Kemi, tell your mum how it makes you feel when people touch you," Marion interrupted, regaining order.

I can't believe she's asking me to do this in front of them. We spoke about physical contact in confidence; this has nothing to do with today. This was supposed to be about Christmas dinner!

Shifting uncomfortably in my seat, I remained silent, my eyes searching Marion's in shock and confusion. *What are you doing?*

"Kemi," she continued, trying to reassure me and all the while gently turning the screw, "it's important that you explain how physical contact makes you feel. If your mum can understand how it makes you feel, then she will be able to understand why it is important for you not to be touched." *How dare you! You're throwing me to the wolves!*

Finally, after a lengthy silence only interrupted by the rhythmic ticking of Marion's desktop clock, I spoke. I explained that the inside of me felt ugly and dirty and . . . well . . . wrong. I disclosed that I believed if someone touched me, they would be able to feel my filth and that I wouldn't be able to hide it from them any longer. I was sobbing by the time I had finished talking and exhausted from the powerful release of emotion that speaking honestly brought. In that moment there was genuine shock and sadness from my mum. I saw it; it wasn't an audition this time.

She agreed to try not to touch me anymore. I didn't feel confident that she would be able to maintain her abstinence. In the rare moments when she did show true and sincere empathy, they remained exactly there - in that rare moment. She could never carry her empathy outside the moment.

The rest of the meeting went fine. I agreed to eat roast potatoes at the Christmas dinner, as long as no one brought up my eating. My mum said she would get my dad to agree. Rab had acted like the perfect partner, as expected. Marion said that it might be a good idea for me to consider going away for a few days to get a break from the kids. She would later regret her encouragement.

Rab remained on his best behaviour over the Christmas period. Mr Nice Guy was ever-present; he was integral to Rab's method of convincing me to accompany him to Blackburn for Hogmanay. Burying my sadness at the thought of being separated from Michelle and six-week-old Dayo, I eventually agreed to go.

Rab had been really keen for me to go. He wanted to introduce me to his friend and his girlfriend and was eager to make a good impression. We were to stay with them in their flat for three nights.

# # #

We travelled down to Blackburn, England, by train on Hogmanay and met up with his friend, Freddy, who turned out to be lovely; not at all like Rab's other friends. His girlfriend, Louise, was really nice too. Freddy lived in an apartment above his dad's pub. We went for drinks in the pub, before deciding to go up to Freddy's flat to relax for a while and freshen up. We were to return to the pub later to take in the bells at midnight. So far, the night had gone well and I'd managed to keep the thought of my children being miles away out of my mind.

Freddy and Rab went through to the kitchen to pour drinks, while Louise and I retreated to the living room, heels in hands. We chatted away while I sieved through her CD collection, trying desperately to find something to replace her choice of song, *Robson & Jerome's* rendition of *'I Believe'*. As I ejected the CD to replace it with *Coolio's Gangsta's Paradise*, the briefly silent interlude occurred at the precise time to reveal a snippet of the conversation taking place in the kitchen between Rab and Freddy.

"Billy . . . Stu . . . lunchtime," were the only three words I heard before *Coolio's* intro kicked in. *Why is Freddy talking about Billy and Stu . . . they're Rab's friends . . . does Freddy even know them? Are they coming here?* I was confused and hurt but couldn't - and wouldn't - make a scene. I supressed my urge for answers.

Rab and I were in the bedroom getting organised to return downstairs to celebrate New Year's arrival. I felt agitated and frustrated. I'd left my five-year-old daughter to be shared between her dad and his parents; I'd abandoned my six-week-old baby to be shuttled between both sets of grandparents and I'd travelled miles away from my family and home - against all of my instincts - to be down here with Rab; not his mates. Eventually my lips were breached.

"Are Billy and Stu coming tomorrow?" I questioned, sitting upright at the foot of the bed, having just put on my shoes.

"Whit[17]?" Rab snapped, slightly off balance, partly due to alcohol and partly down to him struggling to wriggle his foot back into his shoe without untying his laces.

"I know they're coming," I divulged, watching him sway at the side of the bed, "I heard you talking in the kitchen."

"So fucking what . . . do you fucking own Blackburn?" His tongue was becoming looser and his patience thinner.

"No," I calmly replied, "but I wouldn't have come if I'd known they were coming. I don't understand why you wanted me here if they were coming."

Defeated by drunkenness, Rab sat down at the side of the bed, his lower back facing me as he sagged over his knees, attempting his shoes again.

"Aye, well I don't want you here."

Tears poured out of me. Floods of tears. *Why did I come here? I don't know this place . . . I don't know anyone here.* I was trapped, hundreds of miles away from my children. I was devastated.

Consumed in my thoughts, I didn't see him coming. In one fell swoop, he lunged across the bed at me, gripping me tightly by my throat, throwing me backwards onto the bed before straddling my chest with all his weight. With his hand still on my throat, clamping like a vice, I was pinned. I could feel the blood pressure swelling my face. He pressed firmly across my mouth and nose with his other hand, before leaning in and forcing his face up close to mine.

"Who the fuck do you think you are?" he frothed. "You're not fucking causing a scene here! I could stop you breathing right now. I could chuck you out in the street and nobody would even care. Nobody knows you here."

Through my blurry, tearful eyes, I could see his veins bulging across his forehead and his infuriated, red face. I could feel my face being crushed under the weight of his clammy, tear-filled palm. I thought that at any second, my throat was going to collapse from the force being driven through it. *I can't breathe. He's going to kill me. I'm going to die.* Then suddenly, and unexpectedly, he released his grip.

"Fuck this; this is Hogmanay! I'm getting the fuck out of here," he

---

[17] Scottish slang, often used in place of 'what'.

declared, before spitting in my face.

He climbed off my chest, allowing my lungs to expand with every gasp that I took and walked out of the room.

I lay there, incapacitated by fear. My nose throbbed, my jaw ached and my throat already felt bruised, pulsating with pain every time I swallowed. I could hear Rab's voice and then Freddy's voice, followed by the sound of a door closing. Then silence. I waited in the room, immobilised, for what felt like an eternity. *Have they left? Have they all left? Where is Louise?* The silence was broken by a huge roar from downstairs in the pub, accompanied by a series of fireworks going off somewhere nearby. *Must be midnight.*

Probably another hour passed and I remained in the room, latched to my despair. Then I heard a door open, allowing the noise from downstairs to momentarily boom into the flat, before being muffled again as the door closed. I heard footsteps entering the flat. *Who's that? Has he come back? What's he going to do now?* Terror filled me. The footsteps drew closer, before stopping at the other side of the bedroom door. *Knock, knock.*

"Kemi?" Louise beckoned. *Oh my God . . . what will I say? I don't even know her.*

"Yeah," I replied, mortified.

"Kemi, it's Louise. Can I come in?" she requested gently from the other side of the door.

"Yes," I conceded, accepting that I really had no choice; it was her flat. The door slowly opened, gradually exposing Louise as she sheepishly entered.

"I don't know what's happened and I don't need to know," she began, sounding sincere. "This isn't right, him going out and leaving you here."

"I don't care about what's happened," I explained, "I just want to go back home to my children."

As I searched my bag for a tissue to clean my face, Louise began telling me about the night's developments.

"Rab's friends . . . Billy and Stu? They're downstairs partying . . . " *They're here already?* I dabbed at my eyes with a *Kleenex* trying to hide my distress. "I think they said they're heading back at lunchtime for a party in Coatbridge." *They're what? I've got to get out of here.* I began searching my bag again, rummaging with panic. *Fuck! He's taken the lot . . . the money, the bank cards . . . and the train tickets.*

Dejected, I began counting the sparsity of coins in my purse. £13.26.

"I've got no money," I said aloud to myself, letting the reality sink in.

"What, has he taken all the money?" Louise probed.

"Yeah . . . but he probably doesn't realise," I suggested trying to play down my embarrassment.

"Oh, he knew," Louise counselled. "He was bragging that he intentionally argued with you just so he could ditch you."

I was humiliated that a stranger was delivering these revelations. *He's planning on returning to Scotland without me? He's intentionally leaving me here?* Louise wasn't trying to be spiteful, she was just being brutally honest to reveal her opinion that Rab was a dick. I don't think her boyfriend knew what he was getting himself caught up in when he invited Rab to Blackburn and Louise had certainly not envisioned her Hogmanay turning out like this.

I can't stay here two more nights . . . I don't even know these people. How am I going to get home? Baby Dayo would by now be with Rab's mum and I was petrified Rab would try and take him home, where he'd no doubt be drinking and partying with his friends.

"Look, is there anybody that you can phone?" Louise suggested, halting my racing mind.

I knew I couldn't let my parents know what had happened. My dad would have been furious and my shame would not have allowed me to look into those disappointed eyes again.

"I've got £50 - here," Louise said, closing her purse and extending her arm towards me. "I'll give you that. You can post it back to me later." I awkwardly accepted her offer.

No sooner had I done so, I was on the telephone, finding out train schedules for Scotland. I could get the 7.55am to Glasgow.

Next, I phoned Tayo - my one and only emergency contact - and told him what had happened.

"What do you need me to do? Do you need me to come and get you? Oh, shit! Kem, I've been drinking!" I remember the concern in his tone.

"No Tay, I'm getting the train," I rambled, needing to get my instructions out, loud and clear.

"I need you to pick me up at the train station and then take me straight to Rab's mum's house. I need to get back to Dayo before Rab does."

"I'll fucking go and get him in the morning," Tayo asserted. "Don't worry Kem, I'll go and get the wee man."

"No way, Tayo," I rebuked, "then Mum and Dad will find out. No. No one must know what's happened," I pleaded, not wanting to attract any more shame.

We agreed that he would collect me at the train station in Glasgow. We would then drive to Rab's mum's house in Coatbridge to collect Dayo before Rab could get to him. Tayo would then take me back to my house, where I would stay in hiding for two days, until I was expected to be back. I wouldn't allow Tayo to stay with me - his car parked outside would only draw attention. However, I did agree to him visiting me every day. He made me a promise not to tell my mum what had happened. Thankfully, Rab never returned to the flat. I didn't see him, or any of his friends, before I left Blackburn.

The train was eerily empty, with very few people travelling on New

Years' day. Most people were at home with their families. This increased my sadness at being so far away from my children. It wasn't good for me to be without my children, as it made me lose all purpose. Without them, I was worthless. Sitting at the mercy of the train's timetable, unable to hurry my journey along, I was afforded one piece of respite; Rab and I were over.

Upon my arrival, it was such a relief to see Tayo waiting in his pristine, black-exterior and immaculate, red-leathered interior, *BMW*. Tayo's cars were always spotless and always smelled amazing. Just being in his car and being with him, allowed my heart to beat at a more peaceful pace. His chilled, calming vibe smothered me, consuming me. It helped that he was with me, supporting me to go and face the dragon that was Rab's mum; to rescue Dayo before his dad could get to him.

Tayo shifted his eyes, first from my neck and then into my eyes.

"Kemi, you need to pull this up," he imitated fixing his collar while indicating towards my neck with a nod of his head. "Are you alright?" he asked carefully and caringly.

I fixed my polo-neck to conceal the mass of bruising. We never spoke about this kind of stuff. I would never put that on my little brother and he would never pressure me to talk about it. We had an unspoken understanding.

Tayo called Rab's mum, as agreed. I didn't want to get into the details of what had happened over the phone. We knew that she wouldn't question Tayo about it because like Rab, she needed to preserve her 'good' image to the outside world.

I saw her move from the window as we pulled up outside her house. By the time Tayo had parked and we were making our way down her path, she was already waiting at her door. I could feel my body tighten with dread.

"Has he been okay?" I asked, as I bent down to see Dayo sitting patiently in his car seat, his little smiling face looking back at me, delighted to see me.

In that moment, all the stress completely disappeared. I had made it back before Rab. Tayo took Dayo's baby bag and buggy to the car before returning to collect Dayo, in his car seat.

"Yeah, he's a delight. Very easy baby," Rab's mum replied, getting the phoney civilities out of way.

"We've seen Rab," she happily revealed. My heart sank. "He had to come by here to get some clothes, because of what you've done," she said with great condemnation. She stood there, arms folded, face drawn tight.

"What?" I retorted, filled with anger. *Is this woman actually going to try and start with me?*

"I know exactly what has happened," she continued, undeterred.

I just stared through her. I was not having her lecture me about her 'innocent son, the victim'.

"No, you don't. Thanks Rosemary," I said through gritted teeth, before turning my back and walking away.

When I got home, I called Michael to tell him that my plans had changed and asked him to bring Michelle home a day early. He was quite happy to give her back and she was happy to be coming back earlier than expected. She was only used to being away for a couple of days at most.

I spent two euphoric days alone with the kids. No interference from my mum or Rab. I remember thinking how wonderful it would be to live like that every day. I felt I could live without support from either of them. I had found peace and contentment. It was blissful, despite it only lasting 48 hours.

It took one week of Rab's grovelling, repeating the same old lies about how he had changed and that he would never drink again, before I finally agreed to allow him to come back. By now, he had convinced me that his violence and cruelty was at the hands of the alcohol; it was not his fault, but rather the drink's and all that he had to do was stop drinking.

By the time I attended another session with Marion in early January, Rab had already returned to my home. I'd gone into the appointment with the intention of not sharing what had happened in Blackburn, but she knew something was wrong. I'd last seen her just over two weeks ago and in that time I'd easily lost a stone in weight.

To begin with, she gently challenged me on my eating and asked why I hadn't been keeping up with my food diary. It didn't matter if there weren't many entries in it, just even the littlest comment about anything was appreciated. I was agitated and disappointed with myself, as I didn't want to disappoint her, but I'd always felt defeated any time I wrote anything in that diary. It only served to remind me that I'd eaten something at some point.

Then she went on to talk about Rab, asking how his alcohol consumption had been over the festivities. I had previously confided in her that I felt he had a drink problem, but I'd never confessed his violence.

I told her about Blackburn . . . minus the violence. I revealed my struggle to get back home and the joy I found spending 48 hours alone in my house with my children. She listened intently while I spoke, divulging my censored version of Hogmanay and the two days that followed. As I finished speaking, she took an assured deep breath, a smooth, unwavering inhale through her nostrils, causing them to flare and her chest to rise. A steady release of air through her compressed lips followed.

"Kemi," she began, while extending her right arm out towards me, hand palm up.

"You had this time, just the three of you, not feeling any of the upset," she demonstrated, closing her right hand into a fist and allowing it to bob hypnotically for emphasis, "and now, you're back with Rab," she stated taking her left hand, mirroring the same movement, "but you don't actually seem happy about it," she concluded. Both our eyes fixed on her left hand.

"Why are you here?" she probed, "and not there?" Both our gazes turned to her right hand. "Why did you pick that? . . . " she pondered, again staring back at her left hand, " . . . and not this?"

I couldn't answer her; I didn't know the answer. I don't think I believed there was a choice - a left and a right. Silence dominated the room while we both stared at her right hand.

That's how Marion worked with me; she never told me I'd done the wrong thing, but her subtle questioning of my choices and why they had been the options that I had chosen, unknown to me at the time, was planting a seed. Marion, very carefully, unpeeled the layers of my lack of self-worth. She exposed how I had been affected by the deeply entrenched beliefs I had about myself, as a direct result of the racism I'd endured, and raised her concerns regarding Rab and my mum. She was not a fan of my mum - nor Rab for that matter - and she could see how their controlling alliance was the biggest feeder of my anorexia.

At this time, I didn't sleep well, as I didn't want to share a bed with Rab. If I didn't go to bed early with the children beside me, I would stay up all night, thinking. I thought about all the people who would be happier if I just took the ten-minute walk from my house to the motorway and let a car kill me. But I couldn't. I had these two, mixed-race children who needed me; they were my only reason for living. More importantly, it was my job to protect them, as I knew they would need it. This country just would not accept their existence as equal to whites. I had to somehow protect them from this.

# # #

Up until this point in my life, there was only one person who taught me about myself: Auntie. However now, here was Marion. She stepped into that role and knew parts of me better than I knew myself. I remember the first time she explained starvation to me. This I was great at. I knew how to keep my body going by eating just a little, twice a week. Sometimes I would allow myself a little fruit, as it wasn't filling. To feel like I had eaten was unbearable. Marion was trying to show me that I was in deep pain, that I was starving myself to numb my feelings. I remember she told me that when the Jewish people were killed at the hands of Nazi Germany, very few were screaming as they walked towards their deaths, as they had been starved for so long that they had lost connection to their emotions. She knew exactly what she was doing. She was trying to keep me as safe as I would allow her.

# # #

By the time Dayo was five months old, I was horrified to learn I was pregnant! Two months pregnant! The panic I felt meant no amount of starving would suffice. A few days after I found out, I had a dream that a little boy came to me and told me he was the son I was carrying and that he was coming to save my life. When I woke up sobbing, I knew this baby had meaning for me. I can truly say that the beautiful boy that was born seven months later, was the same child that had visited me in my dreams.

Having Marion's support really helped me during my pregnancy. Rab didn't like it. My parents were taking my illness seriously now, although my mum could never see her contribution to my disorder. Rab knew how to play the game and most people believed he was Mr Nice Guy. He wasn't; he was a bully and a racist and Marion could see it . . . and Rab knew it. Marion would subtly challenge my beliefs, both in my relationship with Rab and my mum. Despite the fact that my mum would never admit to her faults, I was starting to see that she did love me, in her own, messed-up way. She did try to adhere to everything Marion asked of her.

I'd never been forcefully challenged on my eating, but I'd had to agree to eat something once a day and stop taking diet pills. Despite finding it extremely hard to consistently do either of these things, I somehow managed never to take the diet pills during my pregnancy. However, I was barely gaining any weight and ended up being put onto liquid supplements to help, as I found it easier to drink than to eat. I was so scared that I was damaging my baby.

Rab would disappear for days at a time throughout the pregnancy, as he continued to go on drink and drug binges. I continued to look after the children. Rab didn't work at this time and any money that was brought in was because I'd earned it. I'd even taken an additional job for a short time, working in a kebab shop in the part of town Rab came from. It was the most rundown, racist place I'd ever came across - a place in Coatbridge called Townhead. I received so much racism from the customers, most of them Rab's friends. It was hell and he thought it was funny.

On our way back from a session with Marion, Rab told me he didn't love me. I was eight months pregnant and devastated and so told him I wanted him out of my house and my life. He just laughed.

I was finding it difficult to hold back my anger by the time we arrived home, but was adamant I wouldn't create a scene while the children were in the house. I kept out of Rab's way and occupied myself with the children to burn off my frustration. We played for a while then had dinner before I gave them both a bath and got them into their pyjamas ready for bed.

While they played around in my bedroom, enjoying their last 15 minutes before bed, I got changed into something a bit more comfortable. Being eight months pregnant made it so difficult to feel comfortable in most clothing, so I put on my trusted long, red, silk nightshirt with buttons down to the start of my bump. I instantly felt cosier.

I was standing in the bedroom with my back to the door, taking in the beautiful scene of my children playing, when I heard Rab come into the room behind me. *I hope he's isn't planning on staying up here.*

I hadn't noticed Rab's mood-change since our return home; his rage had been building and as I turned to see why he'd come upstairs, the first thing I saw was that look: feral predator.

Terror poured through my veins. I knew what was coming. *Not in front of the kids.* In my split-second, head-start my eyes scanned the room. I could see 14-month-old Dayo toddling around and Michelle playing with her toys by his side. *They're going to see this. He can't do this - I'm eight months pregnant!* He came fast and hard, slapping me across my cheek with such velocity it sounded like the cracking of a thick branch. My face instantly began to sting with an intense heat that kept growing.

"Who the fuck do you think you are bitch, saying that you're going to chuck me out?" he erupted, foaming frantically at the mouth.

Michelle let out the cry of a wounded animal, its piercing tone dominating my attention. *Michelle!* Instinctively, I tried to turn to get to her and Dayo, but as I took my first step, Rab was on me, grabbing me by my nightshirt, pulling me back towards him with such ferocity the silk material ripped off in his hand, throwing me forward with the immediate absence of resistance. Regaining my balance, I again tried to get to the kids, but Rab was relentless. He grabbed me by my hair this time, forcing my head down and my body to lean forward, folding me onto my bump, restricting my breathing. The next thing I knew, I was on my back on the bathroom floor, with Rab crouched over me and his hand over my throat. I don't know how I got there. I could see Dayo by my side, wildly screaming. *Where is Michelle?* I tried with all my strength to get him off me, but he just wouldn't budge. He continued to pin me down, all the while fiendishly laughing at my attempts to break free.

"Don't you ever tell me you're fucking chucking me out again! You can't fucking chuck me out," he intimidated, just as Michelle came upstairs and into my sight.

"Grandad's coming," she screamed. "He's on his way."

At this, Rab got up off me, releasing me from his grip and calmly walked downstairs leaving the three of us to instantly huddle together. I could feel their tiny, little hearts speedily thumping. My face was still pulsating, my scalp nipped intensely, as if my hair had been ripped clean out of it and my neck stung from the friction burn caused by my nightdress being dragged. I do not know how long I spent on the bathroom floor consoling Michelle and Dayo before their tears stopped.

"Mum, is he going to leave?" Michelle asked, looking into my eyes for reassurance.

"Yes. He is." I replied with conviction.

Rab was still downstairs by the time my mum and dad arrived. As they entered the front door, Michelle went sprinting downstairs, to get to her Nanny before Rab could. She wanted to tell her everything that he had done.

I remained with Dayo in the bathroom with him fast asleep on my lap. All his crying had tired him out.

"It's alright Michelle, I'm here now. I'm going to sort out all this mess. Just you go back upstairs," I heard my mum say, before Michelle came back into the bathroom.

I could hear my mum, dad and Rab talking downstairs. I put Dayo down in his cot and told Michelle she could watch a DVD before putting on my dressing gown to go downstairs.

When I walked into the room, the talking stopped. Everyone turned to look at me. They all shared the same expression: disappointment; and it was aimed at me.

"He needs to get out of here," I addressed my parents. "I don't want him around here anymore."

"Kemi, you're pregnant - you can't get upset," my mum advised, ignoring my words. By now, I was consumed with so much anger, its charged energy allowed all to pour out.

"I don't care! He's just had me by my throat on the bathroom floor, in front of those children," I fizzed, shaking with anger. "He's ripped my night dress!" I continued, pulling back my dressing gown to reveal the evidence. My nightdress flopped open, its collar torn in half, exposing my chest to my shoulder on one side. "Look what he's done!"

I saw Rab dramatically hold his over-exaggerated, shaking head in disbelief; his theatrical reaction openly suggesting *I'm* the crazy person in the room. My dad, other than to offer to go and sit with Michelle, sat in silence. My mum broke the silence.

"Oh Kemi, just stop this. Just stop it right now. You're mentally ill!"

"What?" I replied in utter disbelief.

"Yes, Kemi! You're mentally ill! That's why you go to Marion!" my mum barked, sounding defiant.

"I go to Marion because I have an eating disorder, Mum, not because I am mentally ill," I corrected, aggrieved at her stance.

"You're just acting psychotic," she continued, sticking to the script. "This is absolutely ridiculous how you are behaving. Rab has told us about your behaviour. I mean, you can't behave like that in front of the children." *No fucking way!*

"Behave like what? What are you talking about? What have you told them?" I stared at Rab. I was seething. He paused, quietly staring back at me, revising the lines for his role.

"Kemi, just calm down," he began in a concerned tone. *Ah, Mr Nice Guy.* "I don't want you to get upset again. I mean . . . I don't mind if you lose it with me . . . I can take it; it's just when you do it in front of the kids . . . I mean, it's just not right."

"You fucking, sly bastard! Get out of my house! Now! Get fucking out! Right now!" I roared wildly. My mum stood up out of her seat, posturing dominance towards me.

"I'm not having this! I'm phoning Marion myself and you, young lady, will get sectioned. Is that what you want?" she threatened in an attempt to silence me. *Did you really just say that? He's attacked me and I'm the sick one?*

I told them all to leave, but as always, they didn't listen. Instead, they started to discuss my mental health - in front of me - and how difficult it was for Rab! I was so overwhelmed with anger and frustration and desperation; I couldn't believe this was happening. I needed to get out of the room and away from them. I didn't feel good. My head was reeling trying to take in all that had just happened and my legs felt weak, while my throat throbbed as a result of Rab's attack and my shouting. I was drenched in sweat. My nightdress clung to me, so soaked by emotion that I thought for a moment that my waters had broken. I couldn't do this anymore.

"I hate you. I hate you all. He will be leaving my house, even if it's the last thing I do."

In complete despair, I retreated and returned to my bedroom upstairs. Sitting alone, sobbing on my bed, I could still hear them continuing to discuss me and what should be done to try and control my outbursts. I was filled with horror. *They're going to try to get me sectioned.*

Before my parents left, my mum came up to my room and informed me that she would not accept me being a single mother with three children to two different fathers. That would be too much shame for her. I listened to her lecture on what I was to do and how I was to behave. I didn't argue – there was no point - my mind was already made up. This was my house; I paid for it, not them and certainly not Rab. I would decide who lived here.

The following morning, whilst getting Michelle ready for school, I tried speaking to her about what had happened. I didn't know what I was going to say, but I knew I had to make her feel safe.

"Mummy needs to speak to you about what happened last night, sweetheart."

I did not want to upset her before she went to school, but I knew I couldn't ignore it. I had to address it. Her feelings needed to be validated and her fears settled.

"It's okay . . . Nanny has already told me you're not well," Michelle sweetly replied, trying to reassure me.

"Not well?" I encouraged. I felt sick with dread. *What has she said?*

"Yeah, in your head, Mummy; in your brain. Nanny said that's why Rab got angry."

I was frozen with shock. Michelle had been taught that I was the problem. My child was happily telling me that Rab's attack was okay because *I'm* not well! I had no control in my life; none. I couldn't even truthfully explain to my daughter that she had witnessed an attack; my mum had already convinced her that there was something wrong with me.

Sitting with Marion later that day, I told her I needed Rab out of my house and unloaded what had happened the previous night . . . minus the violence. I was in such a state and she validated it all, however, she questioned whether this was the right time for me to take on additional battles, being so far into my pregnancy. I agreed before making her - and me - a promise that I would eventually get Rab out of my house.

# # #

My beautiful boy, Sola[18], was born on 17th February, 1997, weighing just 4lbs 10oz. I loved him deeply. He was so good, with no demands. He would always wait patiently for his turn with Mummy, simply showing me deep love. He was not going to be affected like his older sister. I kept both of my boys close by, always. My mum had more and more control over Michelle by now and my daughter was learning how to get whatever she wanted by invoking Nanny. I loved my children equally, but because of my mum, I always felt like a massive failure.

---

[18] Pronounced: *Shaw-lah.*

I didn't know I had a choice; but I did

I turned 25 two weeks after Sola was born. I thought I was finding it easy to be a mother to three children; but in truth, I was the sickest I had ever been with anorexia.

I had my routine: get up, weigh myself; get the kids up, get them breakfast; get Michelle organised for school and the boys dressed; prepare Michelle's lunchbox and take her to school, with Sola and Dayo in their robust, navy blue, double pushchair that my mum had bought. Baby Sola would lie in the pram compartment to the rear of the pushchair with Dayo sitting upfront, 'driving the bus'. It felt like I was pushing a bus. The double pushchair, with all its passengers and all their accessories, was very heavy. I didn't mind however, as this would be the first of my many daily workout sessions.

We lived at the bottom of a big hill and Michelle's school was beyond the top of the hill, so I would get a good session. I would continue on, even after we'd dropped Michelle off at school, and walk for another two miles, before returning home usually just before 10am to weigh myself. I would then reverse this route when collecting Michelle.

After weighing myself again, I would spend the rest of the morning doing housework and playing with the boys, while Rab remained in bed. He was not working at this time and would never be up before midday at the very earliest. Throughout my day, I cycled . . . a lot. I cycled everywhere. Sometimes I would cycle to the shops on the High Street, nearly three miles away, only to intentionally 'forget' to buy something I needed, so that I would have an excuse to get back on my bike and cycle back later that day. Each trip to the High Street involved a visit to *Boots*, the chemist, to weigh myself on their scales. I was obsessed. I was filled with so much energy for once and could never burn it off. My mind was just as lively, looping the same tracks over and over: kids, don't eat, exercise and weigh.

I'd even started to cycle to my appointments with Marion - four miles there, four miles back.

She told me I was suffering from post-natal depression, complicated by the anorexia and something that she called, 'elevation'. She was concerned; I was so consumed with my routine with the kids that not eating, exercising and now weighing myself had become compulsive. I was on the scales at least five times a day, every day. I wasn't sleeping - I couldn't, so instead, I would sneak out at night to cycle. All this and still I never felt exhausted. All of this led to her calling my mum in to attend another session with me - but not Rab.

I remember sitting in Marion's waiting room with my mum. She appeared concerned.

"If you don't eat, you will die," she began, in a whisper, "then what would happen to the children?"

She took my breath away. I'd never believed my anorexia would kill me - or at least I hadn't allowed myself to - but in that moment, she'd forced me to.

I was filled with terror. The most terrifying realisation wrenched at my diaphragm, causing an involuntary intake of breath. This gasp was not the result of my sudden acknowledgement of my mortality - that anorexia could kill me; and no, it wasn't a fear of death itself. This was far more petrifying. I was horrified at my new realisation: *if I die, she'll get my children.* This thought had not existed until that moment.

We went into Marion's room and instantly began discussing my medication. The *Prozac* I was prescribed was not working; it was not having the desired effect. Marion felt that the 'happy pill', prescribed to combat my post-natal depression, was actually suppressing my appetite and causing me to have 'elevation'. She was now talking about *amitriptyline* – a tranquiliser.

By the end of the session, I'd agreed to change my medication and to give my scales to my mum. We'd also agreed, after lengthy negotiations, that I could keep my bike, but only on the provision that I stopped using it excessively: no more night-time rides while everyone slept; no more cycling to my appointments with Marion and no more daily High Street cycles. Just two trips a week. Strictly.

The reason I agreed to Marion's demands was simple: I could not die and sentence my children to be raised by my mum. I didn't want to eat, but now I was more determined not to die.

My mum took me to the pharmacy to collect my prescription before heading home. I fussed over the children with excitement upon arrival, before making some coffee. I had no sooner entered the living room where my mum and Rab were comfortably sitting, when she began.

"Kemi, you need to go and get me the scales," both her tone and eyes lacked sympathy and compassion.

"I know. In a minute," I said with apprehension. *Don't remind me . . . how can I get out of this?* I was filled with desperation, racking my brain trying to find a solution, but I knew I had to accept this as being futile.

I would weigh myself all the time. Obsessively. It didn't matter if it was the fifth, tenth, or twentieth time that day; I could always justify it. My scales were my eyes. You see, having body dysphoria, which came with anorexia, meant that looking in a mirror was a terrifying ordeal. Mirrors told lies. Any regular mirror to me, would reflect a distorted representation of my body, much like the Crazy Hall of Mirrors that you see at funfairs. However, unlike the fun-seekers, my reflection did not bring me laughter or enjoyment.

When I saw myself in a mirror, my eyes would tell me I was really big and heavy. They said I was hideously grotesque; that my weight was straining to be contained, stretching the elasticity of my brown skin to the point where it could rupture, allowing all my weight to come gushing out.

My scales reassured me. They confirmed that what I was seeing wasn't real. They never lied to me. I might not like what they had to say, but they were always honest and so they became my trusted ally. If I drank, I weighed. If I ate, I weighed. If I exercised, I weighed. My scales and I knew each other intimately, right down to the very last ounce.

Although I was infatuated with their charm, they were not my friend. I did not enjoy their company. I usually visited them with fear and apprehension and departed with an acutely heightened level of self-loathing. They, with hindsight, would dictate my moods, which in turn controlled my temperament and behaviour. They were very damaging - mentally, physically and emotionally - but they counteracted my distorted visual perceptions.

Addressing me, much like a scornful headmistress would a petulant five-year-old, my mum domineeringly began to speak:

"Kemi, you will go and get me those scales, right now." Her tone of self-appointed authority ignited my burning annoyance. *Yeah, okay . . . you're so concerned, aren't you? No, you're loving this! Enjoying having even more control.*

"I will go and get the fucking scales," Rab piped in.

I could see he was itching to get involved, to show both his untiring support for my mum and his free rein to exert dominance over me.

"No, you will not," I chastised instantly. "This has got nothing to do with you." His eagerness remained in his chair. *Oh my God. What will I do now? She's actually going to take my scales.*

"I will get them," I affirmed before starting my resentment-filled journey to retrieve my truth-speakers.

Desolately, I brought them downstairs. *This is really happening. How will I know my weight?* I entered the living room, cradling the scales, looking down at them, filled with grief.

"Right. Go and put them in the boot of my car," my mum barked.

I found this to be adding insult to injury; like making an alcoholic pour away their own bottle of wine. It broke my heart closing the boot of her car and watching it drive off out of sight and out of my life.

This latest flex of control especially hurt. 'The scales thief' began to visit every day, spending a couple of hours at a time checking-up on me. I now faced my perpetrator daily and every time she visited, she served as a constant reminder of her actions.

It had been two days since I'd sacrificed my scales and I had been in mourning. During her daily routine of 'inspecting Kemi's life', my mum did something quite unimaginable. Whilst watching me trying to make us both some coffee and toast, she randomly asked me to go and bring some shopping in from her car.

"There are some wee treats in the boot for you all. Kemi, would you go and grab them. They're in the boot." *How lazy. Who does she think she is? Can't she see that I am busy?*

"Sure, no problem," I sarcastically replied rather pissed-off with her.

I was sure she was only sending me to retrieve shopping to heighten my sorrow. My new medication was wiping me out, leaving me feeling like a zombie, especially in the mornings. My anxiety had increased. It had been 48 hours since I last weighed myself and my mirrors were now frequently whispering to me, daring me to look. On top of this, my mum was intentionally forcing me back to the scene of the crime: her boot.

As I reluctantly opened the boot, I was greeted by two *Marks & Spencer* shopping bags . . . and my scales! *What? Oh my God! Why are they still here?* A million emotions ran through me all at the same time. Elation and ecstasy bounced throughout my being. I was transfixed; nothing else existed anymore; just my scales and my desire to climb back into the dock to be judged by them.

It was pouring with rain, but I was oblivious. *What are you waiting for – you'll never get this opportunity again?* I couldn't just go out and buy another set of scales - I wasn't allowed out by myself. By now, I was always chaperoned, either by Rab or my mum, anytime I needed to go shopping. They had agreed this for me.

I sat the scales on the soaking pavement, causing the rain on the downhill gradient to momentarily gather before having enough flow to run down the sides, forming two separate streams. My heart was racing, charging with both an anticipation of being reunited and an apprehension at what my old acquaintance might have to say.

I recalibrated the scales; adjusting to zero to allow for an accurate reading on the steep gradient - they had to be on point. My tunnel-vision was momentarily widened by my thoughts, bringing me an awareness of my surroundings. *Hurry up, Kemi. It doesn't take this long to bring in the shopping! She could come out at any second.*

I regained focus and got on the scales. Through held breath, I lowered my eyes, too scared to look and yet compelled to: 7st 7lbs! A wave of euphoric relief joined the rain in washing over my soaked self. In the 48 hours of not having my scales, my weight had not changed!

As I bent forward to pick up my frank, but honest ally, my previous urge to climb on was now rapidly dwindling with the satisfaction of fulfilment, allowing my mind to start focusing on what might happen next. *Hurry up, Kemi. She could come out at any moment. Oh my God, Kemi, the neighbours! They could've walked past or seen you from their windows!* I was filled with shame, but not regret. As I stood up from retrieving my drenched scales, I saw my mum standing at my living room window, watching me. Our eyes met, but I didn't flinch. My momentary contentment of not having put on any weight meant that I didn't care what would happen when I got back inside my house. It was worth it.

I placed the scales back where I found them and took out the shopping bags before closing the car boot. As I started back down my path, I dared another glance towards the window. She was no longer there. I took a deep breath, preparing myself for the condescending onslaught I was about to receive. As I entered the door, I had already begun to practice my counter argument. *Yes, granted, I did go on the scales, but why were the scales still there in the first place? And why would she send me there, knowing the scales were still in the boot? They've been there two days and she didn't think to move them?*

I went into the house and she said nothing. Absolutely nothing. No drama, no lecture and no reprimand. In fact, no mention of what she had witnessed, or that I had witnessed her witnessing me. I was confused and started to doubt myself. *Did she see me? Maybe she didn't. I mean, it was raining.* I decided to not question it any further and just welcomed the relief the absence of her berating brought.

I left it for a few days before checking her car boot again. In that time, I'd convinced myself the only reason my mum hadn't mentioned to me about catching me using the scales, was because she knew it was her fault. They were still in her car, so it was her mistake. My mum never made the same mistake twice, so when I slipped out to check the second time, I wasn't expecting to find them. They were still there. And there they remained. In full knowledge, she continued to intentionally manipulate; I could keep an eye on my weight and she could keep me thin.

# # #

I'd only been on my new medication a week when it became clear that it wasn't working. It was turning me into a zombie whereby, other than doing the bare minimum of looking after the children and myself, I couldn't do anything else. I was completely numb - void of emotion and permanently nauseated. Even if I wanted to eat, I couldn't. The effect of changing my medication had become a nightmare.

After one week of being on the new pills, followed by one week detoxing them back out of my system, I was called in for another meeting with Marion, Debby and my mum at the hospital.

"Kemi, we want you to agree to go into hospital for a week," Debbie suggested, sounding concerned. Their three pairs of eyes scanned me, bracing themselves for my reaction.

"No, I'm not leaving the kids. I'm not doing it," I said, attempting to extinguish any flicker of hope that they may be shielding.

"Kemi, please. Just listen to us for a moment," Marion implored, lowering her normally booming Glaswegian voice.

"Kem, please listen. Listen. They're only trying to help you," my mum joined in. *Yeah, but you're not. Leaving the scales in the car so that I'll stay*

92

thin and knowing I can't say anything, or I'll lose them.

"Kemi," Marion re-joined, "we just want you to come in for a week, so that we can try to stabilise you on your medication without all the stress of the children's needs."

"The children aren't stressful," I contested, before looking directly at my mum and revealing, "It's everyone else."

"I know, Kemi," Marion counselled, "but the time and energy you're spending looking after the three children is preventing you from having the time and energy we need you to have in order to correctly balance your medication, your mood and your eating plans. Just come in . . . I promise it'll be over in a week and you can see the children every day." She did sound sincere. Marion didn't lie.

"And . . . if I don't," I probed, "will you have me sectioned?"

This had been a great fear of mine. I'd been threatened with this for so long by both my mum and Rab: "You have a mental illness, so you must be mentally ill" being repeatedly used to silence me and make me conform.

"What? Of course not!" Marion gasped, as if I had just accused her of committing the most horrendous crime. "Kemi . . . you're not mentally ill; you have an eating disorder."

Up until this moment I hadn't known the difference and had believed them to be exclusive. I could see my mum shifting, agitated in her seat. She had instantly become visibly uncomfortable, as if the meeting, at any moment, could be focused on her and her behaviour. I finally realised that they'd all been empty threats; all those endless arguments in which I had been made to back down; all on account of my so-called 'mental illness'.

I agreed to go into hospital. I didn't agree with thinking it was the best thing to do, but I knew Marion and Debby had never lied to me. So, I nullified my mum and Rab and transferred their control of me over to Marion and Debby.

They gave me a day to get organised and spend time with the children. Rab was not happy with me for agreeing to go into hospital and my mum seemed particularly nervous. They definitely didn't want me to go in, but they were not revealing to me why. Both of them were scared of losing me from their clutches.

I saw Marion and Debby every single day while I was in hospital. I was free to walk about; I wasn't a prisoner, but they didn't want me to leave the hospital grounds. We could get a lot of work done, the three of us, having full access to one another, for seven full days.

When I agreed to go into hospital, the seed that Marion had earlier planted, began to grow. I didn't agree to go in thinking that I would get better. I didn't think at all; I listened . . . to my gut. It was one of those times where you just did something, without rhyme nor reason: just a hunch.

Since Sola's birth, I'd started revealing more to Marion and while I hadn't confessed to Rab's violence, I'd told her everything else: his drug

93

involvement, his drinking, the other women, his nastiness and his lack of help with anything.

However, during that week in hospital, something changed and I found myself revealing the whole picture. I'd finally confirmed her suspicions. We discussed the fact that I would need to get well to have a better chance of getting rid of Rab and she made me promise to phone the police if ever he attacked me again.

Every second away from the children was absolute hell and I had all day to think about them. I couldn't and wouldn't eat. I ate nothing and would instead hide my food in *Ribena* cartons. Marion and Debby could see that being away from the children was detrimental and was only making matters worse.

I agreed to go onto another medication, which would prove to be just as unsuccessful. However, after a couple of weeks of being home, because of the relief I experienced from revealing all about Rab to Marion in hospital, my moods improved. I was put back onto a low dosage of *Prozac*, which by then, along with my 'lighter' mind, did help to balance me out. I was just so happy to be back with the only meaning to my life: my children.

I did try to follow my eating plan and to report all that went on to Marion – "no more secrets" - however, it all became too difficult within a couple of months when suddenly, everything surrounding me became more threatening. Rab had started 'working' for my dad and there was violence involved; I was beginning to see another side to my dad's business.

Before long, I began restricting my eating, again. During this time Marion said that I had to make a choice: stay committed to the programme or leave. The pressure to eat was becoming too much for me to deal with. I was eating more than I ever had - which terrified me - but it still wasn't enough to feed the tiniest of birds. They were wanting me to eat more and I couldn't. So, I left; and in doing so I kick-started the downward spiral once more and continued to break my promise of phoning the police.

# # #

Shortly after this, a girl called Katie phoned me, saying she wanted to meet up with me. She was a mixed-race girl who had been at school with Tayo (and had been infatuated with him for years). She grew up with her white mum and didn't know her black dad. She had been brought up in the notorious Townhead area of Coatbridge. She had to fight everyday of her life too, but unlike me, Katie *was* a fighter; boys or girls, it didn't matter; she would defend herself.

She had always been drawn to my family, but we didn't really know each other. I'd heard that she'd had a baby with Andy, the mixed-race, adopted boy I'd known from school, but that it hadn't worked out. When we did eventually meet up, one of the first things she said to me was: "Kemi, I'm sick of this fucking, racist place." That instantly created our bond; we had to be friends. And that's exactly what we became.

We were together most days. We started to take our children out together to parks, swimming pools, anywhere and everywhere. It was easier to go out as a unit as she wouldn't take shit from anybody. If someone was racist to us, in any way, she would address it, instantly. She was so angry and couldn't keep it contained. I loved her very deeply and her friendship made me feel safer.

While my relationship with Katie grew stronger, I was consciously developing a separation from Rab. We barely spent any time together. He was off when I was working, or he was working and I was off, or if we were both off, I would be with Katie and the kids. I didn't have enough strength to make him go and had, by now, on account of him now being entrenched in my family's business, resigned myself to the fact that he would never leave. So, I was creating another life for myself, apart from him. I couldn't bear to be around him. I despised him. He made my skin crawl. Rab and my mum would often say to me that it was ridiculous to think that I could ever be without him. Who would want me? A single mother to three children, by two different fathers? I'd believed them, but I didn't want to be with any man ever again anyway. That is why I, still to this day, cannot understand why I did what I did.

"Kemi, can you come and sit down a minute, so I can speak to you about something?" Rab asked encouragingly, patting the sofa seat to guide me. *Great, what is it now?* I could tell this conversation carried weight; seeking permission was not commonly practised by Rab.

"Yeah, what?" I cautiously enquired, taking the seat that Rab had reserved, its cushions offering no comfort to my now tense body.

I could tell he was, well, not nervous, but perhaps twitchy. He was sat perched on the edge of his chair, feet on tip toes, with his thighs skittishly bouncing with erratic energy.

"You know how I'm working for your dad now and making a lot better money?" he opened, allowing himself to cross his legs at his ankles, trying to regain composure over his spasmodic limbs. "I think that you can see that my drinking has got a lot better." *Where's he going with this? Drinking better? What, four weeks? That doesn't mean anything.*

"Yeah?" I wasn't agreeing, I was encouraging him to hurry up and get to his point. His stating of apparent facts was unnecessarily dragging out the conversation.

"Well," Rab said with a pause, before uncrossing his legs, to return to his bobbing tip toes. "I think it's time we should get married."

I was floored. Did he actually just ask *me* to marry *him*? He sat there, now very still and quiet. I was lost for words. Silence filled the space around us, shining a spotlight directly on me. I searched for words.

"What?" I finally managed, verbalising my confusion. I had heard him

95

perfectly clearly, yet his words were spinning around my mind like a merry-go-round.

"Well, for the kids and that. You know?" Rab advised, justifying his proposal.

His words were not becoming any more coherent to me. We were living such separate lives by now that I could not understand his motives for asking to get married.

"Okay," I replied, aiming to end the conversation. I didn't allow myself the time to properly process what had just taken place. I was just so content to stop talking.

"What, you will?" Rab asked again, double-checking that his ears had not failed him.

"Yeah, okay," I confirmed, showing no emotion, as if I had just been asked if I wanted soup for dinner.

I was fine with it. It wasn't a big deal. Nothing was changing. I'd still be living my separate life and it wasn't like I could get him to leave my house. He wasn't going anywhere.

"This is great news. I need to go and phone your mum," Rab advised excitedly, sounding like a child eager to please its teacher.

"Oh, please don't do . . . " but before I could finish my sentence, he had already dialled her number.

What have I done? Why the hell did I say yes? Reality began to kick in. I sat paralysed, frozen with complete shock. Already filled with regret, I could feel this was going to be blown up out of all proportion.

"I've asked Kemi to marry me . . . and she has said 'yes'," Rab lauded to my mum, still sounding surprised with my answer.

I'm not sure what my mum's initial response to Rab was, but by the time he forced the phone into my hand, I could hear screams of joy and elation escape the receiver from a good four inches away from my ear.

"Kemi, you'll finally be an honest woman," was the first, clearly audible words that my mum offered me. I felt sick and made my excuse to get off the phone. *What have I done?*

Within the hour, my mum and dad were sitting in my living room, uncorking a bottle of champagne to celebrate. I remember sitting there, watching the three of them rejoice at the prospect of legally bonding the families. I knew then why Rab had asked me to marry him: so he could be further embroiled in my family.

It all happened so quickly and before I knew it, I was to be married. The wedding was to take place in Gretna Green, in the Scottish Borders, and then back to the local *Hilton Hotel* for the reception. My mum had organised everything: the venue, the flowers, the food and the guests, some of whom I didn't even know. I took nothing to do with it - she wouldn't have let me, even if I had wanted to. The only aspect worthy of any interest was the time and effort my wonderful, little, Scottish gran was putting into making me a traditional Nigerian dress. The whole wedding was totally out of my control and I was spiralling. I had no Marion to catch me this time.

My cousin Yemisi, Auntie's daughter, came for a holiday the week leading up to the wedding, just as she had done every year since she'd been at boarding school in the UK.

I loved my cousin very much and always looked forward to when she came to stay with my parents. We would spend most days together while my parents worked, giving us some real bonding time together. I had always looked up to her. She was older than me, Tunde and Tosin; not by much, but enough that she was above us - not in an ignorant, superior way, but more in terms of life experience. Being that bit younger always meant our maturity - or rather immaturity - prevented us from being equally ranked with her. Despite this, she was always accepting and openly kind. She was tall and elegant like her mum and is still to this day one of the most beautiful women I have ever seen in my life. She would plait my hair and was the first person to give me a weave, before I even knew what a weave was!

I remember one visit we had together when I was about 19 or 20. She had been working in America and I remember she arrived with straight, black, bobbed hair. I was mesmerised. She looked like a pop star. I couldn't understand how she had managed to turn her tight, afro hair into straight, flowing hair. I could see it wasn't a wig - it wasn't like the one my Auntie Joan had given me when I was a child, as I could see whisps of her afro hair at her hairline. I had only known three styles for girls with afro hair; cornrows, plaits and . . . well . . . afro. After numerous attempts at trying to explain to me what a weave was, she took me to her room. I remember sitting on the bed, watching her methodically unpack her case, searching for an explanation to pacify me.

"Kemi, any black woman you see with straight or long hair has these amazing creations," she said still maintaining a tone of enthusiasm towards me, whilst neatly arranging her clothes into formation on the bed, much like a soldier. "Whitney has them. Diana Ross definitely has them." My ears perked up at the sound of my 'mother'. *Diana has them? They must be good!*

"But Yemisi, how do they work?" I urged for the final time.

"Child listen," she said, in the tone of a true girlfriend, whilst flicking her flowing, straight hair over her shoulder and waving a bag of shiny hair tantalisingly towards me. My eyes lit up. "Do you still want blonde hair?"

She cornrowed my hair into a big spiral around my head, getting narrower and narrower, encircling my crown, and then sewed the weave through the cornrow, making it appear to be my natural hair - my 'natural' blonde hair. It didn't look natural on me. It was mousey brown with blonde highlights. Nonetheless, I had loved that Yemisi had spent this time with me. Spending time with her had always been very precious and that's why it was so bitter-sweet that she made her visit at this time: my wedding. She came with her husband and their little daughter, Tofe[19].

There was a dinner arranged for the evening before the wedding for all the family and friends who were travelling to Gretna. I travelled down by car with the three children and Tayo and went straight to my room upon arrival, ignoring my mum's instruction to come back downstairs. I just wanted to be left alone. Her constant nagging to "come downstairs", where all the food would be presented, resulted in an argument and she wasn't listening. I could feel rebellion growing inside me. The more she fought to get me downstairs, the more I resisted.

She hadn't listened to me at any time when I'd told her I didn't want to marry Rab leading up to the wedding. She'd just told me I was having 'another mental episode', which would always shut me down. But this time, I wouldn't be shut down.

"I don't care if you want me to come downstairs. I'm not coming down," I asserted from on top of my bed, my legs wrapped like a mermaid in the thick tartan throw that had been draped at the foot of the bed.

"The guests are downstairs!" she snarled through gritted teeth, jaws clamped tightly like a hyena, whilst sulkily stomping her feet like a toddler. "Family! Downstairs! All here to celebrate your wedding."

And what will they all think? This was her real concern. Her only concern. She didn't care how I felt. She didn't want to know; she dismissed it.

"My wedding?" I replied, her words injecting me with adrenaline, sitting me bolt upright, before kicking my legs free. "This is your wedding. I don't even know all the people you've invited. The only say I had was my wedding dress."

"Yes," she agreed as she walked towards me, stopping just a few feet away to lean in closer and eyeball me, "and look how ungrateful you are for that. I mean, I even agreed to it being a Nigerian traditional dress."

How dare you? You think you've done me a favour by 'permitting' me to wear a 'black person's' dress? Her ignorance stung.

"I don't want to get married and I'm fucking not getting married," I insisted, staring directly into her unmoving eyes.

"Oh yes you are," she shrieked, sending bubbles of saliva into orbit before going into melt down. "Have you any idea how much money I have spent on this wedding? You selfish bitch! £20,000! So, you will be getting married in the morning. Stay up here if you want, the whole family knows you're not well, anyway!"

I was frozen in silence as she left the room. Within a couple of minutes, there was a knock at my door. It was my cousin Yemisi. There wasn't enough time to try to hide my tears, before she came and sat beside me, holding my hand.

---

[19] Pronounced: *Toe-fee.*

"Kemi, you don't have to do anything that you do not want to do."

It was as if Auntie was holding my hand, talking to me. On many occasions she had offered me those same words. This brought me deep comfort, as being with Yemisi always made me feel closer to Auntie. I was, at this point, so much more damaged than the 11-year-old that had travelled to Nigeria all those years earlier. The concept of not doing something I did not want to do was something I had yet to learn.

That night, before I went to sleep, I remember being in the hotel suite with the children, wishing I could take them and run away. But I had nowhere to run to that was any safer than where I was, so the next day, I was married and believed my fate was sealed.

Over that next year, looking back, I can see I was preparing for something big, but didn't really know what it was at the time. I was in so much shock and struggled to come to terms with the fact I had actually gone through with the sham-of-a-wedding. However, I knew I had to get out of it; somehow. I knew there was only one person who could help me with that: Marion. So, we reunited and I started to do some really good work on me.

I still had my strong friendship with Katie and whenever I wasn't working, the children and I spent most of our time with her and her son. I'd started doing some shifts for my dad and when Rab started working more and getting more involved, I eventually learned what actually went on in my family's 'business' and why Rab was so valuable to them: my dad was heavily involved in organised crime. I began to realise that everything I'd believed about my family had actually been a lie and Rab, the man I wanted out of my life, knew all of my family's ugly secrets; the secrets I was only just beginning to learn about.

This motivated me even more to get well enough to spare my children from the life I'd lived. I had no control over Michelle who was being manipulated - and being taught how to manipulate - by my mother, and there was nothing I could do to stop it. Michelle's behaviour was now creating a problem between me and her dad, with him blaming it on our mothers having too much control in our daughter's life. I knew this to be true, but I was helpless. Any time I tried to discipline Michelle, my mum would interfere and reject my mothering in front of Michelle and instead, take her away shopping to buy her things as a reward. Many a time Michelle told me she would only come back when I was ready to say sorry. I had to. I felt she wouldn't come back if I didn't.

I stopped working for my dad not too long after I restarted. It was such a relief; I hated working with Rab. I remember my dad asking, "why not do something in sports?" as that had always been my passion. I'd educated him that there was no point in learning any trade, as who would employ me over a white person? His response was simple: "Be your own boss." Marion agreed. She would often tell me that if I channelled all the energy that I put into my eating disorder into something else, I could achieve anything. So, I decided I would consider an HNC in sports therapies at the local college.

# # #

By now, Katie had fallen pregnant and wanted me to be her birthing partner as the father wasn't around. I was delighted and it just so happened that her baby was due at the same time as I was due to start college. I remember sitting on her couch on a Sunday - the day before college was due to start - crying. I told her I couldn't go to college. I was really struggling at that time with my eating. It was making me feel out of control again. I felt overwhelmed, believing that my body was literally, physically growing out of control. She just listened and concluded very matter-of-factly: "Well you don't have to go."

That night, while I was getting ready to go to bed with the children, Katie's mum phoned me to say that Katie was in labour and asked if I could go to the hospital.

I arrived just after 1am and words cannot describe what I experienced that night. It was one of the most amazing things I'd ever been part of and I told her that as I cuddled my new godson. It was a completely different experience partnering someone giving birth, to actually giving birth myself. I told her she was the most amazing woman I knew. She just looked at me and said: "Kemi you are amazing and if I can do this, then you can go to fucking college!"

I went home after the birth and got freshened up before attending my first day at college. Nothing in my life would ever be the same again.

Part two

My new life

20th August, 2000. It'd been 11 months since my sham of a wedding and a few months since Rab's latest violent episode towards me. This was his longest period of abstinence. I don't know if that was because of his ever-growing involvement in my family's business or because of what I'd told him the morning after the assault. I'd been up early that morning, having not really slept, and got the children ready for school. Rab was still sleeping off both his exertions and his alcohol consumption from the night before.

"Rab," I said sternly, awakening him as I made my way to leave the house, "that was the last time you will ever touch me." I don't know where it came from - I was so clear and strong - but I knew I meant it, and so did he.

When I returned home from the school run, he didn't hit me. He didn't even mention it. I have to say, I can remember feeling disheartened. I'd expected to be met with violence on my return and had planned to call the police and have him removed, but he never gave me that opportunity. By now I was starting to feel like I did have the choice to get rid of him; even if it meant getting rid of my anorexia first to achieve it.

#

When I returned home from being Katie's birthing partner to get the children ready for school and little Sola ready for his first day at the college's nursery, I began shaking with fear; a combination of nervous excitement and utter dread. However, I felt driven, as if compelled by some unknown desire, along with a determination I couldn't quite understand. I had a gut feeling, almost a knowing, that this was my calling. All I had to do was take the first step.

I dropped Michelle and Dayo off at school and made my way to the college with Sola. Sola wasn't accustomed to being without me and was devastated when I had to drop him off at the nursery and leave him. On the rare occasions when he wasn't with me, he would be with his dad or my mum, but here he knew no one. I felt so cruel leaving him there, but the staff were all so lovely and helped to reassure me. However, it had taken over 20 minutes to get Sola settled and I was now running very late.

I remember running to the auditorium where my very first lecture was being held and trying to sneak in quietly at the rear of the class without being noticed, but without much success. As I slipped through the heavy, double fire-doors, they gave a groan of longing for hinge oil that reverberated throughout the whole room! Suddenly, I was acutely aware that all eyes were on me. *How embarrassing!* I wanted the ground to open up and swallow me. Instead of sneaking in through the back door, I had barged in from behind the lecturers at the front of the auditorium! I quickly shuffled to the first vacant seat I could find, with my head firmly bowed low, avoiding any eye contact.

Unknown to me at the time, my entrance had caught the eye of a young man in the room, leaving him intrigued. He remembers this as the moment he first had the thought: "I will marry that girl."

After being organised into our classes in the auditorium, we were then sent off to attend our first tutorials. My first class was filled with the usual introductions to new classmates. As I looked around the room, in walked the most beautiful, mixed-race man I had ever seen. As he walked towards me, I couldn't look away. It was one of those times when, try as you might, you just can't peel your eyes away. As he got closer, our eyes met. I couldn't breathe. His large mouth with full lips opened with a very warm smile and his eyes cheekily told me they liked what they saw. *Oh my God. What is happening?* My hands were clammy, my heart was racing and butterflies somersaulted in my tummy. I realised in that moment that I was feeling excitement. I hadn't felt like this since I'd given up sports and dancing.

I had been so long without this emotional-physical response that my life force, if you like, in that moment kicked in and I didn't know what to do. By the time he had passed, I had to get up and leave. I hurried down the corridor towards the bathroom and was so relieved to find no one else inside. I got inside a cubical and just sat there. *Oh my God! Kemi, calm down . . . this is ridiculous!* I had never had a response like this to any other human being and I didn't know how to control it. I felt as if I'd discovered some secret emotion inside of me, one that I couldn't shut off.

I eventually got myself together and returned to class, reminding myself that I was married and that someone like *him* would not be interested in someone like *me*. As I entered the class and took my seat, I could see him watching me. *How rude. God, you need to help me.* Shocked by the thoughts that were polluting my mind, I finally settled into my seat.

We all had to take turns to introduce and tell a little about ourselves to our new classmates. *Ah, this should help.* I listened to his words: "I'm Craig Ferguson. I'm 20 years old and I live in Airdrie." He looked at me the whole time he spoke, as if he was addressing only me. In that moment I was so relieved to be brown, as you couldn't see that I was blushing. *Ah, he's too young.* He continued to steal looks in my direction and would hold it long enough so that I would notice. As the person before me completed their introduction, I gathered my thoughts. *You've shown your hand, okay.* His sweet persistence was not familiar to me and was making me feel awkwardly self-aware, like a schoolgirl. I would play my ace of an introduction and end our game.

"I'm Kemi Ogunyemi. I'm married with three children and I feel it's time for me to do something to improve myself."

I felt victorious delivering my status. *He'll lose interest now.* When I looked up, I met his ever-gazing eyes eagerly listening while he gently rested his chin on his thumb and ran his index finger along his plentiful upper lip with intrigue. He nodded and smiled as if to say: "nicely played."

I was disappointed that I'd ended 'something' for the remainder of that class, but I advised myself that it'd been the right thing to do.

As the class ended for lunch and everyone began busily shuffling about with purpose, I felt a bit at a loose end. I didn't know anyone. As I got up from my seat gathering my belongings, the girl who had been sitting next to me and who had smiled kindly as I returned from the toilet, introduced herself.

"Hi, I'm Andrea," she said, in a cheery and welcoming tone. She couldn't have been more than five feet tall, but she exuded the warmth of a friendly giant.

"Hi, I'm Kemi," I replied, instantly opening up to her calm and bright personality.

"Would you like to get some lunch together?" she suggested with an inviting smile, "unless you have other plans." I didn't.

"Yes, I'd love to," I agreed, feeling both nervous and relieved to have someone to go for lunch with.

"That guy . . . Craig Ferguson, is it?" Andrea began as we weaved our way to the canteen, through the strange corridors filled with swarms of bodies, "he seems very interested in you," she disclosed with a smile, her friendly eyes alive with her findings.

"What?" I replied, trying to sound oblivious. *Oh my God, did she notice something?*

"He came and asked me who my friend was when you left the room," Andrea revealed with a smirk as wide as the Clyde.

"He's just one of those cheeky guys who flirts with everyone," I suggested, trying to smother Andrea's theory. "I think he'll back off now; I said I was married with three kids. Anyway, he's too young."

I hurried my reply, trying to convince Andrea - and myself - what I was saying was true whilst feeling disappointed at the same time. As we sat at the end of a very large, quarter-filled table to have our lunch, we engaged in the usual, socially-accepted small talk.

"So, three kids? God, you look so young," Andrea complimented, whilst unwrapping the brown paper that concealed her homemade, cheese and tomato sandwich.

"Thanks. Yeah, I started young," I replied, unscrewing the lid on my bottle of water, before taking a nerve quenching sip. "I had my daughter, Michelle, when I was 17."

"Did you say you are 28?" Andrea recounted, wiping her mouth with some kitchen roll to remove any socially-unacceptable debris, in an overly, self-conscious manner.

"Yes," I confirmed, watching her fold the paper in two before tucking it up under her sleeve.

"God, you look about 20!" she announced sincerely, breaking off a piece of her sandwich with her fingers and carefully placing it in her mouth.

"God, I'm glad I'm not 20," I laughed outwardly, hiding the internal shiver I felt down my spine at the thought of how sick I was back then.

"Kemi," Andrea suddenly blurted out, sitting her sandwich down to quickly change the subject with urgency, "guess who's heading our way?" she whispered teasingly, looking directly over my shoulder, before leaning in to hear my answer.

"Craig?" I replied, mouthing his name for Andrea to lip-read, not knowing how close he was behind my turned back. As my heart's tempo beat faster with anticipation, I knew he would be smiling on his approach. He seemed so confident and cheeky.

As he took the seat beside me, he hit my eyes straight on with his big, overly-darkened, brown eyes. *Oh shit. Stay cool Kemi.* I certainly didn't feel cool.

"So, *Kemi,* is it? Nice name. Is it Nigerian?" he opened, his eyes still penetrating mine.

"Yes, nice guess," I replied, deflecting my eyes away from his, impressed that he had recognised my heritage.

"I'm Craig, Kemi," he continued, trying to regain visual connection. "Very pleased to meet you. So, which one of your parents is Nigerian?" he enquired as he slung his bag strap over the back of the chair, signalling his intention to remain put and in conversation.

"My dad's Nigerian and my mum's Scottish," I informed in between shuttling my gaze back and forth, nervously, from his eyes to my fidgeting fingers that were by now erratically peeling the label off my bottle of water.

"Nice," he sincerely enthused, nodding his head in contemplation. I was impressed that he made the distinction of who I was; that I was mixed-race. We'd recognised this in each other.

"Where are your parents from then?" I bravely probed, deflecting the attention of the conversation away from me.

"My mum's Jamaican and my dad's Scottish," he shared, kicking his feet up on the chair opposite him, making himself at home.

We were both surprised to find out that we had lived in adjoining towns, Coatbridge and Airdrie, and how we had never seen each other before, especially considering that my parents had moved to Airdrie a couple of years earlier and were living three streets away from his parent's house. I was losing myself in this conversation, just crushing all over this guy. Panic soon started to fill me, so I excused my presence, citing that I had to go and see Sola at nursery.

"I'll come with you, if you don't mind . . . I could do with the fresh air," Andrea said, standing up to swing her rucksack over her shoulders.

"Sure. Sorry, Craig, I need to go," I said, quickly getting to my feet. I

106

felt stronger, more resistant, having brought my son into the conversation. I felt it brought us both back to reality.

"Erm . . . oh . . . yes, of course. Catch you later," he said, seeming uncomfortable with my reality, but also saddened by my withdrawal.

As I left, I too felt saddened, like I'd lost something. But I'd never had anything to lose in the first place.

I returned to my classes that afternoon, feeling exhausted by the events of my first morning at college. Seeing Sola had helped bring me back to reality by reminding me of my responsibilities of being a mother. That evening, after I'd collected the children and made them their dinner, my parents came round, dropping off Rab after work, to see how my first day had gone.

For once, I was full of chat and told them how Sola's day had gone before telling them all about Andrea and Craig. While my dad became very interested and had many questions about Craig's parents, I could tell my mum had become nervous. I understood - I was also nervous; nervous that I couldn't stop myself talking about Craig and that I was choosing to express myself while Rab just listened, asking no questions, wearing a genuine look of what I thought might be worry. In some ways I felt defiant; I was finally challenging Rab and I knew if he hit me, I would call the police and be freed of him once and for all. But he didn't.

That night, as I lay in bed with Dayo and Sola's little, hot bodies warming me, my mind was free to think about Craig. No matter how hard I tried, I couldn't deny I was strongly attracted to this man. In fact, I began to realise I'd never felt like this before about anyone and it scared me. I didn't want to feel like this. I felt hopeless and trapped. Even if I wasn't married, I was still a mother of three children, and on top of that, to two different dads. As soon as my mind went there, it was easier for me to fall into my self-loathing train of thought. *Don't be ridiculous. Craig would never want someone like me: damaged goods.*

With the familiar lump of shame in my throat, I made myself a promise to stay away from Craig. I knew I had little control of myself around him and that he would only complicate matters. I was now clear that Rab and I were over and that I needed to get him out of my house. This was my whole reason for going to college; to better myself. I had to stick to my plan.

The class had a very small intake that year, and we all gelled together really well. I enjoyed being part of this new group of people and even liked hanging out with them if ever there was any out of college socialising. Sola had settled into his nursery very quickly after his initial resistance. He even started to enjoy our little daily journey to college together, where he wouldn't have to share me with his siblings after they had been dropped off at school.

This was a big time for both Sola and Dayo. Dayo, had just started primary school and was already becoming aware that he was 'different' from the other children. He experienced racism in his first week. I knew the school well, as I had been there many times complaining and dealing with the racism Michelle had received. It was strange, as I would still put up with a lot of racism towards me, but when it came to my children, I had zero tolerance.

The boys had always been together but now they missed each other deeply whenever they were apart. They were so close that people would often assume they were twins. Dayo was a very special child, very sensitive in every way. He had little foibles that, even at four and a half years old, I knew were some sort of coping mechanism. I had to send him to school with wet wipes as he needed to have his fingertips moist all of the time and he would point-blank refuse to wear trousers so, even in winter, he wore school uniform shorts that only went to his knees. He had the most beautifully blond, curly afro and he loved it, but it had to be long - he was very particular about that. Both boys liked to play with Michelle's 'girl' toys, especially Dayo and because of this Rab insisted Dayo was gay. He wanted to 'change' him, but I wouldn't allow it; they were my children and I was determined that they would grow up feeling comfortable with themselves in their brown skin.

After what Michael had done regarding Michelle's name, I had been adamant that the boys would have Nigerian names with meaning. It was important for their identity. Dayo is a unisex name and means 'joy'. Olusola[20], Sola's proper name, is also a unisex name, and means 'a show of wealth'.

Growing up, I'd had an Uncle Sola who'd had a very strong presence. He had the ability to command any room with his energy, without ever demanding it. I didn't name Sola after him, but there were definitely similarities between both of their souls. Sola was more comfortable than Dayo in who he was and would always challenge the racism he encountered in a timely way.

Life at college was very social and I was starting to experience life as I hadn't before. There was also this beautiful man who'd started to make his feelings very obvious to me.

"I'm not sure, Andrea. I'm thinking he might just be teasing me," I suggested, reading her face, hoping she didn't agree.

"No Kemi, I don't think he is. It's quite obvious that he likes you," Andrea replied, looking and sounding sincere. "I think he's being completely serious."

I now had to search deep within myself; I was intrigued at what *he* saw in *me*. It was so incomprehensible that someone like *him* would have any interest in someone like *me;* he knew I was married and had three children, but he was serious. I was terrified as, even though Rab had cheated on me

---

[20] Pronounced: *Oh-loo-shaw-lah*

108

several times throughout the seven years of our relationship, it was not something I had ever considered. However, as time went on, I could no longer ignore that this was becoming a definite possibility. I was so confused. I felt quite fragmented; as if I had different aspects of me, all part of the same person, but in conflict with each other.

College was providing me with a lot of sport and teamwork, which had always been something that made me feel alive, and there was a part of me that finally, really wanted to live. My work with Marion was going very well; I was thin but not in an ill way. I was stable and I was on an eating plan – one that I could stick to and didn't make me feel out of control. Marion and I both knew it would only be a matter of time before I left Rab. I hadn't told her about Craig at this time. Well, I'd mentioned him, but only as a friend.

When I wasn't in my college life, my feelings were all over the place, like an emotional roller coaster, and I felt shameful. However, when I was in college life, I was someone new, someone who was not a victim. I was starting to believe I could have a life without Rab. I was so much stronger now than I'd been a year earlier.

I was finding it harder and harder to be around Craig, but he started to be everywhere I went. I couldn't stop thinking about him and he was all I could talk about with Katie, which she found very annoying.

We would go for drinks, lunch and walks, all with the other classmates, spending time getting to know each other. I knew it was only a matter of time.

I loved my course. I was learning so much about the body; how it moved and how it recovered, and the massage aspect of the course had become an obsession. Massage was a big part of the course; we had to do it most days and this was where my passion really lay. This is when I decided I wanted to study how to repair the body. I was determined to make a success of my life for myself and my children. I was changing, growing in confidence. It was around then my mum came to me to speak about my failing marriage.

"Kemi, what do you mean it's over?" she said in blind disbelief. "You've only been married a year . . . don't you think you should be working on saving it?"

Saving it? I wasn't willing to have any discussions regarding saving my shambolic, violent marriage.

"You can work on my marriage if you want - but I'm done," I simply quipped back, ending the debate.

She was horrified but didn't argue, as I think she could see I was changing. Plus, I wasn't considering a life without *her*, just Rab. She was right; I was changing, but I wasn't ready to address the damaging, toxic relationship I had with her. I didn't know there was anything to address. I had always accepted her control and cruelty - I hadn't known anything else. Looking back, I now find that incredibly alien because at the time, I did know from deep within me, that I could never have treated my own children the way she'd treated me.

By now, I was really starting to worry about what might happen between me and Craig. My situation didn't seem to bother him; he'd even asked me if I was happy. I didn't answer him. I didn't want him to be seen as the reason for ending my marriage, and I didn't want him to think my marriage was ending because of him. I knew I was finished with Rab - I'd known that since before I met Craig. Regardless of how I felt about him, he was not why my marriage was ending.

It was 17th November, Dayo's fifth birthday, and I remember going to the pub to meet up with the class after I'd put the children to bed. I'd had butterflies in my tummy that whole evening and after having tried on my fifth change of clothes, I'd given up and decided to let Michelle choose my outfit.

"Oh mummy . . . please wear the red one," she urged excitedly, her eyes besotted with the deep V-necked, crimson dress.

"Okay angel, I'll wear the red one," I reassured, hiding my anxiety.

Oh God. The red dress sat very close to my body, hugging me, leaving me feeling exposed. I hated that feeling, but Michelle's decisiveness had stopped me from trying on at least another five more outfits!

That was normal; that was how I always got dressed, ever since I'd thrown out the 'whispering', full-length mirrors. Now, I had only a small mirror - fixed high to the wall - that only allowed for my head to be reflected. So, a ten-year-old's opinion made perfect sense to me.

I stopped off at Katie's for a quick smoke and a vodka to calm my nerves.

"Miss Ogunyemi, you are looking for trouble. This little Jamaican will not be able to resist your black magic!" We both laughed. As I left her flat to get into the taxi, we said our goodbyes:

"Kemi, just be happy," she said with great wisdom.

"Katie, that is what I intend," was my honest reply.

When I arrived, I could see Andrea waving excitedly, waiting to greet me outside. My legs were like jelly as those butterflies returned, taking over my entire body. As we entered the pub, Craig turned instantly and met my eyes with a look of knowing and intent; we both knew we were past the point of turning back.

"Kemi, you look stunning," Craig complimented, his brown eyes captivated.

I didn't know what to say. I felt a little embarrassed and exposed, but I didn't show it. This man did not know this part of me and didn't need to. He was right here, right now and that was all I could do: be in that moment.

"Come, sit down," he encouraged, his firm but gentle hand ushering me by my lower back.

He led me through the pack of strangers to where our classmates were seated, offering me the seat next to his, before disappearing and swiftly returning with a double vodka for me. I got very merry that evening - not drunk, I'd like to add. I did not lose my senses through alcohol - just pure desire. We all joked and enjoyed each other's company. Craig was very attentive, making sure I was comfortable and enjoying myself. I was enjoying the attention.

Later in the night, I went to the toilet and as I opened the toilet door to return to the lounge, there he was, waiting. I didn't have time to say anything as he stepped forward into the doorway, gently putting his arm around my waist. I lost control of my legs for a split second. Then, before I knew it, his soft and full lips were on mine. I melted into his embrace and lost myself for that moment. When I finally halted the tryst, we just looked at each other, bonded. I felt so deeply connected to this man, but I would not admit it to him.

"I need to go," I blurted, as I tried to manoeuvre away from him, my feelings exploding. *Oh my God Kemi, what have you done?* I wasn't in control. I'd crossed the line and now I was panicking.

"Kemi, please don't rush off," Craig pleaded, now looking very concerned. It was the first time I had seen his face without its smile. "I'm sorry," he offered, his brown eyes confirming his sincerity.

"It's cool," I shrugged dismissively whilst nervously smiling, suggesting his apology was not required. "Don't worry about it."

Don't worry about it? Kemi, what have you done? I turned and walked. And kept walking. I walked straight out of the pub and hurriedly got into the first taxi I could reach. As I took the ten-minute taxi ride home, I tried to gather myself together. *What have you done?* I felt tears building up inside me. I tried to appease them. *It was just a kiss. He probably kisses lots of women. It's happened now, just let it go.*

Rab was already in bed when I got home, so I got the spare quilt out of the cupboard and slept on the couch. This was not an unfamiliar arrangement, but usually my motives were for other reasons. This time however, I could not sleep in the same bed with him; not after what I had done.

I didn't sleep well that night and when Katie phoned at lunch time to ask how my night had gone, I cried.

"Oh Kemkem, come around here," she pleaded, looking to offer me support.

"I can't. I'm waiting for Michael to collect Michelle," I explained.

"Well, what time's that at? Come after he's been," she suggested.

"Okay. He'll be here at 1.30, so I'll come over with the boys around 2pm."

The boys were delighted to be going to Katie's. Her eldest, Will, had become inseparable from Dayo and Sola, and my boys loved her new baby, Teddy.

It was a relief to unload on Katie that afternoon. While the boys merrily built castles with *LEGO* in the living room, and baby Teddy had his nap, Katie sat and listened to my self-inflicted woes.

"Oh Kem . . . it's just a kiss. Do you think you might be overreacting?" she counselled, pouring us both a coffee.

"No Katie. I should have waited," I assured, feeling somewhat guilty.

"For what?" she asked, with a tone of bemusement accompanied by a furrowed brow.

"I'm ending my marriage," I began, "Not because of this, but really, since I got married . . . "

"I've never understood why you got married in the first place," Katie interrupted, not looking for clarity, just sharing her thoughts.

"I just don't want anyone to think it's because of Craig. I'm just going to have to stay away from him." We paused in silence to stare into our cups.

"Good luck with that, Kemi," Katie snorted, doubting my self-will. We both laughed. I hoped I could stay away from Craig, at least until Rab was gone.

By the time I returned to college, I had convinced myself that Craig wouldn't be a problem, as I hadn't heard from him over the weekend, which was unusual. I decided he had as much regret as I did. I was already in class when Craig arrived late. He didn't really give much away when he sat at the desk next to me and Andrea, to whom I'd also confessed. Halfway through the class, as I was pretending to be following what was going on, I felt a nudge on my arm.

"Kemi," he whispered. I could feel his eyes on me. *Oh my God, keep it together Kemi.* Feeling very much older and out of my depth, I maintained my pretence of listening to the lecturer.

"Yeah," I whispered, still facing forward, refusing to make eye contact, imitating being an engrossed student.

"Can you wait for me outside of class? I need to speak to you."

I could still feel his stare as regret and dread both filled me. I did not want to speak to him. I knew what he was going to say and I didn't want the humiliation that I felt would come from us speaking.

"Okay," I agreed trying to sound cool about the whole thing.

I told Andrea to go on ahead and that I would catch her up as we left the classroom. She didn't need to ask why, as Craig was already loitering. We walked along the busy corridor, together in silence, until eventually there was no one else around. He indicated to stop.

"Well?" I began, willing his rejection to speed up, so I could just get out of that moment.

"Are you okay?" he asked sincerely, studying my face for any discrepancies that may contradict my words. *Oh no, he's going to pity me now.*

"Yeah, I'm fine," I replied quickly, my face wearing its best attempt at disguised dishonesty.

"I've been worried all weekend," he explained in the now quietened corridor. "I wanted to text you to see if you were okay. You left before I got out of the toilet." He stepped even closer.

"Look Craig," I rebuffed, turning side-on to avoid his eyes, "you don't have to worry about me. I'm a big girl, you know." I afforded him a glance as I checked my watch, wanting somewhere else to rest my eyes.

"Kemi, please don't be like that," he softly urged, trying to posture himself into my line of sight.

"We need to go, Craig, we'll be late for class," I responded apologetically, as I readied myself to leave.

"Can we go for a walk at lunch time? Please Kemi?" I was torn. I could see his eager, yet concerned, desperation.

"Okay," I reluctantly agreed. We walked to class together, again in silence. I didn't want to speak and I didn't want to hear what he had to say. I was glad for the silence.

"Are you okay?" Andrea asked concerned, as I sat down.

"Yeah. Cool," I replied with a flash of a smile. *Oh my God! Oh my God!*

"Really Kemi?" she tried again. I just looked at her blankly. I was good at this; not letting people know how I really felt, but she saw right through it. "Kemi, you really like him," she concluded.

I remained in silence, feeling sick for the rest of the class, worried about the pity and rejection I was going to receive. Craig waited for me outside the college building. It was a typically damp and cold, Scottish, wintry day. We went for a walk along a quiet walkway in silence for about 15 minutes.

"Kemi," he opened, stopping us both in our tracks to look directly into my eyes. "I'm sorry I kissed you in the pub . . . " I couldn't speak. *Here it comes.* " . . . but I don't regret kissing you . . . just doing it in the doorway of a pub toilet," he sniggered. I was paralysed with shock. *What did he just say?* "Well?" he invited me to respond.

"I don't regret it. I wanted it. I just panicked . . . my life is so complicated and it won't be fair for anyone," I confessed finally maintaining eye contact.

"But I don't want to *not* see you Kemi." The silence amplified his deep inhale. "I know you're not happy," he offered hesitantly, not wanting to overstep his position.

I didn't argue. We started walking again and before long I was once again lost in his embrace.

Craig and I continued to see each other and on 22nd December, we spent our first night together, in a hotel. Rab had a Christmas night out and I'd arranged for the children to sleep over at my mum's, saying I had a college Christmas party.

We had our own little Christmas, exchanging small gifts that wouldn't draw attention from the outside world, and talked for hours getting to know each other better. That night I couldn't sleep. It was now 4am and Craig was out cold. What had been a magical night was now starting to be filled with dread. *What if someone saw us? What if Rab didn't go on a bender and is actually waiting at home and I'm not in? Shit! I have to get out of here!* I dressed in the bathroom so as not to wake Craig and called a taxi.

As I looked back at him, I knew I wouldn't see him again until New Year at his house. We'd planned to meet up after 'the bells', as they say in Scotland. He lived just around the corner from my mum and, as always for New Year, I would be at my mum's house with the children – but without Rab. Craig's parents and sister would be out, freeing up his house and I would tell my mum I was going to Katie's.

Craig didn't know I was planning on asking Rab to move out. It was important that he didn't know. It wasn't about him; this had to be about me.

When I arrived home at about 5am, the house was in darkness and empty. Rab, true to form, had not come home. I was delighted. My long-awaited plan was falling into place. I couldn't sleep. I was so happy when I thought about Craig and convinced myself that even if we didn't work out, I was happy with what I'd experienced. He'd made me feel alive and happy and he thought I was beautiful, funny and intelligent! Yes, I could live with just these memories if I had too.

Rab returned home two days later. It was Christmas Eve morning and he went straight to bed. He didn't get up again until night time, while the children were excitedly getting Santa's milk and cookies ready. He came and joined in and I played along, waiting for my moment. He was still in a fragile state and dealing with his hangover by the time the children went to bed that night, so I decided I would wait until after Christmas. If he was going to be violent, it would not be in front of my children on Christmas Day.

As usual, we all went to my mum's house for Christmas dinner, where we would stay overnight. The children would normally stay over on Boxing Day night too, so that Rab and I could have a night out.

When we returned home on Boxing Day evening to get dressed to go out with Rab's friends, I told him I wasn't going.

"What do you mean you're not coming?" he demanded, filling the room with contempt and tension as he patted his coat pocket searching for his wallet.

"I'm not going because I don't want to be with you anymore," I delivered bluntly.

"Oh, here we go. Is this because I had a bender?" Rab dismissed, shaking his other pocket now, listening for the jingling of house keys.

"No . . . I don't care about that," I confessed, "I just don't want to be with you."

His confused disbelief stared at me in silence. No more pocket inspections. I got worried when he didn't get angry. *Why can't you just make this easy for me?*

"Rab, I mean it," I reinforced breaking the silence.

"I'm out of here . . . I'm not listening to you. Stay here if you want, I don't give a fuck," he said, slamming the door behind him. I snuggled into the sofa relieved to have said it, but concerned that maybe he didn't believe me.

I arranged for Tayo to come over and have a smoke after Rab stormed out. I'd told him I was throwing Rab out when I was at my mum's house for Christmas. He was the only person that knew what I was doing. He was the only person I trusted to share my secrets.

I hadn't spoken to Craig for a few days. He'd last called me the morning I'd left him asleep at the hotel; he was hurt to have woken up to find me gone without saying goodbye. I'd felt really bad. I hadn't wanted him to feel like that and told him I was sorry, but that I had panicked. He understood, but I knew he found it hard only having stolen moments. He was so proud of me and he wanted to tell everyone that I was his African queen. He understood that I couldn't see him during the Christmas period because I had the children, but we looked forward to being together at New Year.

Rab didn't come home for a couple of days after my confession and I used this time to figure out a plan. I would pack some bags for him, to last him a couple of weeks and tell him that I needed space to think. He made it easy. He phoned me after three days, screaming abuse. With his bags already packed, I sent him a text message saying that he could pick them up, but that he wasn't getting back into the house, as I needed time to think.

He'd made it so easy for me with his predictable behaviour. He, however, had underestimated my unpredictability, as by the time he'd sobered up and read the message, I'd already changed the locks. When he phoned, I explained I couldn't have him back just now and that I needed space.

"I'm not saying it's over," I began, "I just need some space. I'm fed up with being treated like this. If you really are sorry, you will give me this time." I could hear his breath and his resistance to my suggestion, but he had to agree as he couldn't be sure of my next move.

"Okay . . . I'll come and pick up my stuff," he resigned sulking.

"No," I quickly interrupted, "your bags are ready and Tayo's here; we'll drop them off to you."

"Er, what? Oh, okay." His confusion was quickly replaced with realisation.

As I hung up the phone, I felt free. I had done it; he was gone! He didn't know it, but he would never be back in my house as my husband ever again. The dropping off of the bags was very uneventful. I told him I didn't want to talk, so he met me at his mum's front door to do the handover.

"I'll be in touch . . . when I've had time to think," I said as he took the bags before dropping them at his feet.

"Kemi, I'm sorry," he offered.

I believed him, but I didn't care. As I got into Tayo's car, I was just relieved to have finally freed myself.

The following day I went to my mum's house to spend new year. I told my parents all that had happened over the festive period and that I'd asked Rab to give me some time to think. They were both very concerned.

"What do you mean you need time?" my mum choked, startled at my revelations.

"Well, I do. I don't need to be treated like this and this will teach him that," I misled.

I didn't want to get involved in the full truth at this moment. I was only concerned about meeting Craig later that night and unnecessarily worrying them could delay that.

"Mum don't worry. I'm much better, so he should treat me better," I offered hoping to appease.

"Okay . . . but you need to sort this. He's too involved with the family business now, so don't be getting any ideas," my mum advised.

"Mum, I said I just wanted time. I don't want to have to watch him recovering for a week because he's drank too much," I continued, cementing my misdirection.

"Oh yeah, you're right. You don't need to put up with that," she concluded.

I knew she would accept this argument as she hated his laziness.

After the usual New Year's family traditions, I got into a taxi to go and meet Craig. I was so excited, but I wasn't sure if I was going to tell him about Rab. I didn't want to freak him out, or have him think I'd done it for him. I pushed my indecision to the back of my mind as my taxi pulled up outside the dimly lit house.

By the time I'd stepped out of the car, he was there, big grin beaming. He nearly lifted me off my feet he was so pleased to see me. As we settled by the fire in his parent's lounge, with just the Christmas tree lights on, I felt quite unsettled. Craig could see that.

"You don't feel comfortable, do you?" he asked, looking concerned, whilst sitting down his glass of *Jack Daniel's*.

"Oh, I'm sorry. It just feels wrong being *here*," I replied, feeling awkward.

"It's okay," he reassured. "Would you feel more comfortable in my bedroom?" he offered innocently.

No sooner had the words left his mouth, did he hear how they came out. I just laughed. He really was trying to be helpful, but it had sounded like a cheesy line; a cliché.

"No. Not like *that*," he clarified with a hint of embarrassment.

"I know," I reassured.

We went to his bedroom, which wasn't any better, but after a while of catching up on all our Christmas news, minus my marriage news, I finally began to relax. It was always so nice to be with him. I felt so different, as if my life before knowing him had never existed. As he measured my hand in his and commented on how little I was, what had been a very tender moment suddenly became uncomfortable. I needed to change the subject.

"I've asked Rab to leave, and he's gone," I blurted out.

"What?" he exclaimed with a deep swallow. "Are you serious?" His eyes scanned mine searching for deception.

"Yes," I began, exposing my eyes to show their honesty, "but it's been a long time coming . . . and it's not because of you," I informed, trying to show him that I was a strong woman that doesn't go from one man to another.

"Kemi, I don't know what to say? I've had quite a bit to drink; is this real?" he questioned, longing for confirmation.

"It's real. I've been planning it for some time now," I revealed, satisfying his need. "But Craig, let's not talk about this tonight," I gently requested. I didn't want to be talking about that toxic part of my life; this was separate and I didn't want him to see that side.

"I'm sorry, I've just so many questions . . . but they can wait."

As he pulled me back in close and as I lay in his comfort and strength, I questioned how could I ever have a relationship with this man I was falling in love with; with all my baggage. The rest of the night evaded any further discussions of Rab and my freedom. When the time came for me to leave, Craig walked me out to my taxi.

"Kemi, can I see you tomorrow?" he asked, opening the rear door of the taxi.

"I'm sorry, I can't. I'm at my mum's house until the 2nd." I could see his disappointment.

"Well, the 2nd then?" he urged with optimism.

"I don't know . . . I have the children, but I'll text you," I said as I climbed into the taxi.

"Kemi, we need to talk," he advised, looking into my eyes while taking the car door in his hand.

"Okay," I agreed as he gently pressed the door closed.

As I watched him waving as we drove away, I realised I wasn't ready to talk. I didn't want to be discovered.

Before I left my parent's house on the 2nd, I told them that I wouldn't be taking Rab back, that whatever went on in their 'family business' was nothing to do with me and that I would not be changing my mind. My mum knew I meant it and was suspicious.

"So, I take it you are seeing the Jamaican now," my mum scornfully suggested.

"Yes," I calmly replied. "And think very carefully before you say another word. This feels right. For once I have someone who truly cares for me.

117

Supports me. Understands what life is like to be mixed-race living in Scotland. I can see this relationship growing to include the kids. And what then? Are you still going to question my choice? Do you not want to be a part of that?"

A momentary silence landed, broken by my mum's pursuit of having the last word.

"But Kemi," she began.

"Leave it Daisy," my dad intervened, "it's her life." He sounded rather full of approval.

"You're only saying that Samuel because this guy's black," my mother snarled, "that's the reason you're fine with this," she accusingly declared.

There was no response from my dad. The silence was his confirmation. I took comfort in knowing she was right.

When I returned home, I agreed to let Craig come to the house to talk after the children were asleep in bed. He arrived at 10pm as arranged and didn't need to knock as I was waiting to let him in. He looked quite nervous as we entered my living room.

"Nice. I like your home," he confessed. "It feels like you."

"Thank you . . . I think," I replied, feeling more relaxed here than I had at his parents' house.

He appeared to be more relaxed by the time I returned to the sofa with a cup of tea for us both.

"I know you've just separated and you should probably have space - but that's not what I want. But, if it's what you need, then I will be your friend until you're ready."

"What? That's quite a statement," I replied in shock at how serious he seemed.

"Kemi, I'm not playing. I don't want to lose this connection we have. I know you feel the same."

I didn't know what to say. I did feel the same, but that was madness. I couldn't wrap my head around how this could be happening. He held my hand in both of his.

"Kemi, I loved you the moment you walked into that auditorium. I told myself: "I will marry her". Don't panic . . . I'm not asking you - I'm just telling you how I feel, because if I don't, I might regret it."

I couldn't speak. I was trying to hold back tears and feared they might breach if I spoke.

"This is crazy," I finally managed, "but I do feel the same." *I love you too.*

My life would never be the same again from that moment.

Separation and divorce

"Rab, you're here to see the children - not me," I reminded him, rebuffing yet another attempt to debate our current situation.

"I know, and I *do* want to see them. It's just that I want us to sort this out too," he admitted.

"No Rab, I'm not speaking to you about it until after I've had my two weeks to think. Please, stop," I urged.

"Okay . . . I'll give you some time," he reluctantly accepted.

"Thank you," I said, releasing a shallow breath of relief.

Why do I feel so bad for him? He seemed so desperate to come back. It was strange, the sympathy I felt for him. It didn't come from a weakness within me, because I was beginning to see just how strong I'd grown since my wedding 16 months earlier. I was very clear in my mind that I would not have him back; but still I felt guilty. I knew this would be devastating for him. I was coming to see that he did love me, in a very unhealthy way, like my mum. He saw me as something that belonged to him and I was seeing that I belonged to no one, except my children.

Rab had been staying with his dad and his dad's girlfriend. Rab's dad also had a drink problem, so when Rab phoned me the night before the two weeks were up, I wasn't surprised that he had been drinking.

"Hello Kemi," he blurted out as soon as I'd answered his call and before I had a chance to say anything.

"Rab?" I responded, my defences rising as they always did whenever I knew he'd been drinking.

"Have you had enough time now? Can I come home tomorrow?" he asked deluded, not by the alcohol, but by the expectations of the previous conclusions to our fallouts.

I considered putting this conversation off until the next day, the agreed date, and by when he would be sober, but I decided instead to deliver my decision in that moment. I took a deep breath, composing myself. The children were sleeping, which brought relief as they would not be witnessing this conversation.

"No Rab," I began, clear and firm, but with a gentle tact. "I'm sorry. I don't want to be married to you."

There was a pause on the other end of the phone - a silence that seemed to drag on forever.

"Are you serious?" he questioned with disbelief. "How can you say this? You're throwing away seven years together?"

I was shocked to hear him speak like this. *How can you think the last seven years are something worth saving?* I didn't want to be too honest, as I felt he would see this as me being cruel.

"Rab. I'm not happy," I reinforced, not coldly but delicately honest. "I

119

haven't been for quite some time now."

The silence returned, lingering just long enough to make me wonder if he had put his phone down.

"Why do you have to bring up the past Kemi?" he finally queried, sounding defeated.

"Rab this isn't just the past. This is how I feel now." I took a deep breath. "I've changed so much and I don't feel the same anymore." *All true. Take that however feels best.*

"Are you shagging the Jamaican then?" he spat down the phone, his whole demeanour now confrontational. I wasn't shocked by his question – I'd been expecting it.

"Rab this isn't about anyone else. This is about me and the children. We need to be happy and safe," I explained calmly and honestly. I didn't want him to think we were over because of someone else, that would just make him think I would go back to him if it didn't work out.

There was silence once more. I could hear his breathing, made heavier by the alcohol.

"Do you not love me anymore," he asked, offended and in a self-pitying tone. *I don't know if I ever did.* I was tied to this man because of our children.

"I do love you, as the father of our children and we will always be their parents, but no, I'm not in love with you," I confessed.

"You're a fucking, dirty, lying slut," Rab erupted, each adjective gaining more disdain than the previous. "I know this is about the Jamaican." He was fired up by now, charged and losing control.

"Rab, I'm not going to speak to you when you're like this," I advised, not threateningly, more just establishing my boundaries. My days of listening to his drink-fuelled rages were now well and truly over.

"Oh, you *will* fucking speak to me, slut." He was so angry. I could see him in my mind's eye, his irate face glowing bright red by now.

"If you put the phone down, I will come down there. I'm sick of this shit; you're keeping me out of my own home and away from my kids." He was out of breath by the time he finished his rant.

Your fucking kids? What have you ever done for them? And excuse me, but it's my fucking house. What have you paid for? I was ignited. Fuming. But I held my calm. I no longer needed to entertain this behaviour and I certainly would not be participating. He was on his last chance.

"These children are *my* children. Make no mistake about that. And the house? This is *my* house." Internally I was so charged, but my voice remained very calm, clear and succinct. He *had* to hear what I was saying. "If you come down here, I *will* phone the police. I mean it, Rab." My heart was racing by now, but my words remained steady.

"Who the fuck do you . . . ," were the last words I heard as my hand shakily put the receiver down. I was so worked up. I felt sick with relief at finally, and unequivocally, stating I did not want to be married to him anymore.

I called Craig to put him off from coming for our usual 10pm visit. I didn't want to spoil our time together by telling him what was going on. I was trying to savour the separateness of my two very different lives and did not want to pollute the secret one we had started for ourselves.

"Hi Craig. I'm sorry, but I need to cancel tonight," I got out very quickly. I didn't want to get into the finer details, but I didn't want to lie. "Rab phoned and I've told him."

Craig knew of my plan about telling Rab that it was over after the two weeks separation, but he didn't understand at the time why I was scared of Rab.

"What?" he coughed with surprise. "How did that happen? I thought you were speaking to him tomorrow."

I filled him in on the fact that Rab had phoned me, drunk, and that I had just told him straight.

"What did you say about *the Jamaican* then?" Craig found Rab's choice of nickname amusing.

"I told him it was nothing to do with *the Jamaican,*" *I chuckled,* momentarily, before returning to sombre. "I said it was strictly about me changing and not feeling the same."

I felt under pressure not telling both of them the whole truth. Craig wasn't aware of Rab's violence and Rab didn't have confirmation of my relationship with *the Jamaican. I have to do this my way.*

"It's not the time to mention us." I was going to be fully honest with them both - just not tonight.

"Okay . . . but why can't I see you? You sound upset - I want to be with you and make you feel better," his voice sounded sincere.

Please just leave it. I couldn't lie to him. I knew I would have to come fully clean.

"You can't come over." I took a deep breath, considering my next move. With its release, so too did my words fall out. "He might come over and I would have to call the police," I finally confessed with apprehension, bracing myself for his reaction.

"What? Wait a minute!" I could hear him in his silent pause contemplate and conclude why I was scared of Rab. "Why? Do you think he would hurt you? Kemi, has he hit you before?"

"Yes," I said, quickly and quietly, getting out my confession before I changed my mind, "but Craig, I don't want to get into that, please." He wasn't forcing me to speak - more offering his ears.

"Kemi, why wouldn't you tell me this? God, Kemi . . . I'd no idea. I thought you were scared of him . . . but I didn't think this."

He was trying to help and understand, but I was feeling shameful from my confession and wanted to get off the phone.

"I'm sorry Craig, I need to go. I'll speak to you tomorrow." I could hear

121

him taking a deep breath in.

"Okay Kemi, but we need to start talking. Okay?" he reassured.

"Okay. Thanks for understanding."

We agreed to see each other the next night and I was grateful for his understanding and gentleness. He never pressed me. He would make requests, not demands. He was leading me safely through my story, when I was ready.

I would eventually tell Craig the truth about my marriage. He would just listen, holding me when it got too much. I told him all about Rab - more than I'd told Marion - and I also told him I was in recovery from anorexia and that I was still in therapy. By now I attended therapy just once every three weeks and was no longer on any medication.

He was very understanding about my past and never judged me. I felt understood and loved for the first time since Auntie. He could see deep into my soul. He knew my struggle. He too had had to find his own ways of living in this country that didn't accept our skin colour. We found safety and understanding in one another and a deep level of intimacy, which I never knew existed. I really did start to heal some of my sorrow.

I felt like I had just come out of a war, while it felt like Rab was just entering one. He did not make things easy. He didn't pay any money towards the children - he'd never supported us financially before, so I was happy to continue to be the only provider for our children, and he told the children Craig was my boyfriend and that it was because of Craig that I had thrown him out.

"Mummy, Mummy, Mummy, Mummy," Sola excitedly pitched as I tucked him into bed while he drilled two, tiny fingers into my upper arm, like a woodpecker chipping at bark. He always did this whenever he was wanting my attention.

"Yes, little man. How can I help you?" I asked with widened eyes, reminding him that this was a sore way to get mummy's attention. When our eyes met, we both laughed.

"Mummy, you know how you said you still love Dad?" Sola opened, looking for confirmation, "and that sometimes people just don't love each other enough to live together anymore? Remember you said that?"

"You don't though," Dayo declared rushing into the room to interrupt Sola's line of questioning. These two were so close and inseparable and yet so very different.

Sola was very clear and direct if he had something to say, whereas Dayo was gentler and more thoughtful, often preparing what he wanted to say to soften the blow. He would always wait for Sola to start the conversation on behalf of them both, but if he felt he could better verbalise, he would take over, relentlessly rattling out his thoughts, opinions and conclusions without pause and his monologues often took a long walk for a shortcut.

I sat myself on Sola's bed with Sola cuddled up on my knees and prepared myself for Dayo's monologue.

"Mummy, are you listening?" Dayo agitatedly probed, double-checking I'd heard his opening declaration while he cuddled into *Laa-Laa* – his favourite *Teletubby*.

"Yes, darling, I heard," I said, turning face-on to offer him my full attention. "Please continue."

"Yes Dayo, get on with it. Blah, blah, blah," Sola chimed in, wriggling with impatience.

"Mum - tell him," Dayo urged, feeling aggrieved.

"Sola, be kinder to your brother, please," I requested.

"Sorry Dayo," Sola offered through his dummy-filled mouth as he quickly popped his head up from my chest. Like a *Whack-A-Mole,* he quickly disappeared back down again to cuddle in while repeating his self-developed, dummy-suckling, sleep-inducing mantra: "gully, gully, gully." His self-soothing chorus served only to frustrate Dayo further.

"Mum - tell him. He's annoying me on purpose with that dumb noise," Dayo whined. I was trying not to laugh at my children's interaction; without knowing it, they were like a double act.

"Dayo . . . it's okay, he's just getting settled. Please . . . carry on with your story."

"Yes . . . he's getting settled . . . just like a baby," Dayo proudly provoked with a cheeky grin.

"Yes, I am," Sola retorted, equally as proud. Sola was nearly four by now, but he was the rightful heir to the title of 'baby of the family' and he was not for giving it up.

Dayo took a long, deep breath to recap before continuing.

"Dad said you don't love him. He said you threw him out because you have a new, *brown* boyfriend," Dayo finally revealed, delivering his last word with a huge exhale. *Oh my God. How could he? How did I not see this coming?* I hid my shock.

"Mum, *is* he brown like you?" Sola asked, still tucked deeply into my body, his attention focusing on the 'brown'.

"Boys," I began before taking a deep breath. I didn't want to lie to them, but I also had to judge what they were able to understand at four and five years old.

"I do have a special friend called Craig . . ." I started to explain.

"Yes, Mummy - but is he *brown* like *you*?" Sola interrupted, unable to continue the conversation until he had received his confirmation.

"Yes Sola," I confirmed. His little head relaxed into me satisfied with my answer. "He is brown, like Mummy. We have been friends since Mummy started college . . . but Mummy wasn't happy before college started, and that's why I can't be with Daddy anymore. Even if I wasn't friends with Craig, I still wouldn't be with Daddy." I hoped I'd explained the distinction clear enough for their young minds to understand without causing upset.

"What does 'special friend' mean? Do you kiss him Mummy?" Dayo asked bluntly yet innocently.

"No, no. No way does she kiss him," Sola defended, insulted at Dayo's preposterous question. Sola hated to share his Mummy and knew he was Mummy's only true love. "Dayo, shut up."

"Mum, tell that wee idiot!" Dayo urged, enjoying his defamation while looking to me to deal with his brother's rudeness.

"Okay . . . boys let's settle down now, please. Sola you're not allowed to be rude. What do you have to say?" Sola raised his now clammy head, eyes still closed, out from our cuddle.

"Sorry Dayo," he said reluctantly, before retreating back to his cuddle. Taking in another deep breath, I continued.

"Okay. Let's leave kissing questions until another time. A special friend is someone who you like the best out of all of your friends," I offered, hoping to appease without having to get into the finer, more intrinsic details of a special friend's role.

"But we've met all your friends - we haven't met Craig," Dayo disputed with logic. He was so sharp and never missed a trick.

"Well . . . I can fix that - if you'd like - but Sola, you've already met him." Sola sat upright like a meercat and looked me straight in the eyes.

"When, Mummy?" his animated face contorted trying to recall such an event.

"He gives us a lift home sometimes from college," I reminded.

"Craig?" Sola said, scanning through his memory files. Upon retrieval, his eyes widened with delight. "Ah, *that* guy. Yes, I know *that* guy. Dayo . . . he's cool, *and* brown, and he has a red car!"

Red was Sola's favourite colour, so obviously Craig must have been cool!

"But Mummy," Sola began, taking my face in his tiny little hands, turning me until our eyes locked. "He's not brown like *you*," he demonstrated, his palms gently rubbing the skin on my cheeks, "he's brown, like *me*," he said, releasing my face to now pat his own cheeks.

Sola loved to point out different tones and shades of brown, unaware that brown was brown, regardless.

Dayo looked relieved to hear that Sola knew Craig, however, I could tell he was concerned about his dad and how he'd react. Unfortunately, Dayo had been affected by Rab's violence towards me, which had left him scared of his dad and his volatility.

As I tucked them both into bed and kissed them good night, I promised to arrange a meeting with my 'friend', Craig. I half closed their bedroom door and took another deep breath. *That bastard! How dare he?* I'd not intended on having *that* conversation with the boys so soon after Rab moving out; I hadn't wanted to confuse them, but Rab had put me in that position, by selfishly using the children to make himself the poor victim. I now had to go and speak to Michelle. *What the hell has he been saying to her?* I went downstairs to find Michelle in the living room watching TV. *Okay Kemi: round two.*

"Hi Michelle," I began, sitting down beside her on the sofa, "can I speak to you about something?" I was nervously hesitant to hear what she knew.

"What? Is it about what Rab said about you?" she asked in a matter-of-fact manner without taking her eyes off the TV. I felt myself brace.

"Yes, darling. About that," I confirmed, preparing to disclose the same information to her that her brothers now possessed.

"Craig from college is your boyfriend now?" she interrupted, eyes still transfixed on *Sister, Sister*. She wasn't seeking clarification on my relationship status; she was checking we were talking about the same thing.

"Yes that, and no, he's not. Not exactly," I explained, composing myself to resume my disclosure. She looked at me with a half-smile, finally allowing herself to afford me her full attention.

"That's what Nanny said." Her eyes searched mine. She was questioning me. I could hear it in her voice. In her mind, if Nanny said something then it was fact.

"Nanny?" I replied trying not to sound concerned. *What the hell has she been saying?*

"Yes, Nanny," Michelle confirmed, her whole body now facing me, throwing a cold shoulder to *Nickelodeon*. "She said you had a boyfriend from college called Craig." *How dare she!* I refused to show any sign of contempt.

"Michelle, sweetheart, he's not quite my boyfriend, but he is a special friend." She looked up, intrigued. "Would you like to meet him?" I asked gently.

"Yes. Okay," she replied, her eyes alive with excitement.

I pulled her in beside me, wrapping my arms around her, cloaking her in my cuddle. I loved these quiet times with Michelle; just the two of us. I would get her to myself each night when the boys were in bed and when there was no Nanny to interfere. Sometimes I would forget she was older and had different needs from the boys. I was aware she needed me to be stronger; to stand up to my mum before it was too late.

I was shocked when I heard that my mum had told my ten-year-old daughter about my 'friend'. I didn't question Michelle about what Nanny had said, as my mum questioned her all the time for information on me and I didn't want to add to that. My mum had exposed her to too much; things that a little girl shouldn't be hearing about.

"Nearly time for bed, Michelle," I said as *Sabrina the Teenage Witch* came to an end.

"Can't I sleep in your bed, Mum?" she asked, with her little, full lips pouted and her eyes impersonating the cutest of puppies. I had to agree.

125

"Love you, up to the sky and back. God bless. Sweet dreams. See you in the morning." This was our nightly mantra.

"Night, Mummy. See you when you come to bed," she replied, cuddling into my covers in the foetal position. I turned to leave, satisfied that I had handled the evening's revelations delicately well, and began closing my bedroom door.

"Mum?" Michelle beckoned, her voice sounding fragile. "You won't let Rab back, will you?" She took my breath away. I came back into the room and leaned over her.

"Never. I promise you, Michelle. I will never let him back," I said, with definitive reassurance.

"Good," she concluded firmly.

As I left the room to go downstairs, I felt an unbearable guilt in my gut. That little girl should never have been exposed to Rab and I had allowed it. I still, to this day, carry that guilt.

The children met Craig the following weekend. I had Katie and her boys join us. Sola and Michelle liked Craig. Michelle sat with Katie, Craig and me and joined-in in our conversations, sussing out Craig. After a while she went out to play on the street with friends and the boys got Craig to play football in the garden. Dayo was not pleased; he wanted to play basketball, so Craig convinced Will and Sola to switch games. This definitely earned Craig Brownie points and going to get them all *McDonald's Happy Meals* sealed it.

From then on, Craig just grew into our little unit. Dayo remained cautiously concerned. He worried about what his dad might do, but with assurance and time, he learned to feel safer. Sola just thought Craig was cool, and 'brown like him', so it was easier for him to let Craig in. Michelle had also thought he was cool, granting her acceptance. He had natural boundaries that made them all feel safe.

I introduced the children to Craig much sooner than we had planned. Rab and my mum had taken the choice of timing away from me and I wouldn't lie to the children. I thought the best way to handle the situation would be to let the children get to know Craig, to decide for themselves and to allow things to take their natural course.

We had all been through so much together and now these were happier times. That spring and summer were magical. My feelings for Craig were so strong by then, but I didn't know what to do. I'd never felt that way before - but I'd never been happier. I made the decision to listen to my gut and it said it felt right. I'd spent so much of my life feeling wrong, so for once, I chose to feel right.

Rab continued to be spiteful, so, in one of our phone calls in early spring, I told him I wanted a divorce.

"Good . . . I'm done with you anyway," Rab spat out, like a petulant toddler does its dummy. He was angry and dismissive and if I'd been able to see him, I knew he would have been red in the face. "But *I* will be divorcing *you*, you slut, for having an affair."

By now I was used to his vernacular, but still took offence at his audacious hypocrisy.

"What . . . are you serious?" I responded, in disbelief.

"Aye, I am," he answered with his own deluded disbelief, as if *he* was offended by *my* questioning. "This is what happens when you fuck a Jamaican, slut." His hateful tone sounded eager to unleash. He couldn't help himself.

"I'm not listening to this, Rab. Fuck you." I cut him off, slamming the phone down. I was so angry. He was such a hypocrite. I knew then he was going to try to make me pay for 'cheating' on him.

He was shocked that I had done this to him, even though he had cheated on me continuously throughout our relationship. I never denied my affair with Craig - I owned it, as it's my belief that along with the gift of choice, comes the weight of responsibility to own the consequence of your actions, and I wanted my children to learn to own their actions. They had to know this. It'd taken me a long time to learn I had choice and I didn't want them to be blinded to its consequences like I had been.

# # #

To begin with, Michelle would go along with the boys to visit Rab one day a week, and more often than not, they didn't want to go. Rab would take them to his mother's house where it was believed to be okay to smack the children. Rab and his mother had continuously ignored my views on the matter, leaving me feeling powerless. I'd been very clear about it - I didn't smack my children, so neither should they. It was no longer the 1970s and I was the proof that smacking was a very damaging experience and vowed that it should not be used as a deterrent, consequence or punishment.

At the time, the court and the lawyers had all agreed with my views, so during our divorce, Rab was only given one-day-a-week access to the children, with no overnight stay. This would continue to be the case until the court was satisfied that he no longer smacked the children or allowed anyone else to. Marion had advised that I should divorce him on grounds of domestic violence, but it wasn't that straight forward. He would fight that, and I just wanted it to be over and for me to be free of him. Ultimately, he divorced me for adultery.

"How could you allow *him* to divorce *you*? Kemi, you should've used domestic abuse! What will people think?" my mum angrily interrogated, thinking only of herself.

My mother, like my father, was obsessed with reputation and believed, once again, that this label would be too much, on top of my blackness.

During this time of court and lawyers, Rab had taken all three children to the park one day. Not long after they returned, Michelle approached me.

"Rab was bad to me today when I was playing football with Dayo. He pushed me and kicked me when I was on the ground and said I was being too rough."

How could he have done this to her? I felt instantly sickened, not just at her pain from the violent act, but also at the humiliation she must have felt. It brought back the memories of when the man instructed his son to "go and hit *it* and see if *it* cries".

After I asked Michelle to repeat all that had happened, and once I had the children settled in bed, I phoned Rab. As the phone rang my stomach was in knots and my heart was pounding. I knew the reception was not going to be a welcoming one.

"Hello," Rab answered, his monotone displaying his mood.

"Hi Rab," I began, "I need to speak to you about today's visit with the children . . . " I was angry and confused but kept restraint.

"Fucksake - what now?" he interrupted, abandoning his indifference.

"Michelle said . . . ," I began, now loosening my grip on my restraint in reaction to his tone, "when you were playing football today and she was tackling Dayo . . . "

"Yeah, we were playing football, what about it?" Rab abruptly interrupted again.

"Just listen," I continued sharply. "Michelle said that you pushed her, which made her fall to the ground and when she was down you kicked her." There was a brief silence. My back was tense, and my hand ached from gripping the phone so tightly.

"Are you fucking serious? Are you telling me that you actually believe this?" Rab replied defiantly. He sounded offended and not in his usual self-pitying way.

"Well Rab, with your background I have to question it. Why would she lie?" I probed. This was serious and I needed him to convince me.

"Because that's all she ever fucking does," he scathed. "You refuse to look at it. Look at some of things she's done and she's only ten." He sounded so condescending.

"I'm not listening to this and I will be notifying my lawyer in the morning," I advised, before putting the phone down.

My lawyer wrote to Rab's lawyer, requesting answers and reminding Rab that he was still under review by the court for refusing to stop smacking the children. I hadn't heard anything back from his lawyer by the time of his next access. When Rab came to collect the boys, he took great pleasure in telling me his response.

"My lawyer got your letter . . . I'm dropping Michelle from the Visitation

Order," he smirked, looking very self-satisfied. "He's advised me that she's a dangerous little girl and her lies could affect my visits with my boys." *He's still not getting it. One week later and he's still making the point that there's something wrong with Michelle.*

So, Michelle ceased to go. I was devastated at how his lawyer could say this about my child and my mum was furious that Rab would take his advice.

"The bastard! How dare he say that about *my* Princess? Who the fuck does he and his dicky, wee lawyer think they are, talking about *my* Princess? He's just made himself public enemy number one!"

If truth be told, I was relieved that Rab had dropped Michelle from the legalities. I was annoyed that he had, but even more relieved. I didn't want her around him, as there was now a clear difference in how his mother treated her compared to her brothers, and by now Rab's mother was heavily involved.

I wasn't sure I could defend Michelle entirely, as I was not totally convinced that what she was saying was one hundred percent true. Yes, Rab was handy with the children. But to kick her? And in public? That would be exposing himself and he didn't do that. Maybe she just wanted a way out of the visits to his mother's.

Rab decided he wasn't going to pay to support his children and the court practically agreed, concluding that he'd to pay only £5 a week in total, for both boys, as he was no longer working. I didn't want his money and didn't take it. He'd never supported us before, so there was nothing lost as far as I could see.

I remember speaking to my lawyer about the racist language Rab's mother used in front of the children. I was told that *I* would be seen as being petty by the court, as though racism was considered unimportant and that Rab and his mum would only deny it anyway.

This was to be my first experience with the court where, as a woman of colour, as long as I didn't bring up racial discrimination, they would listen to me. I would also learn the importance of being present. In my absence, and on paper, I would only be seen as my race. My lawyer advised that the court had already listened regarding the smacking, so basically, I had to be grateful.

# # #

During the summer, Craig moved in with me, to his parent's horror. His mother and brother didn't really like me and had been very vocal about it. They said it was because I was older, with children. That I could understand. However, I could smell racism a mile away. Craig's mum, like my dad, came to the UK in the 1960's. She'd come over from Jamaica to work as a nurse in the *NHS* and in her words, had met her 'handsome white prince', before moving to Scotland. I can understand how difficult it must have been for her coming to Scotland, all alone and knowing nobody; I've felt that isolation.

Craig and I had started a beautiful life together. He was devoted to me and the children, so much so that he'd made the choice to pause his studies to get a job to help support us, allowing me to continue my studies. When I first met Craig, he showed so much belief in me that I couldn't quite believe it. He would tell me how intelligent I was and that I could achieve anything I wanted in this world.

After college, I continued to further my studies at *Glasgow Caledonian University*. Craig's belief in me made me question what it was he was seeing, but I slowly started to grow some belief in myself. Unfortunately, there would not be enough growth for me to be able to save my relationship with Michelle.

# # #

I was eventually divorced in 2003. Craig, the three children and I had built a lovely life together. Craig was such a 'modern man'. He had no problem doing whatever needed doing for the children, or around the house. He gave the children's fathers total respect and wanted the children to decide how he would fit into their lives. All three children adored him which was very difficult for my mum to accept. She couldn't understand or control Craig. I don't think it helped that he was a very young man taking care of her grandchildren as his own - something she'd been unable to do for my older brother Tunde.

Rab got his own high-rise flat through the council and was supposed to have the boys on either a Friday or Saturday. For one reason or another this wouldn't always happen, which was fine as the children didn't want to go most of the time anyway. Rab was very controlling and quickly angered and the children were exposed to things at his flat that they should not have seen.

Sola was especially vocal about not going to visit his dad and whenever he refused to go, Dayo would refuse to go without him. That way, rather than saying he didn't want to spend time with his dad, Dayo's excuse was that he didn't want to be apart from Sola. Dayo was not as confident as Sola and struggled to communicate his feelings to his dad. He couldn't bear to hurt anyone's feelings - especially his dad's, through fear of how he may react. Rab would often exploit Dayo's consideration, making it very easy for him to manipulate the child.

On one of the visits to their dad's flat, Rab's intolerance of their afro hair compelled him to shave their heads down to a number two buzz cut. This had been fiercely contested by Sola and heartbreakingly accepted by Dayo. Dayo was very traumatised by this one single act. The following day, when the boys returned home, they were still inconsolable, especially Dayo.

Dayo's beautiful afro hair was a huge part of his identity and I was furious. However, I was also deeply saddened. When I looked into their tear-filled eyes, I remembered how my mum had felt about my afro hair as a child and how she had made me feel like it was a burden. I'd like to point out that Rab, unlike my mother, was educated, by me, in black children's needs, especially in the basics of how their hair is kept. This was a racial violation of my children. This was not unconscious, racial bias; this was an in-your-face, blatant act of racism. Rab cut my children's hair as he felt it would make them less black.

I contacted my lawyer and reported the trauma that Rab had caused and advised that I wanted his visitation rights looked at again. Rab's response had been: "I'll do whatever I want to my children."

My lawyer once again told me that this was too petty to take to court. She instead wrote a letter to Rab, warning that if he did anything else to cause the children trauma, I would be seeking to have his visitation revoked. This worked . . . for a little while. Rab didn't like to be over-exposed in public.

My family and Craig

Craig's dad was a police sergeant in Easterhouse, Glasgow and his uncle - his dad's brother - was also in the police. This wasn't good for my family; their daughter living with a policeman's son. When you consider my family's business was in organised serious fraud, my choice of partner, to my family, could not have been any riskier.

To begin with, Craig and I were oblivious to the relevance of this. We were just two people who had fallen in love. We understood each other's identities and the wounds caused by society's lack of acceptance.

I hadn't told Craig anything about my family's business - as far as I was concerned, it was none of our business and I am not one for gossip. I hadn't told him about how my mother treated me or how she had interfered, ignored or overruled my attempts to raise Michelle. This was a part of my life that I tried to keep hidden from him. It was something of which I was ashamed. I felt I hadn't been a good enough mother to my daughter. Not because I couldn't love her - this I found easy - but because I had not been able to stop my mum taking control of her too.

Craig initially thought my mum seemed nice. He was always polite and respectful to her and quickly acknowledged her matriarchal position. However, he did start to notice how she inserted - and asserted - herself whenever I was dealing with Michelle.

"Kemi, Michelle is your daughter . . . why does your mum always undermine you?" he questioned me openly.

He wasn't being nosey, or intentionally speaking out against my mum. He just felt protective of me. He was gently challenging me to see if I agreed with his observation; that he felt I was being treated unfairly. I could feel myself getting defensive and strangely, protective of my mother.

"Craig, it's complicated. When I had Michelle, I was so young and needed a lot of support, and when I was sick, my mum was there and helped me out a lot with her. I think she thinks I can't cope without her," I offered, feeling vulnerable.

I didn't want him to judge me as being a terrible mother, but I had to explain my mum's over-involvement with Michelle. My mum had recently lost her Post Office and along with it her title of Postmistress, which shamed her. The illegal activities of my dad's business had seen to that. She, by nature, was consumed with embarrassment and fear of what people would be thinking and saying about her and the 'blackies'. The toll was too much and she experienced a full mental breakdown, right in the middle of the menopause! This was why I was protective of her behaviour.

"Kemi," he began with reassurance, "you're the strongest person I know. You're a great mother."

He wasn't telling me what he thought I wanted to hear. He was telling me what he truly believed. I found it very hard to accept compliments, especially from Craig, when they were regarding my mothering. I felt like a fraud, such were the results of my mother's scepticism and I would always change the conversation.

My mum had confessed to me one day when the children and I were visiting, that she was concerned about Craig's dad being a police officer.

"What if he finds out about your dad and the Post Office? The shame, Kemi."

She was crying inconsolably, almost frantic-like and I felt sorry for her. No child likes to see its mother crying.

"Your fucking stupid father," she exploded, her erraticness switching its attention; Craig's dad to one side, my dad now in the crosshairs.

"He's a dick, you know. A real fucking loser."

I didn't like hearing how useless my dad was. I hated how she was so spiteful. *As if you're innocent in all of this.* However, my dislike for her spitefulness did not prevent me from remaining sympathetic. So, I deployed the skills that I had developed so many years earlier and remained obedient.

"Mum, shall I go and open some more wine?" *Not wine Kemi, she's already tipsy.* "Or maybe a hot drink would be better," I offered, looking to both comfort her and to allow for my exit during the intermission between her acts.

"Yes, Kemi. That's what to do. That's my girl," she deliriously exclaimed. Her enthusiasm sounding as if my beverage was the answer to all her problems. Her malfunctioning was eerie. She was all over the place.

"You know, I didn't want that wanker Rab working for your dad, but your dad did . . . do you know why?" She wasn't asking me if I knew the answer; she was inviting and permitting herself to reveal further displeasures towards my dad.

"Mum, please," I interrupted, "I don't want to hear this." The children were in the next room and they did not need to see Nanny unravelling, revealing all about their grandad.

"Yeah. Can never say anything bad about *Daddy.*"

She switched to me, her eyes ice cool and full of distaste. I could feel the laser beam on my forehead. I didn't know if it was the wine that was unleashing her tongue or if she was actually breaking down. She paused. I wasn't sure if she was regaining her composure, or had momentarily forgotten who her target was.

"You know that bitch Rosemary will be talking about us . . . about the fucking blackies. All because of *your* fucking loser husband telling her all our business."

I was out of her sights. It was Rab and his mother's turn. Mum's normally snow-white complexion was harshly reddened, causing her cheeks to appear chaffed, and her breathing was shallow, not sufficient enough to allow her to catch breath.

133

"Who cares what *they* think Mum . . . *they're* not important," I counselled, hoping to put her mind at ease and end her tirade.

"And *you!*" she shrieked, locking her target and addressing me with disgust, "with a fucking policeman's son! Next we'll be getting raided!"

What the hell is she going on about? What have they done? I was confused at her attack and was glad to see my dad enter the room; I needed answers.

"Dad, what's going on?" I urged, now feeling very concerned for their predicament.

"Nothing princess," he condescendingly dismissed, as if this was a conversation for the adults. *I hate you calling me that.*

"Is *she* okay?" I found myself questioning him, ignoring his original stance, and as if my mum was no longer present.

"Yes. She shouldn't drink wine during her 'episodes', that's all," he offered with a light, nervous smile. *Bullshit.*

Craig would be coming to pick me up shortly and I didn't want him walking into this. She was out of control, so I was relieved when she took herself off for a bath.

This was how I learned of my parent's concerns about Craig and his police officer father. Despite me lacking the intel of their business, they were cautious - they weren't telling me anything. Even if I did notice or suspect some things, which I did, I never spoke about them and I certainly wasn't going to tarnish my happiness with Craig by discussing *them*. After a while, 'Craig, the policeman's son' became normalised. My mum remained vigilant, but she did accept Craig and behaved much better around him.

# # #

Craig got on very well with my brothers, especially Tayo. Tayo was a constant in my life at home, so he and Craig got to know each other very well. They began to hang out a lot, going to the gym and running track together. This made me very happy, that these two, the only men I trusted in my life, were becoming genuine friends.

Craig got on well with my youngest brother, Wale, too, as they turned out to be the same age. I found out, sometime later might I add, that Craig had originally fibbed in college about his age when we first met! Instead of being eight years my junior, he was in fact the same age as Wale, making him ten years younger than me. By the time I found out however, I was already deeply in love and didn't care. He was still the most grown-up person I knew.

# # #

134

After my mum had got over her 'little episode' as she would call it, I began making my own decisions and choices, without her permission or counsel. I was changing and she was losing her control over me. That was not part of her plan. I'd become so dependent on her before I met Craig, that I never did anything without her approval. The only part of me she didn't have control over was my boys. I didn't allow her to take control of them away from me, as she had done with Michelle.

She could see that there was a change in me, but didn't recognise my new strengths - confidence and self-worth - and so struggled to believe I could cope without her. Looking back, I don't think she had a choice. Well, not a choice with good outcomes at least. My change was so stark that I think she realised, regardless of whether she thought I could cope or not, she had to let go of some of her control, as she was not willing to lose me.

So, I gained some independence and built a new acceptance of myself, as long as she got to keep a piece of my self-worth. I was gaining confidence, but I still didn't see that her constant, quiet judging and loud criticism of me as a mother was damaging. I'd just learned to accept it. I was confident that I tried my very best as a mother, in spite of her interference.

Craig wasn't stupid; he continued to challenge and question my relationship with my mum. I remember him telling me it was uncommon that a mother-of-three had her finances controlled by her own mother. However, this was all I knew and I had never questioned it before – no one had; except Marion.

I was still attending sessions with Marion every month and she always tried to work with me on regaining my independence from my mum. My recovery had gone well, so much so, she suggested I was ready to finish my therapy for anorexia. I was gutted. She'd been such a massive part of my life for so long.

"What? But . . . how?"

I couldn't speak. I had been expecting it. We'd talked about it, but now that the time had arrived, I was left questioning myself as to how I could cope without her. I felt like a child losing its bicycle stabilisers.

"Kemi, I am so proud of you," Marion beamed. "Look at you. I remember you didn't think you could go to college and now you are about to qualify from university." She paused to check that I was receiving her message.

"Kemi, you just need to go and smash life and you certainly don't need me for that."

"Or me," Debby echoed, wearing the same smile of pride.

"I will miss you both so much," I began, finally finding my words with teary eyes. "I wouldn't be alive today if it wasn't for the two of you."

I hugged my two crutches, feeling them support me back, before letting go and walking away in strength; unaided.

I joined Marion and Debby in opening their very first anorexia group-counselling session. I was there to offer support to those affected and to show that recovery was possible; I was someone who had recovered.

I went to the group every few weeks for a few months, before Marion and Debby thought it was better for me to step completely out of my past and be free to live my new life.

#

When I finished my studies, I was qualified to specialise in the repair of muscular and ligament damage and the trauma we hold there. My grandparents were very excited for me, especially my grandad. He'd always believed in me and was so excited that I'd found my calling in the world. He was even more delighted when I fixed the bad knee he'd suffered with for so many years!

"Kemi, show me your motion, tra la la la la."

My dad was very business-like about my intentions, coming from his background in accountancy and finance, and thought I had a solid business plan. My mum had been very happy for me when I was studying and even told me she was proud of me when I was sitting my final exams. However, she thought it was absolutely farcical that I could now go on to grow my own business.

"That's hilarious, Samuel, have you heard her? Kemi's latest fantasy: she thinks she can open a clinic and people will just come."

I don't know what was driving me at this time, but I knew deep to my core that this was what I had to do, and that people would come. I began looking for somewhere to open my first clinic. Craig was so supportive and encouraged me all the way. He would drive me around looking for premises to work from and even made leaflets advertising my services. When I was unable to find a suitable workplace, I had the idea that I could work from my parent's house.

It was an old Victorian house in the Westend of the town. There was a perfect room at the rear of the house with its own entrance and bathroom, so the main house would not be disturbed. It was the room Craig, I and the children slept in if we ever stayed over. The house was situated perfectly on a very busy road, very near a roundabout that often backed up with slow moving traffic. I knew I only needed to put an advertising sign outside on the front railings. I had dreamt about it, and those types of dreams normally came true. Convinced by my plan, I approached my mum and sounded her out over the proposal.

"Well, I want £400 a month and I want two month's rent upfront," she informed, squinting her eyes to focus for any baulking.

"So basically, you want £800 upfront?" I replied, refusing to show as much as a flinch to her demands.

"Yeah. Where are *you* going to get that from?" she grinned.

I knew then she didn't believe I could do it and this felt like another attempt at her trying to control my life yet again. She knew I was on very little income and that Craig was the only one of us working, but she was clear that I couldn't start until she'd been paid. Craig went to his dad to borrow the money and he happily obliged. She didn't care that the money had come from Craig's dad - just that she had the money. And it worked out for Craig's dad too, as he'd always wanted to be 'one up' on my mum, so everyone was happy.

By now, Michelle was at a High School in Airdrie, *St. Margaret's*, the same school Tunde had attended when he returned to Scotland. My mum had wanted her to go there as it was a 'good Catholic school', and with it being a five-minute walk from her house, it also meant she could see Michelle every day. So, it made sense for me to move the boys to the primary school around the corner from my parent's house. If I was to be working from there, I would be able take them to school in the mornings and they could come back to my parent's house after school, where Craig could pick us all up. Even if I hadn't finished working, Craig could collect the children and take them home for dinner and homework before picking me up later when I was finished. It was all falling into place.

So, I put my sign outside and within ten weeks I had a full diary! This was all through my sign, and best of all, word of mouth. My life was taking a turn in a direction that I'd never seen before, and I was starting to gain some self-worth by helping rid my clients of their pain; it was the perfect exchange. I was building a new life with Craig for my children and for the first time I could see that I could have a future. Maybe.

I now had value; something to offer, and it brought tolerance of my existence. However, I was still experiencing racism; people shouting abuse in the street, being followed in shops, or having my change thrown on the counter - the usual everyday existence of someone of colour living in Scotland. My experiences of racism were so common it had become normalised - a part of my everyday life - so much so I'd become blinkered to it. It was all I knew. However now, with my clinic and the acceptance I was receiving in it, I could limit these interactions and control my exposure to some of the racism. There was, sadly, still one part of my life where I was losing total control: my daughter Michelle.

I could see that her way of coping with the racist world we lived in was to be with the children that society had already rejected - the children from the care home in Airdrie. I wasn't completely aware what Michelle was falling into, as by now, with my mother having consistently 'protected' and enabled her, she knew how to control and manipulate. I knew that alcohol was involved and I later believed that there had also been drugs, but I had no control whenever I tried to discipline her. She would go and stay with my mum, for days at a time, until I couldn't take it anymore. Then, *I* would say sorry just to have her home.

My daughter had been very angry ever since she was about eight years old and, except when in public, would physically lash out at me whenever I tried to discipline her, resulting in me 'freezing' like I always did whenever I was confronted with any anger or violence. By the time she turned 13, she was bigger and a lot stronger than me.

Her behaviour was simply accepted by my family - nobody would ever challenge her, because if they had done so, they would then have had to deal with my mum as a consequence. I'd seen this same behaviour in my youngest brother, Wale, when he was younger. My mum's 'rule' regarding both their behaviours was no different from her attitude towards everything else; as long as the outside world didn't see the behaviour, it was okay. But it wasn't okay.

By this time, any problems that my mum would admit to Michelle having - as rare as they were - were always blamed on me: 'I wasn't being a fit mother' or, 'I didn't love Michelle as much as the boys'. These mantras played into my own insecurities, making me back down rather than have the confidence to challenge my mum. I always believed there would come a time when I would be able to challenge my mum. I hadn't considered I could run out of time for my daughter.

My mum would always say that Michelle's behaviour was my fault, because I hadn't loved her 'properly', and I would always believe her. I'm not making excuses for what happened with Michelle - I take full responsibility. I was too young and too damaged to have a child at 17. From day one, my mum had constantly downloaded this programme in me, installing it in me. However, by the time I realised, it was too dangerous and too late to take my power back from my mum. Michelle still pays the price for this to this day.

# # #

By 2003, we'd started looking for a new home. Financial restrictions had always meant I'd had to rent, but now that I was making good money, I wanted to move to Airdrie to be closer to the children's schools and my work. At that time, I was having recurring dreams of a little girl. I instantly recognised her – she was our daughter - so I wanted our new home to have somewhere that I could work from after the baby was born.

We looked at quite a few houses and made some offers but never seemed to get anywhere. Then, in the winter of 2003, my Uncle Simon built our brand-new home. As I grew up, the differences that had separated us during my childhood seemed to fade into the background. How funny that one of my childhood perpetrators, someone who had his part in forming the 'old me', was building the dream house for the 'new me'. He loved that he could do this for us.

The house was just five minutes along the road from my parent's house. We were so happy and moved in by the Spring of 2004. I remember going to see the house with my mum while it was being built. After having looked around the house with the children, showing them their new bedrooms, Michelle entered the master bedroom where my mum and I were talking.

"I want this room," Michelle said, her eyes enchanted by the en suite bathroom and private dressing room.

"No Michelle," I reminded. "This isn't your room - you know this is my room."

"But why do *you* get *your* own bathroom . . . and dressing room . . . and a bigger room than me?" she demanded to know.

Her intention wasn't on throwing a tantrum in disappointment; she was sincerely baffled as to why I should be entitled to the master bedroom.

"Because I'm the grown up," I answered with a definitive tone, suggesting the debate was over.

"But why can't she have this room?" my mum crowbarred, prising open the dispute. Both their eyes watched for my reaction.

"What?" I exclaimed, my face distorting in disbelief at the blatant undermining.

"*Why* are you not giving her this room?" my mum reaffirmed, trying to sound oblivious to her ridiculousness. "You know that she thinks you love the boys more than her." I could feel Michelle staring through me as I locked eyes with my mum.

"No. I don't. Can you *please* stop saying that?" I commanded through clenched jaws. With arms folded and feeling heavily sponsored, Michelle took a step closer to Nanny.

"Yes, you do," she echoed, following my mother's lead.

What had, until this point, been a special visit to our future house, now turned into a battle-zone.

"Okay, I'm not discussing this anymore. This is *my* room," I concluded before shutting the conversation down. I'd stood my ground; this was my house, and my mum would not have any control here.

I'd continued to have a good relationship with Michelle's dad, Michael, and we'd supported each other in our ever-losing battle to keep control of her. He was always clear that he believed we had no control over Michelle because of our mothers – that they were the problem, not Michelle. I knew this was true and it felt like we were powerless.

# # #

Craig and I had been planning our first ever family holiday. Up until now we had only managed weekends away with the children. We decided to go

Center Parcs, but rather than spending a whole week in the one location, we decided to split the week across two different *Center Parcs:* Penrith in the Lake District and Elveden Forest near Cambridge; that way the kids could get to see different parts of England, along with having all the fun they wanted at *Center Parcs*. We were all so excited.

Then my grandad fell ill.

It came out of the blue and shocked the whole family. He'd always been so strong and had been taking care of my gran, who was clearly by now, starting to show signs of dementia. We were all surprised when he deteriorated very quickly.

He'd been taken into hospital a couple of weeks before we were due to go on holiday and was struggling to remember names and faces. However, when Craig and I went to visit him, he recognised us both straight away, confessing his happiness that I'd found Craig and delighting me by calling me his *Brown Girl in the Ring*. This would be the last time I saw him, but not the last time I'd hear him. In times of despair, I can still hear his voice soothingly singing to me.

"Kemi's my brown girl in the ring, tra la la la la."

In the most recent of days, he'd been saying that my late Uncle John was waiting for him. We were due to go on holiday on the Friday, but I no longer wanted to go knowing he was dying.

"Kemi you must go on this holiday," my gran sincerely pleaded, "you've worked so hard. Your grandad's so proud of you - he was delighted for you all when you booked this holiday . . . we'll both be very disappointed if the children don't get to go. Just go and have a nice time. Your grandad will be fine."

By now, Craig was back studying and was about to start working in the clinic with me. Trying to reschedule the holiday would not have been realistic. So, with much trepidation, I agreed to go. We made the journey to Penrith, where we would be staying until the following Monday. From there we would travel to Cambridge, before travelling back home the following Friday.

My mum agreed to keep me updated with any developments and I spoke to her several times during the journey to Penrith. No new developments. We spoke again on the Saturday and Sunday. No new developments. I knew grandad was still ill, but she reassured me he was okay. Despite the lingering fear and dread, we all had a lovely time in Penrith.

We had to get up extra early on the Monday morning to travel to Cambridge. I didn't speak to my mum that day, which was very unusual, but things were so hectic with the packing and the travelling and the unpacking again, that I hadn't had the time to question why she hadn't been in touch.

"Kemi's my brown girl in the ring, tra la la la la."

We arrived at our lodge by darkness. We went straight out to eat after unloading the car and then back to the lodge and to bed. That night I had a dream.

My Auntie Joan visited me at the lodge where we were staying. She took me by the hand and led me into the lounge which was flooded by a bright light pouring through the French doors. That's when I saw my grandad. Auntie Joan told me it was time for me to say good-bye. As he faded, I was woken by Craig. I'd been crying in my sleep. We remained silent as he cuddled and comforted me back to sleep. We didn't talk about it, but we both knew my grandad had died.

"Kemi's my brown girl in the ring, tra la la la la."

I awoke in the morning to my phone ringing. It was my mum.

"I know he's gone," I answered, without as much as a hello. When she confirmed it, I felt as if the bottom had fallen out of my world.

Even although I wanted to return home to be with the family, the funeral wasn't going to take place until the day after we were due home, so it was agreed that it was important for us to finish our holiday for the children's sake. My mum asked Craig to be one of the coffin bearers, as by now my gran thought of him as one of the grandsons. She'd arranged his kilt while we were away. Craig was so proud and flattered by her request and felt accepted into the family.

I remember the day of the funeral so clearly. Craig, my three brothers and my four white cousins all proudly carried my grandad's coffin and laid him to rest. I remember thinking my grandad always saw all things as equal, so it was very fitting that four brown boys and four white boys laid him to rest. He would have been very proud.

"She looks like a sugar in a plum. Plum, plum."

# # #

Around this time, I met a 'unique' man. I was introduced to him by a client of mine, Tom. Tom was an area manager for the hotel chain, *Holiday Inn*, and lived up the hill from my clinic. When I returned to work after the funeral, Tom mentioned during his session, and not for the first time, his friend, William. He was a spiritual medium, who was well known in Scotland for helping the police crack the 20-year-old cold case of a missing girl who'd been murdered. He'd been on *Channel 4's Cutting Edge* and *Unsolved*, and someone had even written a book about it.

I'd mentioned to Tom a while back that my mum and Craig would love a session with William, but that I didn't want to go along. Anyway, when Tom came that evening for his appointment I was taken aback.

"William's given you an appointment for Saturday; and your mum and Craig," he said.

"What? I didn't want an appointment," I firmly reminded him.

"Yeah . . . but William wants to see you," he replied with a hint of excitement.

"Why?" I queried, confused.

"I don't know - I'm just the messenger, but you must be intrigued. Are you going to go?" he enquired with even more excitement.

So, hesitantly, I agreed to go along. I thought that as I'd just lost my grandad, maybe I would get some kind of message.

When we arrived, I was greeted by a short and stylish man, no more than 5ft 8in, wearing an oversized gingham shirt, navy blue jeans, a pair of Italian leather shoes and a reinvigorating aroma. Before I'd even laid my eyes on him, I heard his loud and effeminate, Glaswegian accent greeting me from behind his closed door. He introduced himself as William with a firm, but caring shake of his soft hand. William was very happy that I'd come - he had a lot to tell me.

He went on to recap things that had happened in my life; things I'd never told anyone. He also described in fine detail the dream I'd had saying goodbye to my grandad. I instantly felt a real connection with William, and we would grow to become good friends, leading me to always consult him regarding the making of any major decisions.

At this same time, my cousin Tracey was due to be married and had asked me to be her Maid-of-Honour. Our relationship had changed a lot since I first arrived in Scotland, with our friendship deepening over the years. Her dad, my Uncle John, had died shortly after we moved to Coatbridge from Caldercruix. This had been deeply painful for the family and I think affected me more than I realised at the time. He'd truly been a father figure to me when my dad was absent. My mum and dad had reciprocated their love and support to Tracey and Lee, and Auntie Maxine too, by enveloping them as part of our family, just as my uncle and auntie had done for us so many years earlier.

As teenagers, Tracey and I had become good friends and she loved hanging out with me and Joanna and enjoyed the company of the many boys who were part of our group. We even introduced her to her first true love – a relationship that lasted four and half years. Everything that had happened between us when I first came to Scotland, I felt, had no part in our relationship now. That is why I was so shocked when we travelled to Dublin for her Hen Do. Both of our mothers were also going, along with another cousin, Yvonne, with whom I was to share a room.

We were all out having fun and cocktails when one of Tracey's friends told me that Tracey was really worried about my hairstyle for her wedding.

Her friend actually started the conversation by touching my hair, which I hate, and any person of colour will understand. I was going through my 'Alisha Keys stage' – wearing my hair in corn row plaits or just out in an afro. It had taken me until then to completely accept myself; to be comfortable with myself and my hair.

"What are we going to do about this? It's just too African," she said to me whilst invading my personal space, her unwanted paws trying to stroke my hair to satisfy her curiosity. I was devastated. *I thought we were past this.* Tracey said nothing.

"Yes, well . . . don't worry . . . *we'll* figure it out," my mum said. I was so devastated. *What? How can this be happening?* I was a successful woman with my own business and was about to buy my own home for the first time. All of a sudden, I was eight years old again. My other cousin, Yvonne, could see my distress and took me aside.

"Fuck her! She's just scared you'll upstage her. This marriage won't work out anyway."

So, with two other friends, we left the group and went dancing and drinking. We left the next morning.

Something very special happened when I returned from Dublin. As I entered my house, suitcase in hand, I was suffocated by a mixture of *Zoflora* disinfectant, incense and candles. Craig must've been up since the crack of dawn getting rid of the smell of hash from the night before, when Tayo and Wale had visited.

"I'm *very* impressed, Mr Ferguson," I said draping myself into his arms. I'd missed him so much. Having never been a night apart from him since he moved in, I just wanted to feel close and at home before the children needed my attention.

"Kemi . . . I want to ask you something," he said in a solemn tone accompanied with a hint of apprehension. I could feel the atmosphere tense. I just wanted to feel comfortable, what with Tracey and her friend still playing on my mind, and yet, here I was being confronted with anxiety in Craig's arms.

"Oh?" I reflexed, becoming worried as he pulled away from me; he never rejected my draping on him. I was no longer thinking about Tracey.

"What's wrong?" I questioned, feeling my heart race and my senses heighten.

"Nothing's wrong," he stated very seriously, failing to reassure. "Kemi, I want us to have our baby, now, before there's too much of an age gap from the other children," he said, with a long and heavy exhalation that seemed to deflate his shoulders, allowing them to drop from up beside his ears where they had been pinned by nerves. His eyes were open-wide; honest. I could tell he had done some deep thinking in my absence.

"Yes. Yes, of course," I agreed. I didn't know whether to laugh or cry, but there was no doubt about my happiness.

"I love you," he said as he welcomed me back in his arms.

Craig and I had had many conversations about having a baby and marriage, but we'd wanted to wait until after we'd settled into the new house first. It was important to Craig that we got married. It'd been five years since I'd married Rab. I'd been left feeling that marriage wasn't so important, but I respected that Craig didn't have my past and sought my commitment.

I knew I loved him and was totally bonded to him in a way that I had never felt before about anyone. The children adored him and really did look to Craig as being the dad that lived with them, and Rab as the dad they visited. Sola was only three when Rab moved out and couldn't really remember him having ever lived with us, so he bonded with Craig, deeply, and found it easy to name him Daddy Craig.

However, Dayo could remember his dad's presence at home and the violence he'd shown. Craig worked hard to win Dayo's trust, and finally did. Craig was very clear in his communication and boundaries with the children. They hadn't experienced this with Rab unfortunately. Craig would include them in everything. We were a family that did everything together. I was no longer a single mother with an absent husband. I had a wonderful man whom I loved deeply.

I was delighted to find out Tracey had fallen pregnant soon after her wedding. I was so excited that we would be having babies at the same time. I looked forward to falling pregnant and telling her. And yes, I did go to her wedding - with my hair plaited, adorning ruby beads at their ends to match my long, ruby halter-neck dress. Tracey was happy with my hair.

I always forgave Tracey, as you would a sister. She was just trying to be accepted and I didn't make it easy for her with my 'black' ways.

Tracey went on to have a daughter later in the Autumn of 2004.

Pregnancy

We moved into our beautiful new family home in March 2004. I hadn't fallen pregnant and was becoming very anxious about it. I worried that I'd done too much damage to my body with my eating disorder. I started thinking that I'd damaged my body so badly that it did not recognise, or trust, my new way of life; somehow *it* doubted that I would be able to maintain my health. So now, *it* was intentionally preventing me from falling pregnant.

I was spending a lot of time with my thoughts and Craig had been observing me, trying to keep my old demons at bay. I began keeping myself busy with more and more work. I could work day and night if I wanted, as the clinic had become so successful. It had become a profitable distraction, and not only in a monetary sense. My business was the first place I'd found success and some self-worth. I'd created this, by myself, outside of my family, and it always helped me feel better. I loved the job satisfaction; being able to help people feel better mentally, physically and emotionally. This had always come easy for me. I didn't have the power to heal myself, but I could help others heal.

Craig would gently try to enter the part of the world I struggled with, but I sometimes found it hard to grant him access. I feared what he'd think if I told him the truth; that I didn't feel worthy to be a mother. I hadn't protected my children from witnessing Rab's attacks and I was unable to rescue Michelle from my mum's damaging behaviour. I believed I'd tried the best I could to be a good mother; I just believed my best wasn't good enough. These thoughts I kept prisoner, in isolation. No-one needed to hear them. For if I shared them, especially with Craig, he would surely agree.

# # #

It was 'date night', as we affectionally called it. Usually a Friday. The kids would normally be spending the night at my mum's allowing Craig and I some intimate, adult time minus the responsibilities of parenthood. We would talk and eat take-away food, watch tv and listen to music, drink wine (when not trying to get pregnant) and cuddle. Date night didn't need to be spent out socialising in pubs and clubs. In fact, the intimacy behind our own four walls of the new house was preferred. We could be alone to enjoy each other, undistracted by the outside world.

"Baby girl?" Craig asked cuddling into me, his voice warming the back of my neck. I knew from his tone that he was about to focus on a delicate subject. *Shit! He wants to talk about what's wrong with me.* I'd been feeling in mourning at the arrival of my period earlier that day. It was bad enough that my uterus refused to thicken, but now I had to clean up its mess too.

145

That was adding insult to injury. Waking up to find my sheets looking like a bloody, Rorschach test, followed by knowing the effort it would take to try and soak them clean, only served to further humiliate my failings to become pregnant. And now, on top of my shame, Craig wanted to talk about it. I reluctantly rolled towards him, turning to look at him so we could both face my failing.

"Kem," he said as he put his warm hand on my empty, tender and swollen tummy. I broke into tears: "I'm so sorry. She is coming - she's just not ready." He smiled being wholeheartedly sincere.

"She probably wants to be born on a specific date," he said trying so hard to reassure me.

"What if I can't?" I closed my eyes as I disclosed my fear. I didn't want to see his disappointment. "What if I've done too much damage to my body? What if I'm too old? Craig, I'm so scared I won't get pregnant."

His hand left my tummy and journeyed up around my ribs before resting on my shoulder blade, enveloping me.

"Kemi is that what you think?" He leaned in to kiss me on the forehead. "I'm worried it's *me*," he confessed, taking my attention away from my self-disappointment.

"Craig it's not *you*. How could you think that?" I questioned.

"You know I . . . " he began.

"Craig. No." I interrupted before he could finish. "Don't say that. You're right; we will have our daughter . . . she's just making her entrance on her terms. I think she may be a little drama queen." We both laughed. I knew she was going to be strong-willed; I'd felt it when I met her in my dream.

# # #

By the early summer, Craig had already qualified and had been working a few days a week in William's healing centre in Glasgow, during which time they'd become good friends. While at work one day, William told Craig that he needed to speak to me rather urgently. He told Craig the pregnancy was just around the corner and that he would like me to give him a call - the sooner the better.

I'd been getting more and more concerned about not falling pregnant. By now, Craig and I had been living together for over four years. I was healthy and happy for the first time in a long time. I'd studied, qualified and set up my own successful business. I felt secure in my little family. We were a solid, little unit and the children were happy.

William, funnily enough, reminded me of Marion; they were both typically Glaswegian; small in stature with larger-than-life personalities; both came from the same part of Glasgow, both were gay and they both always questioned my mum's behaviour towards me. He was like a more direct version of Marion and for some reason he really liked me. This I

146

found confusing, but I knew he was genuine.

I remember making the call from my mum's house when I finished work. It was about 10.30pm and I was shattered, but I had been desperate to phone William ever since Craig mentioned it. I'd been back-to-back with clients all day and hadn't had the chance to phone, so my anxiety and excitement had steadily grown throughout the evening.

"Kemi," William began after we had exchanged pleasantries. His friendly tone had changed and was now weightier. "You have to think very carefully about this pregnancy."

What is he going on about? He knew how desperate we were to fall pregnant. How much more thought could we possibly apply? I felt uneasy.

"The baby is near Kemi, but she will wait," he continued definitively.

Why is he trying to change my mind? I could feel myself beginning to get annoyed. I was desperately tired - and tired of being desperate to fall pregnant - and here he was suggesting that I should delay.

"But if you go ahead, just now, this baby's arrival will change things; set things in motion that will change all your lives forever. Things will be different."

Isn't that what all babies do?

"William. Yes, of course I've thought about it. We all have. This is what we want," I reminded.

This would be my first pregnancy absent from anorexia, and the first created from a place of love, with two parents who were both mixed-race. It couldn't be any more different? After a delicate debate involving his repetitive same questioning - just reworded - he knew he wasn't getting through to me, so we left it. By then however, I was quite pissed off with him and he knew it.

"Kemi, if the time ever comes when you need me, I am here for you. Remember that."

As I hung up the phone, I felt a sudden bout of angst. I knew there must have been truth in what he said - this was 'William the Seer'. He'd always advised me accurately whenever I'd sought clarity before, however, my desire for our baby blinded me, preventing me from searching for his truth.

Later that year, in July, Michelle went on holiday with her dad, so Craig and I took the boys to the Lake District for a mini break. It was our second day there, a Saturday evening, and we'd travelled to Morecambe for a day trip. We decided to eat out in the nice-looking Indian restaurant that we'd walked by earlier in the day.

"Are you having your usual Kem?" Craig asked while the boys planned their feast.

"Yes. I'll have the tandoori king prawn with chasni sauce, please," I said, setting my menu down.

I sat there remembering all of the times when this would have been unthinkable; me sitting down in a restaurant enjoying eating food. I loved that I could be happily eating out now.

"Craig . . . are you hot?" I asked feeling a little flushed as the waiter sat my food down in front of me.

In the time passed since ordering, I had started to feel a little queasy. The restaurant felt a little warm considering we were sitting under the ceiling fan.

"Thank you," I mumbled to the waiter as he sat my plate down.

"Are you okay? You look really pale," Craig informed, sitting back to allow the waiter the space to fill the table with the hot and spicy dishes.

"I don't know . . . maybe I'm just tired," I advised before eating into a piece of prawn.

The thick tandoori chargrilled aroma powerfully permeated my senses, intruding my airways. I instantly felt nauseous. My palms and brow suddenly dampened.

"Craig," I managed to whisper while getting up out of my chair, relieved that the waiter had stepped away and praying that I would make it to the bathroom in time.

As I stood up, I became light-headed, not quite head spinning, but enough to feel off balance.

"Babe what's wrong? You look terrible?" Craig asked standing to his feet.

"Mummy what's wrong," Dayo asked sounding concerned.

I couldn't answer. I dared not open my mouth. I just rushed to the toilet and luckily made it there in time for my body to rid itself of all that I had eaten that day. I weakly made my way to the sink to freshen my face. *What have I eaten*? Splashing the cold tap water over my now saturated face, I began to recall that I hadn't really been feeling great all day. I'd thought I was just tired, but with hindsight, I'd actually been feeling extremely tired all week.

As I rubbed my belly to soothe the gut-wrenching pain it harboured, my hand surveyed an anomaly. *I don't feel that empty considering . . . wait?* I began counting in my head. *Yesterday! My period was due yesterday!* Excitement now filled my frail body, rejuvenating me. *Could I be?* So many thoughts filled my head as the bathroom door opened.

"Mummy, are you okay?" Sola enquired as he came bouncing in looking for me.

"I'm okay, baby. Just a sore tummy," I reassured. He accepted my answer and moved on to the real question of importance.

"Mummy . . . can I have five scoops of ice cream for dessert . . . please?" Sola's mentioning of food tugged at my gut, making me feel ill all over again. Thankfully there was nothing left to come out, other than anticipation and growing delight at the thought that I might be pregnant.

"Let's go", I said dabbing my face with a paper towel. "You can have two scoops, Sola." He took my hand in his tiny one and we returned to the table.

"Oh God . . . babe, are you okay?" Craig asked upon my arrival. Unable to answer, I shook my head. The nausea was building again, stirred up once more by the collective of spicy aromas.

"Sorry, I need to get out of here," I blurted, before grasping my coat and bag and hurriedly exiting the restaurant.

Once outside in the fresh air, sitting on a bench looking out to the Irish Sea, I began to feel much better. *I'm pregnant . . . I think.* I rubbed at my tummy. *I am.* Craig followed me out about ten-minutes later, doggy bags in hand and both boys with ice creams in little tubs. As he sat beside me and, to my surprise, put his hand on my tummy, he leaned in to kiss me on my head.

"I think we may be having a baby Kemkem," he whispered. I turned to look at him.

"I'm not sure." I was 99% certain, but I didn't want to jinx it.

"Well let's find a *Tesco* or something and buy a test," Craig suggested eagerly.

"No," I responded. He looked at me, confused. "We go home tomorrow, and I want to do it there."

We'd had such a lovely time with the children and, truth be told, I didn't want to take a pregnancy test in case it read negative, stunting our happiness. I was barely a day late and didn't want to face another disappointment.

"We can get one on the way home and do it when we're back."

"Okay. I understand," Craig accepted. He too knew the gut churning feeling of disappointment and was amiable to the delay.

We arrived home the following afternoon and once we were settled back in, Craig went and picked up the pregnancy test. That evening, when the house fell silent after we'd put the boys to bed, we crossed the hall to our bedroom and entered our en suite where the test was waiting. Our hearts and minds had, for the past 24 hours, swung like a pendulum, back and forth from the 'what if' to the 'not again' and now, finally, we would know for sure. I took the test.

We made our way back to the bedroom, Craig cradling the test as carefully as a new-born baby. In those final moments we just looked at each other in silence.

"Time now?" Craig asked, double checking his counting had been accurate.

"Time now," I confirmed taking a deep breath. I watched his eyes scan the test. A shot of life was administered and they began to smile. 'Pregnant' the test read. We stared in disbelief, finally allowing joy to flow through us, washing away all our doubts.

"Kemi, I love you so much. And our little family. Now we will be complete." As I nestled into his arms, I felt very complete.

#

The following morning, I awoke to hear Craig and the boys downstairs. I could hear *Big Cook, Little Cook's* theme tune blaring so I knew it must have been after 10.30. As I stirred in bed, excited and happy, I became aware that I felt sick. The more I awoke, the sicker I felt. I closed my eyes to try and ease the feeling, becoming aware that something wasn't right. *I can't be. It said I was pregnant.* Panic filled me. I was frozen with shock, too scared to get up. I wanted to believe if I just lay there it would go away; it wouldn't be real.

After some hour-long minutes, I accepted I had to face my fate. As I gently sat up and slid my legs out of bed, the sickness grew, breaking me into a cold sweat. *Please body, don't fail me.* I wasn't asking not to be sick, but rather for my baby to be okay. By now, however, I could see a little trickle of blood run down the inside of my leg. I was frozen, again - consumed with devastation, failure and nausea, so much so that I hadn't heard Craig coming upstairs.

"Morning, mummy," he said affectionally, with a smile and a nod to our little secret.

His enthusiasm was instantly replaced with fear as he saw my head bowed down, looking at my leg. He saw what I was looking at.

"Kemi? Are you okay?" He sat down beside me cradling me into his chest. "What's happening?" I looked up to see his eyes filled with terror.

"I don't know . . . what should I do?" I asked with urgency and desperation. My vision was now distorted and blurry from the gush of free-flowing tears.

"Okay," Craig said, abandoning his fear and adopting command. "Let's get you back into bed. I'll phone the doctor and tell the boys you have a sore tummy."

"No, wait," I interrupted, "bring me the phone . . . I'll call him - he'll speak to me. You settle the boys and I'll see what the doctor says." I could feel the adrenaline taking over, giving me focus and direction.

"Okay," Craig said as he held me a little longer. "Kemi, I promise it'll be okay – she'll be okay." I believed him, and he needed me to.

As I waited on the phone for the receptionist to put me through to the doctor, I felt ill. No longer from morning sickness, but from the fear that I was no longer pregnant.

"Yes, I can be at the hospital for 3pm," I replied with relief.

"Now Kemi, I'm sure the baby is okay, but it's always best to check these things out," said the doctor.

The doctor had arranged an emergency scan for later that afternoon.

"Now, we don't really know how far on you are, but I'm sure from my estimations you're five to six weeks pregnant, which should be enough for an internal ultra-sound."

Craig had called my mum and asked if she could have the boys as I wasn't feeling well. She was delighted to have them, so he dropped them off and then came home to take me to the hospital. By the time we were in the very quiet and empty waiting room, I couldn't stop the involuntary tears. I could tell Craig was just as scared, not that he showed it. He had a very practical and gentle way of handling difficult situations, but I couldn't hide my heartbreak.

I lay there during the incredibly uncomfortable scan, not wanting to look at the screen, while Craig never took his eyes off it.

"Well, do Mummy and Daddy want to see their little, healthy baby?" the midwife asked.

When I turned to look, I could see relief on his face and delight in his eyes. I was told to rest for the remainder of the week before returning for a second scan.

We told everyone I'd had food poisoning, but not everyone believed us.

"No, Craig . . . don't worry, I'll drop the boys off to you. I'd like to check in on Kemi anyway," my mum informed.

"Okay Daisy, I'll let her know," Craig surrendered, ending the phone call. "So . . . she's coming. Sorry, I did try to put her off," Craig said feeling defeated.

"It's okay - she knows," I said, also feeling defeated.

We'd wanted to keep our secret exactly that: *our* secret, at least for the early part anyway, but I knew if she asked me, I wouldn't lie. I couldn't - not to her.

"Hiya darling, how are you feeling?" my mum quietly asked as she entered my bedroom.

"I'm okay - just tired. Thanks for having the boys . . . were they okay?" I asked, trying to steer the conversation away from me.

"They were just great Kem," she replied, perching herself beside me at the edge of my bed.

"High as a kite due to the Micky D's (*MacDonald's*) and ice creams they've had mind you," Craig said half-jokingly, while staring at my mum.

"Well Craig, that's what nanny's do, give the grandchildren whatever they want. Don't I Kem?" she said looking to me for backup.

"And on that subject," she began followed by a momentary pause, "now that my girl is pregnant, this new baby will be treated the same," she said with a smile, looking directly at Craig and then on to me.

Craig was a bit shocked. I don't think he'd believed me when I said she was coming because she knew.

"Well, Kemkem?" she looked at me to confirm.

"Yes mum, we're having a baby," I said with genuine joy, relieved that I was and that everything was okay.

I filled my mum in on what had happened and why we needed her to have the children. I could see this was a sting to her; she had always been the one who'd been there for me throughout all my previous pregnancies. I knew this would be hard for her, to give this control up, but Craig wasn't going to let anyone take his role.

"Well Craig," she said looking directly into his eyes, "no grandchild of mine will go to a Protestant school."

"What? Mum!" I spat, completely blindsided.

"Well, all the children in this family are Catholic and this new baby will be no different," she continued to elaborate, justifying her ambush all the while ignoring my interjection.

The part of Scotland I grew up in was, and still is, very bigoted. My mum's family are all Catholic. My mum never went to chapel, but she was definitely a bigot; Catholics were good and Protestants were bad. Craig was raised Protestant, with his mum being a Sunday school teacher, however, he didn't buy into the bigotry - he took people as he found them, regardless of their religious beliefs.

"Mum that is not your choice," I schooled.

How dare you! I was shocked that for once, she'd put her demands on Craig, showing her hand so to speak. She'd been so careful in their relationship so far. Craig knew she was controlling, but she hadn't really directed much towards him - he wasn't Rab.

"Daisy, Kemi's right . . . this certainly isn't your decision; it's for Kemi and me to decide," he stated clearly and gently, as he always did.

"Our baby will go to the same school as her siblings, not because of religion - I don't care about that, but I do care about the children all being the same. No differences."

My mum was shocked, and even though she'd got the answer she wanted, I could see she wasn't happy; he had taken power away from her.

# # #

Thankfully, I never experienced any further bleeding over the next seven days. I took the doctor's advice and had complete rest. When I returned for my second scan, we were both amazed to see how much the baby had grown. What had resembled a tiny peanut, now distinctively looked like a developing baby. We were so relieved to see that our baby was healthy.

Now that we knew the baby was safe and well, we decided we'd tell the children the great news. We'd wanted to wait until after the first trimester before breaking the news to anyone, but with my mum now knowing I thought it would only be a matter of time before she told the children, or at least Michelle. We went home and after dinner we told them that we had some exciting news to share.

"Are you getting married?" was Michelle's first response, bright eyed and full of excitement.

"Are you having a baby?" Dayo screamed with excitement, wedging in his guess before Michelle got her answer.

"Yes, Dayo," I confirmed to both Michelle's and Dayo's delight.

Sola, on the other hand, was instantly devastated. He dejectedly slid his tiny body down the corridor wall until he was sat miserably on the floor, feet planted, burying his despairing face into his bent knees.

"I hope it's a girl," Michelle stated with enthusiasm, oblivious to Sola's sorrow.

"Yeah, me too," Dayo agreed with zest.

Sola increased the volume of his sobs.

"She can play with *my* old dolls," Michelle informed Dayo.

Sola stamped his feet, remaining cradled in the corner.

"And *I* could have a baby sister," Dayo replied as if playing a trump card.

Sola cocked his grieving face, not enough to make eye contact, but enough to have his words heard clearly.

"I can't believe *this* has happened," he agonised. The sincerity of his shock was expressed so succinctly for such a small boy.

"Sola. She's going to be a girl. You'll still be the baby boy," I consoled.

He raised himself to his feet, sliding himself back up the wall, to stand defiantly with his arms folded, head bowed, lip pouted and firing me the stink-eye.

"It's good that God wants us all to have this new baby," I continued trying to convince.

"I don't want to talk about it now - and I don't want to talk about it later. I don't want a stinky baby," Sola concluded.

"Can we call her Beyonce?" Michelle butted in, animated at the prospect.

"No . . . can we call her Alice?" Dayo suggested randomly.

"Well, if she *has* to come, she *has* to be called Mary," Sola declared, even further off centre.

After Craig and I exchanged eye confirmation of the hilarity we were witnessing, we calmed the children down and explained that she would have a Nigerian name, like the boys did, as they came with meaning. The children agreed to our proposal that we would provide them a list of Nigerian names and that they could choose from it.

The momentary calm was quickly drowned out by energetic excitement as Dayo and Michelle resumed their questionings, ponderings and contemplations: "What will she look like?", "What room will she have?", and "How do you know it's a girl?"

The announcement had gone down relatively well, with two out of three children delighted.

# # #

I knew that I wanted to return to work after the baby was born. This was very important to me – it'd become my purpose, with positive benefits. So, we would need help from a childminder – and I knew just the person. Sandra and her husband, David, had been clients of mine since I opened my clinic. Sandra had been a personal assistant, but had decided to become a childminder sometime before I met her, while David was a Police Chief Inspector and was about to retire.

I'd known even before I fell pregnant that I would ask Sandra to help take care of our daughter once she was born. I just knew she'd be perfect. She had an already full-capacity childminding service and only looked after a few children at a time. However, I knew that one child was about to leave, creating a vacancy. The timing was perfect and I didn't want to miss my chance. Sandra was delighted to be asked and said yes. I was so happy!

It was so important that the right person helped us with this little one - I'd always been present with the other children. My mum had no problem with our decision to get a child minder, but Craig's mum was very angry not to be looking after our daughter when we were working. I'd already learned, with consequences, that grandparents looking after grandchildren can be problematic, and in my case, it had cost me dearly. I had made myself a promise when I had Dayo that I would never do that again.

# # #

Everyone was happy to learn of the new baby. Well, everyone except for Craig's mum. Craig hadn't been speaking to his parents for quite some time, ever since his mum and brother had treated me and the children so appallingly. When his mum found out through a family friend that I was pregnant, it was reported back to Craig that she 'didn't give a fuck'. I knew this wasn't true. She was just someone whose experiences had shaped who she'd become, and all she knew was defensiveness. I encouraged Craig to call her and give her a chance, as this was to be her first grandchild. He did call to break the news and they were back in our lives . . . for a little while.

Craig was very close to his sister, Leigh, who was amazing with my children. She'd built a lovely relationship with them and regularly took them out for meals and to the cinema. She was a proper aunt to the children. She'd even kept secrets from Craig and me about Michelle - how she'd caught her smoking - as a true 'cool' aunt would do. This we found out later.

# # #

I was finding it increasingly difficult to cope with Michelle's behaviour and my mum's constant undermining of me during the pregnancy. Michelle turned up at my mum's house so wasted one night after a local disco that Craig and I had to go and pick her up. My mum was furious. I was scared. I just knew she'd taken something.

"You can't take her to hospital - what will people think?" my mum repeated for the tenth time.

This was always very important to my mum: other people's opinions. So, we took Michelle home and sat up all night with her, terrified that she might choke on her own vomit should she be sick.

When she was coming round, I told her she was now grounded and that I was sure that her nanny would agree with me on this one. Unbelievably, she instead came to my house at 10am the next morning and took Michelle shopping. She spent over £200 on her for her Christmas party and then took her to her house. I was told by my mum that Michelle wouldn't be coming back home until I treated her like the other children.

In truth, Michelle had more spent on her than everyone else, including me. She would make the lives of everyone hell until she got what she wanted. The house had turned into a war zone. Dayo and Sola would cry because of all the screaming she would do to get her own way, and I would always give up in the end for a quiet life. However, Craig was very good at mediating. I think this was because he was younger than me and could relate to Michelle's feelings and struggles. She would even say that he was the only person in the house who understood how she felt.

# # #

Craig got down on one knee and asked me to marry him on Christmas morning, 2004. We'd planned to get married the following year, after our daughter was born, so I was very surprised by the timing of his proposal. He'd asked my dad's permission and my dad had been delighted to give it. Craig is quite a traditional man with a very old soul, so it was a lovely surprise.

New arrival

I had the most wonderful pregnancy, and for many reasons. For one, I was now with someone who adored and believed in me and supported me and my children. I felt so blessed. I began to feel grateful for everything that had ever happened to me, as they had all somehow brought me to this exact moment in time - a time when I could have a baby with someone who deeply loved me, and who I deeply loved.

This wonderful pregnancy was the first of my four where I wasn't being governed by fear – the fear of my body becoming out of control. My body dysmorphia and eating disorder were still a challenge, but because I was well, I was able to work with it. It was difficult, as I knew my anorexia would always be a part of me; reminding me of my old place of safety, for when the world became too much. However, my world was no longer full of fear. I'd taken back so much control of my life, which in turn, provided me with more confidence, resulting in more choice.

My eating, for the past four years, had been regimented. It had had to be. I didn't feel hunger. I'd stopped that internal conversation when my anorexia was initiated. I think I must have trained this part of my brain to ignore my body's cries for food so finely, that hunger rarely ever registered.

Over many years of trying to understand my behaviour around food, I learned that I didn't love food. There was no pleasure - no attraction. There wasn't a taste my tastebuds longed for. I got absolutely no enjoyment out of eating. It was a chore. However, I'd learned to commit to my body and accepted eating as purely for health and energy, not enjoyment. Food became fuel and my body a vehicle.

I still couldn't just sit down to eat a meal. I always made sure to give myself an hour's notice - a reminder, before any meal. I felt more comfortable with the act of eating for having had this time to prepare myself for each of the two daily meals I'd promised to give to my body. I'd never really been able to eat breakfast at any point in my life, but now that I did yoga in the mornings, my body's systems were stimulated, enabling me to have a fruit juice by late morning. Despite it making me feel like I was failing, I'd learned what my body needed.

I believe that when I fell pregnant, my body began reconnecting me to feelings of hunger. I'd always been mainly vegetarian, but this pregnancy made me crave meat very strongly, so I got into the routine of mainly eating fresh fruit and veg with a little meat.

My body started to remind me with 'notifications'. It was so strange the first time I felt it. In fact, I think I heard it first: a hollow growling from the amphitheatre that was my tummy. At first, I didn't really understand what the pain was. I could feel it travelling up through my solar plexus, making its way into my throat, like an empty opening calling to be satisfied. I finally recognised this was my hungry tummy rumbling and I responded with very little fear.

My body was trusting me. I was feeding it well and it was giving me energy and a vitality that I don't think I'd ever felt in my entire adult life. With this new vitality I planned to continue to work for as long as I could, stupidly believing that I could work right up to the week before the baby was due. By now Craig had stopped working in Glasgow to concentrate all his time in my clinic, so that he could take over when I was having our daughter.

I knew my daughter would be born in March by an elected C-section, due to the complications I'd had with my previous pregnancies. I'd had the same two consultants for my blood disorder and deliveries since I was 17. I was very, very blessed, as these two men knew me so well. I can't begin to tell you the mix of emotions I had when I was told my C-section would be on 4th March - my birthday.

I worked until ten days before the baby was born. The doctor said that he would have to put me in hospital if I didn't stop working. I was already having false contractions and with the baby sitting so low, he thought that I could go into labour at any time.

My days off work were filled spending time with my wee gran. My gran left Caldercruix to move to Airdrie after my grandad died and was living in a wonderful, sheltered housing unit at the bottom of my mum's street. My gran had felt that I needed her help, so Craig would bring her to our house every day before he went off to work in the clinic. Her memory was still deteriorating, but she was better than she had been before my grandad died. I think him looking after her so well had de-skilled her somewhat. She now had very little short-term memory, but she never forgot where the *Marks and Spencer* clothes department store was, and would frequently shop there with her younger sister, Auntie Jessie.

I managed to spend an hour with the boys at home after school before I had to go into hospital. Dayo was extremely excited and repeatedly asked for assurances, pledges and oaths that he would be coming straight to the hospital from school the next day to see the baby. I gave him my word of honour. Sola, on the other hand, was inconsolable.

He sat in the corner of the sofa, his tiny frame folded, knees up to his chest and elbows crossed, whilst eyeballing me not through, but over his glasses that had by now, slid down his sunken face, to rest at the tip of his nose. Despite his sulk, he couldn't resist sitting on my knee when I sat down beside him. It felt like there wasn't enough room, what with the bursting baby I was already carrying, but this eight-year-old needed some 'mummy time'. So, with Sola sprawled across my lap, I began to gently massage his head. He loved massage and I'd found it always helped to calm him down.

"Please mummy, don't go. Please. I've told you, we don't need a stinky baby," Sola pleaded, wearing a frown and a matching pair of pouted lips.

"But Sola, I have to go," I explained, rubbing the crown of his head with my fingertips. "This baby is coming tomorrow and if I don't go to hospital, I'll have to have the baby here and we don't want that, do we?"

"But mum, we don't need one. Why do we need to have a baby?" Sola repeated his daily catchphrase.

"Sola . . . we've spoken about this," I reminded gently. "This baby wants to be a part of this family; she wants to have you as her cool, big brother. And she'll love sharing the youngest role with you, because you're still going to be the youngest boy, aren't you?"

His little mind was thinking it over. His resistant body gave, relaxing with submission. He finally conceded the inevitable: there was no way out of it – this baby was coming.

"Well, I don't see why I have to stay with Nanny," Sola argued, moving on to the next item on his agenda. "I want to stay in my house with Daddy Craig."

Craig interrupted our heart-to-heart to explain to Sola all the organising that he still had to do and that he would have to be up, organised and out of the house far too early for Sola to come with him. However, he assured him that once mummy was settled at the hospital, he would come and see him at Nanny's.

"Until bedtime?" Sola asked, extending out his pinkie.

"Yes. Until bedtime," Craig confirmed, wrapping his pinkie around Sola's, sealing the 'Pinkie Promise'.

"You won't forget the name, mum? Remember, it rhymes with my name: Sola," Sola prompted, now offering me his pinkie.

"I won't forget that little man; I promise," I assured, hugging my pinkie around his. Finally, we were in accordance and with a hug, his meeting was adjourned.

Unfortunately, Michelle had got out of school late, so by the time she came in with her friend, full of giggles and excitement, I didn't get to spend much time with her, as I had to be in the hospital by 5pm, but she was thrilled about coming to the hospital the next day to meet the baby.

I was very scared by the time Craig and I arrived at the hospital - the most fear I'd ever felt in any of my pregnancies. I think being older and healthy for once, along with being properly in touch with myself had heightened my awareness of mortality. I'd become aware that I had so much to lose. I hadn't experienced nor appreciated this in my 20s, but it was definitely my reality now. Even the consultant's visit to answer questions and to explain the proceedings for the following morning didn't settle my fear. If anything, it served as a reminder of all the reasons why I was fearful.

"You scared Kemi?" Craig asked gently as he sat at the side of my bed, clasping my hand in between both of his.

"Yes," I replied trying to hold back my tears.

The thoughts of being ripped, torn apart and opened during my C-section had me worrying about all the things that could wrong. The fact that it was my third C-section didn't make it any easier; it made it worse.

"It'll be okay, Kem . . . these guys know you and they know what they're doing," Craig reminded, trying to reassure me while gently stroking his thumb back and forth across the back of my hand.

'I know . . . I'm just so tired," I presented, pretending to myself to lighten how I was really feeling. Craig, however, knew me too well.

"Just try to focus on tomorrow afternoon when the children come, and when we'll all be together with our new baby for the first time."

He was right and it didn't take me long to dream into his picture.

"I know," I agreed, as he slid up the bed to put his arms around me. That always made me feel instantly safe.

"Kem," Craig finally said, "I'll need to go soon. I don't want to, but I need to see the kids before they go to bed." We both knew Sola wouldn't settle until Craig was back – he'd promised.

Feeling better by the time Craig left, I spoke to the children on the phone before settling myself down to sleep.

I awoke in the morning feeling excited, extremely hormonal and anxious. Not too long after, the butterflies awoke too and began playing tag, tumbling around in my tombola-tummy. My mind then started to tease me by imagining scenarios. Multiple thoughts all with irrational reasoning. This pregnancy had been so enjoyable; too enjoyable. My mind deemed it too good to be true and actively searched for how it was all going to go wrong.

I waited to phone Craig until I could wait no more. We'd agreed that I would phone him in the morning to make sure he was up and organised. By now it was 6am, two hours before I would be getting prepared for theatre, so I gave Craig his wake-up call. *Ring Ring*. It rang out and went to his voicemail. *Why is he not answering? Where is he?* I waited half a minute and when he hadn't phoned me back, I called him again. *Ring Ring*. As my call rang out to voicemail for the second time, I became increasingly panicked. *Here it is. I knew it. Something's happened.* Putting irrational thoughts to one side, I was still worried that he'd miss the birth, so with reluctance, I called my mum. *Ring Ring.*

"Morning Kemkem, how are you feeling?" my mum answered with a chirpy excitement.

"I can't get Craig on the phone," I blurted with desperation, ignoring her greeting.

"Oh Kemkem . . . don't worry. *I'll* call him and your dad will go to the house if he has to," she replied calmly. Maybe too calmly. *Does she know something?*

"But mum, why is he not answering? I need him," I asked inviting a disclosure, or at least a rational explanation.

"Kemi, we will get him – he'll not miss this. He's probably in the shower and didn't hear the phone," she offered, unstirred.

"Okay," I accepted, just to get her off the phone so I could try to phone Craig again. This time it was engaged and within minutes my phone rang.

"Craig. What's happened? I've been so worried," I released before he had the chance to say a single word.

"Kem, sorry I missed your call. I was in the shower," he reported.

I was so relieved to hear his voice, safe and sound, but I still felt uneasy. There was something in his voice that confused me - I could tell he was lying. I didn't know why, and I didn't want to know; I was too scared and emotional.

"I'll be there in 40 minutes, okay?" he promised hurriedly. I could tell he was as eager as me to get here.

"Okay, Craig," I accepted, despite not fully pacified, before checking one last time, "but everything's okay?" My insecurity just wouldn't let me leave it.

"Yes, of course. This is the best day of my life - what could possibly be wrong?" he answered so reassuringly. I could tell this was a truth.

"I'm just scared something will go wrong," I confessed, feeling myself getting even more emotional.

"Kem, I promise everything is going to be wonderful," he assured convincingly. "Now, that's me in the car. I love you and will see you very soon."

"I love you too," I said, hanging up the phone feeling somewhat heartened.

I didn't even have time to put my phone down before 'Mum' began flashing on its screen.

"Hello mum," I answered much calmer than I'd been 20 minutes earlier.

"You sound much better," she stated. "You spoke to Craig then?"

"Yes," I replied, but before I could continue, she interrupted.

"Yes, he fell asleep late this morning. He's decorated your dressing room and made it into a nursery," she divulged in a matter-of-fact tone, intentionally trampling all over Craig's surprise for me.

As I was sleeping, Craig was busily creating a beautiful pink nursery for the baby. He'd decided to have a half-an-hour 'power nap' and laid down at 5.30am. He was so exhausted that he slept through my morning call at 6am. *Ah, that's why I heard untruths in his voice. He wasn't in the shower - he'd slept in!* This realisation settled me, momentarily.

"Mum. Why did you tell me that?" I demanded. "It was obviously a surprise."

"Oh . . . oops, I forgot," she said in the little, child-like voice she always used whenever she was trying to portray her malice as merely being a 'wee joke'.

"I can't believe you've told me." I felt deflated.

"Oh Kemi, there's no need to get your knickers in a twist."

This was a saying that my grandad would use to try and calm down a situation. However, she was using it to suggest she hadn't done anything *that* bad; that I was overreacting. This only proved to annoy me further.

"*I* will tell Craig I made a booboo, if that makes you feel better."

"No," I instructed, "you'll tell him nothing. Mum, if you tell him that I know I won't forgive you," I warned with certainty.

"Okay, I won't tell Craig," she flippantly replied, in a tone suggesting again that she didn't think her disclosure was a big deal.

"Mum," I addressed, demanding her full awareness to make sure I was being received crystal clear, "Craig would be devastated if he knew you'd ruined his surprise." I knew she was hating that I was trying to protect him, but I meant what I said.

When Craig arrived at the hospital, I was so relieved to see him. I needed him: we were a team. This was the first time I'd experienced constant support throughout a pregnancy from the father of my baby.

Our daughter was born at 9.25am on 4th March, 2005 - my birthday - weighting 6lbs 2oz, the same weight I was when I was born. We named her Olutola[21], or Tola[22] for short. A name picked by her siblings because it rhymed with Sola.

While I was in recovery, Craig and I had the whole morning together, just the two of us, with baby Tola. It was pure bliss . . . at first. Craig and I took turns holding her, savouring the precious new life that we had created. I felt euphoric; a lovely combination of the natural high that comes with having a baby, mixed with the numbness from the epidural, so I needed Craig's assistance holding Tola.

Then it began, and without as much as a gentle introduction to serve as a warning. Within the blink of an eye, I was in excruciating pain. One that engulfed and consumed me, rendering me incapacitated, unable to focus on anything other than my agony. Tormented, I could feel the full extent of where the lacerations had ripped and torn at my pelvis, and my body's fiery, burning reaction to its torturous violation.

Craig alerted the staff nurse who immediately wanted to inject me with morphine. My morphine dripline into my hand hadn't been working and I had not been receiving any pain relief since the operation.

I was so relieved when the nurse gave me the shot straight into my buttock, and I remember her being so apologetic for the faulty drip and sincerely sympathetic to the pain I was in. For the next 20 minutes that pain slowly decreased, before finally leaving my body, allowing my attention to acknowledge the sickness that now occupied me; my reaction to the morphine filling my blood stream. Morphine had always caused a nauseous reaction in me, but it was the quickest way to kill the pain, so I hadn't put up any resistance.

---

[21] Pronounced: *Oh-Loo-Taw-Lah.*
[22] Pronounced: *Taw-Lah.*

161

As I slipped into my drug-fuelled, deep slumber, Craig sat by my side on the bed with baby Tola cuddled safely in his strong arms. I felt at peace again and began to let go of my consciousness, at ease in the knowledge that Tola was safe. I turned to Craig, exhausted, and caught his face looking worriedly back at me before my eyelids dropped in submission. I could feel him gently kiss me on my forehead. I was safe.

I awoke a couple of hours later to Tola's cries for mummy to feed her. Craig had stayed the whole time I was asleep, holding and pouring love all over our new daughter, but now she needed mummy. I was so relieved that the pain and nausea had left me, allowing me to raise my arms to receive my little bundle. She was all I could think about. I was totally consumed with love for this little, brand-new human that I'd brought into the world, safely and healthily. All the pain I'd felt was now replaced with pride for myself, as I watched Tola calmly feeding, her cries now satisfied. Craig had to leave the hospital around 2pm to collect the children from school to bring them to the hospital to meet their new baby sister. I was grateful for the couple of hours I got to spend alone with Tola to bond.

When it was time for my next dose of pain-relief, I refused to take the morphine.

"I can't take that. I won't be able to function again if I have that," I said very clearly.

The last morphine had completely knocked me out, making me lose track of time, and it had made me feel so ill that I was determined not to experience it again.

"But Kemi, you've just had a major operation. Everybody takes it for the first 48 hours," the nurse tried to convince.

"No," I insisted politely, but firmly. "I'll take the codeine, but not that," I compromised.

"Kemi . . . ," the nurse began.

"No," I interrupted, "I've had four children now and three C-sections; I know my pain levels. I'm not too bad. I just want to go home to my children and the morphine will stop that. Please . . . if it gets too bad, I'll take it," I assured.

"Okay Kemi. Buzz me if you need anything," the nurse advised reluctantly before leaving the room.

I had just enough time to give Tola her first massage before Craig and the children were due to arrive. This was something I had been desperate to do. I wasn't trained when I had my other children, so I was determined to give this little girl everything I had to share. It was fascinating how her tiny body responded to my hands getting to know her. Although she was tiny, she was strong, but she melted into my touch and slept through all her visitors.

The children couldn't get enough of their new sister, each taking their turn to cuddle. Surprisingly, it was love at first sight for Sola: "*This* baby isn't stinky." I remember everyone was so happy when they came to visit Tola - everyone except Craig's parents. They made the point of coming to the hospital with gifts for Tola and Craig and ignored my birthday. That was the price I paid for not letting my mother-in-law look after my daughter. I didn't care as my little family was now complete.

I got home 48 hours after my C-section, insisting that I was fit. I wasn't. I was exhausted and weak for the first two weeks. Craig continued to work at my mum's house and I spent the first two weeks at home with my gran. She helped with my healing. When the surgeon had closed me up, he had stapled my wound shut, accidently using metal staples, despite knowing I had a metal intolerance. This had caused my wound to react and become painfully infected. Her 'old-wifey remedies' helped soothe my ailments and restored my exhausted body. She was a great comfort, and the boys loved coming home from school to see her.

My mum had gone to Ireland for five days after I came home, affording me some time to settle in with all four children before she could start to undermine me. In her absence, my dad began to visit every day for a cuddle with Tola. He would sometimes sneak out of his house, without telling anyone, for an additional cuddle. They always knew where he'd disappeared to. He began visiting most evenings, spending time with the boys before they went to bed, listening to their stories of all that had happened in their day, before spending hours cuddling and snoozing on the sofa with Tola. They seemed to comfort each other. This gave Craig and me time to eat together when he came home from his evening shifts at the clinic. Craig cooked all the meals and even kept me company during the night-time feeds. I felt safe. I didn't have to think about work or money. All I did was take care of myself and the baby. I'd never been happier than in those first few weeks, when life seemed to slow down.

My mum, however, was not so happy with all the attention and affection my dad had for this little baby; it was independent of her. My dad didn't have personal, one-to-one relationships with any of his children or grandchildren. He'd always been behind her, on the periphery in those relationships, but his connection with Tola was different; he'd created his own relationship with her, with origins and boundaries that he'd established by himself. A relationship over which my mum had no control. I loved that he could have his time alone with her; the time that he'd not been strong enough to have with me.

"I can't believe you're still here," my mum snarked at my dad as soon as she opened my front door. She'd gone home to find his car missing. He'd been AWOL all day and she knew exactly where to find him. "It's so obvious that you love Tola more than the other children," she accused.

"Hahaha," his infectious, African laugh fell out, a natural reflex to her absurdity. She was cold, but he remained snug, lying almost horizontal in the corner of the sofa, ankles crossed and with Tola, chest-to-chest, fast asleep.

"It's so obvious it's because she's blacker than the other three," she sounded off, as if it was a competition.

"Hahaha," my dad laughed again, his belly gently rocking Tola up and down. "She may have more black in her, but she is the lightest!" he laughed, genuinely tickled at the odds.

Tola might have had two mixed-race parents and strong African features, but she was lighter than all of her siblings, with blonde, afro curls too.

"I won't let you treat the children differently," my mum continued, getting annoyed at my dad's refusal to flinch. She was losing her hold and I could only watch on in disbelief at her hypocritical stance.

"I won't have this Samuel," she concluded, looking to him to obey. My dad steadily stood up, scooping up Tola and placing her in my arms before turning to my mum.

"Piss off, Daisy," he said quietly, but firmly. "See you guys tomorrow," he aimed towards Craig and I in defiance, before walking out of the house and leaving an awkward silence behind him, ended only by the fact that my mum left straight after him, kissing the three of us good-bye, while behaving like nothing had happened.

My dad continued to come and look after the children when I returned to work six weeks after Tola was born. It felt great working two evenings a week from my home and having the children safely nearby. I loved that my dad defended his time with his favourite baby, Tola.

#

Sola made his First Communion when Tola was two months old. My mum held the party at her house, as she had a spacious, enclosed back garden, and bought a trampoline and hired a bouncy castle for the children. The children loved it. After all the guests were gone, Michelle, who'd left the party earlier in the afternoon with her friends, returned while my mum, Craig and I were clearing up in the kitchen. She'd been spending more and more time out on the streets with her friends and I was sure she'd started drinking alcohol.

"Kemi," Craig said, indicating for me to look at Michelle, who appeared off-balance and swaying as she entered the house through the kitchen.

"Michelle, have you been drinking?" I questioned, taking a step towards her. The smell hit me from a few feet away.

"No," she responded with a dismissive tone, taking an unstable step backwards while avoiding eye contact.

"Look at me," I demanded, taking another step forward, "I know you're lying - I can smell it."

"Fuck off, Kemi," Michelle slurred, as if she was casually speaking to one of her friends.

"Michelle! Do not speak to your mother that way," my mum demanded,

164

inserting herself, preparing to take control of the situation.

"Mum, please. Let me handle this," I insisted. I was determined I would deal with my daughter.

"Michelle, give me your phone," I demanded with an extended, open palm. I wasn't just confiscating her phone as a punishment, I was taking it to prevent my mum from being able to speak to her in the morning, undermining my authority.

"No. I don't think so," Michelle laughed, standing upright, with folded arms.

"I mean it, Michelle. Give me your phone or I will call your dad," I informed.

This caught her off-guard. She couldn't tell if I was serious; she was too drunk and confused at witnessing me standing my ground in my mum presence. She just looked at me with disdain.

"Nanny . . . are you going to let her do this?" Michelle finally stuttered, reaching for her ally; inviting her nanny to overrule.

"Kemi, you can't get Michael involved," my mum insisted, accepting Michelle's summons.

"Mum. Please be quiet," I said firmly, reinforced with a sustained stare.

"No Kemi, you be quiet," Michelle dared, feeling empowered by the arrival of her sidekick.

"Daisy, Michelle is Kemi's daughter. Can you let her deal with this, please?" Craig gently demanded.

The room silenced. Both my mum and Michelle stood in disbelief. Craig had just questioned my mum; and in front of everyone.

"Michelle. Phone. Now. I'm not playing," I ordered, breaking the silence and interrupting their shock to maintain lead role in the space that Craig had just created.

Michelle stood rooted to the spot with confusion: was she supposed to listen to me or her nanny - who was in control? She gave me no response, so I took my phone from my pocket, but before I could even open the screen, she was on me, pulling at my hand, trying to grab and snatch at my phone, bending and twisting at it. *Do not lose your grip*. Michelle was bigger and stronger than me and if I gave in now, I would never be able to control her. I tightly pulled the phone close into my chest, forcing her hands to surrender it.

"Michelle!" my wee gran gasped upon entering the kitchen and witnessing Michelle pounce on me.

Startled by my gran, Michelle took a step back away from me, only to notice a curtain pole that had been resting against the back wall. She grabbed for it and turned to me. My mum froze in shock, while Craig quickly began ushering my gran away from the scene and into the adjacent dining room. He knew I wasn't going to back down and so never allowed his eyes to turn away from the confrontation. I braced myself, knowing I would maybe have

165

to take a blow to regain control of the situation, but I was adamant I would own the control.

"Michelle, I'm warning you; I will phone your dad. I mean it. You will not behave like this."

Our eyes locked and everything else in the room disappeared. In that moment, it was just the two of us and I could see her mind considering her options.

"Michelle, you have two choices: you give me the phone and get in the car, or I call your dad." I looked deeper into her eyes.

"Take it," she screamed as she threw it at me. I had to swat at it to stop it from hitting me, catching it, but not without spraining my finger. I kept my composure.

"Okay, we're leaving now. Go and wait in the car," I instructed before heading to the dining room. "Craig, please can you get the children ready. Gran, come and help us get the children ready."

My little gran was so upset by what had happened. I hoped her dementia would help make this memory disappear. I would never have intentionally subjected my gran to this drama, but I felt I'd had no choice. If I hadn't done what I had, I felt I would have lost all control of my daughter forever.

The biggest fight of my life

At this point it is very important that I say something about what you're about to read. It terrifies me to share this part of my life, for many reasons. However, for you to understand just how entrenched racism is in our society today, I have to tell this part of the story. It has affected me, my husband and more importantly our four children. It will illustrate to you the lengths that people in power will go to when they want to show - and believe - that people of colour are not equal; no matter how hard they work to live an honest life.

24th June, 2005

It was a beautifully sunny Friday morning. Craig and I had dropped the children off at school and Tola to Sandra, before heading into Glasgow for our 'daytime date'. We'd decided to go to Byers Road, where my dad had taken me to Uncle Segun's salon all those years earlier.

It was our favourite part of Glasgow. Just about every second shopkeeper, along with their customers, were from different parts of the world: Africans, Asians, Caribbeans, Europeans and Scots, all on the same street. It was one of Glasgow's most multicultural areas and we felt comfortable there. We fitted in, blended in, and were never treated like outsiders. The shopkeepers would chat to us and we were never followed in their shops. It was nothing like where we lived.

We window-shopped, amazed at the beautiful (and extortionate) Asian jewellers, while leisurely sipping our *Costa* mochas. We sauntered into *Solly's,* an Afro-Caribbean store, picking out some African foods and spices. We sat outside a delicatessen, in the full glory of the sun, Craig devouring his freshly prepared, toasted panini while we watched the brown people, of all shades and tones, go about their business. This was how we would spend our daytime dates; just being.

We felt rejuvenated heading back home. The good coffee, fresh air and brown people had all formed a lovely date, putting an extra bounce in our step before we returned to normality. We sat fulfilled, without speaking, as James Blunt's *You're Beautiful* played out from the car speakers, allowing me to daydream out of the window and off into the warm sun, when my mobile phone rang.

"Private number," I said, coming back to reality and looking at the caller ID.

"Probably a sales call Kemi, just ignore it," Craig advised, breaking into a duet with the radio.

I wouldn't normally answer private numbers, but for some reason I did.

"Hello?" I answered, half expecting to hear an automated response.

"Hello, is this Kemi Ogunyemi?" a real human, female voice asked.

"It is," I replied, feeling a bit cautious. My tone caught Craig's attention and he muted the radio.

"My name is Gillian," the voice continued, "I'm a police detective from Child Protection."

"What? Are my children okay?" I blurted out, my stomach instantly in knots.

"Kemi, what is it?" Craig whispered, his face screwed with concern. I shook my head to get him to be quiet so I could hear the woman.

"Yes Kemi, they're all fine. Where are you?" the voice asked.

"I'm in the car on my way home from Glasgow. Sorry, what is this all about? What's going on?" I could feel my heart pounding throughout my body, forcing it to judder with nerves.

"Kemi, I'd like to meet you at your home," the voice suggested.

"Why? You've got to tell me what this is about!"

I could now feel my neck and shoulders locking tight, rigid with tension, bracing themselves, as if they somehow knew what was coming before I did.

"Kemi - what's happening?" Craig whispered again, but this time a bit more firmly. I narrowed my eyes and put my finger across my lips, signalling for him to stop talking.

"I'm sorry, Kemi, it's not really appropriate to discuss this over the phone, but . . . ," the voice began.

"I appreciate that," I interrupted, becoming frustrated, "but I have four children, none of whom are with me at the moment. *Who* is this about?" I demanded.

"It's okay Kemi, there's no need to get worked up - honestly, they're all safe. This is about Michelle. I'm waiting in your driveway. I'll speak to you when you get home. Okay?" the voice stated.

"Well? What's going on? What the hell's happened?" Craig asked, visibly frustrated, as I put the phone down.

Ring Ring.

"That was a police officer, from Child Protection," I rambled, looking down to my shaking hand to see who was phoning now.

Ring Ring.

"It's something to do with Michelle." Saying it out loud caused a deep, sickly dread to somersault amongst all the knots in my stomach.

Ring Ring.

"Why the hell is Wale phoning me?" I felt faint. The rushing adrenaline shallowed my breath.

Ring Ring.

"What does that mean? Kemi is she okay?" Craig asked concerned.

The ringing stopped.

"I don't know what it means," I answered abruptly, frustrated at my words' truth. I exhaled before taking another deep breath, trying to calm myself.

Ring Ring.

"Only that it's not going to be good, if that's who's waiting to speak to us. See this bloody phone."

My nervous system was jumpy and I couldn't get a second to clear my thoughts before Craig started to speculate.

Ring Ring.

"Something must have happened at school. I'm sure she's fine," he tried to reassure. "Did they not say anything?"

Ring Ring.

"Craig, I need to answer this bloody phone! It's Wale, again. That's the second time he's called. What is it, Wale?" I abruptly answered with no regard to politeness.

"Kem, what the fuck's going on? The police have just been here," Wale frantically babbled.

"I don't know, Wale, she's just phoned me. I'm on my way home. I'm meeting her at the house. Why, what did she say to you?" I quizzed to see if he had any more information.

"Nothing really," he stammered, "she just asked if we had a number for you and where you would likely be. Why? What do you think it is?" he probed curiously.

"I don't know Wale," I replied sharply and with less patience, shutting him down and cutting off his speculation. "All I know is that it involves Michelle."

"Fucksake . . . what has *she* done now?" Wale sniped scornfully.

"No Wale, it's not like that," I corrected, defending Michelle, "this is Child Protection, that means that somebody has done something *to* Michelle."

"Eh, what do you mean?" Wale asked, with a sudden change of attitude, switching from irritated to anxious. "What else did she say?"

"She doesn't need to say anything else, Wale - she's Child Protection and it involves Michelle. That can only mean one thing," I alluded, feeling my heartbeat pulsating at the back of my throat.

"Ah, but . . . ," Wale began.

"Wale, I don't have time to talk," I interrupted, shutting him down again.

"Ah but . . . ," Wale started again.

"Wale! I'm going now," I said, trying to end the call.

"Kemi, you'd better phone me back and tell me what's going on," Wale ordered in a raised voice before hanging up.

What has Michelle got involved in now? I felt sick as we pulled up outside our house. I could see two women waiting: Gillian, the police officer from Child Protection and a social worker, Lydia Bramley - a name I will never forget. When I introduced myself, I saw her disgust contort her face as she looked me up and down, while refusing to accept my handshake. I was quite taken aback. In that moment I knew this woman, Lydia, felt I was her inferior and not even worthy of a handshake.

Now granted, on paper this looked quite bad for me. Here I was, a mixed-race mother of four children, to three different fathers, living in this big, beautiful house with my fiancé who was ten years my junior. I could see the judgement and contempt on Lydia's face, knowing that she must have done her due diligence on who she was about to meet. However, it wasn't just her judgement and contempt that I felt; I saw her revulsion and recognised it. My soul was fine-tuned to recognise it in a heartbeat. I'd felt it a million times before. It's an involuntary reaction; an instinctive sense developed

170

over a lifetime of experience, and I had experienced it in almost every day of my life.

Regardless of whether it occurs being followed in shops, or being racially abused on public transport, or even in the privacy and company of your own family, the feeling is always the same. It occurred that frequently, it had become normalised, and normally I would take a mental note, acknowledging its presence, before accepting it and moving on. But here, I couldn't move on and away from Lydia. Regardless of what I was about to be told, I knew she'd already made her mind up about me.

When we got into the house, Gillian wasted no time in revealing to Craig and me the reason for her visit: Michelle had made an allegation of a sexual nature against Craig.

I was instantly winded, like a boxer receiving a body shot. My legs began to tremble, forcing my whole body to shake on its unstable foundations. I sank into the sofa and remained silent, listening and absorbing, all the while racking my brain for any proof from hindsight.

"What? What do you mean? *What* sort of allegation?" Craig rambled, sounding confused.

He looked like I felt: deflated, and his mouth was struggling to keep pace with his thoughts.

"I'm sorry, but I can't go into the details of the allegations with you here, Craig," Gillian calmly explained, turning to look to me.

"Well, that's fine, you'll leave Craig, right?" I suggested, desperate to know what Gillian had to say.

"Of course," Craig agreed, looking vacant and picking up his car keys, "when should I come back?"

"This is a risk assessment," Lydia abruptly interrupted, her disgust dominating her tone, "*you* don't come back. If you come back to the house before the risk assessment is completed, and if Kemi doesn't keep you out, the children could be removed into temporary care."

Her eyes lit up with supremacy as she delivered her threat. *What did she say? Did she just threaten to remove my children? What has Michelle said?* My head was swirling and I found myself observing their conversation, but not taking in anything that was being said.

"So, what do you need me to do?" Craig questioned, looking for direction. He looked grey, as if someone had drained the life out of him. "What should I do? Is there anything I can do to help?"

"Can you give me your contact details, Craig, so I can arrange an interview and we can take it from there?" Gillian requested with diplomacy.

"Of course, sure. Do you have a number I can have to get in touch with you? How soon can we do the interview?" Craig asked, as he took out his phone to take Gillian's number. I could see his hand shaking.

"Hopefully in the next few days," Gillian replied.

Craig exchanged numbers then left, looking shell-shocked, and advising that he would go to his parent's house.

Gillian asked if there was anyone that she could call to come around for support and before I knew it, I'd phoned my mum. She arrived very quickly. As the afternoon went on, I realised she was the worst person I could have asked.

"I knew there was something not right with him," my mum character assassinated, in one of her first statements.

"What do you mean Daisy?" Lydia encouraged, speaking to my mum in a friendliness that had, up until that moment, been absent.

I was shocked and devastated at my mum's statements. I couldn't believe what I was hearing and found myself momentarily dumbstruck. *What the hell is going on?*

"Well, I find him very sleazy," she resumed her assault. "I saw him naked one day, in their old house, when he got out of the bath at the top of the stairs!" my mum reported playing the 'victim'. I saw Lydia sit upright at the edge of the sofa, delighted to hear my mum's wild accusations.

"What?" I shrieked at her deluded idiocy. "Are you mad? He was in his own home! The home that you would just walk straight into, unannounced and whenever you liked," I defended with ferocity.

I could feel my body tense further, instinctively adding another layer of defence. She knew well that she had been the one in the wrong for walking in on Craig - not the other way round.

"He's a pervert," she pursued, staring at me.

Her words struck me like a knife to my chest. *What is she doing? Where is this coming from?*

"Mum shut up - you don't know what you're talking about. They're talking about child abuse . . . a child, that means he wouldn't be interested in someone of *your* age," I explained, highlighting her absurdity. I didn't need her sticking her nose in before I had all the facts. I saw Lydia shaking her head, agitated that I was standing my ground.

"Kemi, it's important that I hear what *you* have to say. Is there somewhere we can talk, and I can take a statement?" Gillian offered calmly, trying to neutralise the intensity between me and my mum.

Lydia and my mum left instead, going into the room next-door, so Gillian and I could talk in private. She asked me to think - to think very hard - to try and recall anything, however insignificant, any sign that Michelle could be telling the truth.

"I don't understand this," I sobbed. My head was still swirling, propelling all my fragmented thoughts. "I don't understand how this can be happening. I know my daughter - I'm not claiming to know everything about her - but I know Michelle." I wiped my eyes and cleared my face. "Are you telling me that this can happen, and there would be absolutely no signs whatsoever?" My eyes searched hers for answers, before welling up and streaming again. "I'm sorry," I sobbed, wrestling to regain some sort of composure. "I'm struggling to take this all in at the moment. I just don't understand." I could feel the words tumbling out of my mouth, jumping from one thought to another without process or direction.

"Look," Gillian began sympathetically, "speaking to the mother is of big value in my job. That's why I'm speaking to you; I do believe that we know our children best, but just speak to Michelle when she comes home from school. See what she has to say," Gillian suggested.

Gillian told me that Michelle's friends had made the allegations the day before to a teacher and in turn, the school contacted the police. When Gillian went to the school to question Michelle, she'd run away from her. She eventually managed to speak to Michelle and had advised her that she would be coming out to speak to me.

Gillian continued to ask questions and I continued to answer them. I told her everything and anything of any relevance: Michelle's childhood, my family dynamics and her recent social life.

"So, does Michelle get grounded when you catch her drinking or staying out all night?" Gillian probed gently, in a non-judgemental manner.

"I do ground her, but my mum interferes a lot and Michelle normally goes there until I unground her."

My confession was laden with shame. I could hear how bad it sounded; blaming my mum's interference for my lack of any control of Michelle, but I had to be truthful, no matter what it sounded like.

"I was young when I had Michelle - too young, and my mum helped out a lot. Too much."

I began trying to explain the intrinsic complexities and dynamics of mine and Michelle's and my mum's relationships, and how it had got to this point. Gillian sat at the edge of the sofa, her hand speedily jotting in the notepad that balanced on her knees, whilst trying to offer me full eye contact.

"Has Michelle ever made any allegations before, Kemi? Craig, or anyone else?" Gillian asked, halting her hand to read me.

"Yes," I answered quietly, after a pause, "my ex-husband, Rab - but it wasn't of a sexual nature," I added. "About five years ago, Michelle said he'd kicked and pushed her to the ground."

"And what happened? Were the police involved?" Gillian probed, freeing her hand again.

"No. I spoke to him and he denied it - point blank. He then dropped her from his visitation order. His lawyer advised him that she could jeopardise his visitation rights with the boys."

"Did you believe her?" Gillian asked, pausing again to see my answer.

"I wasn't sure at the time, but . . . no," I confessed, finally admitting it to myself. There was a long silence before I continued.

"My ex-husband was very violent," I confessed, "and Michelle saw so much - too much - and she didn't like going with the boys to Rab's mum's house, none of them did. They smacked the children, and I had to get my

173

lawyer involved to make them stop. But he never 'attacked' them."

"What are you trying to say Kemi?" Gillian asked, probing me to disclose what I was truly feeling.

"Well . . . she didn't have to go anymore after she'd said he'd kicked her. Michelle demands control. I think it's because she felt so helpless witnessing Rab's beatings. She has no boundaries. You can't make Michelle do anything she doesn't want to do. There's no way anyone would get away with doing . . . *this* to her - and for two years? Not a chance. She would've screamed the house down, or at least said something to my mum. I don't think she fully understands how serious this is. I don't think I believe it."

I said what my gut was telling me. *God, she'll think I'm a terrible mother.* I certainly felt like the worst mother in the world, but I had to make sure everyone understood the story that was Michelle, and from a place of truth.

"Will she open up to you if you speak to her?" Gillian asked.

"I'm not sure, but I'll know if she is telling me the truth," I revealed.

Gillian completed taking my statement after nearly two hours. When we re-entered the room, a silence fell as my mum and Lydia glared at me. I was instantly sickened again on remembering Lydia's threat. *She can't take my children.* I was worried about what disgusting nonsense my mum would have been saying in my absence. The two of them seemed to be getting on very well and that made me feel like an alienated outsider. When Gillian and Lydia left, they said they would carry out their investigation and keep me informed, but that Craig shouldn't return to the house in the meantime, until after their investigation was over. As soon as they'd gone, my mum started.

"I can't believe you defended him," she sneered standing over me sitting on the sofa, posturing for dominance. I looked up and matched her stare.

"I'm defending no one," I corrected, "I just want to get to the bottom of what's going on," I stated firmly and with a tone signalling I was not about to get into this with her.

I wasn't ready to let her know my beliefs, and I didn't trust her after her wild allegations. I knew she had her own agenda; I just didn't know what it was yet. I wouldn't, however, have to wait long to find out.

"It's not *normal* for a man as young as him, to want to be with someone like *you*," she announced with a look of sincerity, portraying belief in her own words.

"What's wrong with you?" I scathed, standing out of my seat. "I don't need your input and negativity; I need time to think - before Michelle comes home."

"Yes, well, *I* will be here for that," she interrupted, sitting herself down, as far back into the deep sofa as she could, displaying her intention to remain.

"Oh no you won't," I assured, picking up her jacket and handing it to her.

"I will," she fizzed, reflexing forward and erect at the edge of the sofa, "I don't trust *you* not to defend him."

"What the hell are you talking about? Michelle is *my* daughter, not yours, and I don't trust *you* to be here," I hissed back at her. "If you want to help, you can pick up the boys and feed them and give me a chance to speak to Michelle. Mum don't fight me. You either help or go home." I could see her struggling to remain quiet, her lips twitching, preparing to speak.

"Okay," she allowed, picking up her jacket defeated. With a look of disgust, she departed, slamming the door behind her.

As I sat on the sofa, alone and in silence, I couldn't believe what had happened. I kept experiencing waves of anxiety crashing through my body, only interrupted by the sporadic bouts of nausea that caused a swirling cloudiness in my head and imprisoned me with my thoughts. First Lydia and her demeanour and her threat. Then Craig and that desperate look on his face. He'd tried calling me, but I wasn't ready to speak to him yet; I had to speak to Michelle first. I was worried about him, but I had to find the truth about what was going on before I spoke to him. My thoughts were disturbed by the sound of the front door closing.

"Michelle, are you okay?" I asked sincerely, getting up as she came into the lounge.

"Yeah, why?" she replied, feigning her innocence and avoiding making eye contact. I could tell she was nervous; she'd chosen not to enter the living room, but rather, to linger at the doorway, keeping a clear exit.

"Michelle, the police and social work were here today," I opened gently, feeling my heart race faster.

"Oh . . . I'm not talking about *that*," she interrupted pragmatically, before I heard the boys, followed by my mum, passing the window on their way to the front door. *I can't believe her. What is she playing at?*

"Mummy," the boys ran to embrace me as they entered the room.

"They didn't want to come to my house. They said they wanted me to bring them home," my mum excused as she rushed in behind them, desperately trying to prevent Michelle and I from talking in private. My blood was boiling.

"Hi boys, how was your day?" I asked, firing a stare at my mum. I knew well she'd rushed them home, coincidentally arriving just a minute behind Michelle.

"Mum, why did Nanny pick us up from school today? Where's Daddy Craig?" Dayo asked, sensing that something wasn't right. He was always so observant and could tell when things were off.

"He's at work, Dayo," I said, taking his hand to stabilise him as he wriggled his shoes off. My mum stood silent sharing glances with Michelle. *I need to get rid of her.* "Boys, Mummy needs to speak to Michelle about something very important, so Nanny is taking you to *MacDonald's*, okay?"

175

I said while looking at my mum, knowing she couldn't refuse.

"Yes, Nanny. Please, can we?" the boys excitedly pleaded. I played her like she had tried to play me.

I helped Dayo slip his shoes back on before waving goodbye to the boys as they skipped to the car with their defeated Nanny.

"Michelle, come up to my bedroom please," I said gently, but firmly. She followed without uttering a word. I closed the door behind her and sat down on the bed beside her.

"Michelle, I have to know what's been going on. If Craig has done this, then he will be dealt with, but I need you to tell me the truth." I felt my soul agonise and my body quiver.

"*I* didn't say anything. It wasn't me; it was my friends," she said unmoved and more interested in inspecting her chipped nail polish.

"Yes, but *you* told them; *they* only reported what *you* had said, right? Michelle, I don't understand. Please talk to me," I pleaded looking into her eyes.

Silence was all she gave me. It wasn't that she was too scared to talk, there was no fear to be found in her eyes. No, she was intentionally being aloof, enjoying her control, like a cat playing with a mouse.

"*I* don't have to tell *you* anything, right?" she bragged, leaning in towards me threateningly. "He did it, and *you* can't let him back."

"Michelle, why are you behaving like this?" I questioned, confused at her heartlessness.

"I'm out of here. You're so fucking annoying," she screamed as she charged out of my room and into her own, banging the doors behind her.

I sat on my bed in shock. I could see she was in pain; I'd known it for a long time, but I hadn't known what to do. I was ashamed that I hadn't been stronger for her or protected her from my mum and Rab. But I knew she was lying, and she knew I knew. That's why she wouldn't speak to me. I just needed more time with her, without my mum's interference. I knew she would open up if I could just keep her close. I decided to wait and speak to her after the boys and Tola were in bed.

When my mum came back with the boys, I heard her giving Michelle her food and being told to 'just get out', followed by Michelle slamming her door shut. I came out of my room to meet my mum at the top of the stairs.

"Well?" my mum coldly greeted me, looking to know where I stood.

I just looked her in the eyes and walked past her downstairs. I could hear my dad, Tayo and Wale all congregating in the kitchen, so I took to the living room to attempt some composure. She didn't follow me, but instead entered the kitchen.

"Are you sure, Daisy?" my dad interrogated with urgency. "I do not know if I believe this. Michelle would have said to you, Daisy, and *you* would have seen it."

My mum was furious and started shouting. With no chance of quiet to think, I made my way into the warzone.

"Don't you dare Samuel! Don't you ever, ever suggest that she would make something like this up! Don't you dare," my mum frenzied, her face twisting and blushing from her vehement condemnation.

"But Daisy," my dad barked insistently, "look how close you two are; she tells you everything. She is always running to you." The room silenced, momentarily, before the eruption.

"Oh, Samuel, just fuck off! Fuck off into the living room! I'm sick of looking at you! That baby's crying in there, go and lift her," my mum ordered.

I stood in shock. This day had felt like a living nightmare, and with my dad's refusal to back down to my mum, it took a deeper twist into the surreal. No sooner had my dad left the room when an unlikely sniper popped up.

"I believe it Mum. I definitely believe it - no doubt. He's definitely done this," Wale exclaimed, animated, as eager as a puppy trying to impress its owner, sending me into a confused fury. *Why are you even here?*

"What the fuck are you talking about Wale?" I retaliated, seething and with a scowling stare. "This is *your* mate that you're talking about." He stood there silenced and still. My blood was boiling.

"Just listen to *her*, defending *him* as usual," my mum accused with disgust, attempting to interrupt my questioning and defending her loyal pup.

"What's changed, Wale?" I resumed, ignoring my mum's slight. "You're so certain about this? Why? Craig's been *your* mate. You've never had any problem with him before now – but somehow, all of a sudden, you have no doubt that he's this sleazy?"

His face looked back at me with defiance, but his mouth remained silent. He had no argument.

"See!" my mum exclaimed obstinately and with a misplaced rationale. "I knew you didn't believe Michelle! I knew it!"

"Hold on, can we all just take a minute here?" I said calmly, and with a lowered voice, attempting to restore some order.

"Somebody who abuses children is a predator. It's a sickness; they can't stop themselves. Are you telling me that you believe that's what's going on here - that Craig's sick - and we're not even going to consider looking to see if it's maybe something to do with Michelle's behaviour?"

"See, see! I knew it! I fucking knew it!" my mum spat through her clenched jaw while stamping her feet and pointing antagonistically at me, trying to shut me down.

"Listen, *you*," I ordered, "for years I have tried speaking to you about Michelle's behaviour and her having no boundaries. I think there's something seriously wrong with her. Maybe…"

"I'm not fucking listening to this," my mum interrupted, dismissing the notion as usual. "Let's go!" she ordered, rounding up her troops. "Let's leave her! Michelle can come with us too if you're going to behave like this," my mum commanded in a threatening tone.

"You! Stop right there!" I instructed. She paused, lingering at the doorway. "I promise you right now, if you try and take Michelle out of this house, I will phone the police. I mean it." Her jaw dropped a little, her mouth repulsed with her distaste for the police, causing it to gape.

"I will call Gillian and tell her what you're trying to do."

We locked eyes, both knowing that I meant it. I was trembling inside but remained stoic. Her mouth closed shut, clamped tight by her biting her lower lip. She paused and thought for a second before opting to remain silent. Snatching at her handbag and jacket, she left without challenging me. They all left, and I was left alone with Michelle, the two boys and little, four-month-old, baby Tola.

That evening, when I told the boys that Craig had gone away for a little while to sort out some business, they were both very upset and confused, with Sola becoming inconsolable and arguing that Craig would not have left without saying goodbye. I promised they would be able speak to him in the morning and they just about settled for that, reluctantly, and suggested that they should keep me company in my bed, seeing as Craig wasn't there, while offering their services to help with Tola should she wake up.

After settling the boys into my bed with a movie, I sat down to feed Tola in the living room when Michelle finally came out of her room and sauntered downstairs without a care in the world, hair all styled and in full make-up.

"I'm going out now," she advised nonchalantly, engrossed in her compact mirror, pretending to be too preoccupied with applying her finishing touches of mascara to make eye contact with me.

"What? No, you're not," I spluttered, shocked at her deluded intentions. I slid Tola down into her baby bouncer.

"Eh, yes I am - it's Friday," Michelle qualified with vindication, looking away from her mirror to stare me down. I was shocked, but not surprised. I was now completely certain she didn't have the slightest clue of the severity of what was going on.

"Michelle, you're *not* going out," I asserted. "You've said that Craig has abused you, but you're behaving like nothing has happened. Whenever I try to speak to you about it, you just scream or shout and storm off slamming doors."

"I don't care," she dismissed, packing away her mirror into her handbag. "I'm going out and *you* can't stop me."

"Oh yes I can," I interrupted firmly, taking to my feet.

I'd had enough; my mind was broken, along with my heart. My family was being torn apart and I couldn't make any sense of any of it; and the one person who held all the truth not only refused to share it, but was acting like nothing was going on.

"I *am* going out, or I'll smash this house up!" Michelle threatened with an eruption, the suddenness of which startled Tola, causing her to stir before crying.

"The only place you're going is to your room," I said decisively, refusing to back down. We locked eyes for a moment and I heard the boys bundling down the stairs.

"Mummy, what's all the shouting? Please, stop it Michelle. Mum, tell her," Dayo requested looking frightened, with Sola close on his heels.

"I'm going to phone Nanny. She's the only one who cares about me being happy. She'll sort you out," Michelle yelled, intimidating, and taking no regard for her three younger, crying siblings.

I quickly made for the phone and picked it up before she could request permission to bypass my orders from my 'superior'.

"Dayo, everything is okay, darling. Sola, there's no need to cry little man," I said calmly, hugging them into my hip, trying to reassure them. "Mummy and Michelle just need to talk. Dayo, I need you to take Sola back up to bed and put on another DVD and I'll come up and see you shortly. Okay babe?"

"Okay, Mum," Dayo agreed reluctantly and promptly took Sola, and their tears, back off to bed. I gently bounced Tola in her chair, trying to pacify her cries and took a deep breath in for composure.

"Michelle, you've said you've been abused; that's very serious," I rationalised, trying to make her understand her actions have repercussions. "You're going on holiday with your dad in a couple of days . . . "

"Yeah, and what? You'd better not tell him," she roared, suddenly changing her mood from defiance to fear. Tola bawled in retaliation.

"What do you mean 'better not tell him'? You're going on holiday for two weeks with him, Michelle, of course I'll *need* to tell him; he needs to know," I informed, baffled at her threat.

"No, he doesn't," she bellowed, causing a froth to rest at the corner of her mouth and her face to redden like a beetroot. "Shut up. Just shut up. I'm going out." The boys re-joined Tola in a chorus of crying from upstairs.

"I can't believe you still think you're going out," I said with utter disbelief from the chaos that engulfed me.

"Well, I didn't think *this* would stop me from going out. Give me that phone - I'm phoning Nanny!" she shrieked.

"No! Michelle, go to your room. If you don't stop this, I'll phone Gillian," I warned with clarity. Her resistance flinched. I could see she didn't want the police involved again.

"Fuck you, you bitch! I hate you!" she wailed, slamming shut the living room door before stomping thunderously on each and every step on her way upstairs, sending Tola into a tsunami of tears.

"I wish you were the one that had to leave," Michelle erupted from the landing, before storming off to her bedroom and slamming her door closed, causing the boys to howl. I picked up Tola, cuddling her to feel safe. I sobbed, feeling anything but.

After finally settling Tola, and me, I went and laid down with the boys on my bed, calming them down, until they fell asleep. I lay there broken and feeling my wounds. My emotionally drained soul had taken a beating, my eyes felt grazed and sticky from having run out of tears, and my splintered thoughts were causing my head to throb; *how can this be happening?*

The remainder of the evening was quieter and more still than its earlier act. I fed Tola again, and settled her once more, going through all the motions in autopilot. For once, the house fell completely silent, allowing me to absorb just how alone I felt. Again, my mind raced, this time quicker than my heart. Thoughts of Michelle and the police, and the social worker's threat and Craig. *Craig.* At around midnight, I finally called Craig.

"Kemi," he answered with such desperation in his voice. I could hear his fear and desolation.

"Craig, I don't know what to say," I confessed. I was too scared to say anything.

There was an awkward silence. That was our first. I cast my memory to that morning, sitting in the car on our way back home, before I'd answered my phone, remembering how comfortable our silence had felt then.

"Kemi, I swear I haven't touched Michelle. Please, you have to believe me." I could hear how he tried to let me hear his truth, but all I could hear was his deep pain. I felt suffocated.

"Kemi, I need to see you. Have you spoken with Michelle yet?" he urged. I paused, contemplating.

"Yes . . . " I began, dreading to let go of my next words, "but I can't discuss it with you - I don't want anyone to think that I've been telling you things. I need to remain honest, transparent and neutral, Craig."

"Yes, off course, whatever it takes," he accepted.

I felt so cold, but I had to let this process take place. I wouldn't tell him anything before his interview; he needed to react honestly to any questions the police might have for him. If I'd told him the details of Michelle's allegations, he wouldn't come across as genuine. They needed to see the full shock on his face that these allegations would certainly evoke. I knew it would prove his innocence, but I couldn't tell him that. We ended our uncomfortable conversation with me agreeing to see him in the morning, after Michelle had gone to her Saturday job.

That night I didn't sleep. I lay awake through all the early hours of the morning, trying to figure out what was going on and what could happen. As I lay in bed feeding Tola, and with a warm boy at either side of me, I began to fill with terror. *What if they take my children?*

Baby Tola let out a cry, as if reacting to my thoughts.

The truth

I eventually decided to get out of bed at 6am. By then, my bedroom's darkness had been invaded, breached by a sliver of light released from the foot of the curtain, causing a smoky haze to cascade across the room. The hypnotic, swirling, tiny dust particles almost fooled me into thinking I was dreaming, had Craig's absence from the bed not reminded me of my nightmare. A charm of finches, somewhere close by, had been in fine tune for quite some time, much to my annoyance. It felt like they were intentionally chirpier that morning, to spite me, pretending that all was well with the world. I slipped out from between all the flailing limbs and sweaty bodies, carefully trying not to awaken the boys, before heading silently downstairs with the content Tola.

With the night proving sleepless, I needed a coffee and a moment to gather myself before the rest of the surreal world awoke. Michelle would be getting up soon to get ready for work. Pamela, Wale's girlfriend, worked in a hair salon and had got Michelle her Saturday job about a year earlier. I couldn't believe she was still going in to work as if nothing had happened. We'd argued the previous night about it, but she'd been determined to go, and I didn't have the strength to stop her; I had bigger battles to prioritise.

At about 7.30, I heard Michelle moving about upstairs, before the hissing sound of water spouting from the shower. I finished feeding and changing Tola, before laying her down in her cradle to finish my second coffee of the morning, quietly and alone with my thoughts. I must have been deeply pondering and contemplating all my fears, as I didn't hear Michelle coming downstairs to the kitchen. I could see that she was just as surprised to find me there, alone and sitting in silence.

"Morning Michelle, how did you sleep?" I asked, looking to start our conversation off with a light and friendly introduction.

"Fine," she replied dryly, still wanting to continue her stand-off, while pouring herself a bowl of corn flakes.

The sound of the flakes filling her bowl commanded the otherwise awkwardly silent room. With a splurge of milk and a spoon in hand, she made her way to the dining room without uttering another word. I followed her and sat across the table from her.

"Michelle," I addressed, trying to meet her eyes, "we need to talk about this. You need to start talking to me, now."

I watched her finish her mouthful of cereal, expecting a response. Her eyes never left her bowl as she took another spoonful.

"You can't keep avoiding this. You're going off to work now and won't be back until this evening, and then your dad is picking you up tonight. You're supposed to be going on holiday tomorrow . . . which I'm not sure about anymore, and we still haven't talked!"

I stated this calmly and clearly and in contrast to the frustration that was surging through my body.

"Erm, what are you talking about?" she demanded, resting her spoon in her bowl and finally attempting eye contact. Her sudden interest a reaction to my doubting her holiday.

"Michelle you still haven't spoken to me yet and your dad has no idea what's going on," I expressed with sincerity and desperation. "He'll be coming here to collect you tonight, unaware, and that's not right. It's not fair he hasn't been told."

"*You* won't be telling him," she hissed at me dismissively while rising to her feet.

"Of course I'll be telling your dad," I proclaimed. "Michelle, I'm confused. How can you think you can just go off on holiday with your dad, without him knowing what's going on and as if nothing has even happened?"

The surreal feeling was very much present again and I was stupefied, not quite believing we were even discussing whether or not her dad should know. She stood forward, leaning across the table like a cobra waiting to pounce and looked me straight in the eyes.

"*You* won't be telling him anything, right!" She was getting louder and angrier. "*I* didn't say anything! It's *you* that I hate; you're so fucking annoying! I hate you!"

And with that, she was out of the door before I could say anything else, waking up baby Tola and the boys with her trademark door slam.

I had no time to process anything that had just happened. The house was fully alive again - Michelle had seen to that. As I comforted Tola and greeted the boys good morning as they came bouncing into the living room, I couldn't shake off my acute awareness to the level of hatred Michelle had towards me. The reactive, intense hostility and extreme resentment that she displayed towards me, chilled me to the core. Entrenched in my thoughts and heartache, I switched into autopilot mode again. My thoughts only served to make me cry and I didn't have time for tears. I needed to function, not think or feel. So many people were depending on me to get this right and all I had was the truth. I was terrified that wouldn't be enough.

I settled the boys with some breakfast in front of the TV to give myself some time to get organised before Craig was due to arrive to pick up some clothes. I wasn't looking forward to seeing him for two reasons: the first being Lydia. Even the thought of Craig's presence at the house proved enough to trigger anxiety, remembering Lydia's threats to remove the children. We'd told ourselves that should someone see him at the house, he had a genuine reason to be there: he was collecting his clothes. This, however, did little to settle either of our minds. And the second reason: it had been hard enough hearing how broken he was on the phone and I was dreading looking him in the face and seeing all his pain, especially now that

I was certain that he was innocent and knowing that it was my daughter who was trying to destroy him.

Unbeknown to me, that morning Craig, on his way to collect his clothes, had driven the same route that Michelle took to work to speak to her. When he pulled up in the car she stopped and spoke to him.

"Craig, I'm so sorry, it wasn't me, it was my friends. I only said it so they would speak to me again."

It turned out there had been a falling-out between Michelle and her friends over a fight involving a boy that had happened a couple of weeks earlier, resulting in her being ostracised. Michelle had made up her story so that her friends would feel sorry for her and forget their quarrel.

Before parting company, Michelle had promised Craig that she was going to call Gillian at her lunch break and tell her the truth. Craig believed her.

I would like to make it very clear that this is where I truly believe Michelle's allegations were born. Michelle wasn't taught boundaries or consequence, and I don't think she had the slightest idea how far things would go.

When Craig arrived at the house, I went outside to meet him at the car. He parked at the gable end of the house, obscuring his car from the long private driveway and the main road that it adjoined. He looked terrible. His colour was still missing from his face, making his veins visible through his tracing paper skin and emphasising the darkness that surrounded both his blood-shot eyes. He too clearly hadn't slept.

"Kemi, are you okay? Are the children okay? What are they saying?" Craig rattled, as he turned towards me closing his door.

He was talking speedily and walking just as fast, making his way to the front door. His tone sounded different from when we had spoken the night before. More upbeat and hopeful. Tones I didn't possess and felt nor should he.

"Craig, wait. Stop. Are *you* okay?" I asked with genuine worry. His demeanour was out of place and making my anxiety intensify.

"It's all going to be okay," he assured with a certainty that baffled me. "Let's get inside," he said, before kissing me on my cheek and entering the house. I followed him with confusion and concern.

The children were so happy to see him, with Dayo desperate to update him on how naughty Michelle had been the previous night, "all because Mummy wouldn't let her go out."

Craig spent a few minutes with the children before collecting some clothes. They didn't understand why he needed to collect his clothes, nor why he would not be staying there that night. Craig explained to them that he might need to work later than normal, but that hopefully he would make it back home that evening.

I was shocked. I couldn't understand why he would tell the children

183

something that we both knew for a fact was a lie. He never made them promises that he couldn't keep, and he never lied to them. I led him into the back garden to question his motives, away from the children.

"I told Michelle, that if she just told the truth, things would go back to normal. She's going to phone the police at lunchtime, Kemi, and tell the truth. So, I *will* be able to come home," Craig advised, as he finished filling me in on his conversation with Michelle. I stood open mouthed, dumbstruck and furious.

"Nothing can *ever* go back to normal! Craig, do you not understand how serious this is?" I chastised, fearing the consequences of his understandably desperate, yet unbelievably naive actions.

How could he believe it was that simple? And worse, to have put himself in a position where Michelle could accuse him of further allegations of harassment. I understood his desperation, but with it, I realised he had no idea of the lengths that Michelle could take this to. I did. I knew my daughter, and she had my mum's backing. I was scared for us all.

He stood in silence, vacantly looking back at me. I could see he had believed Michelle would speak to the police, but now, all I saw, was his last flicker of hope die out. After an eternal silence, his face fell dejectedly into his palms to smother his sobs, his self-muting forcing his shoulders to twitch.

"Craig," I summoned, trying to relieve him from his thoughts. He raised his dampened face, "you can't speak to Michelle. Not again. Do you understand?" I said calmly, looking straight into his eyes. I could see reality had landed - and with a crash. He looked terrified.

"Yes." he replied meekly, lowering his head, trying to conceal his tears and fear.

"Kemi, I can't lose you and I can't lose the children. I don't know what to do. I'd do anything to make this better." Tears streamed down his cheeks as he struggled to get his words out.

"Craig," I said gently, wrapping my arms around his collapsed frame. His body gave in to my comfort, gripping me back tightly, like a child being comforted on awakening from a nightmare. "Let's get back inside. The children will be waiting."

"Kemi, I didn't do this," he said, breaking free from my embrace and taking a step back to look me in the eyes.

"We need to go in, Craig," I said removing my eyes, and myself. "Come on, we'll talk more later."

I didn't want to have *this* discussion just now; I wasn't ready to tell him I knew my daughter was lying.

That morning was torturous. A stranger looking in through the window would have sworn they were witnessing a loving family going about their everyday lives. What they wouldn't have seen though were our internal agonies. I sat watching a diminished Craig interacting with the boys and

Tola. Seeing how satisfied and content they all were together only served as a reminder of what was at stake.

After lunch, the boys went and played in the garden with their friend, giving Craig and I time to speak again before he left.

"Craig, I think I should call Gillian, and tell her what's happened," I said softly, so not to disturb the now sleeping Tola. His face despaired, but I wasn't requesting his approval; I had already decided.

"You're right. It's the right thing to do," he conceded with a deep exhale.

"It *is* the right thing to do," I encouraged gently, trying to appease his regret. "It was a mistake, but we have to be transparent."

"Kemi," he began, his eyes wide and searching, exposing his vulnerable soul. "I just feel numb. I don't know what to do." I looked deeply into his eyes. He was lost.

"Craig, you don't have to do anything apart from answer honestly whatever they ask you in your interview. You have to speak up. Show them who you really are."

Michelle never looked to Craig as a father. She was older than the boys and unlike them, she had a more solid relationship with her dad, Michael, so she didn't look to Craig to fill the role of ever-present father. She had however, accepted Craig into the family and he was given his own role. Their relationship was more respect-based as, at times, he was 'the mediator'. If ever there was a disagreement, however trivial, Craig would always listen to her side of the argument. He was always honest and fair with his judgements and she respected that; and he always treated the children equally. I thought that if he was honest in his interview and explained his relationship with Michelle to the police, then the police would see the truth.

I made the call to Gillian, telling her that Craig had spoken to Michelle that morning. Unsurprisingly, Michelle had not contacted her, leaving Craig crushed. Gillian was grateful that I had informed her, but advised that Craig must stay away from Michelle. She then disclosed a new piece of information; she *had* heard from my mum. Michelle had contacted my mum to say that Craig's dad had followed her to work that morning and had tried to speak to her; in turn, my mum had instantly reported it to Gillian.

I was shocked. Neither Craig nor I could understand this. A few phone calls later and we were quickly able to establish this was another lie. Craig's dad had been at work all day - in Glasgow. We couldn't understand why she would make up such a specific lie and yet not mention that *Craig* had spoken to her that morning.

Craig left not too long after the phone call and went back to his sister's house. We arranged for him to come back later that night after Michelle had gone and while the boys were asleep, so we could talk. I was glad he was staying at his sister's. She adored him and he was close to her husband, Stephen, who had been their next-door neighbour growing up. I felt comforted knowing they would look after him.

When Michelle came home from work that evening, she arrived, conveniently, just as her dad came to collect her. She was still acting like nothing had happened in her best performance to date. *This is not normal.* Michael exchanged the usual pleasantries as Michelle gathered her luggage, completely oblivious to what was going on. *This is not right.* I felt guilty not telling him, but what would I say. I was scared and needed more time. Before I knew it, she'd said goodbye and they were both out of the door. As they drove away, I was left with one thought: *I've got two weeks to get to the bottom of this.*

Craig came to talk that night, under the cloak of darkness, again parking his car out of sight. It was a relief to have time to speak without the children needing our attention. We went into my treatment room, the farthest room away from the children's ears and the closest to the main entrance of the property. We feared the children knowing he had visited, in case it got back to my mum and the treatment room was the best lookout for unwanted visitors. He was in a terribly broken state. He didn't deserve this - of that I was sure.

"Craig," I gently beckoned, watching him stare off into nowhere. He turned to look at me, eyes glazed.

"Kemi, I don't want to put any more pressure on you, but I can't live without you guys. I don't know how I would cope . . . "

"Craig," I interrupted his desperate rambling, "I know Michelle is lying," I stated firmly. "I don't know how we fix this, but we will."

I believed what I was saying. I believed that if you were honest, the truth would come out.

"Kemi," Craig released, crumbling as if a weight had been taken off his shoulders, "you don't know what it means to hear you say that."

He embraced me strongly, supplying comfort. I felt his strength, rather than his pain. That night, we sat up talking until Tola awoke around 2am for her feed. Craig stayed while I fed her and by the time he was leaving, we both felt a little better.

The following morning was hectic. Tola just would not settle and as if by telepathy, invited the boys to be in one of those moods where nothing I did was right. I knew we were all just missing Craig. When Craig arrived just after 10am, he was concerned with how exhausted I was, but I didn't complain. I knew he would give anything to spend the full day with the children.

We spent the morning getting the house in order and keeping the children entertained. When we sat down to a coffee, Craig told me that both his dad and his uncle had advised him to say, 'no comment' when he was interviewed. He was uncomfortable with their instruction and I was shocked; that would make him look guilty straight away.

"How could they tell you that? They're supposed to know about the law.

Craig . . . do you hear me? Do you understand what I am saying?" I was furious. The more I spoke the more anxious I became.

"Yeah, well, it didn't sound right to me either," Craig confessed.

"Of course, it's not right," I continued. "The only thing that is going to get us through this is the truth. You have to tell the truth about absolutely everything they ask you, no matter what."

This was how my dad had taught us to behave when dealing with anyone with power; respectful, transparent and honest. I felt strongly that we had to be all of these things to get through this.

"I'm so glad you're staying at Leigh's - your dad's an idiot! Does he not understand the severity of this? You have to be open and honest, and make sure that you tell them everything. And Craig, you need to find the strength to be yourself and show yourself, so that they can understand who you are. Just make sure that you talk openly and that you're honest."

I could feel myself shaking by the time I'd finished directing. My family was hanging together by a thread and everywhere I looked, people were trying their best to cut it.

After Craig left, I felt the overwhelming feeling of despair and fear. For the first time since this had happened, I found myself inconsolable, in floods of tears on the bathroom floor. Gut wrenching wails, so deep and long that I struggled to breathe. I felt so helpless. I was disgusted with myself for not taking control of my daughter earlier. I was consumed by my anguish. *How could a child of mine do this to another human being? What can I do?* Then a thought popped into my mind from nowhere: *William.* I remembered what he had said one year earlier: "If the time ever comes when you need me, I am here for you."

I struggled, trying to get my hands to steady, so I could dial his number. The phone rang out for an eternity, before going onto voicemail.

"William, it's Kemi. You said if I ever needed you, you'd be there. William - I need you now."

As I hung up the phone, I was overcome with guilt. I'd failed my daughter and in doing so, had caused unimaginable damage to the man who loved us; the same man I loved.

Evidence

The next morning, I was jolted awake by the sound of my mobile ringing. I'd eventually managed to fall asleep for what felt like a minute. *What time is it?* The room had changed in that minute, with darkness being replaced by daylight. I reached for my phone while wrestling open my eyelids to permit focus. *7.30am . . . William.* Relieved he was returning my call I fumbled, trying to answer the phone, discombobulated with tiredness and the sudden disappearance of night.

"William," I uttered in a half-awake, broken voice.

"Kemi, you alright?" he quizzed with genuine concern, sounding distressed.

Wearily, I dragged myself to sit upright. My whole body felt exhausted, and my head was cloudy. It reminded me of the derealisation you get when you first step out of bed after having had a bout of the flu.

"Oh William, no. I don't know where to begin. It's Michelle she's . . . "

"Kemi, she's lying," he interrupted with certitude, sparing my anxiety. Every time I spoke those disgusting words, they made me perturbed and ashamed. "You do know that, right?" he stated more than questioned.

"Oh William," I began, before my free-flowing tears halted me mid-sentence, choking me and clogging my airways.

"Kemi, it's okay. I'm here for you. You just cry girl - get it all out," he encouraged.

I took him up on his suggestion and submitted to the salty throttling. When the bawling finally reduced to intermittent, involuntary sobs, he began to speak.

"Kemi, I will come over tomorrow and we can speak properly then. But you need to understand that this isn't about Craig – it's about *you*; she hates *you*."

His words drew a gasp from me. I wasn't surprised at his statement; I'd already come to that conclusion, but now I had confirmation.

"How's Craig?" William asked, triggering my eyes to dribble and my throat to tighten, restricted.

"William," I gulped, "I'm so worried about him. I'm scared he might do something to himself."

I had no one to share this fear with, well, no one who would have cared. I could finally confess what I had been fearing. As if listening in, Tola began to cry.

"Oh, is that baby Tola?" William asked, trying to distract my attention away from my fears. "Okay, I'll let you go, darling. Call me when you can, and we can arrange a time for tomorrow."

"William, thank you."

"Kemi don't be silly, we're friends. Now, go feed that wee princess."

As I sat in bed feeding Tola, I began to think about all that could lie ahead for me and shivered. *One thing at a time Kemi.* I had a very busy morning and could fear those thoughts later. Sandra would be here at 9am to pick up Tola and then I had to deal with the clients.

When Sandra arrived for Tola, I still wasn't dressed, and neither were the boys.

"Morning Dayo," Sandra warmly greeted, as he let her in.

"Morning Sandra, Mummy's just coming. Daddy Craig isn't here - he's working, and we got to sleep in Mum's bed again," I heard Dayo reporting, as I descended the stairs with Tola and car seat in hand. *Shit! No, please don't.* I was too late to stop him. *Okay, I'll just pretend he didn't say that.*

"Morning Sandra, we're a little behind this morning, sorry. We're still trying to get into the swing of things here. God, you forget how time-consuming new babies are, don't you?" I engaged, trying to sound casual.

"Kemi," Sandra softly addressed. I could tell she was searching for her next words to be tactful, while trying not to pry or show concern. "Is everything okay?" I could feel her eyes longing for my attention, but I couldn't allow it; I would have broken down in tears.

"Yes, Sandra. We're all good," I assured, contradicting the high pitching of my last word.

"Kemi would you like me to drop Tola home today, if Craig's away?" This was typical Sandra. She wasn't being intrusive; I don't think she knew how to be. She was simply being practical and thoughtful.

"Oh God, Sandra, sorry, I hadn't even thought about that. Yes, please. That would be very helpful," I replied feeling both embarrassed at my oversight and very self-conscious wearing my bed-head and Tola-stained nightdress. *She must think I'm an idiot.*

"Okay then Kemi, I'll see you around 4.30pm," she said with her warm, motherly smile as she turned to leave.

I followed her to the door and waved her good-bye, now worried that she suspected something was going on. I knew David had just retired, but my mind was trying to convince me that he would have still heard something through the police grapevine. I felt ashamed as I shut the door, before quickly pushing it to the back of my mind, as I still had so much to do.

After getting myself and the boys dressed, they went out to play in the garden with friends, allowing me to call Craig's clients to cancel their appointments, saying he wouldn't be working as he was 'ill'. He had nowhere to work. He couldn't work from home, Lydia's threat had ended that; and my clinic, well, there was definitely no way he could set foot in my mum's house.

Regardless of whether he had somewhere to work from or not, he was in no fit emotional state to do so. He was too petrified to see people. He had started to believe that everyone had heard the allegations and that everyone believed them. Other than coming to the house late at night, he never ventured outside through fear.

He was struggling; desperate to have his interview. I told him I wasn't telling him anything that the police had said to me about the allegations, as he had to have natural reactions to their questioning, and we had to do things properly. So, he had no idea that Michelle had said he had paid her in cigarettes for sexual favours, not sex, and she'd said it'd only happened to her and not to her brothers.

Once I finished the calls to Craig's clients, I cancelled my clients for the next two days to be able to have the time to deal with things, before finally calling Gillian.

I'd made the decision that the only way to help Michelle, and get the right help for both of us, was to be honest, irrespective of what people would think. I sat riddled with nerves at what I was about to say while I waited to be put through to Gillian's extension.

"Hello, Gillian? It's Kemi Ogunyemi." I could feel a slight trembling in both the hand that held my phone and my voice.

"Hi Kemi. How can I help you?" she replied.

"Gillian, I've spoken to Michelle and I don't believe Craig has abused her."

There, I've said it now. I was worried that I may have sounded cold; I knew it was very cold to say that my own daughter had lied, but I had to say what I believed to be the truth, for everyone's sake. The sooner everyone saw Michelle needed help, the sooner the help could be sought.

"Gillian, I have something else to tell you," I quickly followed up with, before taking a pause for a deep intake of courage-filled air.

"When Michelle was two, I found out that a member of my family had been using her for sexual acts." *Oh my God, Kemi, you've said it now.* My hand began to quiver uncontrollably, and my heart was racing, causing a sickly breathlessness.

"Okay. Kemi was this reported?" she questioned stolidly.

"Yes . . . but he was a child - the family member - and only eight or nine years old," I reported, feeling a cold sweat break out down my back. "I spoke to my mum about it at first, but she wouldn't talk about it. She told me not to say anything to anyone and called Michelle a liar, saying she was a toddler and didn't know what she was talking about," I confessed.

"I see," Gillian replied.

"I went to my doctor and health visitor because *I* knew it was the right thing to do for Michelle, despite my mum. I protected her, even though my mum threatened never to forgive me. And I would protect her again, if I believed her, but Gillian, I know my daughter," I stated with finality.

"Kemi, thank you for sharing this and how you feel about it. I know that couldn't have been easy for you. You've been very brave and honest, and I appreciate it."

I didn't feel brave; I was just doing whatever I could to end this

190

nightmare and get Michelle the help I felt she needed. For the remainder of the conversation, I told her about Michelle's behaviour over the weekend and her not wanting her dad to know of her allegations. She found it all a little strange.

I came off the phone feeling a little bit more centred. It didn't last long. I now had to phone my mum.

"Mum, it's me," I replied to her bubbly greeting.

"Yes?" she coldly responded uninterested, now realising who she was talking to.

"Mum, I want you to know I don't believe Michelle," I stated.

Normally, my body would have braced itself, or at least flinched in anticipation of her ridicule and condemnation, but this time I was brazen in my truth.

"Oh surprise, surprise. Kemi, 'Mother of the Year', not," she vigorously mocked, bursting into life.

"Mum, I'm not doing this with you." Despite the adrenaline surging through my body, I controlled my words. "*I* know she is lying, and *you* know too."

"*I* do not," she lambasted, "Michelle could never make something like this up." I could see her in my mind, her face screwing up, getting ready to spit venom.

"Of course, she could," I reacted with defiance. "She said the same about Rab, remember? He's a bastard, no doubt, but we both know she was lying."

"That was different," she tried to assert.

"Mum, no it wasn't. The only difference then was that Michelle wasn't sexually aware," I fired back.

"I can't believe you're letting that paedo-wanker back in," she screeched. She was really getting into it now. Her tongue was warmed up and itching to go.

"You'd better watch what you're saying," I warned succinctly in a lowered tone, "and I'm not letting Craig in. I can't; there's an ongoing investigation and it will show the truth."

"You disgust me, Kemi." Her venom darted through the receiver and I felt her words.

"Yes, I know I do," I said truthfully. My refusal to disagree with her stunned her for a second and in her silence, I continued calmly but firmly. "Mum, you can't see the children on your own anymore."

"What? You can't stop me," she roared in disbelief. "I'm . . . "

"I do not trust you and you won't be seeing any of the children without me being present until this is all over," I interrupted, still remaining calm.

"This is ridiculous," she began to bellow, in a pitch at least an octave higher than before.

"That's your opinion. Let me know when you want to see them. Good-bye." I hung up the phone before she could say another word. I hadn't phoned her to listen to her disgusting views.

She instantly rang me back, but I didn't answer. Instead, I put my phone on silent for an hour, until she stopped calling. I was raging at her ugly words and spent from my adrenaline rush, and no matter how many breathing exercises I performed I could not slow my heart down. However, I felt relieved and free for having told her I didn't trust her. I was determined she wouldn't affect my children any further and I wished I'd done it years earlier.

I felt so drained after feeding the boys and their little friend some lunch; it wasn't even 1pm yet, and there was still so much more to do. After lunch, I set the paddling pool up in the garden for the boys, just outside the conservatory, where I made the remainder of my calls.

Get the worst over first: Lydia. The woman who'd terrified me in my own house with her threat. God, telling her what I thought was not going to be good for me; the way she had intimidated me in my own house with her threats and sneers, but I had to be honest. It was the only way I could see out of this.

My hand was shaking as I waited for her to pick up and I felt sick.

"Hello, Lydia speaking," she answered quite professionally.

"Lydia? It's Kemi Ogunyemi here. I'm phoning you to share some information with you that I feel is important."

"Yes?" she said coldly.

"Lydia, firstly, I need to tell you I don't believe Michelle is telling the truth," I stated very clearly. I knew she knew this was how I felt.

"You can't say that about your own child," she rebuked condescendingly. I felt my neck stiffen in response. I bit my lip and regained my composure.

"Lydia, I'm saying this *for* my child. I have many reasons for not believing Michelle, and I need her to get the proper help I feel she needs." I had rushed my words, but they had managed to come out coherently.

"I have to say, this worries me and makes me very concerned about your other children," Lydia sniped.

Oh, that felt like a threat. I continued to tell her about the family member's earlier abuse and my mum's threats at the time. She had no interest, whatsoever. She never asked questions, like Gillian had done and she certainly wasn't taking notes like Gillian had, as she didn't stop me, slow me down, or ask me to repeat anything I was saying. She didn't care; she had made up her mind. My 'I don't believe my daughter' statement meant, in her eyes, I was a bad mum, ignoring her daughter. She was making me feel like I was doing something wrong and that I would be punished for it.

"Excuse me Lydia," I defended, feeling every sinew in my body torque and tighten at her words, "I have proven that I have protected my children, all of them, in the past, and I will continue to do so in the future."

"Well, I'll be the judge of that," she bragged, trying to put me in my place. I was not accepting it.

"Okay, so you're not interested in the family's history, Michelle's history, or anything that's relevant," I accused.

She gave me only silence. I had a feeling of helplessness. She wasn't listening, which could only mean she was either uninterested, or blatantly ignoring my disclosure. She refused to consider that what I was telling her had any relevance to what was going on now.

So, I ended the conversation, feeling safe in the knowledge that she would find out. *When she does her investigation, this will all be detailed in the doctor's records.*

I made my final phone call: William. I was drained, physically and emotionally and it felt like days had passed since I'd last spoken to him, rather than just a morning. We arranged a time for him to come over the following day.

That evening, Sandra returned baby Tola and asked if everything was okay. I didn't have enough energy to feign and pretend anymore. I was broken. My family was broken. Nothing was okay and I had, by now, accepted it. I broke down in tears and told her everything that was happening. She phoned David, to ask him to come over and before I knew it, she had helped me feed and get the children to bed like a real-life *Mary Poppins*. With the children settled, David stepped into police-mode.

"Okay, have you searched Michelle's room?" he began. He was relatively small in stature but had a commanding presence. His eyes listened to me speak, his pupils narrowing with every detail.

"Yes, but I didn't find anything," I reported. His eyes relaxed, affording a coy smile.

"Well, do you know *how* to search a room?" he asked excitedly, sounding genuinely invested.

"Yes, well, I mean . . . I've looked under her bed and stuff."

His face lit up. He may have just retired, but he looked like he still hankered after the taste of an investigation.

"Come and I'll show you how to search a room properly. You lead the way," he instructed with a gentle, yet eager, enthusiasm.

Once in her room, David went straight to work on Michelle's built-in wardrobes. After removing the clutter off the floor, he patted around the inside carpet, before carefully peeling back a section to reveal a diary and a 10-pack of *Mayfair* cigarettes. I was shocked, firstly at how this unassuming man knew exactly where to look and secondly, that my daughter had gone to these lengths to conceal things.

Next, his eyes scanned the room, like a hawk in pursuit of prey. They stopped, zoning in on the single futon that was really only used if Michelle ever had friends staying over. He unravelled the futon, from chair pose to bed position. He then flipped the cushion-mattress upside-down. As he gently pressed on the seam, it gaped, revealing an area where stitching had been carefully picked. He slid his fingers in searching. He smiled, looking as satisfied as a child on a successful treasure hunt. He removed his fingers, along with a folded magazine.

As he unfolded the magazine, the headline '*I'm Having an Affair with My Mother's Boyfriend*' shot out at both of our eyes. I felt instantly sickened. It had so many similarities it was frightening.

David began talking about what this meant, but I was just numb for a good few minutes - shell-shocked and struggling to wrap my head around what was happening. I listened to him as he read hateful extracts from Michelle's diary about me and how she wished I was dead. Then there was the fall-out she'd had with her friends and why they weren't speaking to her. She'd actually written firstly about telling them that I had cancer for sympathy, along with which friends she would tell and in which order. That entry was dated 20th June. She'd changed her mind and decided to go with a different lie. The reality of what my daughter was capable of was confirmed.

David continued looking and thankfully, didn't find anything else. My heart could not have taken any more revelations.

We went back downstairs to the living room, me, dejected and David, intrigued. He asked me questions on every aspect of every interaction I'd had with the involved authorities, trying to gain a perspective on what they were thinking. I explained to David how Gillian and Lydia had contrasted in behaviour towards me.

"The police were just doing their job, and they sounded thorough enough. No, she sounds fine. Craig just has to have his interview now and he knows he's got to be honest and open."

For all his earlier excitement, David also possessed the ability to calm. I don't know if this was intentional, or just down to his slow and methodical approach to me.

"David, I phoned Lydia today, too. I told her that I didn't believe Michelle and gave her all my reasons why."

"What did she say to that," David enquired, leaning forward in his seat and resting his elbows on his thighs, fascinated.

"She's not willing to look at the possibility that Michelle could be lying. She said I'm an unfit mother and that I can't voice that I don't believe Michelle." I lowered my eyes. I knew I'd done the right thing, but I still carried shame.

"Kemi," David spurted, "she can't say that to you. She can't just dismiss you." *He gets it.* Hearing him affirm my sentiments replaced my shame with anger.

"David, it's like, *I'm* the mother and *I've* brought all these children up, and yet anything I seem to say is completely dismissed as irrelevant," I rambled, visibly frustrated.

"Kemi, not to be rude, but they're not used to dealing with people with intelligence and they're certainly not used to people questioning them. They're not used to it and they do not like it. Trust me, I've seen it throughout my career."

What, so I'm supposed to be quiet? His words sent chills through me. In that moment I realised that the more I fought to get Michelle the help I felt she needed, the more I would be considered a problem.

"Kemi," he continued, "this doesn't feel right to me. I'm saddened to say this, but maybe you're right; maybe this is because of the colour of your skin. Do you want me to assist you with this?"

"Oh my God, David, yes please," I accepted in a heartbeat.

"Okay. First things first: phone the police in the morning, tell them what we have found . . . even take it over there if you need to - it's important that they see this. I know she's your daughter Kemi, but what we've found tonight, and especially what she's written about you, in my many years in the police, I have to be honest, suggests your daughter is a dangerous girl. They need to see this, not just as evidence, but also for your own safety." The chills intensified.

We spoke on for another half an hour, going over all the 'dos and don'ts' as far as he would recommend. He told me to expect this to be a long battle, as it appeared that Lydia was a problem; that she may be out to get me any way she could.

Little did we know as we sat preparing, that Lydia had already been talking to my mum, collecting all the information she would need to try and build a case against me as an unfit mother.

Craig's interview

Here we go again. I awoke, well, rather accepted it was time to get up, and not before too long, Tola had the same idea. The revelations from the night before had occupied my mind and guarded it from sleep, leaving my head feeling fragile and my eyelids reluctant to fully open. There are only so many nightmares you can stomach whilst lying awake in bed. So, wearily I got up and went about the proceedings of the morning, like I had done for some days now, dragging my adrenaline-barren, sleep-deprived and nervously-wrecked self from task to task, heavily dependent on autopilot.

Baby nappy changed, baby fed, baby washed, and baby dressed. Boys fed, boys washed, and boys dressed. Mummy washed, Mummy dressed and baby nappy changed again. Tola down for her first nap. It was 10am and I was knackered, but I knew Gillian would be on shift by now. *Autopilot mode, disabled. I needed to be focused.*

I told her that David and I had found the hidden magazine and the diary in Michelle's room and although sickened, I read her some of the diary's entries. She arranged to come over later that day to collect them. By the time our call ended, I was completely spent. I was emotionally drained by my thoughts.

I began to think about Michelle on holiday with her dad. I'd tried to call her several times by now, but she wasn't picking up. To be honest, I'd felt relieved. What would I have said? *"Oh, hi Michelle, how's your holiday? Good, glad to hear you're having a great time. Us? No nothing, just dealing with the police and a social worker hell-bent on labelling me an unfit mother, to enable her to remove your siblings from my care. Thanks for asking."* No, if we had spoken, it wouldn't have proved positive, which left me feeling defeated. I felt condemned whenever I thought about her.

I still didn't know what was going to happen when she came back home. How was I going to deal with her? I had no idea. I knew she was damaged, but the more I discovered, the more frightened I was becoming. I was starting to see that she didn't think of me as her mum. My mum had always acted like her mother and treated us more like sisters, with Michelle being her favourite. Now, more than ever, I needed to be Michelle's mum, but with my mum's interfering and encouragement of Michelle's behaviour, I didn't know how I was going to be able to achieve that.

#

I was so relieved to see William when he arrived later on in the day. It was over a year since we'd been together, but I still felt our same strong connection when we hugged. The boys had gone with Rab and weren't due back until the next day and Tola was at Sandra's house, so we had time to speak by ourselves.

I'd just finished recapping all that had happened from the horrendous phone call, to Lydia's threat, to my mum's disgusting absurdities, right up to the heart-breaking discovery of the diary the night before.

"Kemi," William started, setting down his half-empty coffee cup, freeing his hands to warm mine, "this won't be easy, but the Social Work Department cannot remove your children from your care."

He looked intensely at me, deep into my eyes and then just off to the side. His eyes began flitting from side-to-side, as if reading a book. I knew what was happening. I knew what he was doing: he was reading me.

"They will try everything, or rather Lydia will. She is going to try and destroy you," he finished with certitude, before refocusing his eyes back into mine.

A cold shiver ran down my spine. I knew he was right and so did my body.

"Kemi," he continued, while subtly nodding his head, as if in agreement with a voice I couldn't hear. *Oh, there's more.* He looked at me stonily, "you have only to stick to the truth, as Lydia - and unfortunately your mum - will lie about you. This will become obvious as time goes on, but you *will* get through it. Kemi, remember, you're a strong, fierce mother."

His face softened as he concluded. William is a very intuitive human being. If you've ever seen the film *The Sixth Sense*[23], you'll know *that* little boy - well that's William. He's had the ability 'to see' his whole life. He'd advised me many times before, in many situations and had always been spot on with his findings. It was good to have him for guidance, but this truth left me fearful.

William hadn't long ago ended his own battle with the Social Work Department. His younger sister, who had a learning disability, had fallen pregnant and had a son about 18 months earlier, and the Social Work Department had wanted to remove the baby from her care. So, for all those months, William and his husband had fought hard, and, with their support, William's sister was able to keep her baby, little Joseph. But it hadn't easy. So, with his words I knew that not only was he 'seeing', but that he also spoke from experience. He understood the enormity of being judged for something you had no control over, i.e. being a minority, still fighting for acceptance.

# # #

William had gone by the time Gillian picked up the evidence later that afternoon. She didn't have time to stay and speak as she was only stopping in on her way to another case. I was so glad to hand over the items; for the

---

[23] 1999 American film about a boy who is able to see and talk to the dead.

police to have insight into what was going on in Michelle's life, but also to have that hate out of my house. That hate had made me feel deeply sick with worry about what Michelle might be capable of doing. We both needed professional help with this - I had no doubts about that.

When Sandra and David brought Tola home the house was deathly quiet. Time had vanished since I'd sat down. I'd been allured by my own tormenting thoughts again. Tola's cries from having just woken up startled me back to reality.

Not long after some much needed hugs with Tola, Craig came in, looking faded, like a prisoner who hadn't been touched by the sun for years. He too hadn't been sleeping for worry. He worried about the police and the Social Work Department. He worried about my family. He worried about everyone - strangers. He worried what would happen to him if people heard the allegations and believed them. He was terrified to go out and especially scared of coming to our house during the day, in case anyone saw him. We both felt shameful. We felt like people were looking at us and judging, believing we were capable of causing harm to our children.

Sandra and David had both had to call Craig to reassure him that he was not breaking any rules coming to the house at this time; there were two other independent adults here and Tola was the only child.

"Craig! Hi, son," Sandra gasped as he crept in the door, instantly taking a step towards him to gently wrap her arms around him, like a mother attending to her child's pain. He crumpled in her arms.

"Sandra," was all he said, as he welcomed her embrace. He didn't need to say anything else - he was in safe company.

"Craig, how are you doing?" David clumsily, yet sincerely, asked, in what I think must have been an 'old school' policeman's attempt at sympathy, while firmly patting him on the back.

Craig just smiled. We both knew Sandra and David quite well, and they both loved Tola. They'd both been clients of mine for years by now and Sandra had looked after Tola since she was seven weeks old. We'd dined at each other's homes on a few occasions and had become friends.

Despite our friendship, David wanted to have a chat with Craig. He didn't think, or believe, Craig was capable of Michelle's allegations, but he had been clear to me that he wanted a conversation with Craig, alone, to ask him some direct questions. The two of them left the room to have their talk.

Finally, they came back into the room, Craig leading the way with David's arm draped around his shoulder. David was satisfied. He went on to raise the point that it had been six days since the allegation had been made and still no social worker had come out to check on the other three children.

"Kemi, this is the type of thing that you hear about in the news, where children haven't been visited for weeks and end up dead . . . and she hasn't even called you - *you've* had to call her, and she says *you're* unfit? Maybe she should come out and check first!" By the time he'd finished his tirade he'd become visibly agitated.

"I know what she'll say, David," I advised, joining his frustration, "she'll say she's not been out because she doesn't have any concerns about the other children, as Michelle said it only happened to her and not the boys."

"Kemi," David yelped, irked at the potential excuse, "that's not for a 15-year-old, wee girl to determine! If there's a predator, a child abuser in your home, no child in your house is safe, including baby Tola," he lamented.

"But doesn't her not coming out mean her investigation will come up with no findings?" I asked naively.

"No, not necessarily. Kemi, you're missing the point. What's concerning me is, if she's not speaking to you and she's not visiting the children, then who *is* she speaking to?" My stomach clenched. I knew it would be my mum. This, I had not anticipated.

"Craig," I said gently, taking a deep breath. He turned to look at me, as did Sandra, as did David. "You *must* tell them about your operation," I stated firmly while not breaking eye contact.

I saw this as evidence and having discussed it with David, he agreed, but this was the first time I'd discussed it with Craig. I could see in that moment I'd hurt him. His eyes narrowed, flinching at my request. Then they scanned the room, looking at his spectators, to catch their reactions, before lowering, embarrassed with the realisation that they already knew. This was not something he'd wanted anyone to know.

"Craig, think about it; the scar is so distinctive - there's no way you could miss it." A new, and less defeated, look of realisation leapt across his face. He hadn't thought about that.

"Craig, this is solid proof," David confirmed. I could see a tiny bit of hope return to Craig's eyes.

"I hadn't even considered it. I've been trying not to think about what could've been said," he said, allowing himself to look at his audience. He paused and took a quick inhale through his nostrils, steadying himself to speak. "It makes me feel sick thinking about it, imagining the unimaginable," he confessed, struggling to hold back his tears. His statement was difficult for us all to witness.

# # #

The next morning, Gillian phoned Craig to arrange his interview and asked him to go in the following day. He had a sound of relief in his voice when he called me to let me know.

I was up early with the boys on the morning of the interview and had spoken to Craig before he went to meet Gillian at a police station in Motherwell. We'd agreed that he would come straight to the house after he was finished. The boys needed to see him - and I needed to see him face-to-face, to see how he was coping. This was too important-a-day for us as a family, so I didn't really care about Lydia or her threat; she hadn't been near my house since her initial threatening visit and still hadn't seen the children.

Craig's interview was at 1pm, so by the time 3.30 arrived and I still hadn't heard from him, I became anxious - very anxious - and wasn't able to eat. The boys had come home, all out of sorts and needing a lot of attention after having spent time at Rab's the previous day, which didn't help, but I'd grown accustomed that – it was their normal reaction and could last a few days. Today however, I could tell Dayo was particularly burdened; he had something to tell me. He'd been wearing the same look on his face since he came home. I'd asked him earlier in the morning if there was anything wrong, but he only went as far as to say he was just thinking. I knew something was bothering him, but I wouldn't force it out of him; I knew he would open up when he was ready. So, I wasn't surprised when he came and joined me feeding Tola on the sofa.

"Mum," he said with grave concern, while gently rubbing and kissing Tola's head. It warmed me to see how much he loved her.

"Yes darling," I replied, looking him straight back in the eye, so he knew he had my full attention. Dayo needed eye contact to maintain conversation – he liked to see he was being heard.

"Mummy, why are we not allowed to see Nanny and Grandad?" he questioned. *What have they said?* He knew I wouldn't lie about it if asked and I could see it was making no sense in his young mind. He needed to know the truth.

"Who told you that babe?" I asked gently, hiding my instant anxiety.

"Dad said you won't let them see us - is that true?" he questioned without hesitation. *Oh, he did, did he?* I took a deep breath.

"Dayo darling, this is true, but . . . "

"Dad let them come and visit us and they said we hadn't to tell you," Sola interrupted, desperate to share with me.

I'd been so focused on Dayo and his revelations that I hadn't heard, or felt, Sola enter the room and sit down behind me on the sofa.

"Mummy, I was crying. I said I would tell you," Sola revealed, snuggling under my baby-free arm.

"Solie, I'm sorry that happened to you . . . "

"And Dad was mean," he continued, not wanting to keep any secrets. "He did the mean face and told me to be a big boy and not a cry-baby." He buried his face in my side, comforting his hurt.

"Why don't you want us to see them?" Dayo asked again, this time watching Tola's little hand tightly gripping his fingers.

"Listen boys. I can't say why - not just yet - but I promise I'll tell you soon." *How do I tell them?*

"But why not *now* Mummy?" Sola's muffled voice queried from my side.

"Boys, look, I haven't said they *can't* see you," I assured with a feigned

200

smile. "I said if they want to see you, then they have to come here, when I'm here too." Sola pulled his smeared face out from his comforting.

"Oh, then . . . what's the problem?" he stated, wiping his face with his sleeve, more than content with the new supervised arrangement.

"Exactly little man," I agreed, this time with a sincere smile.

"*Mum,*" Sola protested, whiningly.

"Sorry - not little man - baby boy," I smiled at him as he snuggled his little head back under my free arm.

"Is that okay for you too, Dayo?" I asked. He was a deep thinker and liked to process his feelings thoroughly before sharing.

"Sure," he replied with confidence. "Look, Tola's finished. Can I hold her now?"

His switching of topic confirmed all was well. However, all was far from well. My mum was now going behind my back and saying God knows what - and not only to the boys, but equally as disturbing, to Rab.

# # #

Craig was broken after his interview. The police had questioned him thoroughly. Afterwards, he'd handed over his phone to the police, so wasn't able to call me when the interview had finished. He instead had driven straight to his sister's house to call me to arrange a time for him to come over that night, once the children were in bed.

"I feel so dirty. Kemi, I can't possibly come over and spend time with the children. I'm no use to anyone like this."

I felt so sorry for him. All I could hear was the deep sadness that consumed his voice, brought on by the stomach-churning details of the allegations, combined with the questions he'd had to answer. It had devastated him.

"Craig, I understand."

I knew this was best for the children; they didn't need to see him broken, but it didn't stop me thinking he needed me to be there with him.

When I got off the phone, I called Sandra to see if she could come and look after the children to allow me to go to Craig's sister's to be with him. Within half an hour, Sandra was walking through my door.

I felt sick the entire five-minute taxi journey to Leigh's house. Craig had sounded so diminished and I worried what state I would find him in. When I got there, it was only Stephen at home as Leigh was still at work. Stephen was an HGV driver and worked the early hours of the morning, so he was normally home in the afternoons.

He saw me from the window and was waiting at the door to greet me.

"How are you, Kemi?" he asked, cocooning me with one of his famous, gentle-giant, teddy-bear hugs.

"I'm a bit fucked to tell you the truth, Stevo," I said frankly. He nodded sympathetically.

"How is he?" I asked, looking for a heads-up on what I was about to find. "He's glad it's over, but he's not good. He's gone upstairs for a lie down," he said, gesturing with a nod of his head for me to go on up.

With a heavy heart, I trudged up the stairs. I paused outside the door to compose myself before entering. I was overwhelmed by the reality of not having a clue how our family could recover from this - and to be honest, I wasn't sure Craig ever would. I thought in that moment that the price for him being with me was too high for him to pay.

As I drew back my tears, I opened the closed door. The room was silently dark, with the curtains closed. It felt like I'd entered the room of a sick person. The musty, warm air hit and engulfed me. I walked over to the bed where Craig was lying, his back facing towards me. He hadn't turned when I came in.

"Craig," I whispered gently, not sure if he was sleeping. He rolled around, wiping his sunken eyes. He looked withered and devoid of spirit.

"Kemi - you're here?" he said, surprised.

"Sandra is with the children and Leigh's going to go round after work," I stated, letting him know we had plenty of time. "I'm all yours," I smiled, as I joined him for a cuddle.

We lay there in silence for what seemed like forever, holding one another, each medicating the other with safety. Finally, it was Craig who broke our peaceful embrace.

"Kemi, that's the worst thing I've ever been through in my life," he confessed, before breathing a heavy sigh to continue. "I was so scared Kem. It's terrifying; how easy it is for your freedom to be taken away."

I could see he was still in shock from his interrogation. I felt even more guilt. This was my child who was doing this to him. I was so overwhelmed I struggled to stay present. I wanted more than anything to be there to support him, but I felt responsible for what was happening to him.

Already knowing some of the details of what was alleged hadn't prepared me for hearing Craig's humiliation and pain when he recalled every detail of his interview. He finally knew all the details, but I can't say it made it better for either of us. It just made our reality even more frightening.

Craig had learned that Michelle had accused him of asking her for sexual favours in return for cigarettes. She'd also said that he'd recorded it on his mobile, prompting Craig to hand it over to be forensically examined. He was told the phone could be gone for quite some time as it had to be sent away to a central testing centre to be analysed, including deleted data.

Craig did inform the police of the operation he'd had as a child and the scarring that he'd been left with. This, along with a few other details, could determine if anyone had seen this area. Michelle hadn't mentioned it. The police decided that they now wanted to re-interview Michelle when she came back from her holiday the following week.

The thought of Michelle being interviewed gave us hope that this may be over in a week or so, and then I could look at getting her the proper help she needed. However, there was a small part of me that didn't accept the hope and was covertly preparing for what was still to come.

Michelle's return

"When will he be here, Mummy?" Sola asked excitedly from beside me while rubbing his tired eyes to encourage them to awake.

The boys had been beside themselves with excitement ever since they'd found out that Craig and I had arranged to go to the Lake District for the weekend.

"9 o'clock, and it's 6.25 now, so you have two and a half hours until he's here," I replied, watching him wakening his body, stretching like a starfish.

"No Mummy," Sola yawned, causing me to yawn, "two hours and thirty-*five* minutes" he corrected with conviction before popping out of bed to shake off any remaining tiredness. *And he's off.* For having such a tiny frame, he was always 'charged' with so much energy.

"Solie, you're so smart," I praised, while smiling at him, watching him zip around my room like a moggie on catnip, supercharging himself through his combination of fighting imaginary 'bad guys' and dancing in celebration at his own triumph.

"I know Mum," he agreed with full sincerity, before disappearing into the en suite on his 'motorbike'.

"Morning Mum," Dayo whispered from my other side, his eyes still closed. Both boys had slept in my bed again, which was now becoming a regular thing. I didn't mind though, I felt safer having them close.

"Morning sweetie, did you have nice sleeps?" I greeted, stroking his brow free from clammy bedheads.

"Yes," he replied involuntary, still half-asleep, "but can *I* use your shower, please?" he requested urgently. Sola's 'revving' into the en suite had stirred Dayo awake just enough, prompting him to quickly call shotgun.

"Erm, why?" I teased, playing dumb.

"Roses, Mum; *I* love them too," he assured, opening his eyes for the first time. Dayo loved to use my rose soap and shower gel just as much as he loved to highlight all our similarities, just in case I should ever forget. "Plus, Mum, Sola makes our bathroom smell like stinky boys. Remember?"

Dayo was referring earnestly to the numerous conversations we'd previously shared regarding his younger brother's hygiene and bathroom etiquette, or lack of. Sola was just too much of a boy for Dayo at times.

"Dayo, *squawk*, it's okay, *Squawk,*" Sola advised, re-joining us from the en suite. He was now pretending to be his favourite dinosaur, a pterodactyl. "I'm having a, *squawk*, bath downstairs. *I* need to, *squawk*, relax before the journey."

Sola loved the downstairs bathroom. It had a corner jacuzzi bath, that, with the introduction of some bubble bath, was the ideal setting for his tiny body to relax and his imagination to run wild.

Where Sola washed was actually irrelevant to Dayo. He was purely and simply after my rose toiletries, and if using 'stinky' Sola as a means to receive permission to the goods, then so be it.

I smiled with joy, watching my children simply being innocent children. They hadn't yet been fully impacted by what was going on. They had started to question Craig's 'working away', and we knew we would have to tell them more, eventually, but we couldn't yet - not until *we* knew what was going to happen. To them, we were going on a short family holiday. For Craig and me, we were going somewhere no one knew us, somewhere we could be a family - somewhere that wasn't home. This was important, especially for the children. We were too scared to spend any quality, family time together anywhere locally, or where we were known. Neither of us felt safe. We never spoke about it; we had just accepted it.

Craig being absent from home was hard for the children. It'd been a whole week since they'd last seen him and when he arrived, Dayo was so overwhelmed that he instantly cried.

"Hey big man, what's wrong?" Craig asked softly, crouching to his knees to peer up into Dayo's bowed face.

"I just missed you," he replied sincerely, throwing himself into Craig's arms to be lifted up into a bearhug.

"I've missed you too," Craig comforted, as Sola came skipping out to the car.

"Dad, Dad! Look at my nail polish - Mum did it," Sola managed to get out, before springing into Craig's arms, almost catching him off guard as he put down Dayo. "You look sad. What's wrong?" Sola asked with concern, as his tiny palms lightly lifted Craig's cheeks upwards, stretching his lips to a smile.

"Oh, nothing Solie," Craig laughed, holding Sola up in his arms, "I'm just tired, that's all, and I've missed you guys so much." Sola hugged Craig tightly, wrapping his arms around his neck and leaning his tiny head under Craig's chin to sincerely offer his sympathy and comfort.

"Mummy's not letting Nanny see us without her being there. Did she tell you that?"

Dayo loved to share information, especially if it was a drama. It wasn't gossiping and nor was it showing off for having known something you didn't - no, it was a sincere update download; to make sure *you* didn't miss out on anything.

"I don't think I knew that big man," Craig entertained, knowing that his attention would make Dayo feel better.

"Well, I'm guessing she's been naughty to Mum again," Dayo speculated wholeheartedly.

"Well, I'm sure Mum will tell me about it all," Craig said, smiling over Dayo's head towards me. I felt a happiness in that moment; I could see Craig coming alive again.

We had two great days away, somewhere no one knew us, where we could be parents, and it felt great having Craig's help with the children. We arrived back home in the evening and Craig had promised to stay and read the boys a bedtime story. After the boys' story time, and as the house grew quiet, Craig and I finally ceased our oath. We'd both agreed, prior to leaving, to try to make our break away a 'free from talk of Michelle' zone. During our final cuddle, and before he left, we began to acknowledge our reality.

"I can't believe you still haven't heard anything from Lydia," Craig opened with a bleak disbelief, his words signalling the break away was well and truly over. Cuddled into his chest, I could feel his heartbeat increasing.

"She *must* be speaking to my mum," I confessed, clutching him tighter to comfort my tightening stomach. David's insinuation had been replaying in my mind, growing into the evermore probable, the longer I hadn't heard from Lydia, and now my suspicions were causing me anxiety. Craig cocked his head, drawing his chin to his chest so he could see my face.

"Seriously? You think that's what's happening?" he asked, his eyes narrowing at the prospect. Ever since his interview, Craig had been tormented by my mum's involvement and expected the worst any time her name was mentioned - let alone alongside Lydia's.

"I'm certain. I've spoken to the doctor and the health visitor and her school and no one has heard from Lydia, so that only leaves my mum." He dropped his head again, resting his cheek back on my head.

"So, what now?" he asked defeated.

"David has told me to call Lydia in the morning and ask her outright what's going on."

There was a moment of silence between us as we both absorbed the potential answers Lydia could supply. We'd been feeling more buoyant since the police had advised us of their intentions to interview Michelle again, but now we lay together in silence, both feeling deflated.

I called Lydia the next morning.

"Hello Lydia, it's Kemi Ogunyemi," I opened clearly, hiding my anxiety.

"Oh . . . Kemi. Hello." She hadn't expected me to call her again, and in her three words she had gone from being surprised to disappointingly inconvenienced.

"Lydia, I'm calling because I still haven't heard from you." I paused allowing her to respond. The silence raged, followed quickly by my annoyance. *You threaten to take away my children and now you've got nothing to say?* "You're supposed to be doing an investigation," I continued, maintaining composure. "It's been over two weeks and you still haven't seen my other children. Who *have* you seen?"

"Kemi, *I'm* in charge of this investigation," Lydia lashed out, her ego offended, prompting her to flex her authority. "Not you; *me*, and *I* will decide when I visit the children." *How dare you!*

"Okay Lydia, but, if you are doing an investigation - and you've not been out here to visit my children - then who exactly *have* you visited?" I questioned again, sensing her reluctance to answer this particular question. I knew she hadn't spoken to any of the relevant services in Michelle's life.

"Wait a minute, *you're* the one under questioning here," she snapped, deflecting yet again, "not the other way round."

"*Me?*" I retorted. I could feel my heart pounding faster now, and I was consumed with a sickening concoction of nervous anxiety and blood-boiling anger. "I thought it was *Craig.*"

"Yes, he is," she quickly rattled, "but *I* have to determine if *you're* a fit mother." *Here we go.* She made it sound as if Craig was now irrelevant. I was shocked, but not surprised. She'd shown her displeasure of me from the very first second we met, but to hear her confirm my beliefs took my breath away.

"What? Are you serious?" I managed to release, winded by her revelation.

"Yes, Kemi. Very." She let out a heavy exhale, growing tired of our conversation. "Kemi, people like *you* just need to be patient. *I'm* in charge and I'll tell you my decisions in due course," she concluded condescendingly. "Now, goodbye, Kemi." *Click.*

Before I knew it, she'd put down the phone. *Oh my God.* My hands were shaking uncontrollably and my thudding heart was trying its hardest to burst free from my chest. Should I have been standing, I would surely have collapsed, as my legs felt wobbly, as if made from jelly. A cold sweat came over me and my mouth desperately longed for moisture. I couldn't believe what had just happened.

I sat there for a few minutes, alone and dejected, still clutching the receiver that was by now blaring a disconnect tone, while my mind ran wild. *Who does she think she is? Oh my God, she's trying to take my children! What has my mum been saying?* I was terrified.

As I tried to process what had just happened, I was filled with a sense of relief that I hadn't specifically asked her if she had spoken to any of the services, or to Gillian about Michelle's interview. I knew she hadn't, but I never got the chance to tell her I knew. Something had told me to wait and watch before I questioned the next time.

I reluctantly phoned Lydia again two days later to raise my concerns about Michelle's return home from her holiday, as she still hadn't answered any of my calls or texts.

"Yes, well, she's been in touch with your mum," Lydia divulged, revelling in her revelation. "She doesn't want to speak to *you*, Kemi - *you* don't believe her, and she's scared of what you might do to her, now that you've decided to ban her nanny from seeing the children." *Ah, so you have been in contact with my mum.* Panic filled me. *What has she been saying?*

"I don't believe you're telling me this; you've had contact with Michelle, and you've had contact with my mum, but you still won't contact me to see

207

the other children; the children you're supposed to be investigating?" I was trembling with anger, not fear. Anger and disbelief.

"Yes," she stated blandly. For the second time in as many conversations, Lydia was confirming my suspicions. *You're out to get me, and my mum is helping.*

"Let me get this straight: I tell you that Michelle has issues, and I tell you my mum's constant interference is the main problem in our relationship, and yet you're speaking to her - why?" I demanded. She took no hesitation in answering:

"Because I'm trusting your mum - not you."

Her words spoke to me on so many levels. I now had no doubts whatsoever that Lydia was taking my mum's word over mine, simply because my mum was white. I had had numerous experiences of this throughout my life and was very familiar with how it felt.

"You're trusting a woman who tried to stop me reporting sexual abuse of Michelle when she was two years old," I highlighted, daring her to defend.

"Kemi, that's your word against hers," she dismissed.

"No, Lydia - it's actually documented, but you'd know that if you'd bothered to contact Michelle's doctor or health visitor."

I could hear my voice shaking. I couldn't believe this woman was so blinded by her own disdain of me. I wasn't getting through to her - she didn't want to hear what I had to say, so I ended our call.

Later that day - and after much soul-searching and brain-racking - I decided to call Lydia yet again and ask her to come and collect some clothes for Michelle as she couldn't return home, not until the investigations were concluded. I was dreading this phone call, but I only had one choice: damage limitation. With Michelle's holiday soon coming to an end, I was petrified to have her back in the house. How could I? I now felt that she was a danger to the entire family; all she had to do was claim the boys had said something and I could lose them all. No, this was now definitely damage limitation. I believed I'd already lost one child and I was not prepared to lose the other three.

Lydia was very cold when she came to pick up Michelle's belongings to take to my mum's house. Apparently Michelle and my mum had already agreed between themselves that Michelle would be staying there that night.

"You do know this will go against you - throwing your own child out of the family home?" Lydia threatened, while extending the handle of Michelle's suitcase to wheel it out to her car. She was seething.

"I have no choice. I can't have her home until your investigation is over; but instead of investigating my children, you're trying to make me out to be an unfit mother." She just sniggered at me.

"Now, you remember; Craig is not allowed around the children." She delivered this provocatively, and with a sarcastic display of sympathy smeared across her face. She opened the door to leave, pleased with herself for having despatched her demands.

"Erm, I think you'll find that Craig has full rights to see his daughter," I contested, causing her face to twist and her feet to halt.

"No, he doesn't; you're not married," she smirked, before going to leave again.

"I think you'll find that Craig has full rights," I stated again, interrupting her dramatic exit, "and as long as I'm present, he will see the children - all three of them."

I said this so clearly and with such certitude that she knew I meant it. She stared at me blankly and only spoke to state that I would be hearing from her regarding the Child Welfare Hearing, then left. I think in that moment she realised that her emotions had got the better of her and that she had underestimated me. Dayo and Sola were both playing in the garden that day, and Lydia never bothered to see them, let alone speak to them.

Once Lydia had driven away, I called Gillian to update her that Michelle would now be temporarily staying at my mum's house and to ask if she knew when she would be interviewing her again. She told me that she would go and contact my mum, and Lydia, to arrange for Michelle to be interviewed at my mum's house.

All hell broke loose when Michelle arrived back from her holiday. She arrived at my mum's house expecting to be staying there for one night, only to see a suitcase waiting for her and to be told by my mum that she wasn't to return home until after the investigations were concluded. I'd tried to call her to advise her of her new, temporary living arrangements, but she still wasn't answering my calls, and I felt it wasn't right to send it in a text message. She must have felt like I had abandoned her.

Gillian tried to arrange for Michelle to be re-interviewed, but when she contacted Lydia and my mum, they'd both refused to co-operate. Lydia had gone as far as to say it would only be to vindicate Craig and that it wouldn't serve Michelle, so she wouldn't allow it. I was shocked and devastated listening to Gillian update me. I'd been under the impression that the purpose of an investigation was to uncover the truth. That had been our only hope to completely clear Craig's name. However, my mum and Lydia had denied us that and denied me the chance to get Michelle the help I knew she needed.

Gillian said as far as she was concerned she had no concerns, and, pending Craig's phone being returned clean as expected, her investigation was over. However, she warned me that the social work had more far-reaching powers than the police when it came to children, and that they could look to continue their 'investigation' for a further three months. Her words rang true to me; *that's what Lydia is planning.*

Craig and I had just arrived back from collecting the magazine and diary from Gillian, and I was still a bit shell-shocked by Gillian's last words to me:

"Kemi, in my experience a lot of kids do eventually tell the truth. Sometimes quickly, some can take years and some don't ever."

It was the latter that had stunned me. I knew my daughter and began to realise that she might never tell the truth. *How could I live with that? How could we all live with that?*

"Kemi," Craig urged, and in a tone that told me there was something wrong. *What now?* I finished taking Tola out of her car seat in the lounge and then joined Craig by the bay window.

"Michelle!" I gasped.

She was alone and approaching the house. When she saw us peering out at her from the window, she just laughed. My blood ran cold. I'd expected her to contact me in some way, but I hadn't expected her to just turn up at the house, unannounced. I made my way to the front door with Craig close behind me. I heard her before I even opened the door.

"Who the fuck do you think you are?" she roared. She was livid and frothing like a rabid dog. Craig caught me by the arm.

"Kemi, not with Tola," he reminded. As I handed Tola to her dad, I quickly scanned the patio doors to make sure the boys were still in the back garden and that they were not aware of what was going on out front.

"Michelle, you shouldn't be here," I informed in a neutral, quiet tone as I took a step outside the door to barricade the house from her presence. I didn't want to match her animosity and risk this escalating out of control. The last thing I wanted was for the boys to witness this; there was no way she was getting passed the front door.

"Fuck you," she screamed at me, "you can't tell me what to do." She was buzzing - high on anger and adrenaline. Her recently sun-kissed, bronze skin had by now turned to a hazardous shade of purple, like an allergic reaction to my presence.

"Michelle, stop. This isn't going to help," I advised. She just stood there, fired up with pure hatred. *How has it come to this?* I could feel my entire body rattling, vibrating with anxiety.

"Michelle, why are you doing this?" Craig asked from behind me, still holding Tola.

"Craig, let me deal with this," I snapped. "Take Tola inside please." He just stood there looking at me. I could see he was stuck in no man's land, undecided whether to retreat for Tola's sake, or maintain his watch over me. "Now Craig." I'd seen this look on Michelle's face before and knew that at any moment she could become violent.

Craig had barely left my side before my jaw suddenly felt a hot pain, then numbness, followed by tingling. Before I'd had the chance to guard myself, I received a full-bodied boot to my shin accompanied with a combination of punches, many of which landed on my wrists and arms that were by now trying to shield my face. It all happened so fast. The next thing

I knew, Craig had wrestled Michelle off me.

"What the hell, Michelle?" he yelled, confounded.

"I hate you!" she scathed belligerently towards me. Her eyes narrowed as she stood cross-armed, allowing herself to catch her breath, before pointing her finger in my face: "I'm really going to fuck you up now; I'm going to tell them he slept with me," Michelle hissed. A flash of excitement shot across her face upon hearing her own plan.

"Michelle!" was all that Craig could gasp before she flung herself towards me again, all punches and kicks, but this time I caught her arms and held on with every ounce of strength I could muster in my horrified and woozy body. I didn't know how I would be able to keep hold of her. She was a good four inches taller, and bigger framed. She was strong.

"Michelle, I'm calling the police," Craig warned, taking a step closer to our grapple while speed dialling Gillian on my mobile.

Michelle relinquished her assault and began to retreat down the driveway, all the while screaming disgusting threats.

"And I'm going to tell them you gave me drugs."

I couldn't believe the things that were coming out of her mouth. With each threat she unleashed, the more irate she was becoming. One thing was very apparent: she was determined to destroy me.

The police went to my mum's house and Michelle was cautioned in the presence of one of my brothers. She was warned she would be charged if there were any further incidents. Neither Michelle, nor my brother told my mum this had happened. After the police had informed me of their actions, I decided to call Lydia to inform her of what had just taken place.

"I'll call Michelle and see if she's okay," Lydia concluded, completely ignoring all that Michelle had said. *See if 'she's' okay? Here we go again.*

"What? Is that all you've got to say?" I probed, infuriated that Michelle's threats were not registering with her. She ignored my question.

"I've set a Child Welfare Hearing for Tuesday the 12th," she advised, switching the topic of conversation. My already pummelled body felt her kick sicken my guts.

"What? How can you?" I questioned in utter disbelief. "Today's the 8th and you've only spoken to my mum and Michelle - no one else; not the school, her doctor nor the health visitor. You haven't even seen my other children."

"Kemi," she interrupted, "you're the problem. *I* don't have to discuss anything with you. I've just popped the details in the post – you should have them by Monday."

When I put down the phone and explained to Craig what had happened, we decided to call David straight away. I knew she was breaking procedure by her behaviour, and David was already making notes.

Children's welfare

"What?" David shrieked down the receiver as I told him about the pending Welfare hearing. "Kemi, she can't do that! Nobody's been consulted. This is ridiculous – absolutely ridiculous. Kemi, we need to prepare. Shall I come this evening when the children are in bed?" he asked with urgency.

I found David's passion and frustration matched my own concerns, and while it was reassuring to feel supported, his sceptical reaction only strengthened my belief that Lydia was out to get me. I felt like I was being setup.

"David, if you wouldn't mind. I think you'd better."

By the time I came off the phone, Craig was already preparing dinner for the children. All the drama seemed to help resuscitate some life into him. He was now beginning to find the energy, motivation and concentration to be able to carry out everyday tasks. Whether that was to help me and the children, or to keep himself occupied, it didn't matter. It was daytime and he was here helping. My over-used body and mind were so grateful for the help.

As I sat feeding Tola, I began to daydream. I thought about how Michelle had come to the house and how she had confronted and assaulted me. My face was sensitive, not only to the touch, but also when I tried to say certain words, and the side of my neck felt tender from trying to restrain her, while my shin had grown a swollen, maroon coloured, golf ball. She was out of control – everyone could see that – everyone, apart from those who really mattered at this moment in time.

While Michelle had been on holiday, I'd been clinging onto the tiny piece of hope brought on by Gillian's intention to re-interview. However now, with no new interview, all hope had run out. I felt powerless. My mum and Lydia were using Michelle for their own agendas, and I'd come to the realisation that they were willing to sacrifice her, at any cost, to get to me.

That whole weekend, David sat with Craig and me, at my dining table, to prepare me for the welfare hearing. David's policing history meant he was an old hat at these things. He'd sat in on many hearings and knew the procedures like the back of his hand. *How would I have managed without you?*

I sat watching David emptying his briefcase into little bundles of papers, all with highlighted markings and colour co-ordinated sticky labels. He was amazing. He'd been documenting and detailing every single incident that had occurred since he first got involved. Everything. Investigation procedures that had happened that shouldn't have, and actions that hadn't happened that should have. All with a meticulous attention to detail. Proper old-school policing.

"Okay Kemi," David opened, clearing his throat while arranging his paperwork, "so, Lydia hasn't followed procedure, and while we don't know what her motives are, it's becoming rather obvious she dislikes you."

"That's an understatement," Craig chimed in. We all shared a solemn glance.

"Now, whether that's because she's racist, we don't know for sure - but *I* suspect that it is," David warned very clearly, staring at me with his steely eyes, introducing an additional intensity into the room.

"*I* know she is," I advised, confirming that we were all on the same page, "but what do I do? She's my only contact now that the police are no longer involved."

"Precisely, Kemi, and that's what's disturbing me the most," David revealed, rolling up his sleeves and sliding his chair in closer to the table. "Logically, I just don't get it. It makes no sense. It's obvious Michelle's been lying, and the police wanted to prove it, but Lydia won't even consider it; why? She hasn't spoken to her school or her doctor; why? And she hasn't spoken to Sandra who sees Tola just about every day; why? These are all relevant witnesses, Kemi, and they all would confirm that you're a good mother, and that the children are well taken care of; and yet she's spoken to none of them. Why is that?" The three of us joined in a momentary silence to reflect.

"So, what do I do?" I asked, praying that he had the answer.

"Nothing," he replied, initially failing to fill me with confidence. "We go to the meeting and see what unfolds." He said it so simply.

"And then what; my children get put on a register and I lose them?" I asked with despair.

"Kemi, you're not going to lose them; and the register - for what? Being at risk? What risk? Craig isn't living here, Michelle isn't living here, and Kemi, the police are satisfied. What's the risk? They wouldn't even know if there was a risk, as they've not even met the other children." A wry smile crept over his face.

"So, does that mean they can't be put on the register?" Craig asked innocently.

"No," David and I answered almost in sync, chilling the room.

Our talking and preparations continued on until around midnight. As David left, he reminded me of all my duties for the next day. I needed to contact the children's doctor, health visitor and schools. I hadn't anticipated getting any response from any of them, as it was the summer holidays, but I would try.

The following day I contacted the school, but as expected there was no answer. I did manage to speak to both the doctor and the health visitor again, but neither of them had been contacted for history or background reports, nor had either of them been invited to attend the Child Welfare Hearing being held in less than 24 hours. I knew then that I was being set up.

#

Tuesday 12th July, 2005.

I was riddled with fear and a sickening anxiety when I finally conceded it was time to get up. As usual, I'd struggled to sleep, or to be more accurate: I hadn't. Depersonalisation had kicked in leaving me feeling frozen in time, observing myself getting through my chores. Later in that bleak morning, once my body and self finally agreed to corroborate, I became increasingly aware that my mouth felt chafed and tingly, with my tongue also raw and inflamed down both sides. I was finding it hard to talk and feared if it got any worse, I would struggle to be able to speak at all.

By the time David arrived to collect me it was 1pm and as I hurriedly bundled myself into his car and out of the rain, with my stomach churning and my hands shaking, I struggled to understand where time had gone. It was then that I began to realise I was in a state of trauma. My morning was a complete blur, yet I'd managed to function and do everything that needed to be done. It was beginning to register just how much this ordeal was really impacting on me. *How long have I felt like this?*

To the outside world I appeared fine; I was functioning, but internally I was broken and my body was trying to reduce my senses to lessen the impact of what I was about to experience. I tried to ground myself back into my body. *Focus Kemi. Breathe. Get yourself together.*

"Kemi . . . Kemi! Are you okay?" David asked with concern. He'd been speaking to me the whole time I'd been sitting in his car, but I hadn't heard one single word. By the time he'd prompted me back into consciousness, we were already there; parked in what used to be *Fine Fare's* carpark; a place I'd known well.

My grandad had taken my gran there every Friday evening for her weekly shopping. I would help my gran by collecting her items as she pushed the trolly, while my grandad would take Tayo to walk the aisles, looking for, and inevitably finding, a fellow, lone grandad for a chat. Afterwards they would take Tayo and me, full of excitement, for sweets as a reward for all our help. We loved it.

Now though, as I sat looking out past the window wipers furiously swiping away the down-pouring rain, and off into my fears, the memory of that excitement was replaced with terror. There were no sugary treats on offer today; just the right to keep my children.

"Kemi," David repeated, this time placing a firm hand on my shoulder. His face displayed a look not quite of scared, but rather more unnerved, and not for the looming hearing, but for what his eyes could see: me.

"Sorry David," I croaked, "I was miles away."

"Kemi, I know it's easy for me to say, but just try to stay in the moment. Don't think about the what-ifs. We'll deal with whatever happens next,

214

when it becomes the now. And right now, they're not going to be taking your children away. But Kemi . . . " He paused and lowered his eyes momentarily before taking a deep breath of honesty, "prepare yourself for the children being put on the child protection register, just in case," he warned gravely.

"I know," I rasped, feeling condemned before I'd even entered the building.

I'd convinced myself that everyone in that room, with the exception of the police, would believe I was an unfit mother. This had been the theme throughout my life. People had always found it easier to think - and believe - the worst of me. Not through evidence or proof, but simply because of the colour of my skin.

"You ready?" David asked, resting his hand on mine, offering support. His face had regained its steel. He looked ready for business.

"Okay," I replied, reluctantly agreeing to be judged despite my stomach's instinct to repel.

"I'm with you Kemi - you're not alone." I smiled weakly, appreciating his support.

As I stepped outside and into the rain, the wet and damp air lashed against me like nature's own public flogging. We headed towards the council offices, making our way along the grimy, graffiti-laden and reeking of urine, concrete brick flyover that adjoined the offices to the car park. The long and silent walk made me feel like a death row prisoner heading towards their final meal.

We signed in and took a seat in the sterile waiting area. The hard, plastic chairs offered no comfort and had it not been for my jelly legs, I would have opted to stand. As we sat waiting, I could feel my breathing beginning to accelerate, becoming shallow and noticeably louder against the silence of the room. *Just breathe Kemi.* The incessant ticking clock from the wall above our heads served not to tell the time, as neither of the hands moved, but rather to prolong my anguish of trepidation. Every second felt like a minute, and yet the time displayed stood still.

The double fire doors to the waiting room swung open and in entered Gillian and another police officer who I didn't recognise. As Gillian passed, she offered a professional, yet friendly "hello", before disappearing into another room. As they closed the door behind them, I heard them say hello to someone else. *Who's in there?* As my mind began to keep pace with my heart, Lydia came out of another door and approached us.

"Good morning," she greeted in a light-hearted tone and with half a smile. *You seem chirpy.* I'd never experienced this side of Lydia.

"Good morning," David replied, springing to his feet. "You must be Lydia; I'm retired Chief Inspector David Stephen." Her chirpiness evaporated during their handshake and was replaced with a flustered look of shock. David's presence had not been expected.

"Oh," Lydia gulped, snatching free her hand, "but this isn't a policing matter anymore" she informed, instantly looking to dismiss David.

"I know," David advised, tapping his file of paperwork. "I'm here as Kemi's support." No sooner had David finished talking, than she turned side on to him and with a roll of her eyes, ignored his presence.

"Kemi, you can come in now," she invited without making any eye contact. *Ah, there she is - there's the Lydia I know.*

She led the way at a frenetic pace, with David and I exchanging glances hot in her pursuit. I could tell he wasn't impressed by her. We followed her into the room that I'd seen Gillian enter earlier. *Breathe. Just breathe.*

I was shaking as we entered. I lowered my eyes and continued to follow Lydia's direction with David walking closely behind me. I could feel all eyes on me, but I dared not to check whose they were. My senses had become acutely heightened and it felt as if someone had muted the room. All I could hear now was a high-pitched ringing, accompanied by a combination of my own gasps for breath and my heart beating louder and louder, thumping against my inner ear, like a pedal to a kickdrum. *Lub-dub, lub-dub, lub-dub.*

My throat was by now throbbing and my tongue was so dry it stuck to the roof of my mouth every time I tried to swallow. Whether he recognised my plight, or it was just his gentlemanly manners, I was so grateful when David poured us both a cup of water from the carafe that sat next to a mixed collection of cups of all sizes and designs. As I painfully sipped away at the water, I dared myself a quick look around my environment. *Just a quick glance, then back to David.*

My scan detected the health visitor sitting next to me. She offered me a warm smile. *She made it!* When I'd spoken with her the day before, I'd learned that she hadn't been aware of the hearing. By then it was 4pm and with such short notice and her already full day of appointments, she'd been unsure if she would be able to attend. That's what Lydia had been counting on. I was so relieved to see her, that I sipped some more water and dared a second glance, to which I saw Gillian and the other police officer, along with David, all sitting on my side of the table. *Okay, that wasn't too bad.*

I watched David take out an A4 notepad and a black *Montblanc* fine-tipped pen, before removing his reading glasses from their case and giving them a wipe. I didn't want to remove my eyes from him; his was the only image that I found safe, but I had to see who my judges were. *Quickly, Kemi, and don't make eye contact.*

I raised my glass and sipped. With my next peek I saw Lydia sitting beside another woman whom I didn't recognise, but from her lanyard I assumed she was another social worker. *And back to David.* His face was now looking across the table and despite his best effort to remain assured, I could see solemness starting to spread, along with a hint of confusion. I felt my stomach drop and my throat clamp shut further like a rusty vice. *What is it?* I scanned across the table one final time, this time forgetting to hide my glance behind my cup, attempting to find what had triggered David's attention.

There was another woman - a minute-taker - sitting next to Michael. *Oh my God – Michelle!* Even more terror flowed through my veins, supplying fear to every single cell. *What is she doing here?* Children were not allowed to be present at these hearings, and yet, there she was, sitting beside her dad, scowling brazenly in front of her audience. My mind was sent reeling. *This is bad!*

As I sat engrossed in my thoughts, I began to realise that most of Lydia's stitch-up had indeed succeeded. There was no representation from education. Considering the majority of Michelle's week was spent at school, her teachers would have been reliable witnesses to Michelle's behaviour and character, but with Lydia's late arrangement for the hearing, and especially with it being announced after the schools had closed for the summer holidays, none were present. Not only were they not present, but nor was there a background report. Nothing. The same went for the children's doctor. Not present and no report. Child minder, none. Sandra had tried numerous times to contact Lydia, but was always told she was unavailable, and she never returned her calls. And yet Michelle, who was definitely not supposed to be here, was. And worst of all, the three children who were 'potentially at risk' had not been seen once by a single social worker. No home visits meant no reports.

David challenged these points and Lydia dismissed them all; it wasn't *her* fault it was now the summer holidays. When he went on to question Michelle's presence at the meeting and its legalities, Michelle stood up lurching across the table at him, interrupting him repeatedly whilst unveiling her aggressive side, before finally challenging him with: "Why the hell are *you* even here?"

The room was now super charged to an electric atmosphere. I felt ashamed by her behaviour, but glad for its exposure in front of the witnesses. Lydia sat in deafening silence, barely acknowledging Michelle's outbursts, whereas Michael was horrified and repeatedly told Michelle to sit down and be quiet. Michael had only found out about the allegations the day before and must have been sitting there very confused and concerned. The whole environment was toxic, but at least *I* knew what was going on – he had no idea.

"Why didn't you come and speak to me?" Michael questioned directly, blocking out the chaos that he found himself surrounded by. These were the first words he'd said to me since finding out.

"I don't know," I replied honestly.

I'd wanted him to know - and it would have been the right thing to do - but I hadn't known how to tell him. I felt a guilt occupy my churning stomach as I looked across to him dropping his head in disbelief. We've never spoken since.

Next, Gillian read out her report, highlighting how she'd been prevented from re-interviewing Michelle by Lydia and stating that she believed that speaking to Michelle again would've proved Craig's innocence. She confirmed in her conclusion that she was satisfied that her investigation into Craig had found no evidence to support Michelle's claims, and therefore she had no need for any further involvement. Lydia didn't once bother to look up from the table the entire time Gillian was addressing the room.

When it came time for Lydia to speak, she arranged her paperwork astutely, while sliding her chair in closer and clearing her throat to address the table. *Here we go.* Wave after wave of anxiety flushed through my body in anticipation of Lydia revealing her hand. *And she's off.*

She caught me by surprise and went straight for my jugular by opening with a redacted, brief account of my "history of mental illness"; my anorexia - the anorexia that I'd been suffering from for many years, and still was.

I wasn't surprised that she opened with my anorexia; I had expected that. What caught me was *how* she divulged it, along with her level of fine detail. Rather than calling it anorexia, she intentionally referred to it as my "*mental* illness". "*Mental* illness" this and "*mental* illness" that. With every intimate detail she disclosed, the more she indulged in making eye contact with me, and the more I became aware that her words had been supplied by my mum. She spoke of things that only my mum knew and even somethings that I thought she didn't. She'd quickly and carefully painted her *mental* image and was wasting no time in delivering her claim.

"She has a mental illness and I suspect she's suffering from postnatal depression too," she lectured, now ignoring my presence.

I took a deep breath, steadying myself to contest her absurd argument, but I was too slow, as my visibly irritated health visitor interjected.

"Excuse me," she interrupted with disbelief while pointing both her hands towards me, as if ushering Lydia's eyes in my direction, to remind her that I was in fact present. "Kemi is not mentally ill and she certainly doesn't have postnatal depression," she corrected clearly. The anxiety in my petrified stomach surged, trying to burst its way past my inflamed throat.

"Is that right?" Lydia snorted, rejecting her with a look of contempt. "Her baby's only four and a half months old - you *can't* know for sure." Her scorn was replaced with a confident smugness.

"I *can* be sure. With all the assessments we've already carried out; her six-weeks postnatal, and her four-months visit, not to mention all the home visits I've carried out and all the weigh-ins for baby Tola . . . "

"Well, she's had it before," Lydia rudely interrupted under her breath while rolling her eyes in an over dramatic fashion, referring to when I had Sola. *How dare you!*

"She *is* mental; I should know," Michelle announced with perfect timing to collaborate with Lydia.

My whole body stiffened as the room fell into meltdown. Voices over spoke voices, disgusting slurs were flung at me quite openly from the ever-glaring Michelle, who, every time I tried to speak, repeatedly shouted over me: "liar".

"Michelle!" Michael finally recalled sternly and with frustration. *What must he be thinking? He knows who you are, Kemi. He knows you're a good mum and he knows what Michelle's behaviour can be like.*

Michelle, at age 15, continued to be disruptive throughout the remainder of the meeting and made further allegations that Craig had abused her and that I'd known about it, and that I'd supplied her with cocaine. Lydia revelled in Michelle's outbursts, noting down all of her wild accusations, while I could only look on in horror; helpless. Nothing I could say would help me. This was no longer about the safety of my children; this was about destroying me.

My family had gone from being complete, to being completely broken, with the joys of a new baby nothing more than a distant memory, and the ever-present pressure of the new 'family' home mortgage repayments draining me both physically and financially. I explained I was having to work both during the day while the children were at school, and again in the evenings when they were in bed, just so I could earn enough money to pay the bills, as I was the only one allowed to work. I asked when Craig could work again, and why he couldn't work while the children were at school.

"I don't care about Craig working, or you for that matter. My only care is for the children," Lydia scolded with utter contempt, as if I was a criminal.

"Erm, excuse me Lydia," David cut in, defiantly dropping his pen with opposition, struggling to contain his bemusement. "I don't think you can affect Kemi's business. Are you prepared for this family to lose their home?"

"It's not my concern if Kemi gets to keep her lifestyle," she scathed, "I'm only interested in keeping her children safe, and that's still to be determined." She glared at me as she delivered her words, sending a chill to my core. *I'm going to lose my children.*

As Lydia brought the meeting to a close, she concluded that with her having concerns for my history of "mental illness" along with everything and anything Michelle alleged, the three other children should be put on the child protection 'at risk' register. However, Michelle wasn't, as she wasn't in my care anymore and was therefore deemed no longer 'at risk'. This didn't feel like it was about Craig anymore; it was now all about me. I was devastated.

And that was that. No appeal, no arguments; case closed. I was all over the place. My mind was in a whirl, spiralling at what had just happened, and my stomach was sickened by the smirks of satisfaction on Lydia's face. David quickly rose to his feet and gathered up his belongings.

"Okay, Kemi. Let's go – don't talk to anyone," he advised, before leading me out of the room.

I'm not sure if his order was to protect me from my emotions, or to stop him from saying something *he* might later regret. I struggled to keep pace with his surprisingly fast, quick-march as we exited the stuffy, sterile waiting room, and I felt a sudden light-headedness, accompanied by a queasiness with my breathing becoming accelerated. By the time I'd followed David into the reception area, he was already a good few feet ahead of me, so didn't see me stopping dead in my tracks.

What's he doing here? A shot of adrenaline was administered, causing a falling sensation to wobble my legs and a cold sweat to trickle down my back. I stood completely motionless, oblivious to all the on-goers forced to walk around me like a puddle. Just when I thought my living nightmare couldn't possibly torment me any further, I was quickly corrected. I'm unaware how long I stood there, rooted, before David interrupted my trance.

"Kemi, what is it?" he urged, concerned at the shock etched all over my face.

I heard him speak, but I was too preoccupied to process his words. I didn't look at him; I couldn't, my eyes wouldn't leave their terror.

"Kemi?" he repeated, this time shorter and sharper, and with a shake of my shoulder. His jolting allowed for time to catch up, and although delayed, I managed an answer to his question.

"Rab."

David turned to see where my eyes landed, just as Lydia walked past us and over towards Rab. Suddenly it dawned on me. The things that Lydia had said, that I knew my mum couldn't have known, Rab knew; and he had shared. As we watched their interaction, we could tell that they knew each other and I could see she was smiling. Rab finally looked over and saw me staring back at him gobsmacked. He gave me a half smile that filled me with chills. I knew what that smile meant: payback.

David and I remained in silence the whole journey to my house, and even beyond, with not a word shared until after I'd collapsed onto the sofa. I no longer had any energy to stand. My head throbbed with an occasional searing, stabbing pain behind my eye and my throat stung like water to a fresh papercut. I couldn't think straight - but I had to. *Rab.*

It had unnerved me to see *that* smile, full of delight, on his face upon receiving Lydia's summary. My brain began its ungovernable carousel once more; fearful thoughts spun around in my mind, again and again, teasing and consuming me to the point I was oblivious that David was now sitting beside me with two cups of coffee. He coughed, not to clear his throat, but to announce his presence and regain my awareness.

"David," I began, snapping back into life, "what does this mean? Why was Rab there? He had the boys – so, where were they? Do you think . . . "

"Kemi," David interrupted gently, halting my rambling and making me want to cry. He hadn't offended me; I just felt that if I kept talking, I could distract my tears from flowing. "Kemi, listen. In all my years of the service, I have *never* experienced anything like that before," David stated gravely. "This woman is gunning for you and she's too stupid to even try to hide it. She can't take your children, or she would have done so today." He looked at me wide-eyed, scanning for any response that I'd heard him. A new sensation entered my body, helping to side-track my tears. Anger.

"David, she's going to try and use Rab against me," I warned with unequivocal certainty. "She's . . . "

"Kemi," he interrupted again, "forget Rab for a minute – you're missing the point."

This was the first meaningful conversation we'd engaged in since leaving the council offices, and it was now becoming patently clear that he'd waited to the confines of my four walls to discuss his observations. Looking through his notes, he began shuffling uncomfortably with what he had to say.

"*Due to Kemi's mixed-race and mental health, I have to determine whether these children are safe* . . . Kemi, she can't say that. Look, I've quoted her." David's finger furiously prodded at his notepad. "She spoke *and* wrote about your colour . . . documented it, as if it was relevant in regard to you being a good mother."

I was shocked. I'd heard it, but I'd also been conditioned to accept it as 'normal'. Of all the names mentioned in her report, including Craig's, mine was the only one that stated the person's race.

"She can't do that - it's not relevant. Kemi, it's racist and illegal."

"But no one stopped her," I pointed out. "Her boss would have signed her report off, or at least she will. *She'll* think it's okay". I was now enraged.

"But Kemi, that doesn't matter – she's put it on paper. She said you have mental health problems, and with no proof. Then she wouldn't let your health visitor defend you." He took a breath to steady his agitation before continuing. "She had no education, no health-care, no child-care. Nothing. She's even ignoring the police report and obstructing them from doing their investigation. Kemi, Michelle was at the Child Welfare Hearing - the child 'victim' - she should never have been present."

He noticed his own agitated animation, and with embarrassment at losing his composure, forced himself another deep breath.

"She's blatantly breaking procedure to try and discredit you – we know she is - and she's proved us right with her so-called report. We have serious grounds for a complaint, and if you're happy for me to begin, I will start it this evening."

"David, I don't know what I'd do without you," I said honestly.

It was true. At times, it had felt as if it was me against the world, but with David by my side, I now stood a chance.

"Let's focus on this for now," he replied offering a genuine smile, "and not the horrors Lydia could bring on you, Kemi." I allowed a moment to pass to try to focus on his advice, but I was too worked up.

"Well, she's going down the wrong path anyway if she thinks Rab's any use; he wasn't even allowed to see the boys overnight because of all the smacking," I said confidently, to reassure myself.

"You're right Kemi," he exclaimed with a slap of his knee. He could sense I was trying to focus on the positives, as rare as they were, and like an encouraging father to his child, over enthused his praise.

"I mean, it's not as if the boys would ever agree to living with him." Despite knowing my words to be true, the pit of my stomach flinched at the thought.

"Well Kemi," he began, followed by what must have been his first sip of at best, a warm cup of coffee, "that's your trump card: you're an excellent mother and the boys adore you. I know your children – they'd testify to that," he said taking a handkerchief from his pocket to dab dry his greying moustache.

"Yeah, if anyone ever takes the time to see them. David, I'm going to have to tell them *something* now."

I was making a choice to be honest with my children now that I was sure Lydia was trying to take them from me; they had a right to know. A chill ran down my spine as I began to think about *that* conversation.

"I agree, Kemi. It's now *that* serious." He gave me a sober look. "You've no room for mistakes or regrets," he warned.

"Should I call Rab to see what's going on?" I asked.

"No, hold fire. The boys are due back tomorrow. Wait and ask him face-to-face . . . but don't let him know what you suspect. He may be stupid enough to say something about it." David looked to me to see if I was in agreement. He saw my doubts. "Kemi, I know you may not be able to resist calling him, but you need to be careful now; there are a lot of pieces at play here and you are their target."

I agreed. I didn't want to further upset myself and I didn't want to make Rab angry while he had the boys. I knew Rab and I knew I had to let him make his first move before I could decide what I was going to do. I decided I would wait until he brought the boys back the next day.

I didn't have long to myself after David left. Before I knew it, Sandra had brought Tola home and then Craig arrived earlier than normal. He was desperate to hear what had happened at the hearing, but with Tola having been very unsettled since arriving home, I hadn't been able to call him. He settled Tola down for a nap and we finally got time to speak. He was furious at what I had to share.

"This isn't right – it's not fair," Craig challenged. "Why was Rab there? Where was my invite? I've done nothing wrong – the police have said as much – yet everyone gets a say apart from me?"

He was hurting. He'd been accused of an horrendous crime, then exiled from his own home and family, with no idea when he could return, and then he had to idly sit by, watching me slave away to try and stay above water, while being attacked from every direction; powerless.

"I know. David said they're not giving you your rights as Tola's dad; that you should have been informed." He went silent.

"Kemi, I'm going to go and see a lawyer. I need to know what my rights are," he decided.

"I think you need to," I agreed. "Craig, we need to know just how many rights *we* have because I'm pretty sure Lydia will stomp all over them. Being honest apparently doesn't defend or protect you."

The wedding

"I don't know *what* to think, Kemi," Rab confessed down the receiver. While his words were neutral and sounded almost genuine, his tone let him down, reminding me of how Lydia had sounded when she first met David, before she found out he was supporting me and before she showed him her true colours. It was the morning after the hearing and I'd stuck to my agreement with David; as much as my rage had wanted me to phone Rab to tell him that I knew he was part of the stitch up, I hadn't. Now that Rab had called me however, it was taking every ounce of what restraint I had remaining not to call him out, so I kept my talking to a minimum and allowed him to speak freely, hoping that he would reveal the extent of his involvement with Lydia, and if possible, what they all had planned for me next.

"Lydia invited me down to the Social Work Department - I only found out why *after* your meeting. I mean, it's just not sunk in yet," he continued in his best attempt at sounding sincere.

Liar. Lydia said things in that meeting only you could have told her. I knew not to believe him, but knew better not to challenge him; he would tell me more if he believed he was convincing me. *Just play the game Kemi.* I took a deep breath and buried my desire to confront him.

"Rab, Michelle is lying," I stated simply.

I wasn't trying to convince him – I didn't have to. I was simply standing my ground while calmly drawing a line in it. Which side he chose to stand on was up to him. I listened for his next move.

"You can't say that about your own daughter," he rebuked scoldingly, "I mean, what will people think?"

I felt my jaw clench, desperate to unleash all that I knew down the phone at him before slamming it down, but I somehow managed to keep my tone unmoved.

"Rab, I don't really give a shit about what people think; I just care that the truth comes out," I replied.

There was a silence and I could tell that he'd not anticipated such an apathetic reaction, leaving him unsatisfied.

"Should I keep the boys for another night? I don't mind," he offered, pretending to be doing me a favour, "you sound exhausted, and you've got Tola to think about. You don't want to overdo it . . . and get sick again."

Ah, and there it is. The supportive ex-husband concerned for the sick mother of his children act. And with his offer I now knew he was going to go for me using my mental health. *You bastard!* I was furious, but I still wouldn't show him that. I didn't have the energy to fight him and the longer I remained on the phone the higher the chances grew that I would expose myself.

"Okay Rab, have them until tomorrow then," I accepted, before ending the call without having risen to his bait.

The following day, when Sandra came to collect Tola, she suggested that I should come back with them to her house. David had been working tirelessly on my complaint and was just adding his finishing touches, and he seemed keen to get it posted as soon as possible. I couldn't believe the dedication he was showing me. Knowing I had his support allowed me to feel more alive than I had done in weeks.

When we arrived, David greeted me still in his royal blue, tartan pyjamas and thick royal blue, fleece dressing gown, with a hug and a cup of coffee. He looked wired and raring to go despite his attire. He led me through to his office where he sat down at his PC.

"There's a copy in there for both you and Craig," he said tapping at a red ring binder folder with a white label on its front reading 'Private & Confidential' in black, "but let me read it out to you. Stop me if you notice any mistakes."

He'd worked very hard on my complaint, raising points on every failing of procedure we'd encountered, advising the department on what *should* have happened by cross-referencing their own guidelines, questioning them on why they hadn't followed procedure in the first place, and most importantly, concluding by asking why my mental health was under question considering my doctor hadn't been spoken to, and why my race was of any relevance in regard to the safety of my children?

When he finished reading it, he swung round from his monitor to look up at me with a grin of satisfaction.

"David it's brilliant. I can't believe how good you've made my case sound," I exclaimed. Hearing it all read aloud and written in the clearest way possible filled me with a renewed hope.

"Kemi, it's the facts. What's happening to you is a crime in itself and this woman is in a position of power. She needs to be stopped." This I knew in every part of my being.

I spent the rest of my morning with David, Sandra and Tola just being. The boys were due back later in the afternoon and I didn't fancy being at home alone. My home had become a place where I felt both terrified to be alone, and terrified to have company. In truth, it didn't feel like much of a home at all. It was now my workplace, located in no man's land, where I was fair game to be attacked. It was nice to get out of that house for a while.

The morning slipped into afternoon, as did many fresh coffees into my never empty cup. Sandra insisted that I stayed for lunch before heading back to my house. While feeding Tola some yoghurt and myself the *Ryvita* and jam crackers Sandra had prepared, my mobile began to ring.

"It's Rab," I sighed, checking my phone. *He can't be at my house already - the boys aren't due back for two hours.* I felt a sudden pang of anxiety stir. "Sandra, sorry, can you take Tola? Hello," I answered, bracing myself for whatever lay at the other end.

"Kemi, it's Rab. I'm keeping the boys for a couple more days," he blurted out over a backdrop of chaos. His tone was back to its usual self: irritated and domineering.

"No, Mummy, no. We want to come home Mum," Dayo cried in the background. I felt my heartbeat quicken.

"Rab, put Dayo on the phone," I demanded, rising to my feet to pace the length of the kitchen, one step per beat, startling David to spring out of his chair in alarm, his eyes narrowing with concentration and his frown forcing his eyebrows to drop, almost blocking his line of vision.

"No," Rab snorted, dismissing my request. "Dayo be quiet – Kemi, I'm keeping them." His bullishness baffled me and brought my blood to boil.

"Mummy . . . Mummy. Let *me* speak to her," Sola now cried out from behind Rab's voice, somewhere in the distance.

"Rab, I have full custody of the boys," I hissed at him, "and I'll come and remove them with the police if I have to."

"What?" David let slip, concerned by my warning. "Kemi is everything okay?" he whispered in shock.

"Put Dayo on the phone. Now," I repeated, daring him to refuse me again. I wasn't playing. He needed to know that if he was going to try anything, I would be ready to fight back and that he would not win, not at the expense of my children.

"No, he's upset. I don't want *you* upsetting him more," Rab manipulated and rejected once again. I could feel my hand shaking with rage. David and Sandra both watched on, frozen in silence, their faces etched with a preserved distress.

"Rab, if you *do not* put him on the phone, right now, I'm hanging up and calling the police. I'll tell them you're refusing to return my children; how do you think your visitation will go then?" I warned. He went silent, allowing me to hear Dayo and Sola still maintaining their pleas to come home. "Now Rab."

"Mum?" Dayo pitched-in between sobs and gasps for breath, his hoarse croak evidence to how long he had been in distress.

"Baby, please don't be sad. It's okay," I tried to comfort. "You're coming home soon . . . "

"No Mum," he whispered, interrupting both me and his cries, "Dad said we *have* to stay . . . because you're too busy?" I could hear the fear and confusion in his voice and instantly felt a heat sweep over and through me, enraging me. *How dare he use the boys to get to me.*

"No baby, that's not true," I began, feigning a smile down the receiver in hope of reassuring, "your dad must have got mixed up. Not to worry though, it's all fixed now."

"It's okay Sola, we *are* going home - Mum said. No Sola, just wait - *I'm* talking first." Dayo's voice sounded better already, but Sola still sounded

226

confused.

"Kemi, is everything okay?" David whispered again, only this time he brought himself closer beside me and leaned his head into my line of vision, insisting that he scan my eyes. I paused and nodded solemnly, with an eye-roll and a prolonged, deep breath that in turn released slowly, and heavily, down both nostrils.

"Dayo, sweetheart, put Sola on and I will speak to you when you get home – okay?" My pacing returned, only this time shorter and faster.

"Okay Mum," Dayo replied, handing the phone to his brother.

"Mummy, I hate it here," Sola unloaded, brazen and unapologetic. "And I hate Dad . . . he's so mean. He's done his angry face all day – just because we said we wanted to come home. Mummy . . . why *did* we sleep two nights? You know I hate that." I could see his frowning, pouted face.

"Sola, it's fixed now so no need to be upset," I appealed, not only to comfort him, but to halt what I imagined would be Rab's ever-growing irritation at Sola's undiluted honesty. "We'll speak when you come home. Okay?" I encouraged.

"Okay Mum, but . . . " he stopped and paused. "Okay Mum."

"You're such a good boy, Solie. Put your dad back on the phone," I asked with a friendly tone, signalling to him that the panic was now over.

"Okay. Love you Mum," he answered, quite content to move on.

"Love you too baby." I heard Sola sit the phone down. *Okay Kemi, remain composed.* Sandra and David dissolved into obscurity, as did my surroundings, as I cleared my racing throat and closed my eyes to fine tune my ear. I stood still.

"Yes?" Rab grunted, his annoyance choking him.

"Will you have them back for 4pm?" I questioned clearly.

"Yes," he spat with venom before hanging up. *Click.*

"Bastard," I exclaimed, finally permitting my frustration some release. I was shaking with fury, and to the kitchen carpet's delight, I had to take a seat before I could begin to fill in Sandra and David on what had just happened; Rab had well and truly thrown his hat into the ring.

I decided I would speak to the boys when they came home in a way their young minds could accept. I didn't want to scare them, but at the same time I knew I had to be honest, for their safety. With Michelle, Lydia, my mum and now Rab all out to get me, I couldn't - and wouldn't - run the risk of the boys being used or manipulated.

When they arrived home just before dinner, Rab didn't even bother to bring them to the door, but instead opted to drop them off in the driveway before driving off.

"Okay boys," I began from the dining table while watching them both make light work of their Neapolitan ice cream desserts, "we need to have a wee chat about something." I could feel my mouth dry up while the goosebumps on my forearms erupted, causing my hairs to stand to attention.

"Yes Mum?" Dayo said giving me his full attention, while Sola, spoon in mouth, raised me his thumb.

"It's about Michelle . . . "

"Oh, Mum!" Sola interrupted, before hurriedly slurping and gulping down the remains in his mouth. "We were supposed to see her, but you said we could come home, that's why Dad was so angry with you," he quickly stated with a smile, delighted that he remembered what he'd wanted to tell me on the phone.

What? Oh my God! This is a nightmare . . . what would've happened if they'd seen her? What would she have said to them? A cold sweat came over me causing my nerves to accelerate.

"Sola. Dayo. That was naughty of Dad to do that. I don't want you to see Michelle without me – and he knows that." I could hear my voice become shaky. This was not how I'd wanted to start this conversation.

"Why Mummy?" Dayo asked innocently while whipping his ice cream to blend the colours.

"Yeah Mummy, why?" Sola chorused wide-mouthed, revealing his ice cream-clad tongue.

"Boys, when Michelle came back from holiday, she went to Nanny's to live for a while," I continued.

"Why Mum . . . is she annoyed at you again?" Dayo interrupted to offer his theory.

"No darling," I began. *How have I ended up here? Breathe.* "Michelle told the police that Craig had done bad things to her," I said gently. I felt my heart breaking.

"What?" Sola said aghast, his shock slackening his grip, causing his spoon to drop with a clang as it landed in his near empty bowl.

"Mum, why would Michelle do that?" Dayo blurted, angry, shocked and confused.

"Why Mum?" Sola asked as tears freely rolled down from his eyes. "What's going to happen? Will Daddy Craig go to jail?" His head dropped to rest on his tiny forearms, burying his tear sodden face in the table. Sola was now heartbroken. I moved around the table to comfort them.

"No Sola; I promise," I said, wrapping my pinkie around his. With that, he raised his head and buried it in my chest, before I drew the now sobbing Dayo in to join us in our hug.

"Listen boys," I said gently with a reassuring squeeze, "there's a woman who'll be coming to visit us once a week. It's her job to make sure children are looked after properly. She wants to meet you both, to speak to you to see if I look after you properly," I said carefully. I felt Sola's crumpled body wrestle out from under my arm, resuscitated.

"No. No way. Why? You're the best mum," Sola defended, standing to his feet in defiance. The sheer thought that someone could possibly think that his mummy was naughty had infuriated him, and he was having none of it. He was always so protective of me.

"Mum, can she take us away from you?" Dayo asked with genuine concern strained all over his face.

"Never," I replied with certainty, trying to quickly extinguish his fears. "Boys, that will never happen. Okay? There's nothing to be scared of. All you have to do is be honest – that's what Mummy and Daddy Craig are doing; then Lydia will know the truth and she'll be happy." I tried to make my voice sound light and even performed a smile, but their deadly-worried, little faces saw right through it.

"Who?" Sola asked.

"Lydia? She's the lady that looks out for children - to make sure they're safe," I answered with another attempt at a smile.

"What about the police, Mum?" Dayo asked with concern.

"They've spoken to me and to Daddy Craig, and they don't think we're bad, and once Lydia finds that out too, she'll say it's okay for Daddy Craig to come back home."

The questions and the tears went on for quite a while, but by the time they'd both dried up I felt both boys had understood that they must always tell the truth - no matter what - and then things would go back to normal. I'd convinced my children - but not myself.

Craig met with a local lawyer two days later seeking clarity on his rights. He found out that his rights were in fact being breached. He, like Rab, should have been informed that a hearing involving Tola was taking place and he should also have been informed that Tola had been put on the 'At Risk' register. Neither of these had happened. He learned that legally he had every right to continue to see Tola. The lawyer recommended that he should write to the Social Work Department on Craig's behalf to challenge why he wasn't being kept informed and to inform them that Craig would be exercising his parental rights to see his daughter, and the two boys he had been fathering for nearly five years, in my presence. He also advised him it was legally sound for him to commence working from home. We only had one treatment room, so if Craig was working, it meant that either the children were at school, or with me.

By the time Craig had finished updating me on his meeting with the lawyer, he had a spark back in his eyes and sounded more optimistic; positively pragmatic.

"Kemi," he said, sliding closer to me on the sofa to cradle my hands in his, "I think we should get married." He caught me off-guard and at first, I thought he was joking.

"Erm . . . okay," I replied, pretending to take my time to decide. "Except . . . oh no, I can't . . . I'm already sworn to marry my *fiancé* later in the year - or the beginning of the next," I teased.

"No . . . " he smiled, "I mean now." His face straightened and his eyes danced with mine.

"What . . . are you serious?" I asked, shocked by the timing of his proposition.

"Well," he encouraged while freeing a hand to nervously twist at his hair, "we're getting married anyway - if you still want to that is - so why wait? Why not now?" His eyes penetrated mine.

"Craig . . . I don't know," I said dropping my eyes to my feet, "and it's not a question of 'if I want to' - of course I do – always," I assured.

"Then Kemi . . . " he interrupted, "let's. I want us to be a family - a proper family – now," he stated simply, but firmly, resting his case.

I paused. I knew what he was feeling - I was feeling it too. We'd wanted to get married for many reasons, but right now the main one was to *legally* bind our beautiful family; the family we'd created together through our love for one another. I turned so I could look at him completely.

"Are you asking me to marry you, Mr. Ferguson?" I smiled. Craig responded to my playfulness by instinctively going down on one knee while looking into my eyes with strength and seriousness.

"Olukemi Helen Adebowale Ogunyemi, I've loved you from the moment you stumbled into that auditorium, and into my life. Will you do me the honour of being my wife?" He was trying to act so cool, but his cheeky smile couldn't hide his lip quivering. That told me he was feeling vulnerable. I could only nod as the tears of deep love overwhelmed me, rendering me speechless.

As Craig stood and brought me into his embrace, for that moment, we both forgot about all the horrors that were trying to destroy us and our family. In my mind, we would be making a declaration; we would be showing Lydia that we were serious in our unity as a family - no doubts.

"It would be quite a statement," I shared.

"It would be Kemi - but that's not why I'm asking," he defended.

"I know," I reassured, as I snuggled in tighter to his chest, "but it is helpful."

Craig went and put in our Banns at the local registry office and returned with a date for our wedding - Wednesday 17th of August - just three days short of the fifth anniversary of us meeting. Having heard nothing back from his lawyer's letter to the Social Work Department, Craig started to follow his lawyer's advice and began to visit the children more regularly during the daytime.

He took me and the children away for a couple of days to Peebles, a little town in the Scottish Borders, to see if I could get something to wear for our wedding. We'd been numerous times in the past and found it pretty and quaint. Plus, no one knew us there.

While Craig went for a stroll, window-shopping with Tola, I went dress-shopping with the boys. They were so excited to be my assistants and had explicitly advised what I should be looking for.

Dayo wanted a traditional white wedding dress - which made me laugh

- I was never a white wedding dress kind of girl. Whereas Sola, on the other hand, didn't care for the style, as long as it was red.

Walking down the high street, a boy in each hand, I suddenly felt a pang of sadness that my gran was not involved in my wedding, and especially with helping me choose my dress. I felt my throat jump and my eyes well, but then I looked down and saw how happy the boys were to be a part of the wedding. *Keep it together Kemi.* I put my sad thoughts to the back of my mind as I entered the tiny *Monsoon* shop.

Upon entering the jam-packed, yet surprisingly well-aired shop, we were greeted by a pleasant assistant offering help.

"No thank you, I'm just looking," I replied with a friendly smile trying not to show my anxiety.

I hated shopping - especially for clothes. There are always a lot of mirrors in clothes shops: in the changing rooms, hiding on pillars, in between racks and even behind the till. Full length mirrors, short mirrors and mirrors that run the full length and height of the wall. Mirrors everywhere, and all under bright fluorescent lighting – no hiding places, or very few at most. Clothes shopping had become a game of hide and seek, with me trying never to be caught in their view or that of the shop assistant.

"Mummy's looking for a wedding dress," Dayo desperately divulged with excitement, instantly giving away my hiding place to the enemy.

"Yes, a red one!" Sola added confidently, as his little eyes widened. "Mum, there!" he gasped, pointing to the deep scarlet material that dressed a mannequin hanging in the far corner of the shop. She wore a beautiful scarlet dress with a layered, fine net of the same deep scarlet and matching bodice with delicately sewn silvery pearlescent beads.

"Ah," the shop assistant said as she approached the hanging dress, "this is the only one we've had in, although . . . ," she looked me up and down, "it looks like it would fit you perfectly. Shall I take it down for you?" she asked while starting to undress the mannequin, revealing that the dress was in fact a two piece.

The bodice could have stood up on its own, such was the rich material and expert craftsmanship, and the skirt had a flawless waist band and layered skirt that kicked out perfectly to rest just below the knee. The boys were silenced by its beauty, signalling we all agreed this was the perfect dress.

"The changing room is over there if you'd like to try it on," the assistant keenly advised moving onto the next, natural progression of the shopping experience.

"No," my high-pitched voice squeaked, causing a look of confusion to sweep over her face. I hadn't meant for my answer to be so severe – it was a panicked reflex, but I quickly tried to recover. "My husband has our baby – she'll be needing fed soon. She'll be screaming the place down by now," I excused, trying to avoid the distortion room. I was terrified its mirrors would lie to me and ruin my wedding dress. I would not take that chance. Suddenly the tiny shop didn't feel so well ventilated and I broke out into a hot fluster.

"You said it was a size 10, yes?" I continued, keeping her on the backfoot. She nodded, still confused. "Perfect," I assured with a masquerade smile. "Could you please wrap it, and bag it too - in case my husband is the one who comes back to collect it," I rambled trying to hide my panic. "I don't want him to see it."

"Yes, of course," she agreed, still looking perplexed. I could see she was struggling to comprehend how I could be spending so much money – and on a wedding dress no less - and not be trying it on.

"Thank you - I really do have to go - the baby," I said as I gathered the boys and opened the door, leaving, feeling quite embarrassed. I explained to Craig what happened – the stomach-churning anxiety that came on like a flick of a switch, so he went back to collect it.

He took it home and hung it up in Tola's nursery, before being instructed not to return to her room until after the wedding. My beautiful dress hung there, untouched and out of sight, for nearly two weeks before I could find the courage to try it on.

The next day would be our first visit from Lydia. I'd advised her in advance that the time she intended to visit meant that Tola wouldn't be present, but she didn't want to rearrange. I invited her to join us in the game of *Connect 4* I was in the middle of playing with the children when she arrived.

"No Kemi, I'll observe," she politely rejected.

Dayo and Sola looked on puzzled; how could this woman just sit there observing, with no desire to join in or interact? After a while she suggested that the boys continued to play while we went to the adjoining open lounge area to speak more freely.

"Kemi," she began in a lowered voice, "you can't let Craig come and see the children - or work - it doesn't matter what his lawyer says." She informed me as if she was doing me a favour – a heads-up.

"Erm, sorry Lydia," I replied, feeling baffled by her approach, "but you're wrong. Craig *can* work from here; the boys will be back at school and Tola will be with Sandra."

"No." she interrupted harshly while profusely shaking her head.

"Excuse me, Lydia. You have no right to try and destroy my business - that feels personal," I challenged with a neutral tone so as not to prick the ears of the boys, but with a stony expression so that she knew I wasn't backing down.

"What? No, it's not personal," she dismissed with a coy, plastic smile "that's how it works," she insisted as if it was fact.

"Craig has the right to spend time with the children. It's doing them harm not seeing him, and he's never alone with them," I advised her; I wasn't asking permission.

"No - you can't do that," she flustered.

"Check fathers' rights Lydia," I replied. By her refastening of the coat that she'd refused to take off, she'd decided her visit was over. She said good-bye to the boys and left.

The week before, my dad had come to my house, unannounced, to speak to me. When I saw his car pull up the driveway past my living room window, I hurriedly ran out to defend what I assumed would be another attack of some sort.

As I got to the driver's window, I could see he was alone. He tried to open his door to get out, but I positioned myself to stand in the open doorway, preventing his transition from seated to standing, leaving him sat awkwardly with his legs stretched out of the car.

"Dad what are you doing here?" I asked agitated.

It's taken you two months to come and see me. I was angry that he hadn't come and seen me earlier and had instead chosen to leave me to the brutality I was enduring - heavily influenced by my mother. *You are so weak.* He knew me, and he knew I wouldn't lie about my own child, yet his silence had supported my mum. *Pathetic.*

"Hi Kemkem," he opened, with a tone that belied our current dynamics, "I'm here to see you, and the boys, and to take them to spend time with your mum."

"Have you lost your mind?" I asked in utter disbelief. "Dad this is serious. This is going to destroy my family - and you know she's lying." I threw the words at him in a primal, defensive voice. He lowered his head in silence unable to look me in the eye.

"I'll have to leave here - after I've proved my own daughter to be a liar. A liar Dad!" I scolded. I could feel my body torque with tension and unadulterated fury.

"If you'd bothered to care about her, you would have helped, rather than leaving me to the wolves and forcing me to expose her publicly. I will have to leave. Do you not understand, or do you just not care?" I rattled directly at him.

He raised his head, but still said nothing. Disappointment filled me, making me light-headed. The face-to-face realisation of my own father willing to sacrifice me, and his granddaughter, just so he could keep his head warm and cosy, buried in the sand, fuelled me.

"Dad just leave - and don't come back," I said, looking down at him, straight in the eyes, feeling the same familiar feeling of abandonment filling me, like it had my entire childhood. In that moment I realised it had never gone away, even after he'd come back into my life as a child. I'd just buried it deep in my memories, heart and soul.

I walked away, dejectedly furious. As I approached the house, I could see Dayo skipping up the driveway, passing my dad as he drove down. He

233

stopped to talk to his grandad through the car window, and in true Dayo fashion, shared information.

"Mum and Craig are getting married. Are you coming?"

Normally this would have caused a whole array of anxieties, but now, I felt I no longer knew my dad, nor what he would do with the information, so I just ignored Dayo's announcement and closed my door.

# # #

I had a rare moment to myself in the early morning of the eve of the wedding. I'd managed to creep out of bed without disturbing the deep-sleeping boys, or Tola, who lay in slumber in her cradle beside my bed. Tiptoeing, I entered Tola's bright pink nursery. I didn't need to put the light on, as the early rays of the morning sun beamed through the *Velux* window, providing just enough light to see. I was so nervous as I quietly closed the frosted glass door behind me.

There was a small, pink mirror in there that stood upright on the floor in the corner of the room, coming only a quarter of the way up the wall. I'd decided this would be the best way to let me see only the bottom half of my dress. If that'd went well, I would take a second look in my bathroom mirror which would show what I looked like to the waist.

I took a deep breath and braced myself. I wasn't worried so much that the dress wouldn't fit - I was pretty good a looking at something and gauging if it would fit or not. No, this was very much about *how* I would look in it.

I'd intentionally waited until then to try it on, that way if it was a bad experience, I only had one torturous day fearing my dress before my wedding. Logically, I knew that I wasn't overweight, but whenever I saw myself in a full-length mirror, it would show my body bulging - with the more I looked, the bigger it becoming, making me feel like I was taking up too much room; like you could see too much of me.

I slipped my nightie to my ankles and carefully unclipped the skirt from its velvet hanger. The pearlescent silver, round beads danced around the lower edge of the delicate netting that layered the deep rich scarlet skirt. I felt its generous weight. *Gran would love this detail.*

My hands were shaking as I stepped my bare feet inside. I breathed in and closed my eyes as I lifted it onto my waist to fasten the concealed zip on the side. The skirt waist band sat high on my waist, fitting perfectly, and with room for me to breath.

I opened my eyes and reached for the bodice. It was soft against my skin - a soft rigidness. As I fastened its concealed zip, I was delighted with the gentle ruffled gathering of material and pearlescent beads patterned at the breast that I hadn't noticed in the shop. I let my hands trace up and down the dress that now contoured to my gently vibrating body. It felt amazing. I loved how it felt. *I love this dress!* It felt like it was made for me.

I took a deep breath in and permitted my eyes to scan the mirror. I could see my dress . . . just slightly past the waist! I panicked. I didn't think its reflection would show that far up my body. I closed my eyes quickly. *It's okay, Kemi. Look again.* As I opened my eyes for the second time, I could see this exquisite dress sitting beautifully against my brown skin. Even with bare feet I felt like a queen. I stared at myself, enchanted, while my breathing quickened and became shallow with excitement. The kaleidoscope of butterflies in my stomach became evermore sedated with contentment.

I opened the door quietly and made my way through my bedroom to the bathroom, still adopting tiptoeing so as not to stir the children. I entered my bathroom looking down to my feet so I could position myself tactically before peering into the mirror. I raised my head and slowly opened my eyes, as if bracing a peek at a scary movie. Delight filled me. The mirror revealed the bodice of my dress, and rather than being disappointed by its reflection, I was filled with joy, excitement and pride at my preparation paying off.

"Mummy, you look so beautiful," gasped a tired and half asleep Sola, as he silently wandered in behind me. As I hugged into him to share our delight, I was one less worry free.

Craig's Uncle Orlando and Aunt Karen, and their two children, were down from Inverness for the wedding and were staying at the house with me. We'd been spending a lot of our weekends in Inverness with them recently, as it was somewhere we could be a real family. They were a great support to us at that time.

That day was hectic – but a happy hectic. Craig came round to spend the day with us at the house, along with his sister and our friends, Sharon and Frank. They'd become friends of ours since we moved into the new house. They'd moved to Scotland four years earlier after fleeing from their native, troubled by race-relations, Zimbabwe. We'd met through Frank's mother, who had been a client of mine as well as Michelle's maths tutor for the past two years. They'd been very supportive of us and I was touched that they'd become part of our circle of safety.

After chatting our way through the afternoon and socialising in the garden into the evening, Craig and the men went to Leigh's house for a traditional, but quiet, night of drinks. We hadn't felt it safe enough for him to go painting the town red. I remained at home having drinks with the girls. They did a fantastic job of distracting my mind from all my fears.

That night, with the boys having easily decided it was the better choice to sleep in their own room with their older cousins, I lay in bed with just tiny Tola beside me, thinking how strange it was to have so much fear, not only consuming my every waking moment, but even enough to steal its way into my dreams. However tonight, as I fell into slumber, I had a little contentment: I would be marrying my soulmate the following day.

That morning was full of preparation and excitement. Leigh came over to pick up the boys and take them to Byers Road to collect the flowers from a florist we loved there, while Sandra and David came over to help and be part of our special day. At about 11am there was a quick, thudding knock at the front door.

"Who's that?" I gasped out loud while sitting upright on the sofa where I'd been having coffee with Orlando. Anybody who should have been here already was, and I felt a sudden foreboding set in.

"Shall I get it?" Orlando asked rising to his feet, trying to calm my obvious nerves.

"No, no. I'll get it," I replied, looking to the ground to hide the trepidation that must have resided on my face. He followed me as I made my way to the door. I took a moment to compose myself, anticipating an attack on the other side. I braced myself and opened the door.

"What? There's no-one here . . . wait, what's that?" I looked down to find a beautiful bouquet of flowers and a cased, vintage bottle of champagne with a card.

"Dear Kemi, I will be waiting for you at 3pm to become your husband. I love you babygirl, always x".

"Smooth," said Orlando, with a big, beaming smile as he read the card. "That's my boy," he said proudly.

When we arrived at the registry office, the registrar told David that my mum had been in earlier to warn them that they shouldn't marry us - that we abused children. The woman must have been horrified! I don't know the full details of their conversation – and I don't want to know - but I do know it ended with the registrar asking my mum to leave the building and warning her that if she returned, she would call the police.

The registrar had only met Craig, me and the children twice, but had concluded that my mum was off her head and had promised her that she would do whatever it took to keep our day special. She kept her promise.

David walked me down the aisle to meet a very beautiful Craig, strutting a smokey-grey, with a hint of a sheen, *Ted Baker* suit and matching waistcoat, with the very excited Dayo and Sola proudly waiting by his side, and baby Tola being held by Sandra. I remember thinking how blessed I was to have my friends and Craig's family here for us, supporting us in witnessing and celebrating our special day. We had the most amazing day, shared with the circle of twelve people that were becoming our family. Not one uninvited guest turned up to ruin our day.

I remember waking up that night in terror. Craig had stayed, with only us and the children at home, and as I lay in bed, fears began to spring into my mind. *What if Lydia finds out he slept here? What if she comes and takes the children away?*

She didn't. The next morning, we were up by 6am and out of the door by 7am, heading for Dunoon, where we would be honeymooning with the children for five days in a beautiful log cabin. When we returned from our honeymoon, Craig began to spend more time at home during the day. We were making a stand and now, Craig had even more rights.

Dishonest Lydia

When we returned from our family honeymoon the following Tuesday, it felt strange to say goodbye to Craig as he left the house to return to Leigh's. He joked that our marriage must have been the shortest on record – we'd only been married five days and already we were separating. The fact that he could joke about it was a good sign. He returned from our honeymoon stronger. We all had. We were legally a family now, and that brought us some comfort.

"Can't you just stay with us?" Sola questioned Craig, as he tucked him into our bed before leaving.

"Little man, I wish I could, but I can't. We have to prove we are a safe family first, remember?" Craig said while trying to hide the disappointment in his voice.

"You stayed when we got married," Dayo reminded, supporting his brother's cause. It was funny to hear both boys refer to the wedding as 'our' wedding and 'we' got married. But they weren't wrong: our marriage was as a family.

"I know, but that was a special occasion," I offered gently, feeling Craig's struggle to appease the upset starting to build in the boys.

"That's dumb . . . and I don't like . . . stupid Lydia; she doesn't even . . . speak to us . . . or ask us anything; how . . . does she know anything?" Sola vented.

By the time he'd finished offloading, he was struggling to sound coherent through all his tears. Again, Dayo played the supporting role and joined in with tears of his own. We couldn't offer them any comfort, so we just lay with them until they fell asleep. We could never have told them the severity of the situation: that I could lose them. We both hated these helpless times when we couldn't make it better for our children.

I called Lydia the next morning. It was now nearly six weeks since my children had been put on the register, and nine weeks since the initial allegations were made, yet Lydia had still not seen baby Tola.

Usually, anytime I called Lydia, my stomach would be full of nauseating knots, but today, the longer it took for her to answer her phone, the angrier I grew. *Child 'protection'? Pft . . . what a cheek!*

"Lydia speaking, how can I help you?" she finally answered, interrupting my resentful thoughts. *Help me?*

"Morning Lydia," I began, in a neutral tone; I wasn't in the mood to fake pleasantries, "it's Kemi Ogunyemi. I'm calling to let you know that Craig and I got married last week." *Fire in the hole.* There was a deafening silence.

"What? What have you done?" she asked me, as if I had switched the game midway through her playing her hand. I had.

"Lydia, as you know, I was due to marry Craig later this year, but we

238

decided to bring it forward." Again, a silence raged down the phone.

"Do you realise what you have done?" she asked, struggling to shake off her surprised reaction.

"Yes," I confirmed with delight, "I've married the man I love." Silence returned for a final appearance, but this time, *I* took a breath and broke it, "and he now has full legal rights to Tola -who I will make sure is here on Friday – seeing as you won't reschedule to see her at any other time."

"Well . . . erm . . . I was actually going to suggest another time." My news had definitely ruffled her; she was struggling to stay focused.

"Well now you don't need to," I interrupted. "I'll see you Friday. Bye Lydia." *Click.*

I put the phone down with satisfaction. By the end of the day, another letter of complaint was sent to the Social Work Department advising them that I believed Lydia had colluded with, and then instigated Rab to apply for custody of the children.

# # #

I started spending time at Craig's sisters house and sometimes took the children so we could be together as a family. We felt safer there. We never left her house, but it was nice to be able to just be, without the ever-present anticipation of being attacked that lingered at our house. We continued our Friday family drives to Inverness to stay at Orlando's for the weekend. There, we could go out in public as a family feeling safe, and we had witnesses, should they be needed, to say that we were treating our children with love and kindness. The boys missed Craig and they continued to struggle with him not sleeping at home. These 'retreats' helped them to temporarily forget about home and made us all feel better – safer: a family.

In the September, to my horror, I received a letter from my lawyer advising me that Rab had applied for a family court hearing to challenge me for custody of the boys. I'd known it was coming, but my anticipation didn't lessen the blow or reduce the ever-growing fear of losing my boys, especially as I suspected Lydia's involvement.

I'd been keeping my lawyer up to date with everything that had happened since Michelle's allegation and I was cc'ing her in all my complaints to the Social Work Department. I arranged to see her before the hearing.

Craig and David arrived together to discuss our way forward, after I'd put the children to bed; it was better that way – they would only have become upset at Craig not staying the night.

"Kemi is this a joke? She's going out of her way getting Rab involved. Enough is enough! She needs to be stopped or she'll destroy you," David stated, looking directly at me. Craig nodded in agreement. A silence filled the charged room.

"I know, but what can I do, David?" I asked sincerely. I was already doing everything I could; being honest - but it wasn't making any difference.

"You start to live with conviction," David snapped, my defeatism causing him to lovingly react, minus the sugar-coating, "and Craig - you need to start working again - from here. Take some of the pressure off Kemi - and you bloody start attending these Friday visits. Lydia needs to see how the children love you and feel safe and comfortable around you." He was frustrated. He sat back in his chair, irritated by the solution to the problem. I looked at Craig and knew he agreed.

"But . . . " I began.

"Kemi," Craig interrupted, "it's time to make a stronger stand now - right now. It's the only way."

I knew he was right, but I still felt like I was entering the lion's den. By the end of the night, we were all in agreement that the boys' needs came first - and they needed Craig to be more present in their life. We decided to follow Craig's lawyer's advice. As long as he didn't sleep overnight, and as long as I was present when he was in the children's company, Craig would return to working from home.

We decided we should tell the boys he would be spending more time at home. We also thought it was in their best interests for them to know about their dad's intentions. We planned to tell the children in the morning. Craig would come around after breakfast, and we would take them out, far away, for the day, as the schools were on holiday. The boys knew Craig was coming resulting in Sola being awake and alert from 6am with excitement. By 6.45 he could wait no longer.

"Please Dad - I miss you, big millions," Sola whined his high-pitched plea, stirring me awake.

"Sola - who are you speaking to?" I asked, confused at starting my day witnessing Sola talking on my phone so early in the morning, through my half-shut, sleepy eye.

"It's okay Mum – it's Dad Craig. He's coming for breakfast - aren't you Dad?" Sola continued his three-way conversation. I saw by his smile that Craig had agreed.

"Let *me* speak," said Dayo, sitting bolt upright like a Hollywood vampire. Sola, now filled with excitement and energy, passed the phone to Dayo, before leaping from the bed to do his animated *Crash Bandicoot* run up and down the bedroom, joyfully oblivious to the now awake, and crying, Tola.

By the time Craig arrived just before 8am, looking quite refreshed considering he'd only left at midnight, I still hadn't had my morning coffee and still felt quite tired, so I was glad to have his assistance. After breakfast, we decided to speak to the boys while Tola had her morning nap. We all sat together on the big L-shaped sofa, with both boys tucked deep into the corner and Craig and I on either side.

"Okay boys - we need to speak to you about something important," guilt sucker-punched me, knowing that I was about to ruin what had so far been a blissful, family morning.

"What things Mummy?" Sola whispered worryingly as his *Spidey Senses* tingled.

"Well, we have some good news and some not so good news." Their faces peered back at me, both as disturbed as each other.

"Oh man," Sola despaired, dropping his head and burying his face in his palms, "why does there have to be bad news?" He looked, and sounded, so dejected.

"Mum, can we have the good news first, please?" Dayo asked, looking decidedly tense. I held his hand. It felt clammy; sodden with dread.

"Well . . . Craig's going to be home every day from now on - he'll be working here . . . so we'll be able to have all our meals together. Is that good?" Their faces lightened.

"What? Yes! Amazing! So, you'll come this early every day, Dad?" Sola enthused, now bending over backwards to look up directly into Craig's face.

"Well . . . I'll need to – unless you want to be late for school!" Craig joked with delight. Sola gave him the biggest hug with the same look of excitement on his face as on Christmas morning.

"I know the bad news," Dayo interrupted suddenly, looking pensive. "He's still not sleeping here," he said defeated, folding his arms and dropping his shoulders in protest.

"That's true - but it won't be for much longer - I promise Dayo," Craig said, sliding Sola closer in towards Dayo so he could stretch his arm around both boys.

"Boys," I said, followed by a pause filled with a deep and heavy breath of apprehension, "the bad news is about your dad: he wants you to live with him." They both sprang upright, confusion and alarm now consuming their faces, accompanied by floods of tears of panic.

"That's ridiculous!" said Dayo, showing off his range of big words, which at times could be a misnomer. This time he used it perfectly.

"I hate him," Sola spat through angry tears. "I'm never going with him again." They both sagged back into the corner, and into our embrace.

"Mum, can he get us?" Dayo questioned quickly, so quietly it was nearly a whisper. His eyes foraged my mine for honesty. "No," Craig and I said in unison.

"Dayo, your dad can ask, but he'll never get you. I promise you that. No one will ever take you from me; never," I said calmly, but firmly, with a mother's passion. I prayed I would never break this promise.

The boys were so upset and scared. The truth was they didn't have any real memories of ever having lived day-to-day with Rab - except for Dayo's memories of witnessing his dad beating me.

#

When I arrived at court, I saw Rab signing in at the reception with his lawyer - his *new* lawyer. He was no longer using the lawyer that'd represented him during our divorce - the lawyer who'd advised him to drop Michelle from his visitation order as she was a dangerous child. In that moment I knew for certain that Rab was being encouraged, and guided, by Lydia.

At the hearing, my lawyer argued Rab shouldn't be granted any further custody rights. She advised that he barely adhered to the already existing visitation order and that it was already difficult enough for the boys to visit with him, as they were now scared that he wouldn't bring them back home, resulting in them often refusing to go. Both boys had told Rab they didn't want to see him until he stopped trying to take them away from me. She cited all of the history of our time together; the violence and the alcoholism, plus the lack of steady input, effort and financial support since we'd been separated.

Rab argued his case, not with pleas of 'it's in the boys' best interest' or 'I just want to spend more time with them'. No. His claim was that had he not been advised by Lydia that it was in his, and the children's, best interest to pursue custody, he wouldn't have done so. She'd informed him that he would be entitled to claim more benefit allowances along with a new council house. I stood shocked as he freely confirmed what I'd suspected from day one. It was clear that the boys' welfare was not his motive for his actions, and he now realised that his request had made him look like a fool – and he hated exposing his real self to the outside world.

In conclusion, the sheriff decided there was no reason to amend the pre-existing visitation order, other than to advise that whilst I was expected to encourage the children to visit Rab, due to how distressed they'd become, they were not to be forced into going.

# # #

Michelle would go on to add to her original allegation and now reported to Lydia that not only did Craig and I take drugs, but that we supplied them to her, as well saying that Sola had also been abused. I believed that Lydia knew Michelle was lying, but she wouldn't drop it. She was relentless and brazen with it.

One day, the boys' headteacher phoned me at home. She sounded distressed.

"Kemi," she said with a tone of apprehension, "Lydia's just turned up asking to interview the boys. I thought I'd better call you – it's not been pre-arranged - you do know she needs your permission to speak to the boys . . . and to pre-arrange an appointment with the school, right?" My heart jumped and my knees buckled, forcing me to sit my instability down.

"Are the boys okay?" I replied, feeling groggy.

"Yes - she's not seeing them - we don't have your consent," she explained sounding almost as apprehensive as I felt.

"Well, as long as you're in the room as a witness, I'll give my permission," I proposed. There was a short silence from the other end of the phone that allowed the sound of my heart beating to amplify throughout my head.

"Are you sure? You don't have to," she said sounding almost disappointed that I was conceding my consent. "She's gone outside regulations – this isn't procedure – and I've told her so." I could hear sincerity in her concern for my situation.

"I know it's not procedure . . . you're right, but if I refuse, she'll just write in her report that I've got something to hide." My back stiffened, spasming in response to the discomfort of the corner I was being forced into.

"This is ridiculous," she announced, with a loud audible sigh.

"I know, but that's how it is. Can you please let me know how it goes?"

"Okay, Kemi, but this is ridiculous," she repeated, sounding rather irked at my treatment. *Oh my God – what is she playing at now? Phone David.*

"What? Are you fucking kidding me?" he exclaimed, with such velocity that I got a fright. "Kemi, how blatantly stupid is this woman. Does she think she'll get way with this? What is she trying to do - get the kids on their own so she can make up lies about you?" The more he spoke, the more I raged. "Kemi, this situation is getting out of hand. This racist woman's out to get you - by any means possible. You get off the phone and wait for the Head to call you back, and I'll go and get started on your complaint."

When the Head called me back, she explained what had happened during the interview.

"Kemi, you should be so proud of those boys. They made it *very* clear that they know the difference between right and wrong and Dayo asked Lydia when she was going to stop coming to his house, because his 'Mum and Craig are good?'" This was not the first or the last time Dayo had asked Lydia this question.

It was at this point that Craig took David's advice and started attending Lydia's home visits. She no longer had the choice to interact or not - he included her in every conversation with the children. He even got her to play a few rounds of *Connect 4*.

We were making an open and honest attempt for her to see what we were really like - who we really were, but still Lydia never took reports from anyone who looked after my children, and she still hadn't interviewed Sandra regarding Tola. Lydia was still trying to paint me as an unfit mother, completely ignoring the fact that my daughter, Michelle, needed professional help and protection from the people who were using her to get to me. Her tunnel-visioned mission to discredit me as a mother continued to put my other children at risk.

By now, I was at breaking point. I'd had enough. I was a newlywed with an absent husband. We'd not been able to enjoy our new baby as a family.

Michelle was on a war path and my family were supplying her with the ammunition. Rab, despite his failed attempt to get the boys, was definitely hovering and waiting to pounce again and Lydia – well, she'd crossed the line for the final time. I was getting it from every direction and felt backed into a corner. I had nothing to lose. I chose to come out fighting the only way I could: with truth and honesty; to come completely clean about the people my daughter was living with: the honest and complete truth about my family.

The truth about my family

Lydia had no idea who she was making alliances with.

As I have mentioned before, my dad was involved in organised crime; he was the Führer of financial fraud scams and all of his businesses were, in one way or another, a hustle. Rab had worked for my dad in many capacities, ranging from being 'the muscle' that did the heavy work, to having his name being used in some of the scams my dad ran. This was the main reason my parents had been so opposed to me separating from him; he knew too much.

As I lay in bed unable to sleep with my mind full, I tried to make sense of all the madness that was going on in my life. My thoughts drifted to my family, and like a flipbook, numerous images of memories fluttered in my mind's eye, all sharing a theme: their lack of care for me and their controlling behaviour towards me. The pages stopped turning and I was reminded of the time I discovered my parents had taken a £15,0000 loan in my name without my knowing.

In my first year of working from my mum's house, and before Michelle's allegations, I was with a client one day when the front doorbell rang. I excused myself, as the only other person in the house was Tayo, and he was asleep upstairs having worked a nightshift in his taxi.

As I answered the door, I saw two men looking back at me. Both were dressed in black suits, black ties and black raincoats, with one of them holding a black leather portfolio. I knew instantly they were not here for a nice visit.

"We're looking for Miss Olu . . . keemee . . . Ogun . . . yeemee?" one of them began while finger tracing his paperwork and trying his best to pronounce my name correctly. "Is she here?" Panic filled me, but before I knew it, I found myself responding.

"She doesn't live here," I offered with sincerity. I wasn't lying - I didn't live there. The one with the paperwork scored something out in his notes.

"Do you have a contact number for her?" the other one asked.

"What's it about?" I inquired. The one with the paperwork gave me a quick flash of the identification card that hung around his neck. They were sheriff officers.

"We're here on behalf of *Black Horse* finance, regarding a loan Miss Oguny . . . eemy took out against a car."

I can't even drive! I can't believe they've done this to me - again. My parents didn't care how they got their money, as long as they got it. Even if it meant forging my name, and then defaulting the repayments, to do so. *I'll be blacklisted for this.*

"Sorry - I don't have a number for her - I've no idea where she'd be," I advised, trying my best to look calm. "I'm actually in with a client just now - I need to get back to them." They gave me a contact card and asked if I could pass it on if I saw her. I agreed and closed the door. *Oh my God!*

I passed Tayo as I shakily made my way back to my client. He'd heard everything, but didn't look surprised as he rested a handful of empathy on my shoulder. We shared a moment without speaking; he, better than anyone, understood my pain. Mine was nothing compared my younger brother's.

Tayo is a beautiful soul - he always has been - but unfortunately at that point in his life he had mostly worked in the family's businesses, some of which were registered in his name. My parent's house was bought in his name and he was now bankrupt and blacklisted because of them. My parents had destroyed his name, so he was now trapped with them, their lies and deceits. We'd had 'no right to question' them - so we didn't. *Poor Tayo.*

I wasn't long back in my bed and in the present, before the flipbook came back to life again. Pages fluttered memory after memory, all reminding me of how my dad had put me at risk on numerous occasions.

When I worked for him in his pub, there was a handsome, charming man who always came to chat with me. My dad eventually warned me to stay away from him – informing me that he was a very dangerous local gangster. He told me what the teardrop tattoo under his eye meant. I questioned how I was supposed to stay away from him: it was a pub; I was the barmaid and he was a paying customer.

"Just do it," was all he ordered.

I was about 19 at the time, and single. I'd been at home getting ready to go out clubbing with my friend Lesley, when suddenly there was a knock at the door.

I was caught by surprise as there was a concierge service and it was very well manned, 24 hours a day; no one got to my door without them buzzing through to me for permission. My intercom had not buzzed.

"Who could that be?" I asked Lesley as if somehow, she'd know.

"How'd they get in?" she replied more pertinently.

"Must be one of the neighbours," I concluded as I started to make my way to the door with Lesley following close by. I looked through the keyhole.

"Oh my God - Lesley, it's *him* – that guy from the pub," I whispered. My heart began to race. I'd spoken to Lesley about how he would chat me up in the pub, but I hadn't told her anything my dad had said. She moved me out of the way so she could take a look. *Why is he here?*

"Kemi . . . he . . . is . . . gorgeous!" she whispered back with widened eyes and a dropped jaw. When I looked again, he was smiling. *He must have heard us.* I could now see he was with someone who I didn't recognise.

I took a deep breath to force my fear to the back of my mind, braced myself and opened the door. I knew I had to go along with whatever this was; I just prayed it would end well.

"Joey, what are you doing here?" I questioned in a friendly tone. My heart starting thudding.

"Hello Kemi," he said while looking me up and down. He shot a smile right at me with his eyes locking onto mine. He was intense. I knew he fancied me – he'd never hidden it - and now, more than ever, I knew I had to stay cool. I was now scared of this man. "I've brought you a video player," he said calmly, pointing to the brand-new *Sony* box his companion was holding, "some champagne . . . and, of course . . . this." He pulled out a small food bag filled with some pungent, green grass.

"Well gentlemen, you'd better come in," Lesley interrupted. He didn't take a step, but instead waited for me to give my permission – his eyes still holding mine captive. He always acted every bit the gentleman in my company. I nodded in agreement, relieved that Michelle wasn't at home. *Oh my God, what's going on?*

Once in the living room, his friend proceeded to set up the brand-new video recorder.

"I remembered you said in the pub yours was broken, so I thought I'd bring you one . . . to make you happy," he said with confidence. I feigned a warm smile. *Where is this going?*

"I'll go and get some glasses for the champagne," I said, excusing myself from his intensity. I made my way to the kitchen, trying to act cool, hiding my terror. *What is he expecting to happen? Breathe, Kemi. Stay cool.*

I collected the glasses and turned to leave the kitchen, but there he was, standing in the doorway watching me and blocking my exit.

"You gave me fright," I said startled. He took a step towards me, to stand so close that I thought he would be able to hear my heart banging and feel the ground vibrating under my trembling, fear-occupied legs.

In that moment, looking at the detail of the tiny, teardrop tattoo below his eye - the one my dad told me meant that he'd killed someone - I didn't know if this night may be one that would scar me for the rest of my life.

He took my chin and gently lifted it to look at him. His eyes stabbed mine. I didn't want them to – but I couldn't look away; I was frozen.

"Kemi," he whispered so gently intense, and causing goosebumps to rise all over my body, "I like you. I know you're a good girl - that's what I like most . . . and you're beautiful of course." He leaned in and gently kissed me on my lips. No words were exchanged as he turned away to lead me back into the lounge. *What am I going to do?*

As I followed him back into the lounge, I could see the video recorder was now set up, and the other guy and Lesley were getting very friendly sitting on the single seater smoking a joint. I sat on the sofa, and as he squatted to sit beside me, he quickly rose back up to his feet.

"Oh, excuse me ladies," he said, removing an intricately carved, black handled, crocodile-tooth serrated, massive knife from inside his waistcoat. He sat it down on the sofa beside me. *Oh my God!* I could see Lesley's shock - not fear.

I could feel the colour drain from my face, but Lesley sat like an innocent, naive schoolgirl, admiring the weapon. Being the daughter of a police chief inspector, she'd grown up relatively sheltered, and *so* wanted to be a 'bad' girl. However, her naivety meant she didn't understand the subtleties of what was actually taking place right in front of her, and so, returned to her flirting with the other guy. I hoped her naivety would still be intact by the end of their visit. *Act cool.*

I decided to gloss over the fact that *Rambo's* knife was currently sitting inches away from my leg. *What exactly is going on?* I knew I was part of something - something bigger than me - but I had no idea what. My mind raced through fear-laden scenarios, while my face played its best bluff.

"If I dated you," he said, sitting down, "I'd treat you well."

He slid in closer beside me, his arm draping over my shoulder, and the knife, threateningly resting in between us. I fought hard to stop my body exposing my fear with its rigidity. I'd learned it was better not to let your attacker know you knew they meant you harm. That very second his phone began to ring.

"Sorry, I need to take this," he said, before standing to his feet and leaving the room. *Thank God!* I sat there, paralysed, unable to remove my eyes from the shiny, clean blade and its ferocious teeth.

"Yes? *Now* we understand one another! Good . . . okay, I'll leave now that we're good," I heard him say from the hallway.

A different attitude from what had left re-entered the room – his intense, confident calmness was replaced with a more upbeat approach, and to my relief, he was leaving. My mobile began to ring, but my eyes were already too preoccupied supervising the knife to check who was phoning me. My eyes only left his blade once he'd secured it back inside his leather waist coat. *How did that fit in there?*

"Kemi, thank you for your company, and you too Lesley," he said as he motioned to his friend that they were leaving now.

"Hope you enjoy the presents," he said as I stood to follow them to the door. I knew I wasn't safe until they'd gone. Lesley, still completely oblivious, followed his friend to the elevator, and they began to kiss while waiting for the doors to slide open.

"Kemi if you where *my* daughter, I'd never expose you to this life," he said with a seriousness while standing in my doorway. He took me aback. "I'll call you next time - take you on a real date." My heart sank as I knew he meant it.

"That'd be nice," I replied, watching him entering the elevator. He winked as the door closed. *Thank God!* I rushed back inside my flat ahead of Lesley and locked the door as soon as we were both in. My phone began to ring again.

'Hello?" I said shakily, struggling to sound calm.

"Kemi - has he gone?" my dad asked with concern.

"What? Who?" I said, slowly realising what my part had been. *You! That was about you!*

"Joey," he said simply.

"Yes," I choked, holding back a sickening feeling.

"Okay. You won't be working in the pub anymore," was all he said. I didn't ask why. I felt sick, and angry, that my own father could have put me at risk like this . . . again.

Joey went to prison not too long after, so I didn't have to worry about 'the real date'.

My parents hadn't protected me from the things I'd witnessed – things not suitable, or safe for a child - so why would my children be any different. I'd tried speaking to my dad as I knew he didn't really believe Michelle, but his loyalty to my mum would always overshadow him doing the right thing. He was just as scared of her as the rest of us.

Lying in bed that night, wrestling with all those memories led me to make a decision: I'd contact the police and speak to the Serious Organised Crime Division (SOCD) to tell them all I knew about my family. I needed to discredit them.

Once Craig's dad found out about my intentions, he phoned me.

"Kemi, are you sure you know what you're doing? I've always liked your dad - and I've always known who he was - but I'd never want to be the one to tell all." There was a momentary pause. "Kemi, he's family; he's your dad," he finished with concern.

"Family? Chris, really? You know what these people are trying to do to me, and with respect, you have no idea what they've done to me throughout my life. No Chris - family doesn't come into it. Who the hell do they think they are? They think they're better than me . . . they're the criminals; not me." I spoke so fast and with determination I was breathless by the time I'd finished.

"Okay," he conceded.

"Chris, I appreciate your concern, but I know what I'm doing; I grew up in that family. I have to stop them attacking me; this is the only way," I said before ending the conversation.

I didn't care what he said. He'd put his own son at risk by poorly advising him to repeat 'no comment' in his interview with the police. We hadn't spoken to him since as, in my mind, my father-in-law loved drama more than his son. He'd been spreading what was going on around town, putting Craig more at risk.

I was very aware of the risks I was taking by talking to the police about my family's activities; the people involved could bring me even more danger. However, my family was trying to assassinate my character with fiction, so I had no choice other than to cast aspersions with facts.

I knew the SOCD had powers, the like of which I'd never encountered before, but when they arrived, they were very clear that they couldn't help me with my case against the Social Work Department. That didn't matter –

they were still very important to me. This, to me, was an exposé; plain and simple. Not only was my mother helping to coach Lydia, but she was also prepared to sacrifice my children too. I would, by any means necessary, expose everyone involved for who they truly were.

My dad was very clever – he was the best at what he did - and they had never been able to catch him. They were delighted with everything I told them – and I told them everything - but, as always, my everything wasn't enough for the police to get him or his organisations. Despite this, I did somehow feel safer with the police knowing everything that was going on.

This was, of course, putting me more at risk, but at this point I knew that my time in this racist place was over. When I cleared my name, I would be leaving this town.

Not long after my meeting with the police, huge-lettered obscenities were spray-painted on my private driveway for all to see; while on another night someone tried, and failed, to break into the house via my back door while the children and I were asleep in bed. I hadn't heard a thing and only noticed the damaged lock and handle the following morning. I didn't know if this was Michelle's work, my family's, or my dad's business associates. We lived in great fear, but I knew I had to move forward with the truth.

Baby Tola, at only five months old, and the two boys were on the Child Protection Register. This would stick to them forever if we stayed here. Here, they would always be looked upon as abused children; that couldn't happen. Mixed-race children already grow up at a disadvantage. It was my job not to let this happen.

So, at this point it didn't matter how much danger I was in. I was prepared to die for the truth to come out, for the sake of all my children, including Michelle.

David

Rab was becoming desperate. He'd made a fool of himself with his unflattering display in court during his miserable attempt to get custody of the children, and was now hell bent on causing me trouble. One Friday evening, he and his sister turned up at my door out of the blue.

"I want to see my weans[24]," he demanded, as I opened the door.

He looked driven - sounded confrontational - yet he was putting on the façade that his request was a reasonable and rational appeal. Directly behind him I could see his sister sitting in her parked car outside my front door, barricading my driveway so no one could enter or leave. I knew instantly they were here looking to create a scene.

"Rab why are you here; you've got the boys tomorrow?" I reminded, with Craig standing behind me.

"I want to see my weans," he repeated dismissively. I could feel a shot of adrenaline release into my bloodstream.

He wasn't listening. He didn't come here to listen – he came to be heard – regardless of how it affected the boys.

"Let him see his weans Kemi," his sister barked. She was now standing outside the driver's door with a face as red as her car from all the hate and venom it was harbouring. She was itching to have a go. "He's got rights you know."

"Yes . . . ," I rebuffed, "but not today."

They both continued ranting, talking over one another and raising their voices to lecture how I was being out of order, enjoying their plight and being unreasonable. The more I advised that they shouldn't be here and the more I requested that they leave, the more hyper his sister became: agitated; combative.

"Dad? Why are *you* here? *We* don't want to see *you*," said Dayo. His face was blank and his tone was honest. With my eyes having been firmly fixed on the tag team, I hadn't noticed him come to the door – pushing his way to the front of mine and Craig's queue.

"I just wanted to see you, wee man," Rab began, his over-exaggerated, forced smile trying to hide his hostility. It failed.

"Well, *we* don't want to see *you*," Dayo insisted looking him straight in the eye. "You're not being nice to Mummy and Craig - you're trying to take us away to live with you. We don't want to live with *you*."

Although his tone was still honest, it now carried a distress. He was always so thoughtful with his words and always took people's feelings into account before he spoke. It was heart-breaking to see even he'd had enough. *How dare you.* I was furious.

---

[24] Pronounced: *wee-ins* (Glaswegian slang for children).

251

"Dayo, sweetheart, go inside and watch TV with your brother. It's okay - please, I'll fix this." Craig gently led a teary Dayo to the next room.

"Aye, you fix everything, don't you?" Rab butted in, sarcasm stamped all over his face and voice, "but you'll no be fucking fixing the allegations."

His tone changed; anger and menace, with a hint of delight now dominated his speech. Craig returned to my side and asked Rab to leave, telling him that both boys were now crying. Rab ignored Craig's request and continued.

"Aye, how are you going to get yourself out of this one?" His voice was getting louder and louder with every word uttered from his tightly clenched jaw of detest.

"Aye, I know you . . . you . . . fucking black bitch," his sister erupted.

"Right, that's enough," Craig interrupted, "Kemi, in. You two are out of order. You'd better leave. Now. I'm phoning the police," he warned, closing the door in Rab's face.

A raucous boom echoed between the house and the driveway wall, with their shouting and obscenities still being heard through the closed door. They were not leaving.

I phoned David and brought him up to speed, while Craig tried to comfort the inconsolable boys.

"Kemi, get off the phone and phone the police right now; this isn't on. Tell them they're still outside your house harassing and racially abusing you, and that there are children present. Put the phone down now . . . I'll phone you back shortly."

The police arrived promptly to find Rab and his sister sitting in her car still blocking my driveway. After ordering them to move the car, and a quick statement from me and Craig, they were both arrested and escorted to the police station where they spent the whole weekend waiting to appear in court on the Monday morning to enter their pleas. A date was set for later in the year for them to face their charges.

I don't think Rab believed I would ever go to the police. He had done so much to me in the past and I'd never involved them. However, I was no longer that same person. The injustices that I found myself facing, both then and throughout my entire life, had caught up with me. I was fighting back. If you were coming for me, you'd better come ready; I was now in lioness mode. I'd had enough.

# # #

David continued working tirelessly on all my injustices. His eyes had been prised wide open as to how deeply rooted racism was in Scotland. Being a recently retired chief superintendent, he was shocked at what was happening. After witnessing and experiencing the horrific events of that first Child Welfare Hearing, David had continued to challenge everything that was wrong with my case, calling it, "racist from the very beginning." I don't know why I was so blessed to have David and Sandra in my life; I don't like to think about what would've happened had they not been.

At first, we lodged complaints to the Social Work Complaints Department, however they never addressed any of the complaints raised. No answers to our initial complaint regarding how the welfare meeting had been conducted. No answers to why my mental health had ever been in question, let alone broadcasted as the gospel truth. No answers to why my race was relevant. No answers to the complaint highlighting my suspicions that Lydia was advising Rab to go for custody. No answers to the complaint confirming Lydia had advised Rab.

The only responses we ever got was to say they'd received my complaints and would reply in due course. They never did.

Next, we involved the Scottish Social Service Council (SSSC) who overlook the Social Work Department. It's their job to protect people who use council services, raise standards of practice by council employees, and strengthen and support the professionalism of the workforce within the council.

We wrote to them to investigate the Social Work Department's handling of my complaints – expressing that they weren't keeping to their own guidelines of procedure and timeframes when investigating and replying to a formal complaint.

The SSSC responded to say that we had to exhaust the Social Work Department complaints procedure before they would be able to investigate my case. We were getting nowhere. No one wanted to answer my questions.

So, we wrote to the Chief Social Work Advisor, the head of Social Work in Scotland, asking him to investigate how I was being treated. We provided him with copies of all the previous complaints raised to all the various parties and copied-in the Scottish Public Services Ombudsman, the Children's Panel and anyone else who had the power to question what was happening to my children.

The Scottish Public Services Ombudsman replied saying that they wouldn't get involved until after both the Chief Social Work Advisor and the SSSC had completed their investigations. The Chief Social Work Advisor wouldn't investigate my case until the SSSC had completed theirs, and the SSSC wouldn't investigate until the Social Work Complaints Department had concluded their investigation. The Social Work Complaints Department kept replying that they would look into my raised concerns, without ever answering my questions. Nobody was investigating anything.

I'd lost all patience and faith. We'd followed the correct complaints procedures, yet we were getting nowhere. It was at this point that David first had the idea to involve a politician. He advised me that there was a politician proactively fighting injustices endured by the people of Scotland while under a *Scottish Labour Party* government.

I was under no illusions; David explained the angle. There was a General Election due in 18 months and the politician was looking to have his party elected as the governing party in control of the Scottish Parliament. In the meantime, he was helping to cast a light on injustices - and indeed, he was helping a lot of people – ultimately, highlighting any *Labour* failings was his angle.

I knew nothing about politics or politicians. I paid no attention to elections, or what they would come to mean for me and my children in the future, but I was intrigued. Alex Salmond, who at the time had recently been sworn in as the leader of the *Scottish National Party* was the politician David had in mind.

I have to say, he was exceptionally helpful. He insisted on writing to the Chief Social Work Advisor, the SSSC and the Social Work Complaints Department to demand the answers to all my complaints and investigate how the current guidelines were failing. He also insisted on being included in every complaint, letter or email correspondence we sent from now on. He was so determined to highlight my case that he wanted to take my story to Westminster. He even suggested that I take it to the national newspapers.

I wasn't prepared to do that. I'd come to the conclusion that I would have to relocate my family once the Social Work Department was no longer in my life. Once my name was cleared and the dust settled, I would need anonymity to be able to have a fresh start somewhere new. Going to the national newspapers wasn't an option.

The children had been on the Child Protection Register for four, horrendous months by now. It had been agreed at the initial welfare hearing that a review would take place in 12 weeks' time to determine what risks, if any, had been identified and what should happen next. All involved authorities would be expected to attend.

This period was intended for Lydia to conduct home visits and make risk assessments, but with Lydia failing to conduct regular visits, or speak to all the relevant authorities, the 12-week guideline had well and truly expired. I was at my wits end. Then the unimaginable happened. One bleak, wintry day in November, Lydia advised me that her investigation was finally coming to a conclusion.

"All my findings suggest she's not telling the truth," she offered in a dry, matter-of-fact tone. She said it as if no one had ever suggested it before. *Well done; clever you.* "She's possibly a disturbed child, and your mum – she's way too involved." I couldn't believe my ears – I wouldn't. *This is a stitch up.*

"I wanted to set up a meeting with Michelle and the Children's Panel. *I believe the investigation will be dropped, but your mum's not having it. I don't think it's good for Michelle to be living with her anymore.*" *What is she playing at?*

"You . . . and Craig, could let Michelle come home." I was shocked;

254

appalled; confused.

"Will I get support and access to the appropriate help?"

"Not while there's all this . . . *fuss* going on."

Ahh, there it is. She's trying to trade. Taking Michelle back into the home while the other three children were still on the Register, and before Lydia had officially concluded her investigation, would put the whole family back at risk again, as Michelle could easily make another allegation.

I would have loved to have been able to have her back - with the right support - but in order for Lydia to allow that, she wanted me to drop all my complaints against her. I was dealing with someone who wasn't willing to give my children - all four of them - what they needed to repair.

It all started to make sense; that's why the children hadn't been removed from the Register. She'd been waiting for my complaints to blow over and for me to quieten down. I hadn't. I had created noise – political sized noise – and now her actions were starting to catch up on her. With the combined persistence of David and Alex, we could see that the pressure was now starting to mount against Lydia, and this encounter was her last attempt to halt my complaints before removing the children from the Register.

At the end of the day, I rejected her 'offer'. I wasn't doing a deal with this racist woman who took no responsibility for her behaviour. So, David and I, along with Alex, kept the pressure on. We now reported this new development, detailing what she'd offered me.

Shortly after, the Children's Panel did indeed drop the case, stating that there was no evidence to support the allegation. Finally, everyone was coming to the same conclusion. They could see it was all a lie; and that my mum was the problem. Having been on it for nearly six months, my children were removed from the Child Protection Register, concluding 'No Risk'.

However, nothing else. I never received official explanations of why the process took so long. No answers to my questions. Nothing. It felt hollow; unsatisfying. While I was obviously relieved to finally have them removed, I felt a loss.

Time had been lost. Opportunities to salvage had been lost. I'd lost my daughter – and for what? Tornado Lydia had, for nearly six months, wreaked havoc, fear and pain throughout my household - and now my life was just expected to go back to normal in her absence.

We'd spoken to the boys as a family to discuss their thoughts and feelings about us moving away somewhere new in the future. I wasn't prepared to have my children seen as abused children; mixed-race, abused children. Having them growing up in the racism that polluted Central Scotland was no longer an option. We knew it was time to leave now, so we started to make plans. We were telling no one.

By the time Rab and his sister's trial went to Court, my battle was very well known. The children had by now been removed from the Register, and the sheriff had judged it of no relevance to the hearing, so ordered that it was not to be brought up in court. I was delighted.

Rab was facing charges of breach of the peace and his sister was facing a charge of racially aggravated assault. They both pleaded not guilty, obviously, but Craig and I were both witness to what had happened. The children had been there too, but I didn't want them to be involved; they were too young.

When I was giving evidence, I hadn't said that I'd phoned David first. I wasn't hiding the fact, I had forgotten. Ultimately, the defence argued that clearly, I couldn't remember events as they happened, and that either at worst, I had fabricated the whole thing intentionally, or at best, it was possible that I had misheard being racially abused.

As I had forgotten that I'd called David *before* the police, the defence successfully created a doubt, and the sheriff returned a 'not proven' verdict to both of their charges. Under Scots Law, a criminal trial has the potential for three conclusions: guilty, not guilty and not proven. Although a doubt had been cast regarding my reliability as a witness, equally, Rab and his sister's lawyer had been unsuccessful in proving their innocence. The verdict was good enough for me as it stopped Rab trying to cause problems.

Not too long after, one day while family shopping at *Glasgow Fort,* we bumped into Wale's girlfriend, Pam. Pam was the one who got Michelle the weekend job working in the same hair salon she worked in, and we'd all been friends before the nightmares started. I hadn't spoken to her this whole time, so I wasn't sure where we stood with each other, but I suspected with her being Wale's girlfriend she'd ignore us, or at least pretend not to see us. She did neither.

"Could I come around to your house – there's some stuff I think you should know," she asked with a nervous smile while caringly holding onto both mine and Craig's forearms.

I felt her approach was sincere and I sensed an urgency from her, so, intrigued to hear what she had to say, I agreed. She came that evening, 2nd January, 2006.

"I'm so sorry you've had to go through all of this. I'm really struggling being with Wale; nobody believed Michelle - your mum just supported her. It was obvious to everyone in the family that Michelle was lying. I said to Wale I didn't believe her and that this isn't right, how you've been treated . . . but he just told me to forget about it and that it was too late to fix because you'd been to the police and grassed. Kemi, I'm so angry with him - with them all. I just don't know what to do. The family don't care about what's happened to you; as far as they're concerned, you're a grass."

She was sincerely sympathetic. I was furious. I used Pam's phone to call Wale; I knew he wouldn't answer mine. As the phone began to ring, I was trembling with anger.

"Hey Pam," Wale opened warmly and unguarded.

"No Wale – Kemi," I replied. I felt the temperature drop from his end of the line.

"Kemi? Erm . . . what the fuck do you want?" he managed. I could hear the shock in his voice.

"What the fuck do I want? People to start telling the truth. You know she's lying . . . Pam told me you know; that you all know," I erupted, feeling my whole body consumed by rage.

"Yeah, and what? You kicked her out and went to the police Kemi; you deserve all you get." *Click.* He put the phone down. That was the last time we spoke.

Within my anger, there was some fleeting relief. I'd heard it from his own lips: they *did* know that Michelle had been lying all along. And while this did afford some comfort, it only added more pain in confirming that my family – the family I was born into - along with the help of my own daughter, was willing to destroy me. I was saddened, deep in my heart, understanding that the welfare of Michelle, my daughter, was of no importance to my family.

It was a few months later when I jolted awake, alarmed. I'd had another one of my dreams. The ones that were so vividly clear that for the first few minutes awake I'd struggle to differentiate between reality and dream. I'd now been awake for half an hour and my dream hadn't felt any less real. I'd dreamt that my gran had died.

I'd gone to visit my gran with the children when the craziness first began, but my mum had confused and upset her by telling her things that were too heart-breaking for her senility to hear. So, I decided to stop visiting; I would only have confused her more. As I left her wee flat, I knew it would be the last time I saw her. That was one of the saddest days of my life.

As I lay in bed, my nightshirt soaked from the dream induced tears of sweat, I thought about how both my grandparents had been a massive part of my life. They'd only ever loved me. I was their *Brown Girl in the Ring.* We would spend summers travelling around in their little, blue *VW* camper van, attending all the Highland shows as my grandad was a drummer in a band. Tayo and I travelled everywhere with them. When we were with them there was no racism, just love. They'd understood and helped us through everything. I remembered the day I tried to paint myself white - the day my grandad made me the 'long hair' from the tea towel; the times they made everyone call Tayo, 'Shuggy', his 'white' name, at his request, and without questioning him. They just loved us and wanted us to be happy. They tried to make up for all the pain we had to endure.

Eventually, I got up out of bed and got organised as usual. I took the kids to school that day before starting work. By the time I began with my first client I'd convinced myself that I'd just had a nightmare – nothing more - and if my gran had died, despite all the fallout, someone would have told me. Someone did: my two o'clock client.

She was surprised that I hadn't cancelled her appointment given how close I was to my gran. She quickly realised I didn't know until that very moment.

So, I went to the funeral; late. I did this intentionally so I could slip in at the back of the chapel without being seen. I remember looking at the family in the front row - the family I was no longer a part of - and realising that I didn't know if I ever was. This was my punishment; ostracised to the back of the chapel.

I didn't go to the graveside for the burial after the service. Instead, I left the chapel during the singing of her favourite hymn, just before the service ended. Craig had waited outside for me and we drove home in silence.

Walk with Me O My Lord,
Through the darkest night and brightest day.
Be at my side O Lord,
Hold my hand and guide me on my way.
Sometimes the road seems long, my energy is spent,
Then Lord I think of You and I am given strength.

I can still hear her singing this, and in my toughest of times, she brings me great comfort.

My wee gran represented the definition of a lady. In her tiny, wee form she was elegant and graceful and honourable in the most subtle of ways. She was subtle, yet steady in her knowing that I would always be judged. She taught me the importance of *how* I presented myself to the world and how it was important to always present the very best version of myself . . . and of course, in the appropriate outfit. She believed this is what made a proper lady. *She* was a proper lady.

Auntie Joan would later call me, saying she saw me leaving the funeral and that she was so glad I had attended as that was what my gran would have wanted. She said it was terrible that my mum hadn't told me and she sent me her copy of the service booklet. I am so grateful that she did. We left Airdrie soon after.

Leaving

When the children were removed from the Register, I had to accept that it was time to relocate. We'd discussed it, lovingly and with optimism . . . but it had always been discussed as part of the future; "in the future, when we've moved" and "in the future, when we're gone". The future, during our darkest moments, had been our hope - something to focus on; something to look forward to.

While we'd dreamed of the day - and fantasised our preferred locations - I'd never actively looked into it. I couldn't have done, there was always just so much drama consuming my life in the present, and I could only deal with one thing at a time. However, now that the future had finally arrived in the present, I realised I wasn't ready. At least not for another chapter in Scotland. Craig, on the other hand, was ready. He needed out of Airdrie - yesterday.

It was during one of our visits to Orlando and Karen's in Inverness, that I suddenly felt overwhelmed by the prospect of moving. We'd spent so much time together with them in the beautiful Highlands over the past summer, make-believing there to be a suitable location to live. We'd enjoyed our escapism from the 'real world', but now that it was time to leave Airdrie, the future didn't look Scottish. I couldn't entertain the thought of moving to another part of Scotland, no matter how beautiful it was.

I knew if I was going to move, I wanted to move to England: home. I'd longed to return ever since I moved to Scotland. I'd lived my whole existence in Scotland in a constant, low level of fear – always anticipating the next attack, while never feeling accepted or equal. I didn't want my children to feel the way I did; I didn't want this story to become my children's stories too.

I wasn't naïve; I knew there would be racism in England too, but with England having had a larger black community since the 1940's, it had progressed and evolved further than Scotland had in terms of acceptance. Scotland's attitude was years behind and I'd endured enough. I now had the opportunity to get out of this racist country.

We'd just finished Orlando's amazing goat curry with rice and peas for dinner and while the children retired to play video games in their cousins' rooms, the adults relaxed in the lounge beside a napping Tola. As the conversation resumed its theme, I started to feel suffocated. The constant talking of 'us moving north' had taken its toll.

I was done listening. I couldn't do it anymore. The day had been exhausting. What I thought was going to be a family daytrip to the beach, turned into an episode of *Location, Location, Location.* We were in and out of the car, exploring all the local areas, all the local schools, the amenities and the no-go areas - we even looked at a new housing development without a single built house on site. I'd felt ambushed. The stifling had begun then, but now, as we lazed, it matured into a threatening stranglehold, tugging at my stomach and crushing my very being.

"I don't want to live in Scotland," I delivered bluntly, bringing the room to a halt in an awkward silence.

"Kem, I know you don't . . . but we need to at least look into it," Craig said, approaching with a gentle tone, as if reassuring an injured animal that he posed no harm. *He's not listening.*

"Why?" I swiped. "I *don't* want to live in Scotland."

I felt like a child as I repeated my stance - the only thing missing was me dropping to the floor and stamping my feet. My patience *had* been tested. We'd only ever fantasised about living in the Highlands; it'd been a distraction from our miserable surroundings, but now Craig, Orlando and Karen were talking about it as if it had already been decided. I felt as if everyone was making decisions *for* me, about *my* life, and that I wasn't being listened to.

"Kemi . . . there's no harm in looking; it's better to know all our options," said Craig, trying to sound reassuring. "England will probably be the first place they'll look for you."

I felt my back tighten and mistook its reaction as offence to his words. However, within that moment I realised it wasn't offence: it was fear at hearing the truth in his words. *He's right – oh my God, he's right.* I was rendered speechless, choking down my tears of realisation. It felt as if Scotland had sunk its nails deep into me, and was gripping on for dear life, holding me hostage.

"Okay . . . let's leave it. I didn't mean to upset you Kem," Craig offered bringing an end to all talk of moving.

For the remainder of the night, I sat present in the living room, but absent from presence, in a deathly silence, consumed with my new realisation. I knew they'd meant no harm and I understood they'd had my best interests at heart, but I'd not been on the same page as them, and right then, being held captive by Scotland had left me feeling powerless all over again.

The next day, all talk of house-hunting was suspended and I got my family day at the beach – just the five of us. Craig and I drove 30 minutes east from Inverness to a small seaside town called Nairn, where Craig had holidayed as a child.

We parked in an open-plan car park - *the Links* - surrounded by views of a beautiful white sand beach and sea on one side, and the picturesque cricket pavilion, a park and the town's bandstand all on the other. I noticed how some cars had parked with their windows half open - yet no dogs lay inside - while some hadn't bothered to lock their doors. It struck me as odd. I made sure we didn't make the same mistake.

We took a short walk west along the promenade, venturing through two outdoor play parks, with paddling pool and public toilets. The parks had swings, climbing frames and roundabouts – all the usual suspects - yet something else struck me as odd . . . there was no damage preventing the children from using them. No broken *Buckfast* bottle shards, or discarded used syringes to prevent the children from playing on the grass. No racist graffiti or gang tags. Just beautifully manicured floral arrangements. Not a single piece of litter, all bins appeared well fed. The toilets were the same; clean and well kept.

After a quick, yet stiffly contested circuit around the pitch-and-putt, we made our way back east, venturing beyond the car park and along the promenade until reaching a café at the town's harbour, filled with friendly, chatty locals. The boys had never seen so many boats up close before and while polishing off their battered sausage and chips, they took turns at guessing their names.

Once they'd finished their food, we made our way to the sand. We passed joggers, dog walkers, cyclists . . . some of whom were probably well into their eighties – and they all spoke to us; complete strangers – talking to *us*. *This town is odd.*

As we sat on the golden-white sand looking out to the *Moray Firth*, with Dayo and Sola braving the freezing cold waters as deep as their bare, rolled-up-trouser-supporting knees permitted, my heart skipped a beat; I knew this view.

A familiarity set in. It was as if I was staring out at a scene that I'd witnessed before; somewhere I'd been and forgotten. In that moment I remembered. *My dream! I 'have' been here before . . . in my dream!*

Far across the water at the opposing coast stood what appeared to be a cliff; a cliff that had been excavated in the middle, forming two prominent mounds with the *Moray Firth* pouring in between them. I'd seen it before, but I'd assumed its location to be in England. I now knew its name: *The Sutors of Cromarty.*

As I sat there content and relaxed, I realised the town wasn't odd; it just had an odd feeling to *me*. I didn't recognise this feeling and if I'd felt it before, it was so long ago that I no longer recognised its indication. What I'd mistaken for oddity was in fact safety. The whole time I'd been in Nairn it'd felt odd, but now I realised Nairn felt safe.

The openness of the rejuvenating promenade washed over me, exfoliating my soul, offering me a freshness I wondered if I'd ever felt before. I felt alive in that moment. I turned to witness Craig struggling, stooped, bent forward, yet bracing against momentum, trying to keep hold of baby Tola's hands while she insisted on walking - a skill she'd yet to develop. He smiled at me and when I went to smile back, I realised I was already smiling.

He toddled over with Tola, took a satisfying, back-extending stretch before dropping down to the sand beside me, leaning on his elbow and lying on his side. He somehow knew to throw caution to the wind and dare one

261

final attempt. He cleared his throat.

"Well . . . would you like to live here, Mrs Ferguson?" he asked.

"Do you know . . . I think I would, Mr Ferguson," I replied.

Before we left, we made sure to pick up all the local estate agents' brochures to gauge the market, along with the local newspapers to get a feel of the local vibe. *The Nairnshire Telegraph* had a 'can you help' crime section called *Cop This*. This would surely be a good indicator as to how safe the town was.

We were amused – not at the victims' suffering – but rather at the severity of the crimes reported. Back in Airdrie, the local *Airdrie and Coatbridge Advertiser* was always dominated by crimes of high-class drugs, murders and assaults. In our street alone, there'd been two separate violent incidents in the past six months; one female had been sexually assaulted and another had been set upon by a gang. We lived in the 'good' part of town.

The miniscule feature in *The Nairnshire* mainly comprised of bicycle thefts and the mysterious case of the disappearing – before reappearing in a different garden - plant pots, that had the locals suspecting youths as the culprits. The small town had many community projects and organisations and it was clear there was plenty of community spirt. There was even a *Steiner* school in the neighbouring town that would be ideal for the children to attend. And, of course, having Orlando and Karen living nearby would be a great comfort and support to us all.

With England being the obvious destination for my family to start a search for me, I conceded that the Highlands of Scotland would be the last. Nairn would be our new town. We would draw up our to-do list and put our plans into action; but we would have to be careful. Only those who needed to know would know and those who didn't - we hoped they wouldn't. We would have to keep up appearances and act as normal as possible.

When we returned home the first item on our 'to do' list was putting the house up for sale. We contacted an estate agent and arranged for the house to be put on the market, but without a 'For Sale' sign and without advertising, other than on their website. Back then, with numerous property-listing newspapers and magazines, the internet hadn't boomed into the go-to search engine it is today. That being said, there was still a risk in having our house displayed on their website, so we hoped, with the house not having a sign, no one would look on the internet to see if it was for sale.

Next, I had to create my paper trail. I told my lawyer that I felt unsafe living so close to my parents and that I needed to sell my house. I didn't lie. She knew the house being put on the market was to be kept confidential, and I knew she had to do that. I told her that once the house was sold, we would be renting locally for a while until we could find a house to buy that was suitable for us both to work from. I provided her with the rental property's address. It belonged to a client of mine and I knew it would be vacant. They were in the process of renovating with the intention of renting

262

it out once all the works had been completed. The works had only just begun. The paper trail would end there.

Within 48 hours of the house being on the market, the first people to view it made us an offer matching what we were looking for; we accepted. Their own house sale was in the process of completion and they needed to be out of theirs and into ours by the 31st March, 2006, giving us six weeks to find somewhere to rent. It was time to start looking in Nairn, so we arranged some house viewings with the local estate agent.

Craig and I left early in the morning, full of excitement, to drive the three and a half hours up to Nairn. We'd three properties to view before returning home. So far, everything was going to plan. Our house had been on and off the market within 48 hours and no one was any the wiser that the house was selling. All we had to do now was find a house and make it our home.

When we arrived, the first of our viewings had been cancelled as the property was no longer available. *Okay, it wasn't meant for us; there are still two more.* The second viewing, to be honest, I didn't want to even enter. It was stacked, cramped behind the shops on the high street with no natural sunlight or garden and gave off a vibe of neglected and abandoned. After less than five minutes, we headed for the third property, our excitement fading and being replaced by desperation. A lot was riding on the final house. *Please be the one.*

We followed the agent in our car. We drove. And drove. And then drove a little more. We drove right to the outskirts of the town. I knew before we arrived that the house wasn't suitable. I wanted the kids to have easy access to any potential friends they may make and this location had ruled that out. We drove home feeling exhausted and disappointed.

"You worried?" Craig asked, squinting his eyes from both the tiredness of the wasted journey and the glaring low light of the late winter sun.

"No, I'm not," I replied with full honesty.

Considering I would be homeless in less than six weeks, I was steady – calm; content in my strong belief that everything happens for a reason and in its own time.

"We'll find something; our new house can't be ready yet." Craig looked surprised at my serenity and gladly nodded in agreement.

"I just wish it wasn't so last minute," I joked, "I mean, seriously . . . we're not asking for much; just to sell our house, find a new one . . . and a workplace . . . in a new town, oh, and all in under six weeks." We both laughed at our ridiculous predicament, but we knew it just felt right.

Things, from then on, fell into place very quickly.

"Kemi, do you think it's a coincidence that Tom's new job covers the area you're wanting to move to?" William questioned down the phone. I'd phoned him that night after returning from Nairn to update him on the house search. He had an update for me.

My client Tom – the one who introduced me to William - had just landed the role as the new area manager for *The Swallow Hotel Group*. His area covered the Highlands, with Nairn having two four-star hotels. William suggested I tell Tom my plans.

"You're joking . . . what's the chances? Do you think he could help?" I asked.

"Absolutely Kemi, in a heartbeat," William convinced.

I spoke to Tom the same day. He *was* delighted to help and offered us a treatment room in *The Golf View Hotel* for Craig and me to work from, with no rent to pay for the first six months.

"What? Tom . . . I don't know what to say."

"Kemi, it's not all kindness," Tom teased, revealing his business head. "To be able to offer your kind of services up there - especially to the American golfers . . . they're going to love you, so it's a win-win." He finished our conversation saying he would make the arrangements.

I was so blessed and grateful to have had so many people supporting me at this time and was saddened that I wouldn't have them close by after I moved.

All that was left to do now was find a house. The weeks had passed by without any new properties being made available and we still didn't have a house. Then, with only a couple of weeks to spare, a new property came up. We'd been constantly refreshing our web searches, fifty times a day, but kept getting the same results. However, on this morning, a new thumbnail popped up. We called straight away and made a viewing for that afternoon – being told that there was another viewing booked for that evening.

Craig did the journey north by himself as I had a full diary of appointments. By now we were desperate and would have accepted just about anything. Hours of silence had passed before he finally called me, delighted:

"Four big bedrooms; one en suite; the children have a fancy bathroom; the garden's massive and enclosed with a garage, and Kemi, it's in a new development - all the crescents connect by footpaths and cycle paths . . . the children will have friends in safe walking distance."

The house was perfect and the moving in date? 31st March. Too good to be true. He informed the estate agent that we wanted to sign the lease.

We'd spoken with the boys many times about moving and they'd always expressed a keenness to relocate. They too had had enough of Airdrie and all the horrors it had unleashed. This ordeal had taken its toll on us all. None of us felt safe. As often as we'd spoken hypothetically about moving with the boys, we'd never once told them we would be leaving. We couldn't afford for anyone to find out and we weren't asking them to keep secrets.

So, the plan was to arrange for the paperwork to be forwarded so the usual background and credit checks could be performed. Whenever we made any of our viewing appointments, we'd used our aliases – Leigh and Stephen's names.

We would rent the house in their names, leaving no paper trail of ours and we were going to pay a year's rent up front, which meant all we needed was character references. When we were in the process of moving, Leigh would meet the agent and sign the lease using her identification. As only Craig, or rather 'Stephen', had met the agent, Leigh could play herself. We would tell the boys, and Rab, we were going on holiday to *Center Parcs* for a week. That gave us a week to get organised in the new house before anyone would even suspect we'd gone. Everything was going to plan.

Then it wasn't.

The week before we were due to leave for Nairn, we received a call from our lawyer advising us that the couple buying our house needed more time because their sale had been delayed. They asked to delay our sale for a week. We were devastated.

We knew we couldn't do that. We had to stick to the plan and leave on the 31st. We couldn't run the risk of being seen in the town when we were supposed to be 300 miles away in another country. After many discussions weighing up our options, we accepted it wasn't worth the risk and decided we'd just have to walk away from our beautiful home and give up all the money it was worth. We knew the house would probably end up being repossessed if we disappeared without concluding the deal. Financially, we would be left with nothing.

Without the sale of the house, we no longer had enough money to pay the full year's rent as agreed. Even with what we had managed to save up, we were still a couple of thousand short. Thankfully Leigh was able to lend us the money we needed.

On the morning of the 31st, I left Airdrie heading for Nairn, with the children and Leigh - and without hesitation. The only concern I left behind was for Craig, who'd remained with Stephen to pack-up the entire house. Stephen, being an HGV Driver, was going to drive Craig up to Nairn. I was on edge all day, praying they would get on the road before anyone noticed them loading the massive removal lorry in the driveway.

After driving for a few hours, we stopped at the *Ralia Café,* a place the boys liked to stop at whenever we travelled to Inverness, so I could tell them what was actually happening. They recognised it as soon as we pulled into the carpark.

"Wait . . . Mum . . . what are we doing here?" Sola excitedly exclaimed as Leigh unfastened Tola out of her car seat to take her into the cafe.

"Dayo! Dayo! Look where we are!" Sola's bony finger poked at Dayo to get him to look out of the window.

"Mum, why are we here?" Dayo asked with surprised confusion.

"Okay boys, I need to have a serious chat with you," I said, nervously turning round from the front seat to face them.

"Oh, not again," Sola exhaled, showing that his patience had worn thin with all of our serious chats. Their excited and befuddled faces suddenly exhibited alarm.

"How would you feel if I told you we were leaving Airdrie?"

Their faces sprang alive.

"Yesss!" Dayo exclaimed delighted, closing his eyes and double fist pumping.

"What . . . now?" Sola shrieked. He looked as if he'd just been told Santa was on his way.

"Yes, now," I confirmed.

Silence dominated the car while both boys stared back at me with wide-eyes and dropped-jaws waiting for my next piece of information.

"Do you remember Nairn?" I asked, prompting Dayo to nod intensely while Sola held his hands over his mouth to prevent his excitement interrupting me. "Well, that's where we're moving to."

"What . . . today? What about *Center Parcs?*" Sola asked, suddenly remembering he was supposed to be on a family holiday.

"Never mind *Center Parcs* Sola," Dayo interrupted, "Nairn has a beach . . . remember? We'll be on holiday every day!"

"Oh yeah . . . but Mum, *are* we still going to *Center Parcs?*" Sola pressed, happy to be moving to Nairn, but conflicted at not going to *Center Parcs*.

"Where's Dad Craig?" Dayo interrupted again to ask with concern. I felt my stomach flinch thinking about the removal lorry sitting in the driveway.

"Okay, okay . . . one at a time." I took a deep breath while they settled.

"Dad Craig is with Uncle Stephen packing up the house right now - they'll be here later tonight," *God permitting*, "and Sola, no sweetheart, no *Center Parcs* . . . just Nairn."

"Mum . . . have we run away?" Dayo whispered, his eyes reading mine.

"Yes darling," I confirmed with a reassuring smile. "No one knows where we are. How do you feel about that?"

"I feel great with that Mum - I hate Airdrie," Sola answered, quite matter-of-factly and with an eager nod. "There's too many lies."

"Does my dad Rab know?" Dayo asked, now showing signs of panic.

"No darling, he doesn't," I replied. A fleeting silence filled the car, amplifying their first sign of trepidation.

"Will he find us?" asked Dayo. I reached through the gap of the front seats and took his tiny hand.

"No Dayo; I've been very careful." My words did little to ease his young mind.

"Mum, I don't want him to ever find us . . . promise?" He held out his pinkie. I offered mine.

"Don't worry Dayo, Rab will never find us," Sola assured full of belief while patting Dayo on the back.

"Mum?" Sola said, offering me his pinkie. I gave him mine.

They continued the remainder of our journey excited about our new adventure. Their young lives had been so full of fear and uncertainty, and it'd taken such a strain on them, but now they welcomed a life without feeling scared.

We arrived in Nairn in plenty of time for Leigh to meet the estate agent at the house for 4pm to get the keys. After she'd concluded the paperwork - and without any issues - the boys were so happy to finally enter their new house. I'd anticipated a squabble over bedroom choices, but they were both just so happy to be out of Airdrie and away from 'all the lies', that they simply negotiated by themselves before coming to an amicable, joint decision. With Craig and Stephen having not yet arrived, we decided to take the children out of the empty, new house to go for fish and chips at the beach.

When we returned, there was still no sign of the removal lorry. It was approaching 7pm and I still hadn't heard from Craig or Stephen. I knew they should have been well on their way by now, as they'd hoped to be heading north by the afternoon.

By the time, "when will they be here?" and "why is he not here yet" had become repetitive, and after many games of *I Spy* in an empty house and *Hangman* on a limited paper supply, I decided to give Craig a call. I hadn't wanted to interrupt the hectic activity that comes with packing up a house, but my anxiety was really starting to build.

"Hey babe, how's it going?" I asked, relieved to hear his voice.

"Kemi, it's not. We haven't even left yet; there's still loads to do," he exhaled.

I could hear the worry and stress in his voice. *Oh my God, he's going to be seen - if he hasn't been already.* Panic filled me, but I forced myself to sound calm.

"Don't worry, it's okay . . . you can only go as fast as you can. We've come this far. I know God is watching over us," I tried to comfort. *Oh my God, please, please, please be watching over them.*

"Are the children okay? Your text said they were happy to be moving to Nairn." He sounded in a better frame of mind diverting to the children.

"Listen . . . we're all fine," I feigned, needing to get off the phone before my anxiety was discovered. "Don't *you* worry about *us – we're* playing *Hangman!*" We both laughed. I knew mine was fake, I suspected his was too. "I'll see you soon. I love you, Craig." *Please hurry up.*

"I love you too."

The day had been a long one, with both me and Leigh exhausted from entertaining the children. The boys had been as high as kites with excitement, but Leigh and I were done - and with not even as much as a chair to rest on.

Craig and Stephen finally arrived in Nairn at 2am to find all the children very much awake. There was no way they could have unloaded the truck in the darkness, yet somehow, they did manage to find a few mattresses for us all to 'camp' on in the living room. The children thought it was great fun.

We spent the weekend getting the house into some sort of order. Leigh and I dressed the house while Craig and Stephen emptied the lorry and rebuilt the furniture. All this while the boys were wasting no time in making their first new friends.

As we waved goodbye to Leigh and Stephen at the end of the weekend, it all became very real; we'd done it. We were free.

Honest life

It didn't take long for us to completely unpack. The rental house was very similar to the house we'd had to abandon - minus the extra clinic room and nursery, so our furniture had fitted perfectly. It was important that we settled quickly; the children had endured enough over the last nine months and I wanted them to feel safe and free.

I took the advice of the Serious Organised Crime Police and over the course of the next few days, spoke with the local police in Nairn. I was candid. I told them everything; from Michelle's allegations to my family's background - and especially bringing to their attention the fact that I'd given evidence regarding my dad's business. They were surprised - to say the least – but grateful for my honesty.

I also made an appointment to meet the boys' new headteacher; I needed to bring her up to speed. We all attended - even baby Tola. It was important that the headteacher saw our family together before she made any judgement of us. I disclosed everything that had been going on. I had to be upfront; it was important that we were honest and transparent. Should anyone find us, she would already know our side of the story. The headteacher was very warm and understanding and as we left, I hoped that we had come across as genuine. The boys started school the following week and settled in very well, and by the end of the second week they'd made friendships at both school and at home.

The weather was beautiful from the beginning of April all the way through to the end of summer, allowing us to spend a lot of time outside in the garden, at the local parks and, of course, at the beach.

One hot day after school, we took the children to *Findhorn Bay*, a former fishing hub around 15 miles east of Nairn. With the warm, spring sun pleasantly heating the clear, shimmering sea, Dayo and I couldn't resist a paddle.

"Mum, it's great here," Dayo shared as we walked hand-in-hand along the seafront, while the waves poured gently in and out over his brightly painted red toenails, burying them like rubies, and the cool breeze of the sea acted as a fan, reducing the intensity of the sun's rays. "Do you love it?"

"I love it so much Dayo," I said gratefully, taking in the beauty of what was quickly becoming our new life. Never in my wildest dreams did I think it was possible to find so much peace and remedy in Scotland, let alone on a beach in the Highlands during the normally harsh conditions of spring. It was bliss.

"Mum . . . people are nice here." He stopped in his tracks, taking a contemplative pause before continuing. "Mum . . . I don't want to ever go back to Airdrie - do you?" His little face furrowed as his eyes narrowed, looking up to mine for reassurance.

"Never, Dayo. Never," I said as I let go of his hand to pull him closer under my arm while giving him a look of certainty.

"I don't want Rab to find us," he stated firmly, lowering his eyes. The boys had started calling Rab by his first name since the day we moved. I squeezed him in tighter.

"Look Mum," Sola called from behind us while running at full speed, skipping and leaping across the undulating dunes. He and Craig had been encouraging Tola to walk and were giggling at her steady determination not to take either of their hands. "Mum look – seals!" Sola screamed with delight, making his way into the sea with Dayo hot on his heals.

As I sat on the beach with Craig and Tola watching the boys, still in their full school uniforms, wading with rolled-up trousers (Dayo was now happy to wear trousers and not shorts) trying to catch the seals, I knew I was in the right place for my children.

We started working in the *Golf View Hotel* the same week the boys started school. While the treatment room was relatively spacious and perfectly located en route to the hotel's spa, it could get unbearably hot to work in at times as it neighboured the hotel's boiler and heating system. That didn't matter for now – we had somewhere to work from. The staff were very welcoming and accommodating, and made sure guests were made aware of our services. We made some leaflets at home, as we couldn't afford to have any printed professionally, and placed them all over town; sports centres, the doctors' surgery, restaurants - anywhere and everywhere. We had to start our new life with the business hitting the ground running – there wasn't an alternative. If we wanted to stay here, we'd have to take every opportunity to earn.

The collapse of the house sale meant we had next to no savings and every penny counted. Money was a constant pressure – low in supply and high in demand; at one point, we were relying on the big, novelty *Coca-Cola* piggy bank bottle full of coppers and low value silver to support the family. I'd never before in all my life appreciated pennies with so much grace. The years of hoarding 1ps, 2ps, fives and tens had turned out to be a wise investment. The unexpected discovery of the odd 50 pence amongst all the peanuts and chicken feed made us feel like we'd won the lottery.

Thankfully, we steadily started to attract clients; at first, mainly staff members and guests of the hotel, but then we started to build a client base from the hotel's health club members. I didn't know if it would all dry up when the summer trade was over and being self-employed meant I couldn't say no to more business, so I even ran baby massage and meditation classes. While the hotel was providing a steady stream of clientele, I became very aware that we couldn't work from there forever; it wasn't bringing us the locals' business from the town, which we would need to maintain our home here. However, it was good enough for now.

Our work gave us the opportunity to meet a variety of new people - the majority of whom were lovely - and we quickly made some friends: a couple, Andrea and Becky with a daughter, Hannah, the same age as Tola. We had an amazing summer getting to know them, filled with endless play dates and dinners and even the odd sleepover. This all sandwiched in between regular visits from Sandra and David, Leigh and Stephen, and William and his husband. In the rare weekends we didn't have visiting guests, we would inevitably spend time with Orlando and Karen and their children. We were surrounded by the people we loved. Despite all that love, we were always on guard, constantly looking over our shoulders.

In early June, nearly one year after our first complaint to the social services, David and Sandra came to visit for a long weekend. We all had been looking forward to their arrival. The boys had even taken their bikes to school and asked if Sandra could be the one to collect them so they could cycle home along the prom to show her how good they were now.

David remained behind finishing off his coffee as Sandra left with Tola in her pushchair to collect the boys from school. Not long had passed before I became aware that something felt different – official - and with one glimpse of David's distressed, brown leather briefcase I realised he had some business afoot. While my presence had remained absent in Airdrie my story hadn't, with David and Alex continuing to work tirelessly on my complaint. Their relentless pursuit of answers and justice had gathered momentum and now, the Head of the Social Work Council wanted a sit down, face-to-face meeting - with me. I felt a lump drop from my throat all the way down to the pit of my stomach: heart-thudding anxiety.

"Kemi, it's great news," he enthused, "they want to have a face-to-face," David gleefully proclaimed, his enthusiasm laboriously trying to convince my frown to turn upside-down from across the paperwork-clad dining table. He was right; this was great news, but all I could think about was being spotted. By now, we'd successfully been in hiding for two and a half months, but not a single day had elapsed free from at least two dozen fearful thoughts of being caught.

"But David, can I? How can we be sure it's safe?" I mouthed, allowing my anxiety to do the talking, while its high pitch reacquainted with my eardrums. He smiled while giving my hand a comforting squeeze then calmly sat back with a wink. Having diluted his jubilation, he lowered his tone and engaged with honesty.

"Kemi, Alex and I have agreed if you don't want to go - or rather, can't go - we can handle it. We know your case like the back of our hands."

"But David, why in person? What does that mean exactly?" Craig asked, his face awash with every emotion from delight to despair and surprise to suspicion.

"It means they're shitting themselves," David snorted satisfyingly. "*They* know that *we* know *they've* fucked up . . . big time. Alex and I believe, at the very least, they'll admit to some of their mistakes and hopefully apologise." His glee started to recede as his mind wandered. "Or this keeps happening."

I knew what he meant; if there wasn't awareness of their mistakes, then their mistakes would continue to occur. This I knew too well. So, reluctantly, I agreed to go down for the meeting in July.

After yet another sleepless night filled with the worry of returning to my old world, I decided I needed to take some council. No matter how happy my life could seem, at times like this, my fear would always expose itself to me - overwhelming me. It was a virus that lay dormant, indulging in reminding me that it hadn't died, but in fact had evolved; mutated into a parasite that fed off my anxiety, strengthening its existence. The fear I'd learned as a child had never left me; it had grown with me - within me - ingrained in every part of me, and now, as I lay awake consumed, it felt like it wanted sole control of its host.

"Kemi, darling, how are you?" William answered his phone with concern. It was late and this was my third, consecutive attempt to reach him. I'd been desperate.

"William . . . I'm not good," I instantly unloaded, struggling to confine my fear and needing to release its pressure. Our friendship was strong enough to bypass civilities and etiquette. "The Social Work Council want a meeting . . . face-to-face," I confessed quietly, in case fear was listening.

"What? When? No, wait . . . why?" William spat, struggling to keep his mind and tongue in tandem, and not from the effects of tiredness, but rather bewilderment. "Kemi, this doesn't feel good . . . why do *you* need to go? David and Alex can take care of it . . . this feels like an unnecessary risk."

"Could you 'look' into it, William? My fear is off the scale - I can't get away from it," I exhaled.

"Kemi, I'll sit with it . . . but I feel you're not as safe as you think." He paused. "This is a long game. I told you I felt you had to build a new life - but it's not over, and by going it could mean putting yourself into play . . . before you have to."

He delivered his wisdom from a place so deep within that his voice dropped an octave and sounded as if it belonged to someone else, filling me with chills. I knew what this voice meant. This only happened when I was needing to pay attention; to really listen and hear what he had to say. I'd heard.

Notwithstanding my fear, a part of me felt I should be there; it was the opportunity I'd been longing for throughout the entire petrifying palaver. David and Alex had fought hard to create this opportunity and now, finally, I had an audience with the people in power who would determine if I'd been treated fairly or not. I had to go. My voice had to be heard.

I knew if I wasn't present, I could miss my opportunity to be heard, risking my name to be forevermore on some piece of paper in some report somewhere, stating that my mental health and ability as a mother was in question. That couldn't be the case. Plus, I needed assurances that Lydia, and anyone else for that matter, could never have the power to do this to anyone else. The latter was overriding my fear, poking it back into its pit. I decided to go.

"I wish I was going with you - I hate that you're doing this by yourself Kem," Craig said with a genuine conflict. We'd been up most of the night debating and deliberating the 'what ifs' and had come to the conclusion that the boys mustn't return to Airdrie under any circumstances. Getting caught was not an option so Craig would have stay behind with them in Nairn.

"I know, but we can't risk losing the boys, Craig," I said, closing my bag and gathering Tola's blanket and spare dummies for the journey.

I walked over to him and wrapped my arms around his neck. We hugged in silence. There was no point in talking about it anymore; if at any point it didn't feel right, I would just come home. So, nervously, I travelled down by train with Tola.

The fear of being seen dominated my travel and regardless of us sitting in the secluded, two-seater berth at the rear of the train, I was on edge the whole journey; being black in a predominately white country means you stand out - always. So, I chose to sit side-on to Tola, with my back to the aisle. Although I would be blind to whoever walked by, I figured there was less chance of someone recognising the back of my head.

Darkness had descended by the time we finally arrived nearly four hours later, offering some cover and comfort. I waited until the carriage was completely empty before daring to disembark. We were nearly there. One last walk from the train to Sandra's car and we'd be safe. With hood drawn and a scarf covering my face, I scooped up Tola and braved our final voyage. I was so relieved to see Sandra waiting for me in her silver *Mercedes-Benz* by the exit. We'd made it.

We stayed the night at Sandra and David's house in Airdrie where only four months earlier I'd existed. It now felt more like four years. With us having arrived so late, there was only enough time for a quick cup of tea before getting myself and Tola ready for bed. I didn't sleep - I couldn't. I was terrorised by thoughts of Lydia finding out that I was in Airdrie for the meeting, her having told my family and Rab, and them all waiting to capture me like a lynch mob. No matter how hard I tried, I couldn't shake off the overbearing feeling of apprehension. *They know I'm here.*

I lay awake as the minutes ticked by slowly, churning out fear-filled hour after fear-filled hour, the darkness remaining despite watching the bedroom fill with more and more daylight. By the time Tola became unsettled at 5.30am, I decided it was time to get up, but my thoughts followed me out of bed. *They know I'm here; they'll be waiting.* I couldn't think straight. It wasn't until Tola startled me with her delight at seeing Sandra entering the room that my dominated mind temporarily broke free.

"Oh God . . . morning Sandra," I squeaked, my voice pitchy from both tiredness and the tension that strangled my throat.

"Morning Kemi – sorry, I didn't mean to give you a fright . . . did you sleep at all?" she asked with concern while picking up Tola.

"No," I said, feeling like the world was closing in on me.

"David neither," she offered. We didn't need to discuss why; we could all feel it. "Ah, speak of the devil."

"Morning Kemi," David said, entering the room and sitting down beside me.

His eyes looked blurry - almost cloudy - certainly not their usual sharpness, and he was preventing them from engaging with mine for too long at a time. I knew David well enough to tell when he had something on his mind.

"David . . . I can't explain it, but this feels like a set up; it just doesn't feel safe," I unloaded, not wanting to disappoint him but needing to share my concerns.

"I know," David said while patting my hand, finally maintaining eye contact, "I feel the same," he revealed with a deep exhale, sounding as if I'd already been caught.

"I don't think I'm going to go; I can get the 10.10 train back to Inverness - if you can take me to the station, Sandra?" I rambled feeling like I had to get out of Airdrie and far away from its torment.

"Kemi, of course. You get yourself organised and let me get Tola ready," Sandra said without judgement, switching into maternal mode.

"Kemi . . . I think you're making the right choice. Leave this to me and Alex. I promise I'll get you justice," David said, his eyes regaining their steel. "You go and get ready, and Kemi . . . we're not telling anyone you're not coming – not until I'm in there; you'll be back in Inverness by then."

Before I knew it, I was waving good-bye to Sandra from the secluded, two-seater berth at the rear of the train as it started to pull off down the track. The rush to get there in time had temporarily distracted my fear, and while sitting there I was relieved to be getting out of the lion's den, it wasn't until we passed through Perth before I began to feel my body relaxing. I still feel like this even to this day. Whenever I reach Perth heading north, whether by train or car, I always feel like I am entering a different, positive world and leaving my old, negative one behind.

David phoned me that evening relieved to report that he hadn't seen Lydia, Rab or anyone from my family when he arrived for the meeting. The same went for when he left - as far as he was aware. He revealed there had been what appeared to be a genuine reaction of disappointment from the panel when only he and Alex entered the meeting room, but that he couldn't confirm if that was because I had been setup. We'd all felt like I had, and that was risky enough for me.

Their recommendation was for Lydia to receive more training.

"In what?" I protested.

"Kemi, grab yourself a chair. We've got them; they've admitted they failed to follow procedure," David updated euphorically. "We've got enough to take them to court."

He wasn't wrong – I did need to sit down. I was astonished, confused and stunned all at the same time within a nano second of hearing his words. I could hear Sandra cheering ecstatically in the background. My hands began to shake, overdosing in adrenaline. I'd prepared myself for disappointment - I'd expected my case to be made to look trivial before being dismissed. My pessimism hadn't allowed me to dream of this moment. David cleared his throat. Sandra drew silent.

"Kemi," he said gently, his tone cradling me, "they've not admitted to misconduct regarding referencing your mental health . . . or your race," my pessimism had been wise, "but we've still got enough to take them to court," he concluded returning to his jubilance.

"David - I don't know what to say . . . I'm just a bit shell-shocked," I said trying not to sound deflated.

I didn't want to dampen his spirits. He'd worked selflessly and relentlessly to attain justice for me - which he had achieved - it was just that it was a hollow justice. My end game had never been about monitory gain. All I ever wanted was an acknowledgement – some awareness - of the mistakes I'd had to endure, and for a procedural review so that no one else had to suffer the same experience.

"Kemi go and tell Craig the good news – I'll call you tomorrow when you've had time to think about it."

When I came off the phone, I was numb - deadened; flat. All hope had drained from me. I'd been put back in my place. I didn't want to have to go to court, but I now knew I'd have to. As long as there were reports in existence claiming I had a mental illness, my children would always be at risk.

Part three

Stolen

Autumn in Nairn was beautiful. It was a quieter time of year and there were so many changes to experience. Summertime had filled the small town - almost bursting it at its seams - with tourists from all over the world. Visitors arrived in their flocks to experience the historic spa town adored by Charlie Chaplin, the two world-class golf courses, the nearby *Findhorn Foundation* and the historical castles such as *Cawdor Castle*, with its history steeped in the tales of *Macbeth*. Now that autumn breathed life into the town, the few remaining visitors were mainly the migrating, pink-footed geese who arrived full of grace and beauty. Autumn had kissed the emerald green of the forest to gold, making it feel even more spacious and breathable. The town had slowed down to a quieter, cosier pace; a time to wind down and settle in for the oncoming winter.

David and I had continued to build my case against the Social Work Department after they'd refused to admit they had used my race and unsupported mental health claims to discredit me; meanwhile Alex was intent on raising in Parliament the failings I'd endured due to the colour of my skin. Despite their support, I never believed anyone would care about what had happened to me - or my children. This belief was part of my essence; and it ran deep. It had been installed by the time I was eight years old, embedded deeply within me, laying the foundations of my fundamental belief that I wasn't good enough. Before I knew David, I had only ever been taught how not to be seen - and if I was seen, how to behave well, as that *might* keep me safe.

However, since David had entered my life, he'd taught me a lot about what was and wasn't acceptable - and more importantly what was illegal - when it came to racism and discrimination. He had shocked me when I learned that I actually had rights, by law, and that it was against the law to be racist. He was fighting to protect my rights, humbling me with his dedicated passion and determination to achieve full justice and have my name completely cleared of any doubts regarding my mental health.

His determination to right my injustices stirred an anger in me that acted as a catalyst to spur me on to continue trying to get justice for my family. Little did I know just how high a price I would have to pay for trying to make a better life for my children.

#

Back in Airdrie, things were gathering momentum. A private investigator turned up at Leigh's house the week after the meeting I hadn't attended.

"I'm trying to locate a Miss Ogunyemi - she's fled the jurisdiction with her children, breaking a court order. There's genuine concern for her mental

279

state and the safety of the children," the PI laid on thickly, trying to lure Leigh into a fear driven disclosure.

"First of all, I think you mean Mrs Ferguson-Ogunyemi," Leigh cut in, rebuking his tactics, "and no, I have no idea where any of them are – and even if I did, I wouldn't be sharing it with you. Who sent you? No, wait . . . let me guess – Daisy?" Leigh questioned.

"I can't say at this time . . . ," the PI began, changing his bullish demeanour to one of defensiveness.

"Well, fuck off then . . . and don't come back," Leigh ordered, closing the door in his face. I was overwhelmed with panic as I heard her rendition of what had taken place.

"But Kemi . . . there's more," she warned with a dire angst. *Is that not enough? How can there be more?* "Before that idiot turned up, I was just about to phone you anyway. When I was down the street today, I saw Michelle - I literally walked straight into her coming out of the chemist."

The sound of Michelle's name launched my accelerating heart into my mouth, preventing me from speaking and forcing me to listen.

"Kemi, she came right into my face – smiling, giving it all: "Tell my bitch of a mum we know where she is." She said she's looking forward to the boys being taken away from you, and she said it with such . . . hatred and enjoyment. I just said: "Okay Michelle - whatever - get the fuck out of my face," and walked away. I'm fuming. Kemi, I know she's your daughter and only 16, but my God, I wanted to punch her; she's loving all the shit she's causing you guys."

Leigh was filled with so much anger, I handed the phone to Craig so she could vent. I understood this had been a very difficult experience for her; she adored her baby brother and just wanted to protect him. I'd be devastated and furious if someone was doing this to Tayo; but Michelle was still my daughter and I found it hard to hear how others felt about her. It made me want to protect her. I left the room so they could speak freely.

When Craig came off the phone, we just looked at one another with disbelief and fear. I spoke first after what seemed like an eternity of silence.

"She knows nothing," I said with a false determination, refusing to give Michelle's revelation any energy. That would only have added fuel to my already raging, fiery anxiety.

"I know," Craig agreed, trying to convince us both.

"The PI - that's my mum," I whispered.

"I know," he repeated with frustration, revealing his anxiety. "Will you phone William?" he asked more softly, regaining his composure, trying not to flame the fear that we both felt simmering.

"Yes, tonight," I offered, hoping he believed me.

"Kemi, worry is like paying interest on a debt you don't have yet. Don't live with fear. Make a life for you and the children and Craig. Establish yourself in your new world. Live, Kemi, for however long you can before you're pulled back into this game."

William had told me this before I left Airdrie. Deep down I knew what he meant: sooner or later, I would be found. That's why I chose not to call William; I didn't want to know the estimated time of arrival of the terrors from our past.

I had concerns, but reassured myself that I'd been careful and had left no paper trails. I didn't know, and I didn't want to know, the law regarding my current predicament - my fear wouldn't allow me to look at it. So I just thought - and needed to believe - that even if we were found, considering all the fighting I'd done so far to prove I was a fit mother, I wouldn't lose my children. I didn't want to know if I was going to lose them. All I wanted was to be a mother.

Looking back, it was then that I decided I would no longer run. If I was found I would deal with it and protect my children as best I could. I followed William's advice and banished my fears; imprisoned them deep in my subconscious, where they could only escape to haunt me in my dreams. I could only deal with what was actually happening in the now and not something that hadn't happened yet.

So, for the next couple of months we went about living our new lives enjoying the wonderful outdoor life of the hills, forests and sea. I wanted to treasure all that we'd gained. The boys had not only settled into their new lives, but had also truly blossomed with confidence and independence. The move had been great for them; they were thriving with feeling safe.

Back in Airdrie, they hadn't been able to leave the garden unattended, let alone go to the shop unsupervised. Back then, the local shop was just a three-minute walk from my front door, with no roads to cross. However, with all the crime and routine racism, not only were they not allowed to go, through fear, they had no desire to.

Here in Nairn however, there was no such fear – only desire. The estate we lived on interconnected with the next two estates via a cycle path, leaving only one main road (with a pedestrianised, sleeping policeman crossing) to navigate when going to the shop. Despite the shop being a good ten-minute cycle – at least twenty there and back - they loved to venture there and enjoyed talking with anyone they met. Dayo's first words to me, and the genuine disbelief in his tone on returning from their maiden voyage, reaffirmed that we'd made the correct choice to leave Airdrie.

"Mum . . . we're back - guess what? No one called us any names, and no one stole our money . . . can we go again tomorrow?"

Here in Nairn, they were still a minority, but at this time - and for the first time - their race wasn't being used to diminish or punish them. Here, in Nairn, was safe.

The 4th October was a beautifully bright, autumn morning with a fresh, crisp nip in the air, just cool enough to cloud your breath. We dropped the boys off at school, lunchboxes in hand, before Craig dropped me off at the hotel. That morning, the often-overwhelming heat of the adjacent boiler room was for once enjoyable, blending nicely with the post-summer chill to create a misleadingly cosy and safe ambience in my treatment room.

I was working with a client when my phone rang. I was annoyed and apologised, but I could never leave my phone on silent; I had to always be available in case *something* happened.

I ignored it, but when it rang again for the second time, and without barely a second's silence from the first call, my heart exploded and began beating in my throat. I didn't need to wait for a third call - I knew it was Craig, and I knew it was about my children. We had a rule: never disturb each other at work unless it was about the children, in which case we would keep ringing until the other answered.

As I covered my client and made my way across the room towards my doom, something inside me knew I was about to feel pain like I'd never felt before. By the time I'd wiped away the oil from my hands and picked up my phone, it stopped ringing. I just stared at the screen: Missed Call: Hubby. Tears warmed my eyes as the phone rang again in my hand, screaming at me to answer it. As my world spun round, I took a deep breath.

"Craig," I whispered.

"Kemi - you need to come home," he advised in a tone of desperation that, as hard as he tried, his voice just couldn't hide.

Chills ran up my spine demanding that the hairs on the back of my neck stand tall and causing a ripple of goosebumps to blister into existence all over my skin. *They've found us.*

"Why?" I casually asked trying not to raise my client's attention. I was in denial. I already knew his answer, but I was refusing to accept the pain that was about to devastate me.

"Kem, it's the boys - you have to come home."

I could hear the pain and desperation in his voice, but still I delayed, not wanting to accept the reality. *They really have found us.*

"What's happened?" I asked. As the words left my mouth my body braced itself, shooting a deep pain up my neck, igniting my old injury.

He whispered two words; two words that still to this day fill me with terror: "Sheriff officers."

"They've found us," I stated, interrupting him - not wanting to hear any more details.

"Kemi, ask Michael to bring you home – now," Craig said firmly trying to bring me into focus.

All I could think about was how much I didn't want to go home. If I didn't go home, it wouldn't be real.

"Kemi, they have the boys," Craig said solemnly.

My client, Michael, took me home, but the details in between Craig's last words and me arriving are completely lost. I can only remember getting out of Michael's car and entering my front door on legs so weak I didn't

282

think they'd be able to prop me up for much longer.

As I entered the living room, waiting with Craig were two, black-suited men with paperwork. They quickly explained the nature of their visit stating that I'd been found to be in contempt of court; I'd taken my children out of the jurisdiction without informing their father, resulting in Rab being granted full residency of the boys in my absence.

"What? How can you do this?" I managed to say through my accelerated, shallow breathing.

"You'll need to take legal advice on this," was all one of them offered.

"Kemi," Craig interrupted, "the boys are on their way down the road, just now. They left hours ago."

"What? They're on their way back where with who?" I demanded.

"Their father," the other officer said with derision.

"And your mum . . . and Michelle," Craig added, causing my head to spin and stomach to fill with nausea.

"My mum?" I whispered in disbelief. "Please . . . can you just leave? Now." I asked the deliverers of my worst fear in the world. I needed them out of my house.

They left as if nothing had happened.

My boys had been taken from me. A part of me was lost. I sobbed as I felt it dying inside me. Tola crawled onto my lap and with her tiny hands wiped my silent tears away. I was overwhelmed looking into her eyes. Devastation took over me - a familiar desolation that came with the knowledge of what she'd also lost; the big brothers whom she loved; the big brothers who loved her so much. Not only did I know what she'd lost, I knew I wouldn't be able to explain to her – this little girl of not even two years old - why one morning her brothers went off to school and never came back home. What emptiness this would leave in her. The devastation consumed me, reminding me of the pain that I'd endured as a result of the early loss of my brother, Tunde. I sobbed for us both.

When Rab had turned up at the school with the sheriff officers to remove the boys, they'd been met with great resistance - and not only from the boys themselves. The headteacher had refused his request - court order or not. My honesty and transparency from day one, coupled with the boys' visible distress at the prospect of being removed, made her involve the local police and education's legal department. She wasn't going to hand them over without a fight.

Ultimately, this only delayed the inevitable. She couldn't stop them; they had a court order. A court order: something put in place to protect children from danger - not put them in it. The sheriff officers had insisted that I wasn't to be informed of the boys' removal until after they'd driven off. None of it made any sense. How could children be removed from their mother like that?

It turns out it's very easy when the mother is a woman of colour and the people against her are white.

So, how did they manage it? Teamwork. I don't believe Rab would have taken the steps to find us without my mum's unhealthy obsession for control. It turned out my mum knew the law regarding court orders. She'd started working as a paralegal and had sought counsel and, as I would find out later, had teamed-up again with Rab. They hadn't been on the same side since he'd messed up their first attempt to get custody of the boys, but now, as the father he held the key to them finding us. She now needed Rab to make it work.

I hadn't told the boys' former headteacher in Airdrie what I'd intended to do. I thought the paper trail would end with her - and it had . . . until their new school requested their files be transferred to Nairn. Their former headteacher then had an address for the boys' new school and was legally bound to tell Rab.

Next, my parents paid for a private investigator. The PI never visited Craig's parents, or David and Sandra, any of our friends, or any of the people who had regular contact with us - other than Leigh. That didn't matter though; they knew they had only to convince the court they'd made a sincere effort to locate me.

Then they applied for a Change of Residency court order for the boys to be returned to Coatbridge to live with Rab. However, their request was under the pretence that they didn't know where the boys were. My mum, despite being legally obliged to tell the court she had this information, didn't. She knew the court would have contacted me directly, foiling her next move. Instead, she kept quiet, other than to inform the court that her PI hadn't been able to locate us. Without an exact location, the court's next move was to request a court summons be advertised in the local newspapers closest to where she thought we could be living. Despite learning from the school that we were in Nairn, she said she believed we could be in Inverness with Craig's relations. Inverness is nearly 20 miles away from Nairn. A summons was advertised with the date of the hearing set for July.

They took the chance that I wouldn't see the advert and their plan worked. I haven't seen it still to this day. In my absence, the Sheriff found me guilty of contempt of court and changed the boys' full residency to Rab.

I know what you're thinking; surely all kinds of compiled reports and completed background checks would need to have been performed to change a child's residency? No, there weren't any. None. The Social Work Department wasn't even involved, and even if they had been, they had no concerns; I had my apology and they were still under investigation regarding their treatment of me because of the colour of my skin.

No, all they had - and all they'd needed - was a sworn statement from my white mum; an affidavit stating she believed I was mentally ill. No one bothered to investigate her statement. Residency order granted; no questions asked.

By early September, after sitting with the residency order for over two months to make it look like they didn't know where I was when it was granted, they finally applied to the court for sheriff officers to enforce the order, citing that they now knew the boys were in Nairn. They were granted the enforcement by late September.

And that's it. That's how easy it is to take children away from their mother - the only person they have ever lived with. I truly believe this would never have happened to the children of a white mum and a black dad.

Going back

"Kemi, phone your mum," Craig said, snapping me back into the present. Hearing him name my mum made me alert to my situation. "Tell her we're coming to get our boys," he said with determination, as he took Tola from my arms to pack her safely into her car seat.

How could she do this to me? She knew me and must have known this was wrong. Surely, even she couldn't think it was right to treat another human being this way. However, to my mum, this wasn't about right and wrong; this was about me leaving her. In that moment tears overwhelmed me like a relentless high tide, drowning me in a deep grief - not just for the loss of the boys, but surprisingly, for the loss of my mum. I knew then that she'd dealt me a blow she could never take back or justify. We would all have to live with this.

I felt so weak, my body sinking, suffocating under the tidal waves of emotion. I was paralysed with shock, locked in an abyss. I couldn't do anything. With every laboured breath my pain tightened. I felt deflated, collapsed; empty, other than the dense overwhelming fear and anxiety. I knew I had to get the boys back - at whatever cost - but I doubted I had the strength. *Kemi, courage is not the absence of fear, it's the action taken regardless of fear.* "Grandad," I whispered to myself as I made my way numbly to the car.

For once I couldn't get back to Airdrie soon enough, but with every caravan and mobile home in Scotland apparently determined to halt my progress, the three-hour journey back to Hell took an eternity. An eternity intensified by Tola's uncontrollable wailing in the most ferocious, animalistic howl, that only permitted silence in the nano second it took her to gasp for breath to fuel further shrieking. I was lost for clarity confined in that chaotic car, replaying heart breaking scenarios in my mind - not thinking them, but rather witnessing them; a prisoner forced to spectate my own perilous imagination.

Somewhere along the journey mayhem silenced briefly, enough so that I was suddenly aware of being present. Aware of the raindrops sliding down the window, mirroring my tear-sodden cheeks and aware of the vast bleak and barren landscape that mirrored my soul. In that silence, motherhood resuscitated and kicked in and I began to do what I'd always done: fight to protect my children.

I called David and Sandra, and then William. I was gathering my team – I needed them and their support. By the time I'd finished debriefing – reliving my horror through words – I felt a new strength building momentum within me; not from my fears or desperate anxieties abandoning me, but from the joining in unison of my allies. The instinct of motherhood combined with the reinforcement of my battalion acted like a shot of

286

adrenaline, compelling my next act: call my antagonist.

"Mum, what've you done?" I questioned, gripping my phone tightly to rein in my anger.

"Kemi, I've nothing to say to you," she said dismissively. My grasp clenched, absorbing some of my fury.

"You come and kidnap my children and then say you have nothing to say?" I retaliated.

"Kidnaped!" she snorted. "You're so dramatic. They're with me, Rab and Michelle." Her words travelled at lightspeed to land a gut-sickening, body blow.

"I want to speak to my mum," I heard Dayo screaming in the background, his piercing pitch stabbing at my heart.

"Put the boys on the phone please," I requested, at a loss to hide my anguish.

"Mummy . . . let me speak to her," Sola cried in the background, joining Dayo's torment to amplify the tangible commotion down the phone.

"No Kemi - you'll only upset them," she rebuked, condescendingly.

"*I'll* upset them! They're already way past being upset. Do you want them to be hysterical?"

She paused for thought. She didn't have the boys on her side yet and she needed them to see her as being the good Nanny - not the bad Nanny who stopped them talking to their mum. In that moment she became fully aware of how her actions would be perceived by them and the outside world. True to character, her acute need to be seen to be doing the right thing overruled her initial rebuff. She handed the phone over; she couldn't refuse.

"Mummy . . . they're saying . . . they're saying we can't . . . live with you . . . that you're bad," Dayo struggled to relay, confusion and fear forcing his sobbing to break his words.

"Baby, breathe. I need you to be very brave," I said, fighting back my own tears. "I'm in the car right now and I'm coming. I don't know if I'll be able to bring you home tonight, but I'll be at Auntie Leigh's house so that I'm nearby."

I explained that I needed to get my lawyer to fix this, but that it would be fixed. My words seemed to pacify him, with his breathing starting to steady by the time he passed the phone over to Sola. I repeated my reassurances to Sola and he had only one concern:

"Will it take long Mummy, before we can come home?" I told him no. I wasn't lying; I believed this would be the case.

That conversation was one of the hardest - if not the hardest - I've had in my life. Having to tell the boys that I couldn't just come and get them was devastating. My boys were in the custody of the people I'd tried so hard to protect them from and I'd no idea what was going to happen next. The one thing I was certain of, make no mistake: I would get my boys back. I knew this from deep within. I just didn't know what the cost would be.

Before coming off the phone to my mum, I'd arranged to go to her house that evening. My feet ate up her driveway with purpose while my heart pounded with relief at finally being able to hold the boys. With Craig waiting in the car, I rang her doorbell expecting the boys to answer and run into my arms. They weren't there.

Instead, my cowardly dad opened the door. He briefly met my eyes, lowered his face and walked away without uttering a single word. Washing his hands of the situation, he silently passed mum in the hallway on her way to tear into me like she'd done so many times before. She was so cruel.

"Who the hell do you think you are just leaving without telling Rab? He was so distraught Kemi," she spat, weakly portraying sincerity.

Oh, that's the play; this was all for Rab: Father of the Year, because he's always had the children's best interests at heart.

"Are you kidding me? Since when has Rab given a fuck about my children?"

My voice was beginning to break now. I couldn't control it. She had managed to get my children and she didn't care how it affected them; just as long as she got what she wanted: me. In that moment I was reminded of that part of her that hated me as a child. She wasn't going to let me see my children and she was enjoying her control over me again.

"You've taken my children away from me. Do you not understand what this will do to them? And me? Please Mum, don't do this." I was begging now. Humiliated, shameful tears filled and choked me.

"You're not in your right mind Kemi," she stated, in a tone I instantly recognised; a tone I'd heard so often throughout my life during her narrative that *I* was the problem – but that she'd help me.

"If you come back, we'll give you the boys back," she took an exhale and continued with a warm smile, like a salesperson pitching you a bargain. "You'll have to live with Rab, but he's happy to have you back."

Shock now filled me. What was she saying? I felt like I was 24 again - as if I'd stepped back in time to when she and Rab had controlled me. Dread quickly replaced my shock. I was sickened and had to leave. I stood up to look her dead in the eye.

"I will get my children back and we'll never forgive you for this." I walked straight out of the house with her following me in a desperate rant.

"You left me. You're *my* daughter and I'll do whatever it takes to bring you back home to me . . . "

I closed the car door on her tirade and asked Craig to drive. I was furious, scared, sickened and confused, but above all, I was helpless. The only thing I could do was phone Rab and ask to see the boys. He took great pleasure in saying no. My mum and Rab had planned their operation well and together they'd built a strong fortress around my children, barricading them from me. That's when I decided to go to the local police station for advice.

I recognised one of the on-duty officers, and he remembered me and all my troubles. He was astonished to learn my current circumstances and while he wished there was something he could do to help, by law he was powerless. His only advice was to apply to the court for visitation access, as Rab would not co-operate. As I left the station, the officer, still perplexed as to what I was going through, asked me how this could possibly happen. I had no answer. I needed legal advice.

I didn't want to go back to the same lawyer who had previously represented me - I wasn't sure if I could trust her – she was friends with Rab's lawyer, the one he had used in our divorce. Instead, I made an appointment to meet a lawyer, back north in Nairn, who had a great reputation in family law.

We stayed at Leigh's house in Airdrie for a few days, hoping that I would be able to see the boys. With the Home Guard remaining vigilant, I was restricted to infrequent phone calls, with every conversation revealing the boys' ever-increasing distress. All I could do to comfort them was to tell them I was going home to speak to a lawyer in Nairn and that I would be coming straight back to Airdrie.

I met with the lawyer, and just like the police officer in Airdrie, she couldn't get her head around what had happened. "You must have really upset someone quite important," was her only logic. She told me getting the boys back should be relatively straight forward; that the court would surely give the children back quite quickly as they had always lived with me.

She warned however, that if she represented me her fees would likely total in excess of £10,000 once she included all the travel costs and expenses, and that it would be a minimum of six weeks before she could represent me. She recommended that I go back to my original lawyer in Airdrie, that it would be quicker and cheaper, plus, she knew all of my history's complexities. Reluctantly, I took her advice and managed to get an appointment for the next day.

Airdrie lawyer had a lot to say about what had been going on while I was away. She'd been present in court when the children's residency was changed and it turns out I had upset someone of apparent importance: the sheriff. She informed me that the sheriff had been furious that I hadn't attended his hearing.

"Kemi, if you'd only told me what you were planning . . . I could have helped you; but now . . . you're facing a long and tough journey. Make sure you do whatever is asked of you . . . or you could be punished further."

#

Still to this day, I do not understand why it was so important to punish me and destroy my children. I don't understand why the children's needs were never put first. It was all about taking away the power I had as a mother and causing great trauma to two little boys - trauma they would carry well into their adulthoods.

Visits

Over the next three weeks, the phone contact with the boys became less - almost non-existent - with Rab rarely answering my calls. In the scarce times that he did answer, he would limit the boys to just a couple of minutes, under the duress of his strict supervision. He would end the call if he didn't like what they were talking about, and he would end the call if he was getting bored. He would end the call because he could – he didn't need a reason. Those three weeks apart was the longest separation the boys and I had experienced since they were born.

After denying numerous requests from my lawyer, Rab eventually agreed to let me and Tola see the boys for an hour at his house - under his supervision. I couldn't believe this was really happening to us. I was allowed an hour with my children. One hour. Sixty minutes was as long as I could be trusted for. An hour filled me with shame, as if I was an unfit mother – that I was a risk to my children. By now Dayo had stopped asking me about my lawyer. I tried not to think about the small changes I was already sensing from the boys, so instead, I thought about how bad a mother I must be to be punished like this.

I lay awake in bed on the morning of the visit, Tola on one side and Craig on the other, both asleep in a temporary rest. I was restless, gripped with utter desperation to see my boys, despite our visit being under the guard of the man who had terrorised us all for so long. Looking out of the window, all I could see was a cold and grey morning, the kind of which I've only ever experienced in Airdrie. Desolate, dull and depressing. From the moment I stepped out of bed it felt like I was submerged in a thick, grey soup, that I had to drag myself through with every step. Being away from Airdrie had provided a rest from its dense, heavy atmosphere, but that morning I realised I had well and truly re-entered it. I could feel its suction trying to take me under.

Rab lived in infamous, high-rise flats on the edge of Coatbridge's town centre, notorious for housing a lot of alcohol and drug addicts, and where visits from police cars and ambulances were an everyday occurrence. An horrific place for anyone to live - let alone my children. What made the horror even worse was that Rab didn't live alone; he had a flatmate - his drug-dealing friend. I had raised my concerns about Rab's flatmate in court - back when Rab had his failed attempt for custody - and even my mum was aware of who he was and what he did.

As we arrived at *Terror Plaza*, Tola began to cry hysterically as soon as she saw her brothers. She was so overwhelmed. She couldn't understand why her brothers had been taken away from her and why they were here, in a stranger's house. She certainly wasn't going to be able to understand why they weren't going home with her.

Almost immediately after entering Rab's lair, Sola began to unloaded a barrage of questions while leading me by the hand into Rab's living room.

"How long will it be before we can come home Mum?" he asked with desperation, but before I could reply, Dayo interrupted:

"Shh! Sola remember - you're not allowed to ask that," he rebuked. *Oh my God.*

He wasn't trying to help his brother avoid getting into trouble, he was sincerely annoyed at Sola for not following orders. Shock ran through me, igniting a multitude of heartaches. Rab was silencing them. Not only had he kidnapped them – abducted them against their wishes, to live with him, a man that, as far as they were concerned, had only supplied fear and bad memories - but now, he was forbidding them from talking about their wishes to come back home.

Sola had always been a little ball of determination with his own strong mind, and right now, he was still able to express what he wanted. He always had a strong sense of right and wrong and would freely admit if he'd done something wrong. Equally, he wouldn't back down on his beliefs if he felt injustice, regardless of who was in dispute. I feared what the repercussion might be for Sola having asked a forbidden question. I feared more knowing Sola would resist any attempts to have him conform.

Dayo was not the same as Sola. He was more passive, full of empathy and eager to make others happy. He was that bit older than Sola and had his own vivid memories of Rab's violence. Those experiences had brought him an awareness that wasn't as strong in Sola. That awareness was fear.

I think in Dayo's little mind, because a sheriff had ordered that they live with Rab, I must have done something really bad and therefore anything Rab and my mum told him, he believed. I was now the liar. My gentle, little boy was losing his gentleness and it was being replaced with anger. An anger which was being directed subtly towards me. I could feel the pinch, but I could see he was only trying to figure out how to survive in his current predicament. Terror filled me knowing that I was losing him.

While trying to recover myself, still reeling from Dayo's resentment, horror landed a breath-taking body-blow. *What the . . . ?* As I looked round the living room a sickening surge ran from my eyes to my gut. I could see there were wedding pictures of me and Rab! After all these years - seven years - he still had pictures of our wedding up on his wall like a twisted shrine, as if he was trying to keep his distorted memories - his twisted ideas of the happy past - alive. All I could see was how ill and unhappy I looked in each of them.

At one point Rab tried to interact with Tola, but he was very awkward and edgy which made me very uncomfortable. Tola didn't like it much either. When he tried to win her over with a biscuit, she just screamed at him and cuddled into Dayo. Holding Tola melted Dayo. He loved her so much.

"Don't worry Tola, this is my dad. You know him," he said gently, trying to reassure his little sister.

"No, bad. No Dayo home," Tola stated in protest before running to me to lift her up.

She didn't have many words, but we all knew what she meant. As I comforted the crying toddler, I realised despite her being a baby, her senses were fine-tuned.

"Kemi," Rab whispered softly as he sat on the sofa beside me, so as not to be heard by the boys, "I can give you them back."

"What?" I questioned, shocked. I knew he'd never go against my mum, yet my heart lifted for an instant at the possibility. I listened with caution; I knew there'd be a price.

"Well," he began matter-of-factly, "if you come back, you can have them." He said it so sincerely like he meant what he was saying.

"I can't come back; I don't have a home here anymore," I replied.

"No, back here - with me. Come back to me and you can have the boys." He took a deep breath before finishing with a smile: "And Tola of course."

Are you insane? My mum had said the same thing, but I just heard it as nothing more than a throw away comment she said in the heat of the moment; yet here it was again. I was beginning to see how their plan would come together, with baby Tola thrown in for good measure. Panic and disgust filled me.

"Never!" I breathed from somewhere deep inside me. "Never! How could you even begin to think such a thing?"

I felt sick. This man was a monster and he had my children, and with my mum's backing, they'd decided that the only way for me to have my children was for me to return to Rab.

"Well, if you think you'll get them any other way," he bragged with a satisfactory smile, "you won't – ever."

"Yes, I will. I will get my boys back - even if it kills me." And with that, there was no more said on the matter.

As soon as I arrived for my second visit, Sola, true to character, couldn't wait to tell me what had happened the previous morning.

"Mummy, we were waiting to go upstairs in the lift, but when the doors opened, there was a man in it, just lying there, and he had an injection in his neck, and there was massive blood, everywhere, and he was dead Mum," he said with a big exhale, as if the pressure to carry his horror was finally deflating. My horror swelled.

"What? Are you sure?" I asked, hoping he was mistaken.

"Yes Mum, it was very scary . . . I was crying," he confessed bowing his head.

"I'm so, so sorry that happened to you, Solie, and I'm sorry I wasn't there," I said pulling him in close for a cuddle.

"Dad said I was a baby." He rushed his words out hearing Rab and Dayo heading towards the living room with drinks.

Sola's reaction briefed me yet again that he was being ordered not to tell me anything. I didn't mention it to Rab; I didn't want him to punish Sola. Instead, I added it to the never-ending list of concerns for my lawyer's attention.

I later found out from Sola that he and Dayo didn't actually live with Rab; that they only stayed over at Rab's twice a week - three times at the most. The majority of their time was actually spent at my mum's house with Michelle. This caused a great internal conflict within me. The court had granted an order for my children to be removed from me - the only person they had ever lived with – to be handed over to Rab, only for him to then pass them off for the majority of the week. His not bothering to have them added salt to my wounds, but at the same time I took great relief in knowing the boys weren't in the dangerous and exposing environment that was Rab's flat.

I'd known all along that Rab didn't want the boys – and neither did my mum. Rab was only interested in me going back to him and my mum had only wanted me to return to Airdrie. However, they both wanted power over me, and they both wanted me to be punished for my wrong-doings: my honesty.

It was terrifying. I could feel the boys slipping away from me. I was terrified knowing the danger that surrounded them. I was terrified knowing my mum and Rab were working on them, poisoning them against me. However, what terrified me the most was that I knew they could. I felt so powerless to protect my children.

The long drives home after my hour visits were full of mourning. The two empty seats either side of Tola's baby seat served as a cruel reminder of our loss. She would cry the minute the boys said goodbye and would not be consoled. Her cries would just worsen no matter what I did, escalating from a wail to a frenzied roaring so intense it forced her face to turn scarlet in between gasps for air. She wouldn't stop until she'd tired herself into a tear-sodden sleep. It was only then that I would allow myself to crumble. The family car never felt so empty – lifeless. The house felt the same. Quiet, stark; missing its soul. My boys had disappeared and I didn't speak about it. I couldn't. We'd had to tell a couple of friends about the boys being taken, and that my mum was involved, but I just couldn't face talking about it when I was back in Nairn. No one saw my pain. Thinking back, people must have known. We lived in a tiny town where everyone knew everyone's business; but no one ever asked.

Throughout the daytime, the boys' friends would arrive knocking at the door, asking the same question: "Are Dayo and Sola coming out to play?" My answer never changed. I'd feign a smile and release my response through my lumped throat: "They're not back from visiting their dad yet." Their tiny faces of disappointment mirrored my pain. I felt like a failure.

Night-time was the worst. I hardly slept, and if I did, I'd wake up panicked from one of my many nightmares. I couldn't get away from my pain. Excruciating pain, every second of every day, permanently residing in me, occupying and consuming me with shame. It never left me.

Then I started to hear the tempting whispers flirting with me, sweet-talking me, offering me a remedy to my pain. I recognised her enticing voice . . . Anorexia. She was getting closer than ever. I was still eating, but I didn't want to. I remembered I could dissolve my feelings – my pain - by not eating, but right now, anorexia was not a choice; she made me too submissive and I needed to stay focused to get my children back. The belief in my boys returning kept me going, and so I continued to work as if nothing had happened. I needed to; I needed to be occupied in the moment and preoccupied from my tortured thoughts. We'd been building a new life for our family since we arrived in Nairn and now more than ever, we had to continue building that life for the boys to come back to.

We felt we'd been quickly accepted into Nairn; we offered the town a new service and were very good at our jobs and had even made some friends. We felt the town was proud to have our little brown family be part of their community. By early November, we'd continued to establish ourselves in our new community by opening our first clinic outside of the hotel: a little shop at the bottom of the high street, situated on the bridge that crossed the River Nairn.

Rab continued taking pleasure in my humiliation – my inability to see the boys without his presence. He'd even tried to involve Michelle in the visits, but I'd refused; not under any circumstances. My lawyer advised that if Michelle wanted contact with Tola she would need to arrange it herself, through her own lawyer.

It took six weeks from the boys being taken before I could get a court hearing. By the time my hearing arrived, I'd been allowed three one-hour visits.

Children's welfare court

The court battle was set for late November - less than four weeks before Christmas. We drove down to Leigh's the evening before, hoping that Tola would sleep most of the journey south. It was the best way to travel for everyone. Tola was no longer the content and happy child she had been. Laughter and giggles had been firmly replaced by crying and tears. She cried most of the time. She'd lost her independence – her ability to play without constant assistance. She demanded total attention and her brothers daily. "They're at Rab's - they'll be home soon," was all I could offer, but that only further tightened her screams. She never did take to Rab. My daughter was born with good instincts, and feeling her pain broke my heart. I was older than Tola when I lost my brother and no one had told me the truth, so I was determined that, as little as she was, I had to be as honest with her as I could.

After dropping Tola off at Leigh's, I went to see William for guidance. I needed to be prepared for court and any insight he could offer would be gladly welcomed.

"Kemi, I had no warning this was happening . . . now," he said with love, sincerity and frustration.

I could see he was carrying a self-imposed weight of guilt – as if he believed he had failed to protect me. He hadn't.

"You know some things are just meant to happen – no matter what," he reminded.

"So, what should I do?" I implored, feeling betrayed that fate had waded in on my plight against the world for good measure.

"Same as before," he replied adamantly, "just be honest. Kemi just be the mother. You will get them back," his voice tailed off to a sigh before continuing, "but . . . "

"But not tomorrow," I interrupted.

Silence filled the room. If William was correct, I would be stepping into court the next morning knowing that not only did I have a battle on my hands, but that the boys wouldn't be returning home with me that day. However, at least I knew they would return home eventually; eventually I would have them back. I just didn't know how long 'eventually' would take or how much damage 'eventually' would permit to be inflicted on my children in the process.

The next morning, after dropping Tola off at Sandra's, I arrived at court with Craig for support, however he wouldn't be giving evidence - once again, he wasn't allowed to be present. He felt helpless; powerless to do anything. What had once centred around him, was now excluding him. It was no longer about Craig. He had no say, regardless of the fact he was the children's father, 24/7. As far as the court was concerned, he didn't exist.

I felt sick and numb making my way through the entrance. My stomach was churning, my hands were soaked, and my mouth felt so dry my voice strained to breach it. When I registered at the front desk, the receptionist knew who I was without me giving my name. I suppose it could have been luck, guessing my face matched my name.

I was directed to go through a pair of swing doors into a bleak corridor and take a seat outside the court room. Sitting there, on a hard plastic chair that wouldn't look out of place in either an 80's primary school, or some village community centre, I remember being concerned that the dress I was wearing was much looser than it had previously been. I had lost weight and I knew I was thinner, but it wasn't from a lack of food or eating, it was from living on my nerves. The stress was stripping the weight off me and I was terrified this would be used against me – that I would be accused of falling back into my old anorexic patterns.

When the doors finally opened to expose the waiting court room, nothing could have prepared me for the horror that lay inside. The room was eerily silent other than the shuffling of papers and the occasional cough. The court room doors closed behind me, shut tightly, amplifying the silence and trapping me inside. *No going back now.*

The hearing was just that. A hearing, for me to hear; to listen. Nothing else. It was abundantly clear to me that the sheriff was still angered by my previous 'absence' and within a few mere seconds of my entrance he had threatened me with imprisonment for my 'contempt of court'. All eyes were on me, watching me, judging me. I felt like a sitting duck just waiting for the killer shot. My eyes welled leading to a trail rolling down my cheeks and onto my parched lips. I could taste the salty beads.

I wasn't allowed to speak or defend myself. Anytime I did, I was silenced by the disgruntled, older, white sheriff. I tried, through tears, to explain I had fled because I had no choice – that I was protecting my family; but every time I tried, I was shut down and instead received multiple lectures about the pain I had caused 'poor Rab' and my children by fleeing. In my heart I could feel his bias against me; he offered no facts, he provided no reports, and yet he told me I was an unfit mother. I very quickly realised that this was all today was going to be about: making sure I was made to feel like the worst person in the world. My lawyer didn't even try to defend me - not one single word. I was damned in her denial to defend.

Confusion and humiliation consumed me. The trickling beads swelled to a free-flowing torrent, stinging my eyes and blurring my vision. I kept wondering what I'd done that was so terrible that it merited the sheriff treating me in this way. That, and why no one was discussing my boys' welfare.

I smeared my eyes clear to look towards the lawyers. They were the same two lawyers that had dealt with my divorce. The same two lawyers that were involved when Rab's visitations had been reduced to exclude overnight stays after the boys had experienced both racism and smacking while in his care. They both knew he hadn't even bothered to exercise his once-a-week visitation back then. Their silence was deafening. Neither lawyer spoke up for my boys - they weren't even speaking to my boys. No one had my boys' interests or wellbeing as a priority.

Rab's lawyer sickened me to my stomach. He reminded me of the depths of depravity to which a human being can stoop. Five years earlier, he had advised Rab to drop Michelle from his visitation access, warning him that she was dangerous. Even at the height of all the social work's involvement, he had advised Rab against applying for residency as that would have meant colluding with Michelle. But even more sickening, I knew he had children. He was a father, and he was fully aware of how awful Rab was; and yet, here he was, actively preventing my children from being returned to their mother. He was facilitating my boys' traumas - and for what? His legal aid fees?

I had always felt that if the boys had been spoken to, then the powers-that-be would realise that what was happening was all terribly wrong. It seemed to make perfect sense to me; just speak to the boys; find out how they felt. Why wouldn't you speak to them and ask them their feelings? Why, when dealing with the safety of children, wouldn't you investigate? Why wouldn't you request evidence to support a claim made regarding someone's mental health?

None of these things were relevant to the sheriff. He had already removed two brown boys from their brown mum - the only person they had ever lived with - to be abandoned with their white dad, solely on the support of an affidavit from my white mum, and he wasn't going to accept anything I had to say. I was being silenced to cover his injustice; his bias, based on the colour of my skin. It felt like my whole world was falling apart.

By the end of my public flogging, I had been reduced to a dampened, broken wreck and the only amendment made to the boy's residency order was that I was now allowed to see them for two hours every weekend – still under Rab's supervision - and that the visits were to take place in a public area. With only two visits left before Christmas, the sheriff left it to Rab to decide if I could see the boys over Christmas: "Depending on how you behave, seeing as you can't be trusted."

My lawyer had earlier counselled that I had to agree to whatever was offered and she stood by that. She advised me that I had to go along with it, that the sheriff was still very angry with me and if I wanted any chance of having any decent contact with the boys in the future, I had to play the game.

"The fucking game?" I said, "what's wrong with you all? This is about my children's lives - not a game."

She told me if I rocked the boat, they would make me pay. I had been here before: silenced, but I would not be silenced again. I would go on to rock the boat and they would make me pay.

After court, while Craig drove us to David and Sandra's, I sat in silence, frozen in shock, with the persistent replaying of the sheriff's angry and hateful face scorning me. I felt as if I was living a nightmare that I couldn't wake up from. I felt so vulnerable; inadequate; powerless. All I could do was cry. All I had been allowed to do in court was cry. David was shocked and horrified when I was finally able to share with him all that had occurred in court.

"I've never heard of this kind of behaviour where a sheriff changes the residency of the children on a whim - never in all my years of service . . . I mean, on what grounds? And what the hell was your lawyer there for? I think your first instinct was right about her Kemi - I don't trust her . . . she's too chummy with Rab's lawyer."

David was angry. His ranting made me feel something familiar: injustice, again. While my fears were all consuming, the crippling sense of injustice no longer weighed me down, but instead began to spur me on – turbocharging me into fighting back. I knew it was the only way I would get my children returned. I was ready to take them all on. Silencing me – denying me my explanations - was an infringement of my rights as a mother. It was imperative that I was heard, considering who and what was being forced on my children.

David wrote to the head sheriff on my behalf, complaining that I had been silenced - as had my children. He gave the full background story, highlighted all the short-comings that had taken place in court and questioned how the say-so of a white man – and not even a good, white man - supported by a white woman's unchallenged and uninvestigated affidavit, was regarded as being enough evidence to alter the residency order in the first place, despite the lack of a thorough investigation involving all the relevant agencies.

With the sheriff now allowing visits away from Rab's flat, Rab had decided they would now to take place at *Time Capsule*, a swimming pool in Coatbridge. I hated this. Not only because of the sleazy way Rab would look at me, but also because of my body dysmorphia - getting into a swimsuit made me feel very unsafe and over exposed.

We would set off for the first leg of our seven-hour round trip every Saturday to stay overnight at Leigh's, with little Tola usually screaming most of the journey. I didn't have my licence yet, so with Craig doing all the driving, I became desperately worried about the toll it was taking on his mental health. I knew how hard it was for him to just be a spectator, unable to have his say, completely helpless to support his family.

# # #

By early January, my boys had finally been completely brain-washed against me. Rab had kept a close grip on Sola, limiting his conversations with me as well as vetting the content. Sola in turn had started to internalise his trauma and during Christmas began to withdraw even further. By the turn of the new year, he had stopped speaking to me unless I spoke to him first. Dayo had shown anger towards me from early on, so was allowed a freer rein by Rab, as he would openly challenge me on why I was so horrible to Michelle and the family. He even told me he hated Nairn and never wanted to go back. That was soul destroying to hear as I knew it wasn't true, but I could see he was a child in pain trying to survive. At least Dayo could show me how much pain he was in; Sola had retracted so far into himself he could only look terrified in silence.

After one of our Sunday swims in February, Dayo and I were getting dressed in a family changing room with Tola when she began crying for Sola's attention. As he came in to comfort her, he shut the cubicle door on his fingers, jamming them hard and forcing him to howl the high-pitched cry of a wounded animal. As I turned to comfort him, he pushed me away.

"No, I don't want you," he screamed, before running off to Rab. I was ruined. My son was in total survival mode; Stockholm Syndrome[25].

Driving home that evening, seeing all the lambs bouncing around full of life in the fields with their mothers opened my flood gates again. Tears streamed down as I watched on with envy. Why was it so simple for the sheep? I wished my life was that simple.

"Kemi if I had a magic wand, I would make this all go way and we would have the boys back," Craig said softly, observing me watching the lambs.

"Please don't say that - we must see this through. We have to get to some completion . . . some finality . . . where no one can ever affect us like this again," I stated with deep certainty.

For three desperate months I was stuck in limbo - desperate for things to go faster; but with the sheriff's tormenting words: "You have to prove to Rab you have learned your lesson not to flee with his children," I felt as if time was running out and that if something didn't change soon, I would lose my boys forever. By now I had already lost confidence that they would ever be able to speak freely about how they truly felt. They were losing who they were and were now driven by their traumas; the traumas resulting from exposure to those people.

Michelle had taken my lawyer's advice and got her own legal representation, and by December I had received a court summons requesting that I attend a hearing regarding her application for visitation access to Tola. I understood that she would have to see Tola, but I also understood that I couldn't risk having her at my visits with the boys, as I knew from Dayo's outbursts that she was filling their heads with lies. I had been trying to avoid going to court with her and even had my lawyer offer her access to Tola independent of the boys, but straight from the get-go she was adamant and

---

[25] When a victim feels trust and/or affection towards their captor.

intent on being added to my visitation order with the boys. I point-blank refused.

Next, she requested that her visit should take place at my parents' house, as they had also applied to the court for visitation access to Tola. This suggestion was delt with very quickly. In response to my parents' application, I argued they weren't fit to see my children - that they were unsafe - and provided the court with the names of the detectives from the Specialist Crime Division who had been investigating them since before I left Airdrie. Their request for visitation access was dropped.

So, after my parents were no longer an option, negotiations broke down and, in the end, we went court. Again, Michelle argued to be included in the two-hour visitation order I had with the boys. Her lawyer tried to argue that by separating this poor, young girl from her sister, I wasn't acting like a responsible mother. Michelle was nearly 17 years old and from the contempt her lawyer showed me, and her obvious distaste, she came across as simply looking spiteful.

I argued that it was not appropriate to add Michelle to the existing visitation order; that I didn't trust she had good intentions in being there; that the visits were already strenuous enough for all the children; that Michelle, who had only lived with Tola for the first few months of Tola's early life, was essentially a stranger to Tola and that Tola was already being very affected and confused by Rab's presence. The court agreed that it was more beneficial for the sisters to have one-to-one time without the boys being present and so decided the visits were best kept separate.

Finally, Michelle's lawyer had to concede that there was no alternative to Michelle's request and that the only appropriate adult available to supervise her visit with Tola was me.

Her first visit was in the January, however, in the end, I wasn't the one to supervise it. As the court had left the visit arrangements in the hands of our lawyers, Michelle's first visit with Tola overlapped the time agreed for my visit with the boys. I was stuck between a rock and a hard place. I believe this was arranged intentionally, either in the hope that I would agree to Michelle being present at my visit with the boys thus setting a precedent, or that I would give up my visit with the boys to be present at the visit with Michelle thus breaking the agreement of my visitation order.

In the end, I did neither. I wouldn't risk Rab bringing me back to court for failing to visit the boys, so I arranged for Michelle's first visit with Tola to take place at Craig's parents' house. They agreed to Michelle's grandmother - Michael's mother - accompanying her. Craig's parents did very well considering the circumstances, and reported that not only had the visit gone smoothly, but that Michelle's gran had been perfectly cordial and had even pleasantly surprised them with her opinion: "This is a ridiculous situation that should've been sorted out two years ago." This was my only ever insight into how she felt.

It had been very stressful for everybody concerned to facilitate a space for these two sisters to see each other, so after that first visit, I contacted my lawyer and told her that Michelle and Rab would have to agree to the visits being done at two different times in the future, as I had to be the one to facilitate Michelle and Tola's visits. It was my responsibility, and mine alone. I told her that if Rab and Michelle couldn't agree I wouldn't allow Michelle to see Tola until after we'd gone back to court.

By preventing Michelle being present at the boys' visits, I was preventing even more brainwashing of my two sons. I could see my 17-year-old was benefitting from this situation and even found pleasure in the pain it was causing me. Looking back, I think I believed that if the visits had only involved me, Tola and Michelle, then maybe I would have been able to reach her in some way. This never happened.

David continued to complain to the head sheriff, constantly and consistently informing him of all that was going on in the case. He was adamant that we should keep a paper trail of everything that was happening and document all that the court was refusing to let me say.

New battles, same systems

Your case cannot be investigated until after the sheriff has concluded.

Tears filled my eyes. I had held onto some hope that maybe, just maybe, the head sheriff would intervene and right the wrongs of the court sheriff, but after waiting weeks and weeks for his reply, reading the single line response felt like another defeat. All the hours and effort spent by David writing my detailed complaint to the head sheriff had resulted in nothing more than a waste of paper and ink.

To be honest, I wasn't surprised. Effectively, it was a new battle with the same system - and this system always wins. However, having accepted that they might be able to silence me in court, I'd decided that they couldn't stop me highlighting their failings. Even before I received the head sheriff's shirking reply, a second complaint had already been submitted.

Again, I had been silenced in court. Still, the sheriff was not willing to listen to anything I had to say. He was only interested in trying to cover up his mistakes - changing the boys' residency without having properly investigated that it was in their best interest. If I had been heard in court, all his failings would have been exposed, raising the uncomfortable question of why he changed the residency in the first place.

His decision had been arrived at - without any investigation and without any facts - solely on the grounds of his unconscious, racial bias; that because Rab was white, he was superior – better; trustworthy. We all have a duty to look at the unconscious, racial bias that's embedded within our society. If we don't, we're protecting it and are ourselves, committing an act of racism in our silence.

However, make no mistake, just because the sheriff didn't let me speak, it didn't mean his secret was kept hidden. Everyone present in that court room knew my children were suffering, but no one wanted to face it. This, I have come learn, is how racism affects white people. Racism is uncomfortable – horrendously uncomfortable - so uncomfortable that they cannot bear to look at it. So, they don't. If they don't look at it – see it - then it doesn't exist. That allows them to tell themselves that race is not a factor. It's easier to pretend it's not there than to confront it.

So, David had written my second complaint to the head sheriff, again highlighting my concerns that the court sheriff was still refusing to hear me; refusing to hear that my boys were staying four or five nights a week at my parents' house, not their father's, and refusing to hear the nature of my parents' business and the danger posed to my boys by them being in that house. My lawyer was furious when she found out about my complaints.

"Kemi, what were you thinking . . . you can't question the sheriff! I cannot - and will not - be involved in challenging the court. Yes, mistakes have been made, but no one's going to admit to them. Complaining is only going to make things worse. The more often you're in court, the more the waters are muddied."

David would often use the same saying. By now though, I was already in a swamp.

I was now in court every six or seven weeks, reviewing how visitations were progressing. Progressing. Nothing was progressing. My lawyer wasn't acting in the best interests of the boys. She was resistant to anything I put forward to her as being relevant, dragging her feet, not wanting to upset Rab's lawyer. She never challenged anything in court and was happy to accept whatever scraps we were handed. It was slowly breaking me physically and emotionally.

My internalising of the stress was beginning to show externally. I was still losing weight, despite continuing to eat, which only fed my fear and paranoia of being accused otherwise, my hair had begun to fall out on both sides of my head - as if I'd shaved it - but thankfully my lace-front units would cover it and hide it from the outside world; and on top of that, I had a constant stabbing pain in my chest which intensified so acutely every time I inhaled, it could stop me in my tracks. My ever-present anxiety had me drowning in floods of despair. This feeling, accompanied by court appearances, my verboten voice, the soulless solicitors and the chauvinist sheriff, all became an overwhelming tsunami of soul-crushing stresses. And, as if I wasn't subdued enough, court now unveiled an additional vulnerability.

I had provided information to the Specialist Crime Division highlighting illegal activities regarding my parents' businesses and their associates. For safety reasons my home address was never to see the light of day. Despite the court vowing to keep my address confidential and redacted on any official document, it appeared on them all. Rab, my parents and any of their associates would now know where I lived. I had already been failed by the court, but now it was trying to kill me.

Not only was I physically and emotionally destroyed, but I was also financially wrecked. The costs kept piling up. Between the travel expenses, lawyer appointments, legal letters and court appearance fees, not to mention less income due to all the time off work, we were crippled. Thankfully, Craig's dad was able to help us with all the legal costs and for that, I will be eternally grateful.

When Craig reconnected with his dad after the boys had been taken, we learned he had retired from the police and was now working for the Home Office's immigration unit tasked with the identification, monitoring and removal or deportation of immigration offenders. He would only last six months in the job as he couldn't bear the institutional racism and inhumanity he witnessed. He later re-joined the police in their Nuclear Division, accepting a sergeant's position based at Dounreay where he spent four days a week.

With the court having revealed our address, we no longer felt safe in what had briefly been our new, happy home. What had once served us as a sanctuary now felt like no man's land. We never knew who might be watching us, or what their intentions might be. It was then that my father-in-law offered to buy us a house in Nairn, in his name, to restore some level of anonymity. It was our best option - it was our only option, and so we agreed. I felt like my father-in-law was being generous, but Craig felt like he was selling his soul. I felt extremely responsible but didn't understand the full implications of what that meant; I was too consumed with getting the boys back. The deal was for Craig's dad to lend us the money for the deposit and we would pay the mortgage repayments, with us eventually repaying him back the deposit money.

We found a secluded house in central Nairn, perfectly positioned for easy access to the town centre, on the banks of the River Nairn. It turned out to be my financial advisor's house and by 31st March, within five weeks of first seeing the listing on the internet, we had moved in. On top of helping with the legal fees and the house deposit, Craig's dad had even suggested that he offer Rab £10,000 to give the children back, but I didn't want to go down that road. I felt my father-in-law had already been extremely generous and I knew that Rab had to be handled properly, through the court, otherwise he would come back and try to do this to me all over again.

#

Unlike my weekly visits with the boys, Michelle's visits with Tola only occurred once a month, with the first taking place in a soft play area, *Cheeky Monkeys*, in Airdrie. Both Craig and I hated being back in Airdrie. It had now been a year since we'd moved north as a family, disappearing overnight, away from the town and its toxic inhabitants. Returning terrified us.

No one knew of the hostility I'd had with the Social Work Department - I don't even think my mum knew the full extent of what had happened there. No one knew the battle I was still having with the court. We didn't know who knew what, or rather, who believed what. From the outside we'd run away under a cloud of suspicion, only to return minus the two boys, painting the picture of an unfit mother whose children had been removed from her for failing to keep them safe. That's the kindest description of how I felt I was being judged.

"Cold Mummy," Tola shared, whilst cuddling into my side, trying to shelter herself from the cold wind.

We arrived a few minutes early, but rather than wait in the warmth of the car with Craig, to avoid any potential altercations or accusations, we decided it would be better for baby Tola and me to wait for Michelle in the blustery and exposed elements. Exposed was exactly how I felt.

I had no idea who, if anyone, would be bringing her. The last thing I wanted to have to deal with was an entourage. So, I was relieved not to see any of my family, when within a few minutes of braving the breeze, Michelle pulled up and got out of her boyfriend's car. She looked nervous as she walked towards us.

"Hi Michelle," I said with a genuine warmth despite the conditions.

"Hi Mum" she reciprocated, with a sincere smile.

"No. My mummy," a confused Tola interrupted with a mouthful of dummy.

"Tola, it's me . . . Michelle, remember? I'm your sister," Michelle assured, while offering Tola her hand.

"No," Tola recoiled, hugging into my legs to bury her face while beginning to cry and demand that I lift her. Tola had always been a loving baby and toddler, but since her brothers had been taken, she'd stopped engaging with anyone she didn't know.

"Sorry Michelle, she's just a bit sleepy," I lied, trying to take the awkwardness out of the already delicate interaction. "I've just woken her up, so she's still a little bit cranky. She'll be okay in a minute."

"It's okay Mum . . . ," Michelle began.

"My mummy," Tola repeated interrupting her sister, while burying her face firmly into my chest.

It was in that moment I witnessed that my daughters didn't know each other. I'd assumed they wouldn't – I knew they wouldn't - but seeing it made it real and with that came a sadness.

It was sad that Michelle didn't know how Tola ticked, how she responded, what she did and didn't like, and it was sad that Tola had no memory of ever having had a big sister. Tola was only four months old when Michelle made her allegations and they hadn't had any contact since. Tola was now two. They truly were strangers. That sadness replaced my anger and, in that moment, I decided that for all the time we were together, for my daughters to get to know each other as sisters, I would simply be their mother. No judgement; just love.

Michelle responded to this approach positively and withdrew her hostility, just like she had done when she was younger - and whenever my mum wasn't around. When my mum wasn't around, Michelle was my daughter – completely and naturally. While all I could do was hope that us having this time together would eventually soften her enough to be able to tell the truth, I still feared that I'd already lost her; that she was in too deep. I felt compelled to tell her that I understood her – why she had done what she had done - and that if she ever told the truth, there would be no consequences from me; no punishments or repercussions. She was silent, but she heard me and that was what I needed. I hoped it would help her one day if she ever decided to tell the truth.

305

Outside of the visits Michelle's behaviour towards me didn't change and she continued being hateful and vindictive, but I still only saw her as a child being used by people who should have known better. To me, my battle was no longer with my daughter. So, that was how we continued.

Around the same time that early spring, after having admitted to procedural failings, David and Alex had got the case against Lydia Bramley and the Social Work Council to the point where I now had to make the decision of whether to raise a civil hearing.

I wanted the world to know that I had been persecuted because of the colour of my skin and that it wasn't okay, and that someone was held accountable for the levels of bias I'd had inflicted on me – not as a way of revenge, but as a platform for lessons to be learned. Never should anyone else have to experience what I'd encountered. However, as much as I wanted Lydia and the Social Work Council held accountable, I just couldn't go through with it; not now.

It was a bittersweet, anticlimactic ending to all the hundreds of hours of work that David, Alex and I had put in. Just when I had received my apology, my little crumb of vindication, I had to walk away. The thought of any additional battle felt insignificant compared to the battle I was already entrenched in and I needed all my reserve for that.

As David handed me over a suitcase filled with copies of all the paper trails, all the failings and findings, the names of everybody who was ever involved and a copy of everything stored on a floppy disc, I felt hollow and empty. All that pain, frustration and injustice now amassed to little more than a small, leather suitcase. What had been the point? Victory felt like defeat. As painful as it was staring down into that suitcase, knowing I wasn't going to continue my fight for justice, I did take some solace in knowing that its contents existed and that they were safely stored away if ever I changed my mind in the future.

I truly believe that had it not been for Alex Salmond's determination for justice for me and my children, I might never have received an admission of failure. I never once met him face-to-face - that was always done by David - but having his profile attached seemed to make a difference. It frightens me to think what would have happened had he not been involved. Regardless of my views on Scottish independence, I will be eternally grateful to Alex Salmond and David for seeing me as an equal human being.

Patience

It was a further four months before my visits with the boys became unsupervised and increased to a half day, and Craig was finally be allowed to attend. We used this time to take the children to all the places we had loved going to before the craziness existed. Places like *Stirling Castle* or *Blair Drummond Safari Park*. Places where we could be anonymous and invisible together. By then, however, the boys had been completely brainwashed by Rab.

They were clearly terrified by the things he'd been telling them, by his restrictions of what they could talk about and the consequences of not following his orders. While I was deeply worried for Dayo and his ever-growing aggression, and Sola with his almost silent, withdrawn demeanour, I didn't want to make things worse for them.

It was heart-breaking watching them both suffer, but I was conscious not to question or challenge them regarding Rab's influence in what little time I had for a visit. I didn't want to confuse them further or make them feel any pressure to pledge their allegiance. They'd have gone back to Rab at the end of the visit, confused and looking for answers and God knows how he would have reacted to their questioning; I knew it wouldn't have been good.

Their worlds had already been obliterated into chaos; a chaos dominated by people telling them their mum was bad and I wouldn't add to their stresses by having them play piggy-in-the-middle. I knew for the boys to make up their own minds, I would have to wait until I had more time with them alone; the half-day visits were just too short. I had to accept that nothing would change until after I was able to have them for overnight visits. In order to live with this acceptance, I began to survive on faith and patience.

I had always thought I was a rather impatient person, but the preceding eight, excruciating months had revealed the complete opposite. The only thing I could do was be patient. That and pray.

I have spoken with God for as long as I can remember. Some of my earliest memories are prayers - my pleas for acceptance and answers. As a child, Catholicism had taught me not to ask questions, and so by eight years old, I had discovered that the God I spoke with daily didn't live in a religion – God lived in me. This brought me comfort to know God was always so close, watching, and made me believe that God never gives you more than you can handle. At times it might not feel like it and that's why God is always available - for discussion and guidance. Right then, felt like one of those times, so I prayed day and night, speaking to God like a constant mantra.

I believe this helped me survive; having faith kept me alive. The belief that there's a power bigger than me, bigger than us all - that everything happens for a reason and has its own purpose. This belief allowed me to accept my children were not my property, that they were their own beings; that they had their own journeys and lessons to experience in their own lives. No matter how difficult their journey was, we had to walk our own paths and I reminded myself I was only there to nurture and protect them and to teach them right from wrong.

I believed I would get them back. I knew if I continued, with patience and faith, to be consistent in my love and protection for them, whether they lived with me or not, the boys would see that I hadn't changed – that I wasn't the monster people were making me out to be.

# # #

Rab wasn't convinced that he had Sola on side, and he couldn't stop him from appearing withdrawn; he was the cause, so he needed the outside world to believe Sola was withdrawn because of me – that I'd abused him. So, he took the boys, accompanied by my mum, to a Catholic counselling group for children in Glasgow, to have their psychologist assess them in an attempt to prove I was the problem. Rab submitted this report in court.

The report was nothing more than a statement and offered no insight into its conclusion. A conclusion without a cause. The report simply concluded that Sola was traumatised.

That's when David challenged the psychologist's superior, accusing their organisation of providing false evidence for presentation in court at a child welfare hearing. He sent them a copy of the report Rab presented in court, along with the full outline of everything that was happening. In response, I received a letter of apology for the psychologist's conduct, with assurances that she had been investigated and reprimanded. Enclosed was a copy of the real, full report. It stated Sola was deeply traumatised . . . at being separated from his mother.

By June, some eight agonising months after the boys had been taken, I was finally allowed to speak in court. However, 'Operation: Information Blackout' was still in progress. The sheriff who had previously allowed the redacted report to be shown in court was now forbidding me from speaking about, let alone present, the psychologist's authentic report and its true findings. I still wasn't allowed to speak about my concerns for the boys' safety and I still wasn't allowed to speak about them not living with Rab. Suppression was still on the agenda.

At this point I would like to say that all the parties involved - the lawyers, the sheriffs, Rab and the grandparents - had access to my every challenge, every complaint, to my deep concerns for what I knew was happening to my children; and yet still, the sheriff, who controlled what evidence could and couldn't be presented, refused to have them discussed in court.

When I was finally allowed to speak, it was only to allow me to swear an oath – a promise, that if the court allowed me to have my children for weekend visits, I wouldn't let Rab down again with any of my 'silly business'. I swallowed my frustrations and took my oath. Despite my continued censorship, I was ecstatic after court. My faith and patience were paying off. I was eventually getting more time with the boys – a full weekend - and I could sense this was a real turning point.

The sheriff granting me extended visits didn't stop David raising a further complaint to the head sheriff contesting the fact that I was still being silenced. This complaint received two responses: the same original response from the head sheriff – 'Your case cannot be investigated until after the sheriff has concluded' – and a response from my lawyer; she dropped me.

She dropped me during the same week as the boys had their first visit home and at the time, it caused us all a lot of worry and anxiety. I felt let down. Admittedly, she hadn't been doing a particularly good job – in fact, she was barely doing her job - but she knew the case. Now I would need to start all over again, recounting my living nightmare with a new lawyer and all because I had complained about a sheriff.

Looking back, I now have more respect for my old lawyer than I would have had had she continued to be party to my horror. I believe she could no longer stomach it. My determination to expose the psychologist's report is what made her finally say she could no longer represent me. She could no longer be colour blind.

#

I felt like a child at Christmas on the morning of the boys' first visit home. Excitement filled me as I looked around their bedrooms - their bedrooms that had never been slept in, in their home where they had never lived. That night, we would all be sleeping under the same roof in our new family home.

Sola's bedroom had one red wall – red was still his favourite colour - and I knew he would love it. Dayo's favourite colours were pink, because it was pretty, although, he did find orange pretty too, and gold because that had been the colour of his long curls. However, Dayo's room was not to be any of those colours - it had to be green. I had always supported both boys in embracing their feminine side; they had an older sister so of course they would be connected to that part of themselves. Unfortunately, however, by this time, Dayo was rejecting his favourite colours, just like he rejected anything that Rab would see as being feminine.

Rab would frequently use terms like 'that's gay' or 'you're being a mummy's boy' to reject and disapprove of their feminine sides, causing them to feel shame. It was that same shame and rejection that was now being played out in Dayo. He too now showed hatred towards anything feminine, and I felt like I was running out of time to save him. However now, as I closed Dayo's bedroom door, I was content that my patience was paying off. I now felt like I had a fighting chance to rescue and resurrect the Dayo I knew. I knew the boys would gain strength from experiencing some quality family-time at home. The strength to demand to come home.

On the drive down to collect the boys, Craig and I agreed not to ask them questions about what was going on in Coatbridge and to only engage in Coatbridge-related conversations if they brought it up. We didn't want them to feel pressured during their first visit home.

When we arrived, it took a few minutes before I spotted Sola waving from a window. With Rab now having residency of the boys he was entitled to claim even more benefits, and even though the boys were more often than not at my mum's and barely stayed with him, he had been 'awarded' a bigger house in a better area of Coatbridge. This house was meant for the children, but instead, Rab's friend, who sold cocaine, moved in. David complained about this and yet again, it was never mentioned in court. Nonetheless, I felt some relief that the boys no longer had to enter those flats.

Sola arrived at the car first and was already buckling his seat belt before Dayo came into sight with Rab by his side. He was in no hurry. There was no excitement from him, just a reluctance.

"Don't worry son - you'll be back home with me on Sunday," were Rab's last words as he closed Dayo's door. He said it with pleasure, not reassurance; a stamping of his authority.

Despite Dayo's blatant resistance, I was exhilarated to be bringing the boys back home and as soon as we were on the journey north, Sola excitedly began asking questions about his new home.

"What's it like Mum?" Sola asked, his eyes coming alive with great interest. I twisted around so I could reach back and take his hand.

"Well! It has two gardens; a massive one with picnic tables that looks over the river . . . and a secret one - in the roof!" I said in a mysterious tone causing him to laugh.

"Mum . . . seriously, for real?" he enquired, trying to put a straight face on but failing phenomenally.

"Seriously, for real," I confirmed with a squeeze of his hand.

"What about my room? What colour is it?" he asked, beginning to fidget with excitement.

"That, Sola, you will have to wait and see for yourself." He took a moment to himself to gaze out of the window. I could see he was wandering off, following his imagination.

"I hope it's red," was all he said before disappearing off into his mind again.

For once, the normally long and intense drive home was actually enjoyable. Normally the drive home was a silent time of mournful reflection. Normally, the drive home meant I had just said goodbye to the boys. But for once I was bursting with excitement to finally be home.

As we entered our upside-down house, Tola led Sola to the first room off the large, hexagonal-shaped hallway, stood in the open doorway and announced to him: "Shawaz room." Sola's eyes widened.

"Mum . . . it's red!" he whispered.

"Of course. What other colour would it be?" I replied with a smile.

I will never forget what happened next. He turned to face me, eyes full of tears of happiness, and folded himself into me in a clutching embrace. This was the first time he had let me hold him since he'd been taken, and I now knew for sure he would return. It had taken a matter of minutes of him being home – in his new home - for Sola to feel safe.

That night, he looked so cosy and content as I tucked him into his red, squishy, duck-feathered covers.

"Mummy . . . please don't make me go back . . . let me stay here - at home," Sola pleaded, his spluttered words interrupted by his tears.

I felt so helpless peering into his desperate eyes. It was heart-breaking. Craig was looking in from the doorway and as I turned to him, I was filled with even more sadness. He mirrored the helplessness I felt at being unable to provide safety; as a father and as a husband, there was nothing he could do.

"Solie . . . I'm so sorry . . . I can't," I began gently, as I laid down beside him. "Mummy would get into a lot of trouble with the police . . . and that would make it harder for you to be able to come home." I felt like a failure.

"Mummy . . . I don't like it," Sola revealed, before taking a tearful, staggered breath. "It's not fair . . . why does the bad win over the good? Mummy, I know you're good. Why can't I be with you and why is no one helping you?"

For a moment, I had no words of comfort. Here was my son – a child – fully aware of the wrongs that were taking place; the wrongs of which he was bearing the consequence.

"Sola, I have a meeting with the new lawyer, remember? And she'll save the day; I promise."

I honestly believed my words - I had to, I had nothing else. He fell silent of words and cuddled into me. That night, we shared his single bed.

# # #

I will never forget the boys' first night home. I had never seen Sola so unhappy and I had never felt so useless, so incapable of easing his pain; so ineffective as his mother. There was nothing I could do - I could only do as I was told; that and pray. Pray for one of those moments - you know, the eleventh-hour kind - when you think all hope is gone, then, suddenly the darkness breaks and in walks the saviour. David had found me a lawyer with a great reputation in family law, and I was to meet her the day after I'd returned the boys to Rab. I prayed the new lawyer would be our knight in shining armour.

For that whole weekend, Dayo refused to interact with the family or enjoy anything we did. The only person who got close to him was Tola - he adored her and she adored him. He refused to make any connections with anyone else - including me - and he refused to see any of his friends. He was constantly stressed and anxious. I could see that his OCD was playing out and he spent all his time policing Sola, telling him not to do this and not to do that, like Rab's mini foot soldier.

He treated Craig and I with suspicion and whenever he spoke, it was in an accusatory tone, while using words that sounded foreign coming from him; words that sounded more familiar coming from Rab's mouth. In his mind, we were bad and it was his responsibility to inform Rab about everything and anything that happened during their visit. When Dayo overheard Sola say he wanted to come home, he got very distressed, telling Sola he would be in so much trouble when he got home for saying that. Sola didn't care. His visit had given him strength and he was determined he was coming home.

At the end of their weekend visit, before we left for Coatbridge, we gave the boys a mobile phone each. Rab had been limiting my phone calls and would only allow a ten-minute call a week, so having their own mobiles meant we could speak to them as often as they liked. Sola was delighted, but sceptical.

"Do I have to give this to my dad?" Sola nervously questioned. He knew Rab well.

"No, it's yours - so you can call me whenever you want."

Returning the boys turned into a horrible scene. Within seconds of arriving, Dayo reported to Rab that Sola had said he wanted to go home and that he wanted to live with me. Rab got very angry, causing Sola to cry.

"I hate you," Sola screamed, "and I hate it here. I want to live with my mummy." He was so upset he refused to get out of the car.

"Sola, it's okay," I began, trying to persuade him, "I'll be back down in 12 sleeps."

My persuasions made no difference. In the end, I had to watch Sola being dragged out of the car by Rab and into the house, kicking and screaming all the way.

Rab did take their phones away; but not for very long.

Silenced

The next morning, I was to attend an appointment with the new lawyer, Penny, who had come highly recommended by David. He had done a lot of research into her and had even advised us to swap to her some months earlier, but I'd been too afraid at the thought of having to explain things all over again. I didn't believe anyone would believe my story - and I needed them to believe me. William had also been pushing for me to change lawyer. When I called him to let him know my lawyer had dropped me, he seemed relieved:

"So, Kemi, finally this decision has been made for you - from a higher level."

Craig and I hoped Penny would live up to her reputation, but it was hard to keep going when there was no light at the end of the tunnel. I was in a situation where decisions had been made - terrible decisions - that were costing my children very dearly. These decisions had been made based on the colour of my skin, but I was never able to contest that in court. I was in an impossible situation that I had no answer for. I just had to keep going until someone would listen or care.

When we arrived in the lawyer's car park, Craig switched off the engine and turned to face me.

"Kemi, she only has to bring the boys back to us; it's not a lot to ask, and Sola is definitely coming back. Kemi he's a warrior; he will be home soon." There was a tone of certainty in his words.

"And Dayo? He'll say he won't come home . . . then what?" I questioned, unable to hide my desperation.

"Kemi, if there's any justice, he won't have a choice. We only need to get him back home, then he'll return to who he really is. I promise."

"Well, that will be the first time I experience justice."

And with that, we left the car in silence and went into the red-brick building.

As we sat in the waiting area at reception, I looked up to the sound of a creaking door swinging open.

"Morning, you must be Kemi," a small, dark-haired woman said clearly and warmly.

"Hi, Penny?" I said, standing to shake her firm, but feminine, grip. "This is my husband, Craig."

"Pleased to meet you both," she said with a genuine smile. "Okay, please come on in . . . we have a lot to get through. I've received the documents from Mr Stephen – they're very informative - but, I haven't received anything from your previous lawyer."

Craig and I sat down and looked at each other, and then to this stunningly attractive woman. She was very direct, wasting no time, allowing me to feel instantly relieved. I could tell she didn't suffer fools gladly which comforted me as there were a lot of fools involved in my fight.

"A lot has taken place, but if we go down the road of what should and shouldn't have happened, you'll never get your boys back, because Kemi, nobody cares," she explained matter-of-factly. "No one's ever going to admit they've done anything wrong. You need to decide if you want your boys back - and if so, you need to stop highlighting how you've been treated. If you stop, they will give the boys back."

There it was, plain and simple.

We told her about the weekend visit, what Sola and Dayo had said and the conflict between what they each wanted.

"Okay, let's get Sola home . . . and his brother too, if it's not too late."

She explained that she was going to get the boys a curator, which is effectively a lawyer for children, whose primary concern is protecting the best interests of the child. They can take into account the child's wishes, however, they will view these objectively and assess whether the child's wishes are in fact in their best interests, unlike a lawyer.

She informed us the curator would interview Sola, his teachers and all significant adults in his life, to build up a picture before advising his recommendations to the court. She advised that it was best to get Dayo an appointed curator too, but warned if he or Rab refused, there would be nothing we could do to force them. This filled me with fear. She was certain we could get Sola back - and she believed rather quickly. The curator could be a lengthy process, but once the report was compiled, and as long as Sola was able to be honest, him coming home would be a done deal.

I was exhausted after the meeting. Going over all the excruciating facts that was my life had been difficult, intense and full of tears. For good measure, I'd also got to witness Craig's helplessness as he listened to all my pain being relived. He was frustrated. Frustrated he couldn't support me in court and frustrated at not having his own voice in court. His frustration was tiring him - that and all the hours of driving every weekend; and on top of that, his sense of being beholden to his dad. Yes, I was very aware of the effects the pressures in my life were having on my husband once again and there wasn't anything I could do to ease them.

"She must think I'm a cry baby - I cried so much," I said to Craig on our way back to David and Sandra's.

"Kem, it's understandable – its expected. She'll understand, and she'll help us," he offered warmly.

Within three weeks, Penny had organised an emergency court hearing. She was amazing! She put forward the motion for the children to be assigned a curator arguing that Sola was too distressed, that she had deep concerns regarding his mental welfare and that it would be helpful to hear from the boys directly rather than from Rab. The sheriff had no choice but to agree. The boys' visitations were also altered so that they could now come home every second weekend.

My experiences in court up until then had been long, drawn-out sessions of silence and bouts of berating followed by very little, if any, progress. However, that day in court, in less than an hour, Penny had gained me more time with the boys and managed to get a curator assigned. She was very efficient and effective. I knew things were changing. I was still being silenced, but this time I'd chosen not to speak. I chose not to say anything about the injustices I had received.

Within a week of being assigned, the curator had conducted some of his interviews. Rab, as expected, was reluctant to allow the curator to speak with Dayo, but did agree to have an initial visit, during which Dayo stated he hated me and wanted to stay with Rab. The curator managed a couple of interviews with both Sola and his headteacher and he also met with my mum, who finally admitted Sola should be allowed to come home to me.

This hadn't surprised me. I'd had a few phone conversations with her during this time and I'd told her - warned her - to be careful, as the boys would grow up and remember, and understand, who had stolen them and kept them from their mum. I knew she feared what would come out when the boys felt safe again. With Sola now being very open and honest about what he wanted - to be home with me - she had to reposition herself. That and the fact that Rab wasn't sticking to their plan. He was enjoying his power too much and was hell bent on causing me as much pain as possible, regardless of the consequences for the boys. He was out of control, reckless and becoming a liability and she needed to start distancing herself from him to maintain her holier-than-thou façade. The tag-team was breaking up. Michelle and Rab were now the team and honest Sola was their target.

By the time the boys next came home for a visit, it was apparent they were in stark contrast. Sola was ecstatic when we picked them up, but Dayo was very angry.

"Mummy did you hear about me going to my headteacher when I came back? I told her I want to be with you . . . I've told everyone. Mummy, are you proud I'm telling the truth now and not what Dad wants me to say?"

After Sola's first visit home, he had gone to his headteacher and asked her to help him get back home to his mummy.

"I heard my little man; I'm so proud," I said,

"Well . . . I don't want to live with you," Dayo stated bluntly. "I'll never live with you again. I hate you."

This broke my heart. I knew they'd got to him. They had my child and I had lost him. I cried myself to sleep that night, torn between the delight of one boy coming home and the agony that one boy wouldn't.

The next morning, Sola was very distressed, saying he couldn't go back to Rab's and that he was really scared. I couldn't comfort him no matter what I said. He just kept sobbing.

"Mummy please, I beg you, please."

315

This was the most devastating thing I have had to deal with, making my ten-year-old son return to a place of no safety. I spoke with David and phoned the police and Social Work Department in Nairn to see if anyone could help. The police came to the house and spoke with Sola.

"If I were you, I would not be taking this child back," the police officer advised after speaking with Sola.

"It's not that simple; there's a court order . . . I have to, or I'll be arrested . . . then I'd be stopped from seeing the boys altogether." The officer looked confused.

"This is ridiculous! I would not be taking this child back," he repeated, sounding frustrated. "It's extremely unlikely that any court will enforce the order, what with your son being in such a state." However, I knew that was exactly what would happen if I did not return Sola.

The police officer left us, advising that he was going back to the office to raise an emergency report to the Nairn Social Work Department to see if they could assist.

By that afternoon, reports from both the police and the Social Work Department in Nairn were sent to Airdrie's Social Work Department's emergency services, as they had been involved previously. Keeping in mind social workers can overrule anything in an emergency for the best interest of the child, the police assumed they would help.

When we got in the car to head for Coatbridge the following morning, Sola had made his mind up: "I don't care what happens Mummy, I'm not getting out of the car."

The journey down was horrendous. We had to repeatedly stop because Sola kept feeling sick. He was consumed with nerves. We all were. When we arrived at Rab's, Dayo went in to inform his dad that Sola was not going to come out of the car. When Rab arrived at the car, he was really angry.

"Come on son, don't be silly," he snapped, with Dayo by his side.

"No, you make me stay with you . . . and tell lies about my mum and Craig . . . and . . . I hate you," Sola screamed while breaking into tears. The desperation in his tone was horrifying.

"I'll drag you out of that car if I have to," Rab retaliated, displaying his quick temper and lack of care.

"Over my dead body," I warned him, "you'll do no such thing." I phoned the police, and they arrived within ten minutes.

After being brought up to speed, the police could see this was not right – that Sola should not be made to get out of the car - and so frantically made some calls to see what could be done, all the while with Rab in the background repeatedly scorning: "I have a court order; I can drag him out if I need to."

They called Airdrie's Social Work Department – the same department that, by now, would have received the report from the police and Social Work in Nairn, warning them that there was a potential volatile situation taking place - the same department that David and Alex had fought against on my behalf. They didn't even return the call, never mind come out to see Sola. Nobody wanted to get involved.

Without the social work's power to overrule an order, the police officers, with their hands tightly tied, reluctantly, and rather emotionally, conceded that they would have to physically remove Sola if he continued to refuse to come out of the car. Relief shot all over their faces when I asked that they let me try.

After two hours of chaos in the car, the stand-off ended, and I finally persuaded Sola to come out. He was heartbroken. We all were. For once, we drove home in complete silence with even little Tola unusually quiet. I had already spoken to a distraught Sola three times by the time I got home, with each phone call worse than the previous. He was inconsolable. We now shared the same living nightmare.

When I spoke to Penny on the following Monday, she wasn't surprised or shocked to learn what had happened. She said she would chase up the curator to complete his report and ask for another emergency hearing in the meantime. She got one for the following week. Before we went into court, she addressed us both in turn.

"Craig - go to your parents with Tola – you're too angry and too frustrated and you're not going to help matters. And Kemi, I need you to stop crying. Now. I know it's horrendous, how you've been treated, but as I told you already, no one in that room cares. I'll get Sola back for you, I promise, but do not cry in court. Do not show any emotion. Do you understand? I need you to be clear. If I ask anything of you today, it's that you don't let them see what this has done to you. Okay?"

She was as direct as ever and she was right, so I agreed and followed her into court.

Despite the curator not having finished his investigations, Penny was able to put forward his findings to date.

"It hasn't been completed yet, but as you can see, it is in Sola's best interest, in every sense, that he should be allowed to return to his mother," she recommended to the sheriff - the new sheriff.

The original sheriff who I had complained about - the one who had changed the residency and kept me silent - was no longer dealing with my case. I think David had them scared.

The new sheriff said she would have to wait until the curator's report had been completed to make a final decision, but that she would grant an extension to the boys' visitations - that they could come home every weekend until the next court hearing in September. She insisted, because Sola was so distraught, he must be given his phone back. He was.

By late September, when we went back to court, the situation for Sola had become far worse. Rab and Michelle, along with Dayo, were all pressuring him to stay, causing his relationship with Dayo to fracture. The boys had always been so close – inseparable - but now they were clearly on different sides.

The curator's report was thankfully completed in time and his findings were heavily in my favour. Sola's report only stated how damaging it was for him not to be at home with Craig and me. *He's coming home – he's really coming home! Keep it together Kemi.* As conclusive as it was, the report didn't state anything about how Sola had been damaged in the first place – nothing about how the sheriff's decision to change residency was unwarranted, or how it had impacted, traumatised and changed both of my children forever. *Never mind; keep focused. One down, one to go.*

Dayo's report opened with the curator stating that he would have liked to have spent more time with him, but that Rab had refused further access. Despite Rab restricting access to Dayo, and despite Dayo having stated initially that he did not want to return home to the family, the curator concluded that Dayo would also benefit from being returned to his mother. *Oh my God, he's coming home too!* He compared how Dayo had been previously described in school reports from both Nairn and Airdrie, to how he was now, and noted that there were discrepancies regarding what Dayo was saying that he wanted.

As the curator took his seat I was enveloped in silence. All eyes now turned to the sheriff. I held my breath in anticipation and nibbled the inside of my cheek in an attempt not to show any emotion as she shuffled her paperwork and finger-read the reports. *Remember what Penny said – keep it together.* After what felt like an eternity, the sheriff cleared her throat.

"Motion to change residency of Olusola granted. Motion to change residency of Dayo denied."

The sheriff dismissed the curator's incomplete report on Dayo and in doing so, tore out a piece of my soul. For a minute I believed both of my stolen boys were coming home, only to lose one again. The loss filled me deeply, flooring me. Here I was being told not to bring up any of the previous sheriff's failings I'd endured in the past 14 months and in return I could have one son back. Rab tried to fight the judgement, wanting more time with Sola before he was to be returned to me, but the sheriff rejected his arguments and insisted that Sola was to return home to me that very day.

I still to this day feel shame about what happened. I was powerless. The court and Rab both had their own agendas, with my children paying the price, and all because of the colour of my skin. Everybody knew by now it was not in Dayo's best interest to remain with Rab, yet the court sacrificed him so as not to be seen as racist. If they had reversed both boys' residency, questions would have been asked as to why it had been changed in the first place. There was no answer to that question – well, no answer other than unconscious, racial bias.

Concluding the hearing, the sheriff amended the visitation arrangements. From then on, visits were to be alternated every fortnight and we were

318

ordered to facilitate the contact, meaning Craig had to drive a seven-hour round trip, twice a weekend, two weekends a month. For example, on weekend A, on the Friday, Craig would drive south for three and a half hours, drop Sola off at Rab's then turn around and drive back north for three and a half hours. On the Sunday he would repeat this to collect Sola. Then two weeks later, weekend B, he would repeat the same journey for Dayo's turn to come north for the weekend.

The cost had been put in place and we were told that because we worked and Rab didn't, we could afford to do all the travelling. The money Rab 'earned' selling drugs didn't count of course. The court was actively, financially destroying us. Driving all those miles had already put us into so much debt. We had been back and forth, on average, every six weeks to court for the past 14 months, and then there were the lawyer's fees. On top of that - and adding insult to injury - I had to pay child maintenance for the benefits Rab was claiming.

Over the next six months, Rab continued to take us to court whenever he could. He was blatantly trying to cause more distress. I was shocked and relieved when the court finally ordered him to stop wasting their time and to stop trying to destroy us financially.

Lesser of two evils

Dayo was deeply affected by Sola coming home to live - more than I could ever have imagined. He completely lost his identity. Before Rab took the boys, Sola and Dayo had been one and the same. They shared the same friends, the same interests and were constantly together. They were best friends as well as brothers.

Dayo wasn't shaped like most little boys and he carried himself differently. His African physique was more like that of a little, thick brown girl's and he glided like a faerie with every movement. However, since he was stolen, he had been thrown into a permanent state of trauma that shut down his whole body and forced him to hold himself rigid with his fists constantly clenched. He was perpetually scared senseless. His gentle, caring kindness had changed to anger and aggression.

He had always feared Rab, but when he was taken away so easily - given away without question or hesitation - and brainwashed by every adult in his life, he started to believe that the 'baddies', as he had once referred to Rab and his family, were actually the 'goodies'. And now, he felt that Sola had abandoned him in the lion's den. Sola, in turn, felt Dayo had betrayed him by choosing to live with his dad rather than his mum. He couldn't understand it.

Sola didn't have the same bond with Rab as Dayo. Dayo's relationship with Rab was built on a foundation of fear. He had witnessed - and could remember - Rab's violence, but Sola's experience was not the same. Thankfully he hadn't witnessed the same amount of violence as Dayo; thankfully he was too young to remember anything he had witnessed and therefore, thankfully he didn't have the same fear. That is what separated them: fear.

The boys were due to spend the full Easter holidays together, with Dayo coming home for the first week and Sola staying with Rab for the second. When Dayo arrived on the Friday night for his weekend visit home - the weekend before the Easter Holidays - something was on his mind.

"Mum, Craig, can I speak to you?" Dayo asked as he entered the room and sat down on the coffee table across from us both.

Craig and I looked at each other filled with intrigue before casting our focus back onto Dayo. We instantly knew this was going to be important. The once ever-talkative child just didn't speak anymore. With his arms rested on his thighs and his hands tightly interlaced together, he lowered his face and spoke.

"I want to come home now," he whispered without lifting his head. *Oh my God!*

I could see his body was becoming heavy from letting his emotions have room and as I gasped, Craig took my hand to indicate he had this covered.

He could see that my emotions were also rising and he didn't want to scare Dayo off.

"Okay," Craig said simply, "we can get that sorted for you, no problem."

"Dad can't know . . . he'd kill me," Dayo whispered, head still bowed. My leg began trembling erratically and a hot wave of nausea rippled through my body.

"Well, he doesn't need to know - we'll arrange everything . . . and hopefully you'll not need to go back after your week here at Easter," Craig reassured causing Dayo to lift his head.

"How does that sound, Dayo?" Craig asked, now looking directly into Dayo's eyes. A smile spread across his face.

"Mum . . . ," Dayo began as he stood up to make his way out of the living room. He paused for a moment, hovering, "Rab hates you." There was caution in his tone.

"I know," I accepted in a whisper, as he turned to make his way out.

"You've told them? You've been so brave Dayo! Mum and Craig will fix this - I promise," Sola assured.

Sola had been sitting on the stairs outside the living room listening in and was now trying to reassure his brother. I could see this was a role Sola had grown into very well. There were those moments when he really did understand Dayo; at times more than Dayo understood himself.

With the room to ourselves, Craig and I looked at each other in silence for a moment, reflecting on what had just happened. I was so glad of his level-headedness. Dayo was fragile and my outpour of emotions could have pushed him away.

"I can't believe it Craig," I finally allowed myself to whisper, struggling to contain the feeling of joy that was building inside me. I could feel a smile growing across my face to match Craig's.

"Shh . . . they'll hear us," Craig beamed, trying to contain his jubilation. "We'll need to call Penny first thing Monday morning."

It became apparent Dayo's determination hadn't diminished during the night as he openly talked tactics over breakfast.

"What if I just don't go back down . . . I mean, at the end of my visit?"

I couldn't believe what I was hearing. I'd been dreaming of this moment forever, but now that it had arrived, and while my heart was screaming to agree with him, I couldn't. I didn't want to rush the process; it had to be handled properly, for only God knew what the repercussion would have been if it wasn't. As much as I hated my decision to resist Dayo's suggestion, I knew I needed to speak with Penny first before making my next move. So, at the end of the weekend, Dayo reluctantly returned to Rab and acted as if nothing had changed.

Monday morning couldn't come soon enough. I'd fretted with my decision to return Dayo the moment he left Nairn, repeatedly second-guessing myself every five minutes. I was relieved to finally get hold of

Penny early that morning, who, other than the occasional, "hmm, hmm," listened attentively in silence as I relayed Dayo's revelation and my indecisive decision to return him.

"No Kemi, you've done the right thing. This is good . . . I'll arrange for the curator to speak to him again; we'll need to have Dayo's request to come home recorded and lodged." She sounded so positive and instantly removed any doubts I was having.

He's coming home!

Penny being Penny, got straight on to it and within five minutes she'd phoned me back with an appointment.

"That'd be great Penny, we're bringing Dayo back to Coatbridge that Monday anyway. He can have the meeting before we return him and Sola to Rab for their Easter holidays."

"Perfect Kemi, I'll call him back and confirm you're taking the appointment. This is a big step in the right direction!" Penny enthused jump-starting my excitement.

This is really happening. He's coming home!

"Once Dayo speaks to the curator," she continued, "and once the curator's concluded his report, we'll be able to take this back into court."

Court? Court! The brakes were firmly pulled on my excitement. In that moment I realised this was going to be too much for Dayo to maintain. I knew what would happen as soon as Rab found out - he would make Dayo change his mind and he wouldn't come home. I came off the phone feeling deflated – but not defeated. I had a plan.

When Dayo came home for his Easter holidays we had a wonderful week together. He was still insisting on coming home and I could see he was coming alive again - becoming himself again – just talking about it. After all this time, we were finally beginning to feel united.

Dayo had his meeting with the curator before being dropped off with Sola at Rab's. It went very well with Dayo not only being able to confess he wanted to come home, but also that he'd felt guilty for wanting to leave Rab.

"He said he won't get enough benefit money to live on if both me and Sola leave him – he'll lose the house."

This had been the real reason Dayo hadn't come home earlier.

As great as we all felt about Dayo's confession to the curator and his imminent return, I knew there were hurdles still to be cleared; two in particular. If either Rab or Michelle found out before the curator could present his report in court, Dayo wouldn't be coming home – they wouldn't let him; they'd make him change his mind. I was finally now willing to break the court order. The curator had interviewed Dayo and was recommending in his report that he should be allowed to return home to me. Worst case scenario: I'd get dragged into court and they'd have to listen to what was best for my son.

Whenever Sola refused to go to Rab's, Dayo would instead come to Nairn for some extra time. Even when he'd been angry and hostile towards me, he had always taken advantage of any additional opportunities to spend time at home in Nairn. So, with Sola having refused to stay for a whole week at Rab's, it had been agreed that he would only visit from the Monday to the Friday, with Dayo jumping at the chance to come back north for the weekend . . . as far as Rab believed. The plan was for Dayo never to return.

We dropped the boys off and prayed that our dreams wouldn't be revealed over the next five days.

On our way down to collect the boys on the Friday, I received a call from Sola.

"Mum . . . ," he whispered, instantly setting me to alert, "Dayo's not coming home."

Sola was calling me from inside the bathroom and he didn't have long to talk, so he delivered directly and clearly what he thought was important for me to know.

"Mum, Michelle's been here most of the week; I've not had any time on my own with Dayo. Mum, Dayo's told her, and she's told Rab - can you fix it?" He sounded desperate. My heart sank.

"I don't think so Sola," I began, feeling my eyes well, "your dad won't let me near him now. Listen, I'll be there soon. I'll call Dayo right now and see if I can speak to him."

"Mum . . . you can't . . . Rab took his phone off him," Sola said with panic.

"Okay Solie, I'll see you soon. Love you, bye."

"Bye Mum . . . please hurry."

When I came off the phone and told Craig what had happened, we were devastated. We couldn't speak. Silence dominated the car. There was nothing we could do. We both knew for Dayo to now come home he would have to speak up for himself and stand up to Rab; but this was something I was sure Dayo was not strong enough to do.

"Mummy, I want Dayo. Please . . . Dayo said he would be home forever," Tola repeatedly cried on a loop until she finally fell asleep at Perth an hour later.

Dayo was her closest sibling and she had been looking forward to him coming home to live with her forever; but he hadn't even come out to the car to say hello when we collected Sola.

Dayo would try to come home a further three times after this episode, with each occasion ending the same. When it came to standing up for himself and saying what he wanted, he would lose his voice. I knew what was happening; I could see the same pain in his eyes that I'd had in my own for so many years. Rab was physically and mentally abusing my son and there was nothing I could do about it. Dayo wouldn't speak up, he couldn't; he was always too scared of Rab. The angry, often raging, little boy with the weight of the world on his shoulders returned. He was losing himself again and with that, I was losing my son.

As I sit here writing about the terrible treatment Dayo endured, I realise it's still as horrifically heart-breaking to me today as it was at the time.

When he started high school in Airdrie, he experienced violence and racism daily, and no one - not Rab nor either of my parents - went to the school to challenge it. After yet another racist attack from an older boy - resulting in Dayo having a swollen, black eye – I'd had enough and decided to phone the school to inform the headteacher. It was blatantly apparent that she wasn't interested; she would not accept that there was racism taking place in her school. I didn't know what Rab had told the school, but with their ever-resistant attitude towards communicating with me, I can imagine.

I felt helpless; no one would help, defend or protect my son, so I decided I would have to travel down and visit the school in person, unannounced, as no one else could be bothered to intervene. When I arrived, the school still wouldn't accept or address the racism, but instead tried to portray the incident as 'a fair fight'. The boy was 16 years old and had called Dayo a black bastard. Dayo was 12.

Whenever the children experienced racism, instead of protecting and defending them, or even validating their pain, Rab would tell them they weren't black, so they couldn't feel offended. They have afro hair, black features and their skin is light brown; they're mixed-race. Rab just told them that to justify his and whoever else's racist behaviour towards and around them.

I was horrified and angry that he could mess with them like this and I was very concerned for Dayo. I knew some of the abuse he'd been subjected to and although both boys had been opening up to me, I took the decision to speak to my mum about my concerns. I wanted to make sure she was fully aware of all the abuse - especially the mental abuse - as I suspected she knew nothing about it.

When she teamed up with Rab, my mum never thought that he would take control like he had, and she hadn't expected Michelle to end up being so unhealthily involved. This hadn't surprised me at all, but she was now concerned about their close relationship; their relationship without her. She had no control over them and they had no boundaries. She could see how their relationship was affecting Dayo.

I knew she cared about Dayo and despite never being able to admit that she had done anything wrong, I knew she would help, as long as I didn't discuss her role in all of this.

I could see how this would play out. Dayo still stayed at my mum's more often than not and, in order to protect him, I would have to have some sort of contact with my mum. If I was in her life, I could offer some damage limitation to the manipulation he received from Michelle and Rab. If he could see his nanny supporting me, he might gain the strength to admit that what Rab was doing wasn't okay. This was the deal I made: to have some contact with my mum to protect my son.

So, my mum started coming to Inverness with Michelle to visit Tola once a month and if ever I was down in their area for any reason, I would go and have dinner with them. I paid for it all - and not just in the monetary sense. I couldn't be myself. I found that if I was in their company for even just an afternoon, I would step back into my original position in my parents' family, making me ill. My parents had even stayed a few weekends at my house and it destroyed me every time. I didn't do this intentionally; I couldn't help it. I wasn't strong enough not to resume my place in that moment, but my intention and incentive was to entirely separate my family from Rab.

I knew my mum wouldn't do anything to harm or jeopardise our new connection. She had got her daughter back and for her, that was what it was all about.

Sola

When he returned home for good, Sola was keen to re-enrol at the same primary school he had attended before he had been stolen. I had wanted him to join *The Moray Steiner School* in the neighbouring town of Forres, but he didn't want to have to start making new friends all over again. He had already managed to establish friendships at his old school and he had maintained spending time with his friends during his weekend visits home when he had lived with Rab. So that he could settle in as quickly as possible and to minimise any additional stresses, we thought it was best to let him go back to the primary school he had left one year earlier.

However, a lot had changed in that year and he was now experiencing racism, both in the school and the town.

"Mum, it's the same as Airdrie - people are not liking me because of my skin."

He was so glad to be home, but he struggled to come to terms with just how much things had changed. Sadly, at only 11 years old, Sola understood the message that unfortunately, his skin would always be how the world would see and judge him; and not in a good way.

I was a little shocked, rather angry, but mainly very disappointed that this was happening. We hadn't experienced racism in Nairn before - I had in Inverness, but nothing direct in Nairn - and now, what had once felt like such a safe town had begun to drop its act. It wasn't that long before, that a client had asked me if we'd experienced much racism since moving to the Highlands. I remember being able to honestly answer 'no', and that the children hadn't either.

"Yes, it's just the white settlers we don't like up here." I was shocked to find out this meant the English.

Despite the racism he was now experiencing, Sola managed to settle down rather quickly after returning home to the family. However, for as happy as he was to be home, I could tell he was in pain; little, subtle signs that things were not as okay as he made out, but he would never talk about it. He didn't want to discuss his experiences of living with Rab; he didn't want to discuss the fact that he had ever lived with Rab. He had internalised his trauma at being stolen - buried it deeply - and now that he'd returned to safety, he was terrified to acknowledge it existed. I knew it would all come out when he felt completely safe again, so I never pressed him on it.

Sola was in primary seven at this point and was due to move up into high school after the summer. Again, I wanted him to join *The Moray Steiner School* instead of *Nairn Academy,* but racism or not, he had made some friends and he didn't want any further changes. In his last term of primary seven, he attended an introduction week at *Nairn Academy*. The past few months had become very difficult for him at primary school, so he had been looking forward to it with the belief that he could keep his good friends and maybe gain some new ones too.

"Mum, I met a boy just like me - he's kind and he's from Brazil! We're going to be best friends," Sola shared excitedly when recounting to me and Craig how his first day had gone. They had apparently hit it off so well that Sola had asked his new friend around for a sleepover at the weekend. This would be the first time I met Froyabjorn, who at the time went simply by the name Freb.

Freb was a lot smaller than Sola and, as Sola had said, he was very kind and polite. He was very relaxed around the family, chatted away to me and Craig without prompt or hesitation and interacted with Tola as if she was his own sister. Freb fitted in like just another member of our family and before long, was staying over most weekends. Sola would have the odd sleepover at Freb's house, but not very often - he was never completely comfortable sleeping away from home - so we were happy for them to spend most of their time together at ours. With all the fun-filled sleepovers that were taking place, it wasn't long before Alreis, Freb's older brother, began attending too.

The two brothers became both Sola's and Dayo's best friends and would act as a buffer between their ever-growing conflict. By now, Sola struggled even more with Dayo and his choice to stay with Rab, while Dayo had become angrier and resentful at times towards Sola for refusing to go down to Rab's. This, of course, was the seed that Rab had planted in Dayo's mind.

Rab still controlled Dayo and in turn, Dayo tried to control Sola. Instead of accepting Sola's choice to come home for what it was, Rab would twist it and make it into a direct rejection of Dayo by Sola, with Dayo buying into it. Sola feared Rab, enough so that he wanted to stay away from him, but for Dayo, it was the fear of Rab that had stopped him being able to run away from his captor.

The boys having Freb and Alreis helped them to blend - to interact harmoniously . . . most of the time. They all really loved one another. Freb and Alreis were a blessing, not only in my children's lives, but in all our lives.

Tola was still the light of Dayo's life and he just melted whenever she was around. He really would make the effort to include her in all the boys' sleepovers and having been so isolated throughout all the craziness, it was good for her to be part of this dynamic too - whether all the boys liked it or not.

# # #

By the time Sola had been at *Nairn Academy* for two years, all the racism and bullying had become unbearable, so much so, that instead of playing outside or going to the beach, he barely left the house and spent most of his time - too much time - playing on his *PlayStation*. It was his escapism. In his mind it was a safe alternative away from his real, isolated life, but in reality, it was only causing him to become further detached – a mere smokescreen to hide away from all of his pain. He was on it constantly – and I was constantly on at him to get off it.

I had even caught him, on numerous occasions, awake and gaming throughout the early hours of the morning. One such occasion finally led to me confiscating it. I had tried to remind him of all the creative things he had always loved to do and highlighted how he was now not doing anything except for playing on his computer and that he had left me with no other option. He got angry – boy, did he get angry - shouting, stamping and swearing; that's when I decided he needed help to heal. He no longer had a choice; he was now going to attend *The Moray Steiner School*, where Tola had started the previous year.

"I will not be going to that 'hippy' school!"

He started his three-day trial within the week.

Sola had had to accept a change was needed. His way of coping wasn't working anymore, so we took him, reluctantly, along to the school to have a relaxed, 'get-to-know-one-another' meeting with his potential teacher before starting his trial. He wasn't happy; he wasn't rude, but he didn't try to hide the fact he didn't want to be there. That being said, I definitely saw him soften when the teacher confessed before the trial had even started that she, and the class, were keen for him to join.

Steiner schools work differently to 'normal' schools; they give the children a voice, meaning when the trial came to an end, it would be down to Sola to decide whether he would like to join permanently. I knew of the school's reputation for healing children in pain and trusted it was what Sola needed to be able to find himself again - and as his mother, I needed my son to find his voice again. That's why my anxiety heightened; there was so much riding on what his decision would be. I feared if he lost who he was – submitted to the pain he was carrying - he would never be able to survive in this racist and unconsciously, racially biased country. With the school fully informed and up to date with the history of the family, Sola's trial went ahead.

At the end of the trial Julie, Sola's wonderful teacher, called us in for a meeting to discuss his decision. We were nervous going into that meeting. I thought he'd had a ball and Craig thought he loved it, but it was the last day of his trial and we still had no idea if Sola would join or not. His time away from us had made it difficult for him to express how he felt.

As we walked in, Sola stood up from his seat beside Julie and, wearing a big smile on his face, gave Craig and me a big hug.

"I want to join, Mum," he announced, "I'm safe here."

Julie advised that we all had to be ready to support Sola, as now that he finally felt safe, she anticipated he would open up and allow all his pain to come out. I cannot tell you how grateful I felt to be heard as a mother and be supported with my son; to have his needs put first for once; to have someone who was genuinely interested in how he was being affected by the outside world. I had only ever been punished in this country for the colour of my skin, and I think you'd agree that, up until that point, no one had ever cared about any of my children's needs. For the first time in a long time, I had a little piece of safety.

It took about a month for Sola to unravel and when he did the school helped us put him back together. We got him a counsellor and the school brought in their own specialist team to help support him - to give him the space he needed to work through his pain.

As a little boy, Sola had always been very expressive and creative. He was always academic, but now we were beginning to see his creative side coming back to life again, and by the following year he was performing a leading role in the school play. Before being offered the role, Julie and his drama teacher Claire, had called us in to inform us of their intention for Sola to play *Leonato* in their performance of *Much Ado About Nothing*.

We all knew he would be very reluctant to accept the role, but Claire was convinced it was exactly what Sola needed to bring him completely out of his shell. While she wasn't wrong, Sola was initially angry and scared.

"I'm not doing it. People will be staring at me and I'll be rubbish."

Craig and I spoke to him, asking that he at least gave it a try. Ever since he had been at the school, he had been a magnet for all the younger children - they all looked up to him and thought the world of him - and we reminded him that it would give them so much joy. Before long, he agreed, and the rest is history.

They performed the play in the local town hall, the *Universal Hall* at *Findhorn Foundation* and at *Cawdor Castle* before going on tour to Glasgow and Edinburgh. Everyone was talking about him; parents, clients and complete strangers all approached us to say how great he was. My little man was famous! He loved expressing himself through acting, so much so, that he began to attend *Eden Court Theatre* in Inverness after school, to participate in their *London Academy of Music and Dramatic Art* (*LAMDA*) courses.

The school didn't have an upper school at this time meaning Sola wouldn't have a school to attend once he turned 16-years-old, so, I and six others began exploring the idea of starting an upper school. The idea grew momentum and became a reality. However, with the school literally not having the physical space available, the *Drumduan Upper School* was born into existence at the *Moray Arts Centre* on the *Findhorn Foundation's* campus.

It was an amazing experience, not just for Sola, but for all the children. The relocation away from the main school and the younger children, gave them all a sense of independence; of being that bit more 'grown-up'.

With Sola feeling safe, growing in confidence and gaining

independence, he began to work part-time at the *Kimberley Inn*, a local pub in Findhorn, where he went on to obtain much more than just his wages. His interactions with the customers and the guidance he received from the wonderful staff, taught him real life skills and played a big part in how this amazing, young man was developing. With his ever-growing self-belief, he continued to push himself and managed to secure funding from the *Foundation's* youth programme to write, produce and perform a play in their *Universal Hall*, two years running. He was flourishing.

Sola was 17 when his first year at *Drumduan Upper School* came to an end and we could see he was now craving more than the school had to offer. The school had not only been a safe haven for Sola, but it had also helped rebuild him into the confident young man he had become, so much so that he had outgrown it; equipped with the tools, he needed to go out into the world. He had dreamed of doing a degree in acting at *The University of the Highlands and Islands* in Inverness, however, with *Steiner* pupils not sitting exams - instead, they use portfolios to showcase the body of work they have done throughout the school year - Sola didn't have 'results' to use when applying for further education at colleges and universities. A cloud of doubt shaded his dreams.

The University of the Highlands and Islands seemed wary and hesitant when he first approached them. They weren't familiar with this way of applying and not only were they not going to offer him a placement, but they also seemed reluctant to even offer him an interview. We knew if we could just get him in front of them – to have a voice – his passion would shine through any doubts. So, with Sola's deputy head intervening - fighting hard to convince the drama department's manager that the *Steiner* education was legitimate and to persuade them to give Sola a chance - he got his interview.

He blew them away. They loved him that much that they offered him a place on the course right there on the spot. I cannot tell you how proud I was of him. He had fully utilised the very thing that had been taken away from him at the age of nine: his voice. Now, at 17, he was so articulate. He had earned himself his place and was on his way to getting a degree.

"I'm going to go back Mum," Sola decided at the end of his first year at university, "I need to be in a bigger city for auditions . . . to give myself a better chance of getting parts."

Our little boy was growing up and was soon moving out of the family home and into the student halls of residence at the *University of the West of Scotland* in Ayr, where he had been accepted onto their course to continue his dream. I remember the day Craig and I drove him there and I remember how we both cried most of the drive home; both tears of mourning and of pride. Sola was now on his own journey and we would not be part of it on a day-to-day basis, but we were so proud of our little man and all that he had achieved. We had all found some joy.

Joy to my world

The summer that Sola was preparing to leave for university in Ayr was the same summer Dayo finally came home. To my shock and delight, he'd finally stood up to Rab and told him he was leaving him to come and live with Craig and me. He had said to me on numerous occasions in the past that he wanted to return, only for my heart to be broken each time he'd been unable to stand up to Rab, but this time he had found the courage. Rab, as had been expected, was furious, resulting in Dayo having to move out very quickly.

When we brought him home, I hardly recognised my son. His OCD was at its worst, he was angry all the time and, at 19-years-old, was verging on being an alcoholic. I was also convinced that he was gay and that he was suppressing it through fear of the consequences from his homophobic dad. He quickly began to unravel.

He had to have counselling to deal with the abuse he had been subjected to by Rab in the toxic, racist environment in which he had been existing for the past seven years. It broke my heart listening to him reliving and confirming everything I had suspected had taken place; the abuse I had been powerless to prevent.

By the November, Craig and I thought it would be a good idea for Dayo to attend *Experience Week* - a course run by *Findhorn Foundation*. *Experience Week,* in a nutshell, is a collection of strangers of all ages, genders, races and faiths coming together under expert counsel to learn how to know and understand themselves on a deeper level. They learn how to become more empowered and open to love. It's full of fun, laughter, making new friends, experiencing something new, being still, self-reflection and personal development. Sola had attended one before and it had been a helpful tool in him rediscovering himself, so Dayo agreed to go.

In December, we dropped our son off, came home and prayed. Our prayers were heard and Dayo had an amazing week. Strong friendships were made and the opening-up began. When we picked him up the following week, the transformation was incredible. There was just something more present about our child.

It was the week before Christmas when Dayo told us he had something he wanted to share.

"There's something that's been bothering me . . . I'm not quite ready to talk about it yet . . . but I thought you should know in case you've noticed there's something on my mind and are worried."

Sola, who was home for Christmas, came to me after the family meeting concluded.

"Why is he not telling us? We all know he's gay."

"Yes, maybe," I agreed, "but it has to be in his own time."

After a few days had passed, while Craig and Dayo were driving on their way to the shop, a conversation was broached. It's important to note at this point that my husband thinks he's a real joker and always tries to ease others with laughter. He swears there's nothing that works better to break tension than an inappropriate joke.

"Right, come on then, what is it you want to talk about?" Craig asked breaking the silence, wondering if Dayo would open up.

"Sorry Craig, I'm still not ready yet," Dayo replied.

"Well, you do know whenever you are ready, there is nothing you could say that we wouldn't be here to support you through?" Craig offered, trying to reassure him that there was no pressure to talk just now. "You could even say you wanted to cut your pee-pee off and we'd all still be here waiting to support you."

As planned, Dayo laughed at Craig's 'humour' and they continued their journey without another word on the matter being said.

On 2nd January, Dayo again came to me and asked if we could all sit down together as a family as he was now ready to share. We had all, at one time or another - and away from Dayo's ears – speculated on what he wanted to disclose, and we were all desperate to find out. With all of the family huddled together on my bed, what Dayo opened with, no one had seen coming.

"Mum, Craig," he began with a nervous grin, "I'm transgender. I'm a woman trapped in the wrong body."

Something in that moment clicked for me and suddenly everything made sense. That was the last time Dayo spoke. His final confession allowed Joy to finally have her voice.

Craig and I just looked at each other, united with love for our new daughter. At that time, none of us knew anything about gender dysphoria or transgender, but thankfully Joy quickly educated us. It was such a poignant moment, filled with love and relief, that none of us will ever forget.

However, a new fear began to grow inside me: a horrible dread of the heartache that could lie ahead for her being both transgender and mixed race. It didn't matter what gender she was - she was our child and we loved her, and nothing would change that - but that did little to appease my newfound fear; I knew her journey could be a difficult one.

The next morning Craig had been busily researching transgender and gender dysphoria when he came to me.

"Kem, *Google* says almost 50% of trans people in Britain have attempted suicide at least once, and over 80% have thought about it - and there's a 12-18 month waiting list to be seen by the NHS."

It was inconceivable to imagine Joy having to wait a year and a half to be seen by an NHS specialist, while knowing that the emotional pain she was carrying could potentially lead to her taking her own life and being another tragic statistic. In my mind this was a real possibility, so we decided we would just have to work even harder to be able to pay for her treatment privately. That way Joy could be seen by a specialist while she was on the waiting list to be seen by the NHS. There was no alternative; we could not allow her to be another statistic; there was no way we were taking any chances on losing our daughter, again.

There was an immediate change in Joy after her revelation - we all could see it. She had become more relaxed was no longer angry, her OCD became less intense and her alcohol dependency stopped overnight. Although my understanding of transgender and gender dysmorphia was practically at zero at the time, it felt right, as I had not seen this side of Joy since she had been taken away from me. She was very clear from day one that she wanted to move forward in her transition and as a mother, I have to say, my new fears continued to grow inside me. How was I going to protect her? I worry about all my children whenever they're out - they have to endure so much because of the colour of their skin – but worry doesn't cover the depths of fear I had for Joy embarking on her new journey.

We soon got an appointment to see a specialist at a private hospital in Aberdeen where we learned all about what lay ahead for Joy. Her first big step was to receive hormonal treatment, but before she could start, she would have to undergo a psychological assessment in Glasgow. Joy continued seeing her counsellor while we waited for her assessment appointment to come through. We knew we needed all the professional help we could get our hands on to support her, and ourselves, on this new journey.

When the day of the assessment finally arrived, I remember Joy being really nervous and excited at the same time - we all were - but from the very moment the lovely psychologist introduced himself we all instantly felt more at ease, with Joy being unable to hide her smile as she followed him into his office. The best part of three hours passed by without them returning, and I wasn't sure if that was a good sign or not. We all knew just how much rested on the psychologist's recommendations.

Finally, the office door swung open for the psychologist to invite the whole family in. I held my breath as we made our way in. With a few nervous smiles exchanged amongst us, we sat down and listened.

"Joy's done great. I've called you all in to advise you that I'm recommending she be accepted for the hormone treatment."

We were all so thrilled for her.

It would only be a few weeks later, in the May, that we found ourselves back in Aberdeen for Joy to start her hormone therapy. We were told to expect her moods to swing, her body to begin changing shape and her upper body strength to decrease. Well, there weren't really any bad mood swings, but her body started to change literally overnight, with even the consultants astounded at her rapid development. She had always been a beautifully graceful child, but now, and right before our eyes, she was becoming a stunningly tall and graceful woman - and she was happy - the happiest I had ever seen her. Even though Craig and I didn't fully understand all what was happening at the time, we knew it was right as she was present again – laughing and living-up to the meaning of the name I had given her 19 years earlier: Joy.

When Joy had returned home the previous summer, she had decided she no longer wanted to see Rab - that she was too scared of him - however, despite everything that she had been through, she still wanted to let him know about her journey and so decided the safest way for her to do that was to write to him.

When Rab received the letter, he went ballistic. We were all in the car when Sola got the call demanding answers to how 'he' - Joy - could do this to him.

"Not everything is about you," Sola responded before ending the call.

Next, Rab's sister, the one who had been racist to me some years earlier, called instructing Sola, and Joy, that they had to think about their dad and what this would do to him.

I wasn't surprised Rab was making this about himself - he always did. His problem was that he had never seen Joy and Sola as human beings, with their own minds and hearts. He never experienced these young people as the amazing human beings they were. Sadly, for him, he's never got that and five years on, Joy and Sola have no contact with him. I don't know if they ever will.

Over the last four years, our lives have been all about Joy's transition. She did eventually get seen on the NHS for her treatment and her journey has been a very graceful one. We have watched her transition into the beautiful women she was born to be. It has been very tough for her at times, but the support she has received has been wonderful.

On 12th July, 2019 we travelled down to Glasgow to meet her surgeon, Mr Thomas. On arrival it was very sad to see so many young women there, alone and without any support. Unfortunately, that is the norm, however, the care and service that you receive from this amazing surgeon and his team of specialist nurses is phenomenal. Mr Thomas helped me as a mother. He was not what I had excepted, but he was exactly who we needed. He was so reassuring, so confident and so knowledgeable, that I was left feeling like there was no one better than this amazing man to take care of Joy.

To make it a safer environment to be able to give the amazing care these brave women needed, we learned the operation would be performed in the private *Nuffield Health Hospital* in Brighton, England. There, even the local bed and breakfast owners and taxi drivers had all been educated on transgender and gender dysphoria; everyone who we needed to have contact with were experienced. Mr Thomas and his team have even created a catalogue of volunteers for those without any support. The volunteers meet up with the patient to get to know them before their operation, and then take care of them at the patients' accommodation for the first two weeks after their procedure. I couldn't believe all this went on in the NHS. You would never know unless you needed the service.

After her meeting with Mr Thomas, Joy was given the all-clear for her transition surgery to go ahead. This was such a happy day for us. The 12th July, a date I had grown to hate, the date the children had been placed on the Child Protection register all those years earlier, had been transformed from a date I loathed returning every year into a date of great celebration. What had always been a date we remembered with sadness, was now turned into a day of Joy.

Joy's operation was to be performed before the end of the year, as the Scottish Government was cutting the budget for transgender operations (it appears that this is just another thing that the Scottish Government seems to be prejudiced towards; but that's for another story), so the fantastic Mr Thomas was desperately trying to get all of his Scottish patients seen before the budget cuts took effect.

So, Joy now had the green light to proceed with the operation and she had absolutely no doubts whatsoever that she wanted to go ahead with it; but psychologically, she was scared. Joy gets frightened at the thought of - never mind the sight of - blood and wounds, with the faintest scratch causing her to panic about 'bleeding out', as she would put it. So, the thought of the actual operation, or any operation for that matter, terrified her.

To try to overcome her fears, the specialists recommended we try watching videos of the operation being performed on *YouTube*, but I felt I couldn't; Joy was still my baby and if I knew the ins and outs of what the operation involved, I would be too worried and concerned to be able to support her properly. So instead, Craig stepped in and watched the procedure with her.

When they came out of the room from watching the video, Joy was looking better already . . . but Craig was as white as a sheet and had to go and have a lie down!

"On one hand, it was the most amazing thing I've ever seen," Craig said, his cheeks now showing a bit more colour after having recuperated, "but . . . . it will be Joy - our Joy - lying there on the theatre table." The reality of what she was about to go through with was beginning to hit home.

Later that month, we attended our very first *Pride* event as a family - where Joy was one of the main speakers! Joy had joined an LGBTQ+ support group in Inverness and had been attending at least twice a week. We just thought she was going along to the group for some additional support – which she was - but after a while it became much more than that; it was a safe space for her to be herself completely, to grow in confidence with who she was and strengthen her voice, so much so, she mainly now attended to offer her voice to others, to support them. She was even asked to start her own LGBTQ+ group for young adults.

We were shocked by the amount of people who came up to us at *Pride* to share with us how much a support Joy was to them. Craig and I could only stare at each other with pride and silent wonderment, watching her up on the stage speaking to everyone. How had we managed to raise such an inspirational human being? I do not have words to describe how proud I was of her.

Joy had worked as our receptionist for the past four years, so our wonderful clients from all walks of life, some of whom have known her since she was only nine years old, have witnessed her transformational journey, with many commenting on what a blessing she is and that if it wasn't for her, they may never have been as lucky to have met someone who was transgender.

We received the best present the week before Christmas: the date of Joy's operation - 19th February, 2020 at the *Nuffield Health Hospital* in Brighton, England. Sola, who was by now living in London and trying to break into the acting industry, came home for most of January as he wanted to be close to the family leading up to the operation.

This had been a difficult time for Sola in some ways. He was 100% with Joy, supporting her right from the very start, which had gone a long way to help heal their relationship, but at the same time, he was grieving.

"It really does feel like my brother has died," he confessed.

This was sad and he only ever spoke to Craig and me about it. However, despite the grief at the loss of his brother, he was delighted to have another sister!

I remember the last client I had a few days before going to Brighton.

"Oh Kemi, Brighton! That place will seduce you - pull you in. You'll want to live there," Chrisanthe said with certainty.

"Don't be silly; I want to live in the West Country!" I replied. However, she was right.

Chrisanthe knew Joy very well, and Tola too, as she had been her tutor for some time; and she was the only client from whom I couldn't hide my fear. Spending time with Chrisanthe let me see just how much Joy's operation was affecting me. She made space for me to be vulnerable, and although she would come to me for treatment, I would end up being the one crying. She had become a dear friend and organised girls' nights with another good friend, Shirley. For the first time in my adult life, I had girlfriends - real girlfriends.

The days leading up to leaving were unbearable and I'm ashamed to say, for the first time in years, I restricted food to try to dull my emotions. I couldn't get away from my own terror and anxiety and I didn't sleep very well. Looking back, I hadn't really slept for the past three years. I had four empty days to wait after I finished work and without my usual distraction, I found it hard to sit still as all I would do was cry. I couldn't tell anyone that I was scared Joy would die in the operation - I didn't want to give it any energy - so I tried to keep busy, filling my time plaiting Craig and Sola's hair for hours and hours in a bid to try and escape my fears.

We arranged for Sola to come back home on 16th February so we could celebrate his birthday on the 17th, before travelling with me and Joy to Brighton on the 18th - the day before the operation. We were to take Joy to the hospital that evening to get her checked-in and settled, then Sola and I would stay the night at a hotel. Sola would then go back to London the day after Joy's operation, before coming back to Brighton for the weekend. Craig would be staying at home with Tola, but would also be coming down for the weekend. So, on 17th February, we had a birthday meal for Sola and the next day Sola, Joy and I flew to London, to begin our journey to Brighton.

There was a lot of nervous excitement in Joy's hospital room the night before her operation - mine, Joy's and Sola's. We had all waited so long and patiently for this moment to arrive and now there was only one more sleep. However, for as much excitement as I felt, there had also been a 'gnawing' going on in pit of my stomach for most of the day; a deep, dread-filled anxiety. No matter how old any of my children get, they will always be my babies and all day I had known that one of my babies was to undergo an operation the next morning – a major operation. As much as I wanted my daughter to complete her journey, my anxiety had continued to grow to the point that when it came time to leave her, all alone in the hospital, I was terrified.

I tried not to show it, but she saw it.

"Don't cry Mum," Joy said to me as I held her close to say goodbye.

I could only look at her through tears, no words were able to come out as they were now being overtaken with great sorrow for what I might lose: my daughter.

"Look how far we have come. I would never have been able to do this without you," she told me with the grace and calm of an angel. "Mum, I'm *your* daughter; I'm strong, and we can do this," she encouraged, now through tears of her own.

"Mum, she will be okay," Sola said, wrapping an arm around us both.

We all cried that night, both for what we had been through and for how close we were regardless of what life had dealt us so far.

That bleak night, Sola and I made our way through the horrible, torrential rain back to the hotel before going out for dinner, and I can still remember how much more added distress I felt as I stopped to rid myself of all my cash to the friendly, soaked-to-the-bone homeless people. And, as lovely as the little Thai restaurant was, I struggled to eat. Fear sat at our table. It followed me to my hotel that night and it had followed me into my bed, where it kept me awake with its repeated whispers of 'what-ifs' churning around in my head. My family was fragmented across two countries and three locations and I felt scared, alone and fragile. Between hours of

Facetime with Craig and a book's worth of text messages to Chrisanthe, I somehow managed to get through the night.

In the morning, I went for a much-needed cup of coffee and a walk with Sola to kill some time. We were both still so nervous. I had spoken to Joy when she went into theatre at 8am, so that whole morning I knew she was already 'under'. It didn't matter what we did, we couldn't get her out of our heads.

After our walk and coffee had run its course, to distract ourselves we decided to go shopping to find Joy one of her most favourite things ever: a unicorn. At 11.40am, having just completed our search, my phone chimed a notification. As I opened it, there she was: a glorious selfie of my beautiful Joy to the world wearing the most radiant of smiles.

"Mum, I'm finished, when will you be here?"

Sola and I stared at each other in silence before crying tears of joy followed by fits of laughter. We were so blessed! I felt instantly lighter, unburdened; the gnawing had stopped. We jumped into a taxi and were by her side, unicorn in hand, before half an hour had elapsed. Again, we all just cried with 'Joy' (in more ways than one) before calling Daddy Craig so he could also be part of our special moment. I don't have the words to write the entirety of this experience - either for me personally, or as part of a family. That is a whole book of its own.

I cannot give enough thanks to the team of people that looked after us during that week. Everyone from the surgeon, Mr Thomas, through to the hospital cleaners, was so happy to be part of these brave women's lives. We were so blessed to experience this level of support and dedication. We will not only be forever indebted to Mr Thomas, the doctors, the nurses, and all the hospital staff, but also to the taxi drivers, the *Easy Jet* staff and all the staff at both *London Gatwick* and *Inverness Airport* who helped us get Joy home safely. Thank you all.

We were only home for four weeks before the Coronavirus epidemic forced the UK into lockdown. This allowed us the time as a family to be completely there to support Joy in her recovery, without any of the normal, everyday distractions. We will be eternally grateful for this time together.

I would like to take a moment to apologise for not using the proper terminology and language when speaking about Joy throughout this book. For people to fully understand her journey, I felt I had to write her life's story as it unfolded. I am aware of the pain that deadnaming creates and I am so thankful and proud of my daughter for allowing me to tell some of her story the way I have. Joy to my world, I am honoured to be your mother. You are a true blessing. Thank you.

Safety at any cost

After Sola had returned home from Rab, I no longer kept in contact with David and Sandra. To see David reminded me of all the pain I had encountered, which in turn became too painful when coupled with the deep, shameful feeling of failing him that I harboured. After all the support and fighting David had afforded me – extracting admissions of failure from the Social Work Department - only for me to then refuse to take it any further, as that could have compromised getting Sola back, meant that I had sold myself out. I saw that every time I met David - not that he would ever have thought it. Owing to my shame, I allowed our relationship to drift into complete non-existence. As I write this, it is still one of my biggest regrets.

David was like a father to me and there isn't a day goes by without me feeling saddened by my loss of not having him and Sandra in my life.

It was also around this time that I continued to throw myself into my work - the place where I had first felt any true worth for myself. Now I worked even harder, more often than not working 50-60 hours a week. It was somewhere I could be accepted. It was somewhere I didn't have to think about what a terrible mother I had been. Despite having had no options other than the choices I had made, I still felt I had caused all my children great harm and pain; that it was my fault. I never spoke to anyone about it - I was too ashamed to say I had lost my children - so I just pretended it had never happened and thankfully no one ever asked.

I just focused on work and continued to grow, buying the local health shop business which happened to be perfectly located directly across from the clinic. The health shop was something I had wanted and had felt we could make work. The clinical work had been very successful, averaging just under 100 clients per week, with a three-month waiting list. I could see there was an opportunity to both enhance my clients' wellbeing with natural health remedies, while increasing my own profits. The two businesses would promote one another and exchange new customers.

However, with our time having been so constrained to both the clinic and facilitating visits – at that time we were still driving up and down the A9 every two weeks for the boys' visits - we ended up having to employ staff to manage the shop, which inevitably replaced the profits with losses, which in turn ate into the clinic's profits. What was supposed to have lightened the burden ended up putting even more financial pressure on us and so, by 2012 we had given up the lease of the building and manged to sell off most of the health shop's remaining stock.

We continued working from the clinic in Nairn until, in 2014, I could no longer stand the ever-growing racism in the Highlands. Before the Scottish independence referendum, my own personal experiences of racism in the Highlands had been very infrequent and subtle, to the point it had felt as if we weren't even in Scotland to begin with. However, during the build-up to the referendum things changed.

"Go home, you black bitch," a man shouted at me in broad daylight, while I crossed the road to the clinic with little, eight-year-old Tola. I was frozen to the spot, while Tola started to cry.

"Mummy, why did that man say that you're black?" she desperately asked, looking for some reassurance. "You're brown." She was so confused, and I could see the fear in her drenched eyes.

This was to be the start of me orchestrating my life in a way that I could feel safe. I was devastated by what was going on and I was angry that Tola, my youngest child, was now experiencing the same fear her siblings had endured. I had been consciously very careful to limit the outside world's opportunities to subject her to racism and create fear.

A very dear client of mine had heard a rumour of the incident and came to me a few days after the racial attack to ask what had happened. The panic I felt at having to relive my ordeal made it difficult for me to relay to her what had taken place, but she was so lovely, so empathic to what I had experienced, that I managed to take some comfort from having shared. She had been having her own racist experiences, being English and living in Scotland. There were a lot of English people living in the north of Scotland and, for a lot of them, much had changed during this time too. I had even had English clients move out of Scotland because of its growing racism towards them.

One evening, having just finished clearing up after dinner, I received an unexpected visitor. As I opened the door, I was both surprised and confused to see the minister standing there, wearing a warm, big smile while presenting me with a card and the biggest bunch of flowers you could imagine. It turned out that my dear client, Jenny, had approached her minister, who had been a client of Craig's, to bring awareness to the community of my situation. The minister then spoke to his congregation about it during their Sunday service, which resulted in them holding a collection for me.

I wasn't part of their congregation, but they had taken the time to write me the most amazingly supportive card, saying how valued I was in the town and how upset they were to hear what I was going through. I was so over-whelmed by that lovely man standing in my home. I will never forget that.

It was like the referendum had told all the racists I was fair game again. I started being followed in shops in Inverness and I was having more and more people publicly calling me nigger and black bitch. I began losing myself again and not before long, found that I had become too frightened to go outdoors.

I needed to be away from people – more in control of my exposure to people - so we sold the house and moved to a more rural setting near the

340

town of Forres. I started working from home and stopped working from the clinic in Nairn.

Through fear, I stopped spending time with anyone outside my family. There were practically no people of colour in the north of Scotland, so I withdrew from society and became more isolated. I didn't want any of the white people in my life to expose how they felt to me with their views on "there's no racism in Scotland". Looking back, I'm now shocked at how easy it was for me to withdraw from the life we had made; my natural instincts must have removed me from society without giving it a second thought.

I truly believe that the *SNP*, and some of their supporters, come from a place of racism towards the English. I'm no expert, but personally, I do not believe Scotland could sustain itself independently of the UK - but racists don't care about that. I am not knocking those who truly believe independence would make Scotland economically more secure and stronger, that's their right and like I said, I'm no expert. However, there are those in Scotland who desire – crave -independence at any cost. They do exist - I've met them and heard them say so. Their hatred towards England and the English rules them to the point that they would vote for independence, even if an economic Armageddon was guaranteed as part of its manifesto.

Those people care more about their hatred; their belief that they are superior to others. Unfortunately, their belief has been my experience, my children's experiences and those of every other person of colour I have come across in Scotland. I'd always had to live with racism, but now I lived watching my children going down the same, familiar path. From my personal perspective, Scottish independence equals more racism towards people of colour.

Tola's journey

Olutola Barbara Ferguson-Ogunyemi - what a strong name for a little girl. This was the one I thought I could protect. She was the centre of anything good in my life and I was so grateful that she hadn't been exposed to my blood family during those first couple of traumatic years - which was a better start to life than either her siblings or I had. However, between losing her brothers at such an early age and witnessing the constant, emotional pain I endured being dragged in and out of court every other week, I failed to protect her. As she got older, she did carry trauma from her early years, but I had thought that by me being honest with her, the experiences in her life wouldn't mark her in the same way as it had the rest of us.

Tola started the *Steiner School's* kindergarten at six, class one at seven, before leaving at the age of eight. *Steiner* education promotes a slower, more gentle approach to literacy and numeracy, instead concentrating more on imagination, nature and creativity in the earlier years of education. I wanted her to have this gentler experience of schooling, however, with Tola being very bright and a wordsmith like her dad, she was craving more challenge, and as she put it, was determined to go to 'proper' school. We were very reluctant to put her into mainstream school; we had to protect her from the racism in Scotland for as long as we could.

We came to the conclusion that there was only one real option. For Tola to gain more stimulus at school, but without the exposure to the racism that thrives in mainstream schools in Scotland, she would have to join *Gordonstoun* prep school – no matter the cost. *Gordonstoun* prep school is an international, multicultural school with all different races. There, she would have other mixed-race and black children for classmates, which is very important when growing up as a minority. We believed, with the £12,000 a year fees, it would be highly unlikely that Tola would experience racism there, but if she did, the school with its reputation would want to quickly stamp it out.

Tola attended *Gordonstoun* prep school for the next three and a half years and, as we'd hoped, was not exposed to the racism that me, my husband and my other children had all had to endure in mainstream school. This did, however, put a greater financial strain on us, with all our earnings going towards paying both Sola's (who was still in *Steiner* education at this time) and Tola's school fees. Although it was draining us in every way, we had no other choice. The only way to ensure that Tola would not experience racism at school was for us to pay, very dearly, for her education. This in turn ensured I had to work day and night to pay for it.

At 11 years old, Tola, with Joy's support, came to me saying that she now wanted to be a 'normal' girl and go to a 'normal' primary school in the neighbouring village to ours.

"Mummy, if I stay at junior school (*Gordonstoun*), I don't think I will be Tola anymore."

It was terrifying for me to hear that she felt like she was losing herself, but I heard her very clearly and something inside me knew she was right; that it was time for change. Her days at *Gordonstoun* were long; they started earlier and finished later than 'normal' schools and, on top of that was the 35-minute journey at both ends of her day. By the time she got home after school she only had enough time to eat her dinner, complete her homework and have a bath before it was bedtime. At that point we hadn't really thought past her current academic year, as the following year she was to be going on to high school; a mainstream high school, where she could - and most likely would - experience (at best), unconscious, racial bias. That thought had terrified me even more, so I tried not to think about it and instead focused on what I could do to make things better now: find a good primary school.

Thankfully there was a primary school with a great reputation close by that some of my client's children had attended before going off to prep school, so I was relatively confident she would be safe there. However, I was unaware that by protecting Tola from the realities of the outside world, I had in fact made it very difficult for her to navigate how to fit in, resulting in her becoming scared to do anything in case she did the wrong thing. It didn't help when one of the parents told lies about Tola, trying to turn the other parents against her so that she wouldn't be allowed to play with their children. This was Tola's introduction to unconscious racism.

She was aware her siblings had experienced racism and she had witnessed mine, but now she was experiencing her own. Her views of the world had drastically changed to one that was alien to her. She was being taught - and was learning - that she was different. When the time arrived to decide about her high school, I hoped that she would choose to return to *Steiner,* but she was determined to go to the local mainstream high school.

Within the first few weeks of high school the racism started. She was called racist names, told that her afro hair was disgusting and was encouraged to cut herself on social media by some of the girls from the school. She spiralled down in no time at all, becoming more isolated and in search of protection from the racists, aligned herself with the 'naughty' children. I instantly recognised this - I had done the same thing when I was her age to try to protect myself. We made the decision to withdraw her from the mainstream high school and re-enrol her at the *Steiner School,* where eight months later she moved onto *Drumduan Upper School* – the school I had helped create for Sola's class.

In the time we were absent from having any children at the school, the *Upper School* had moved from *Moray Arts Centre,* having managed to acquire a piece of land located next to the familiar grounds of the original *Steiner* campus where Tola had attended kindergarten. To add further familiarity, some of her original kindergarten classmates were still there. However, unlike Sola's experience of *Steiner* education, Tola's was not blessed; in fact, since class two, she hadn't really had a positive experience at all. Within weeks of starting *Upper School* after the summer, it started again. At first it was indirect - young boys thinking it was okay to use the 'N' word flippantly – the same ignorance Sola has been battling against ever since his teens.

Let me be very clear on how I feel about this: the word 'nigger' should never come out of a white person's mouth - no matter the excuse. To still have to explain to white people today why this should be, beggars belief. But here we are and here I am. This word solely exists for white people to intentionally abuse and degrade black people, to terrorise black people and to impose superiority. Simple, no? After centuries of abuse, black people have reclaimed it and, in my view, now have full ownership of its use. We have taken this word and redefined its meaning, for use solely within the black community – exclusively between one another.

However, some of us take it out into the world and expect white people, who are uneducated in our history, not to use it. They see young rappers – young, black rappers - using it; putting it out wrongly into the world and disempowering its meaning, and they mistake its flippant use in media as a sign that it's a safe word for them to use too.

Then there are some white people who think it's 'cool' to say nigger. Their perception of being black is that it's 'cool' – a fashion choice - and they want to imitate it. This is still wrong; it's racially ignorant and makes it harder for us to be seen as people and not some trend. When a black person hears 'nigger' from a white person it tears through our souls. The word carries all our pain - it's in our DNA, and that's why I believe it should only ever be used in the privacy and intimacy of the black community; we have the right to do this. Tola was able to verbalise this belief to her class and peers and while some were able to take it on board, others took no notice.

There was a black, mixed-race boy two years older than her, whose friends would regularly use the 'N' word in his company.

"He said it was okay and gave us 'a pass'," his friends would justify.

I can remember how this had angered and frustrated Tola. These same boys, in the mindset of some of our younger communities that do not understand, would tell Tola she wasn't cool enough to be black, and she felt betrayed and undermined at someone of colour allowing - permitting - white people to be racist. She learned that he was very confused about his identity as they spent more time together, and she was able to educate to him on what was acceptable. He began to stand up for himself . . . sometimes.

In the beginning, some of the boys accepted that the 'N' word had to be off the table, but most of them continued to use it regardless, and even escalated its use from racially ignorant greetings to intentional pain-infliction. They were relentless. They began to straight-out call her 'nigger';

they used racist language about the family and they showed strong disgust and utter contempt for her facial features and thickening body. The school was very small, with Tola's class having only 14 children in it, with only four girls. Her friends didn't support her; they turned their backs on her while she quickly became isolated again, falling into her own dark hole.

Craig and I couldn't believe our baby was having to endure racism and we struggled emotionally to accept it. How could we still be here all this time later? It was devastating and I found it difficult to focus on anything other than what my daughter was going through, all the while feeling powerless to stop it. I obsessed at night, reliving my own childhood memories; the ones I had tried to suppress.

We couldn't understand why all of a sudden this was happening and we needed answers, so we began to trawl the internet in the hope of finding them. That was when we finally discovered the words, 'unconscious, racial bias'. I couldn't believe what I was reading; there was a name for what had happened to me, for how I was treated. I knew in that moment that I wasn't mad for feeling and believing that I'd always been treated unfairly because of the colour of my skin. And with that, I started to feel empowered; I had finally found something that would help me explain what my daughter was experiencing.

The school's management at the time was still the same team I had originally started the school with and like most of society, they were too scared to face the racism Tola was experiencing. I had to force them to look at it, which took nearly two months of repeated phone calls and emails, before they even acknowledged it, let alone addressed it.

In the end, I had to involve my very dear friend who was also my lawyer. He advised that he was to be copied into any email correspondence I had with the school from now on. My lawyer's reputation is known throughout the country - not a bragging right, just a fact - and the mere mention of his name was enough to incentivise the school into action. By the November I finally had a meeting with the management.

Nobody wanted to be at that meeting. The atmosphere was fraught, the management looked sheepish and Craig was furious, so I decided I would speak first. I told them I understood why it had taken them so long to get to this point – that it was down to the fact that they didn't really know how to handle it. How could they? They had 'white privilege'. White privilege describes someone who lives their life absent from the consequences of racism, absent from structural discrimination and absent from their race being viewed primarily as an issue.

I explained to the management that I didn't want the boys punished as I didn't think that was the correct way forward. Instead, I wanted Tola's class - and the rest of the school for that matter - educated on racial awareness and the effects of racism. I had known some of the children since they were four years old and didn't believe they were all truly racist; just ignorant.

"So, why do *you* think this has taken so long?" Craig asked the room. There was an awkward silence.

"I don't know why," one of the trustees answered honestly. "I know it's wrong, but I just don't know why we've found it so difficult."

That is what I call historical shame. We all carry it for one reason or another and it is the fundamental reason we don't move very far forward in this. I explained this at the meeting and they showed signs they were beginning to understand. The Head suggested arranging a sit-down for Tola and the four boys (individually) who were still being racist. I thought this was a great idea and the first real step in the right direction. The meeting concluded with the trustees advising us that they were talking to a group with the intention of bringing them in to deliver an educational package, and asking me if I would be willing to come in and speak to the *Upper School* about racism. I agreed.

Neither the educational package, nor my talk ever happened.

I was still very concerned about the effect this was having on Tola. The school had gone through the procedure of speaking to the boys, many times, and put them on suspension warnings, but this hadn't really made any difference. Despite the school's warnings, the boys continued to be racist towards her, so we asked the parents of the class to meet with Craig and me so we could discuss the seriousness of what was going on.

I was terrified at that meeting; some of the parents didn't even bother to attend, while the ones who did were not fully aware of what had been going on. I found it difficult breaking through their defensive walls, their almost concrete denials to the mere concept that their children could be behaving in a racist manner, but after I'd finished explaining what unconscious, racial bias was, some of the parents slowly opened to the conversation. It was very insightful, with most of the parents at least portraying concern. Most, but not all.

"I can't see my daughter supporting Tola," one of the mothers began. "She sees Tola as being beautiful and having everything . . . and to be honest, I'm not prepared to speak to her about it."

I left the meeting expressing that I didn't actually believe all the children to be racist - more racially ignorant – but warned that if the children didn't stop, I would have no other option than to involve the police.

"I would hate for any of your children to be labelled 'racist' for the rest of their lives."

In the early spring, the school facilitated a safe space for Tola to sit down with the boys, individually, to express how their racist behaviour was affecting her. Thankfully, this was a very healing process for both Tola and most of the boys. However, the daughter of 'Mrs I'm not prepared to speak to my daughter', along with one of the boys, never let up. I watched Tola grow up very fast that year. It was very painful to see her discover and learn how racially biased the world was and to witness her fear and anger growing

346

towards it.

Around three months later, I was shocked when Tola approached me with a question.

"Is it okay for my teacher - my white teacher - to use the 'N' word?" Tola asked while loitering at the utility room door as I sorted out some washing. I had felt her lingering, sizing-up for the right moment. She instantly had my attention.

"Under no circumstances – why?" I asked, feeling a rising anxiety and a simmering anger.

"My teacher said it today during a lesson on LGBTQ+. She told the class that, 'saying faggot to a gay person was like calling someone a nigger'."

Shocked doesn't come close to how I felt. We and the school had worked so hard to eradicate the racism in that class, and here was a teacher teaching those same children that it was okay to use the 'N' word to illustrate something in class. An email was soon sent to the school demanding that the teacher apologise to Tola for her wholly inappropriate use of the racial slur in her poor analogy. I didn't care if she meant it or not, but it was important for Tola and the rest of the class to see the teacher take ownership of her racist error and acknowledge how it had made Tola feel.

We never got a reply. Craig went to the school with Tola the following morning to speak to the Head, but before he could reach the building, they were approached by a teacher whom neither Craig nor I had ever spoken to before.

"Why, *if* Tola is experiencing racism, do I not know about it? How can I fix it if Tola doesn't tell anyone?" This all said while looking directly at Tola, as if it was her fault she was been racially abused.

"Excuse me?" Craig said interrupting her audacity, "who *are* you? Who do you think you are, speaking to her like that? Are you actually trying to blame Tola? There have been several racist incidents; there have been meetings; why don't you know? Does no one at this school communicate? Do you know how hard it is to speak up when you are the minority and being racially abused?"

"Yes!" the teacher began screaming. "Yes, I do know! I deal with racism; I'm English in Scotland."

"Yes, but you're not a little girl being picked on by a whole load of boys because you look different," Craig replied, shutting down her insolence.

At this point, Craig could see the Head hurriedly making his way over to intervene, while Tola had, by now, begun to cry.

"Hi, Craig, . . . ," the Head began as the teacher slunk away.

"This is ridiculous," Craig interrupted. "Tola, go wait in the car – you're not going to school today. Who was that - and why was she in my face? She claims to be one of Tola's teachers, but she had no idea about all the racism."

"She does take Tola's class - once a week. I'll find out why she isn't up to speed, but I can assure you all of Tola's teachers have been sent an email detailing the racism that's been happening," the Head explained hurriedly.

"And my email? We've been expecting a response, but nothing. So, I had to come here to find out why Tola's teacher is using racist language in class, only to have to put up with that from that teacher."

"I'm sorry I haven't got back to you Craig – and I'm so sorry this has happened . . . I honestly don't know what to say. I haven't spoken with the teacher yet, she'd left for the day by the time I got your email, but I will be speaking to her this morning . . . I agree; an apology is needed; leave it with me."

Craig left the school believing a meeting would be arranged for the teacher to apologise to Tola.

It was a further five weeks before anyone from the school sat down with us to discuss their intentions.

During this time, the teacher's use of the 'N' word had acted as a catalyst - igniting the racism in Tola's class to burst into life once again - and within two weeks there was a racist screen saver on another teacher's laptop! The laptop, which belonged to the school, was used for *PowerPoint* presentations and was connected to the projector screen at the front of the class, fully blown-up for everyone's amusement; everyone's apart from Tola's. We reported it immediately and were told the school would investigate instantly. They didn't, and it was not removed instantly. Tola, off her own bat, removed it two weeks later.

Unbelievably, Tola's teacher, the one whose laptop had the racist screensaver, added even more misery. One day in class, the daughter of 'Mrs I'm not prepared to speak to my daughter' kept repeating to Tola that she wanted to say the 'N' word to her, going on about how she just wanted to know how it felt to say it to her and to see if it upset her. This, as you can imagine, was very distressing for Tola, so she tried explaining to the girl that racism was illegal. The girl disagreed and continued to goad her and even called the teacher over for confirmation.

"No, it's not. You can't go to jail for saying the 'N' word," the teacher recklessly replied.

It was only after this latest racist incident that we finally got our meeting with the school where we were told both teachers were no longer employed by the school. However, neither had been sacked nor disciplined. The 'screensaver' teacher had only been on a short-term contract and when it expired the school chose not to renew, while the 'N' word teacher simply left for another position at another school with her name and reputation unmarked.

Oh, and it's worth mentioning, despite being instructed to apologise by the Head and the trustees, she never did. She ignored them for long enough before simply refusing to do it. And her reason for not apologising? She said she had used the word in other schools, both mainstream and private, numerous times before and that no one else had ever complained about it.

348

Either that is a shocking truth, or a cowardly lie. Both are equally disturbing.

I was deeply saddened having to have the same conversations with my daughter that I'd had with her siblings; the same conversations that my dad had had with me; the conversations that would help her negotiate her way through the unconscious racism that still exists; the conversations about how to behave in a racially ignorant society, and why everything that happened to her would always be made to be her own fault. Unless something big changes, this will be what is laced throughout her life. I naively thought I could protect her from racism, but I couldn't.

That being said, I do feel *Steiner* was the best place for her to experience these lessons in preparation for the outside world. Regardless of constantly having to chase them, their intentions and actions, or at times inactions, have inevitably helped my daughter learn what is and isn't acceptable when dealing with racism, and the Head creating a space of truth and reconciliation has taught her how to have an open and honest conversation about racism and its effects. Tola left *Steiner* at the end of the academic year.

#

Tola started home-schooling after the summer. We'd enrolled her after agreeing that she needed a break from feeling unsafe at school. She was to complete a two-week trial to see if she suited the online style of schooling, but by day ten, she had come to me worried that she wasn't taking any of it in and that she missed being around people. With *Steiner* not an option, and with Tola determined not to go back to *Gordonstoun*, I really only had one option left: the local high school, from where she had previously been removed by me.

We had an honest conversation, openly discussing the inevitable racism she would encounter. With hindsight, we both underestimated how much that would be. At the time, she didn't think it was going to be an issue; with everything she had experienced at *Steiner*, she believed she was now better equipped to cope in a mainstream school, plus, she had convinced herself that she had only struggled to find acceptance before because she had been to so many different schools and had never stayed long enough to grow any strong-rooted friendships. This time, she already knew some people at the school from when she had attended before and had kept in contact with some of the girls she liked.

I wasn't so sure, but as a mother, I had learned by now that you cannot stop the outside world from crashing into your children's lives - that you cannot prevent their horrendous lessons. I had always changed Tola's environment to limit her exposure to the pain and shame of racism when she was younger, but by now I understood that *that* pain existed in any environment. I knew I had to accept that I couldn't protect her from it anymore; this had to be Tola's time to figure out how she would exist in her world.

Under the pre-agreements that she would have to take the school bus - I believed this would help her develop some independence as she was too used to being chauffeured everywhere - and that she would have stay at the school and work through any issues that arose, no matter what life threw at her, until after her exams two years later, Tola re-joined the local high school by mid-October 2019.

She quickly learned that she wasn't accepted; plainly and simply because of the colour of her skin.

She managed to make a couple of new friends in the first few days back at the school, but with her principles set at only making friends with people who were real and honest, by the end of the week she was into the negative in the friend count. She didn't care; she knew her principles would make her a very unpopular 14-year-old - and they did - but by now, Tola had had it with unfairness. That's why she couldn't ignore the girl in her class who was body-shaming another girl - her own friend no less - and told her that it wasn't nice to do that. First big mistake. In response, the girl made most of the year turn against Tola.

It was in early November when we dropped her off in town, buzzing with excitement, to go to the fireworks display with the friends she'd kept. However, after only an hour we received a phone call.

"Can you please come and pick me up?" Tola began through staccato sobs, "I've had to leave - there's a girl . . . from my year threatening . . . to beat me up and to stab me. She's drunk . . . and she's with one of the racist boys from *Steiner.*" She sounded terrified. It was contagious.

Craig was there in ten-minutes and took her straight to the police station to report the incident. The following day, he took Tola to speak to the boy's mother about his behaviour, as the drunk girl had said he had orchestrated the attack. However, this was, as we expected, a waste of time, with the mother denying her son's involvement as she was certain he didn't even know the drunk girl. I could feel the familiar bruising on my head resurfacing from where it bumped against the brick wall.

Nothing ever came of it; the girl was never charged and the boy was never spoken to, leaving us all concerned for Tola's return to school, but fortunately, within a couple of weeks, the girl was expelled on a completely unrelated matter.

And so it began, and within a few weeks it had escalated.

"You're a nigger and your dad's a nigger, what's it like?" the group of boys shouted, surrounding Tola as she sat on the floor in the middle of her PE class, while all the other children stood back and watched.

The only person to defend her and pull her out of the circle was the girl Tola had called out for body-shaming during her first week. Tola phoned us straight away and we contacted the school. They advised us to contact the police and this time the boys were charged. We are still waiting to go to court.

Unbelievably, one of the boys continued to be racist to Tola almost every day on the school bus, with the bus driver turning a blind eye. He even went on to throw a pair of scissors at her in class. The school investigated the incident, but concluded they would be taking no further action. He had denied doing it and there were no witnesses, despite it happening in front of some 20+ children. Did my daughter have to be stabbed in class before her complaints would be taken seriously?

I am so proud of my little girl and the young woman she is becoming. She is intelligent, beautiful, kind and beginning to understand people. She continued to go to school every day, even though barely anyone spoke to her because she had reported her racism. My daughter has learned some very hard lessons in the past couple of years and I am deeply proud of her. She still has times when she cries and finds it hard to understand why people are "so mean". She doesn't really trust many white people and says she will never date a white boy. She is only 15. This is heart-breaking for me, but I understand it. This is how a person of colour is made to feel because of their experiences in our society.

In March 2020 we went into lockdown due to Coronavirus and Tola got a 'break' from school. She became inspired by *Black Lives Matter* and her brother is proud of her for using her social media to try to spread awareness of the racial discrimination that goes on in our world, in order to educate others. She has quite a few 'followers', whatever that means, but she has also lost a lot. Sadly, they've all been white.

"They find it hard to accept the truths about racism and its existence."

Tola is now being home-schooled. She will sit her GCSEs in the summer of 2021 and is looking forward to starting her A levels at a college in England.

Mothers

Loving someone of colour and having racial bias are not mutually exclusive. Just because someone has racial bias, it does not mean that they are incapable of loving someone of colour.

I would like to explain my relationship with my mum. I have no doubt that my mum loves me, I truly don't; but unfortunately, her love gets suffocated and strangled by her fear and bias. Her loving me doesn't mean she sees me as her equal; I love all my dogs, but they are not my equal. Her loving me doesn't mean she is free from racial bias. However, my mum is a victim of racism herself.

She was only 20 years old when she met my dad and at that point, her only experience of the world was what she had grown up with in Caldercruix; a tiny, rural, papermaking and mining village with a population of just a few hundred, seven miles outside the town of Airdrie. In her little world she was popular, had attended the grammar school in the much bigger town of Coatbridge, loved to go dancing at the *Pally* and had enjoyed some boyfriends – even once being engaged. When my mum first met my dad, she had never met anyone black before and by her own admission, she was terrified of him.

My dad was handsome, well-educated and had worked in London in the financial sector after university, before moving to Glasgow around 1969 to work in the same company that my mum worked in as a secretary. They started their relationship, with my mum falling head over heels in love with my dad; but he was different: he was black.

Everything she had ever learned in life taught her that he was not the same as white people – not equal to white people. Society told her she was above him and, based on her behaviour towards him whenever they disagreed, she obviously believed it. I do believe she loved him deeply, but society told her this wasn't okay and even after marrying my dad and moving to London, she still struggled to really accept other black people and their cultures. She didn't know the importance of this.

I do believe that she did the best she could with the knowledge that she had at the time; however, being a white mother of mixed-race children with no one of colour in her life to educate her meant she never understood her own unconscious racism. She still doesn't and this continues to be a huge issue in society today. I've had so many white clients with mixed-race children who have no black influences in their lives whatsoever. This can be so damaging. As an adult and with the knowledge of unconscious, racial bias, I can now understand her actions, but as a child it was soul-destroying.

She did show me love when we lived in London - and it was a real love - but when we moved to Scotland, her unconscious, racial bias was blindly led by what society told her. The world shamed her, through her children, for being 'a black man's whore'; something she was called many times. She still carries this shame and it keeps her from seeing the truth of what kind of mother she was to me. She lives blinkered in her world which only serves to keep her further from the truth. I've lived in that world for most of my life and it is one of the reasons I have written this book. I couldn't let her fear control my world, or the truth, any longer.

This is how deeply the pandemic of racism is embedded in all our homes - even the homes of the victims.

I don't regret the decisions and choices I've made in my life, but I do have a deep regret for not being the mother I am today back when Michelle made her allegations. I haven't said much about my oldest child as I don't think it would be fair. My daughter was used by people who were racist - my own mother included. We have all paid a massive price, with Michelle still paying that price today. She is trapped in the toxic family that took me 33 years to escape from and not a single day passes when I don't think of her. I pray she will find her way out. If she ever does, I'll be here waiting, just as I have always been.

When I lost the children, I learned as a mother that we do not own our children. They are a gift and it is our responsibility to nurture and protect them. They are not our property and we cannot tell them how they feel. They are their own beings with their own voices and we are supposed to hear and validate their feelings with kindness and love, no matter how difficult that is for us mothers. I find it incomprehensible that any parent would rather believe their child doesn't have the capacity to truly know how they feel for themselves - about themselves - than accept they are struggling with their own control. In saying this, maybe I'm being judgemental, but I believe it is a good judgement.

By us parents accepting our control limitations, we can begin to accept the truth - that our feelings are exclusively ours and not our children's – which can allow us to hear and accept our children. Joy is that gift tenfold; how could I ever think I knew how she felt about herself better than she did? I couldn't; her revealing her utmost, intimate feelings – and me hearing her - allowed me to get my child back.

Being a mother is the hardest job I have ever had and by far the most rewarding. It is through my children that I have grown the most in my life, learning something new every day: unconditional love.

To all my children, from the depths of my soul, thank you. I'm a very proud mother.

My ride or die

There are not enough words to say how grateful I am for having my husband in my life. For the past 20 years he has completely shared my life. He is my best friend and no one knows me like he does. This book would not have been written in this way had it not been for him. I have written every word – but not always in the correct way. Being dyslexic, my words don't always translate from my mind to paper in the same order, but Craig knows me so deeply that he always understood what I was trying to say.

Each night during the process of writing my first draft, I would share a bottle of *Brother's Toffee Apple Cider* with Craig while he read over what I had written that day. Quite a few empty bottles later, I gave Craig the first completed draft for him to 'correct and tidy' as we called it. It was very difficult for him to read that first draft. A lot of tears were shed even although he knew me and my story inside out. Reading the small details of a loved one's life is very different to knowing their story. My experience of shopping for strawberry bon bons gets him every time.

From the moment I met Craig he believed in me - no matter what the cost was to him. When we had the conversation about what details would need to be written in the book, he had no objections. He is deeply proud of me and has always stood by me in the challenges I have faced, even if he doesn't always quite understand my process; he believes in my choices.

Writing this book together has been very special for many reasons: the sharing of memories, the reminiscing over our love and its beautiful and passionate origin, and for allowing us both the chance to relive a time – the time before what lay ahead – when all we knew was just pure love.

It's that deep foundation of the pure love we share for each other that has brought us this far. I can truly say his is the deepest love I have ever felt for another human being. And for that same human being to believe in me is one of the most precious gifts in my life. It's simple: he's my ride or die.

My husband is an amazing father and always has been. Sola and Joy have had Craig in their lives since they were three and five years old and they love him as their dad. Even in the years when people were calling him a monster, when he was being humiliated and shamed for something he hadn't done, he supported our children and always put them first. He was the one who drove up and down that road to facilitate the visits he wasn't permitted to attend, because that's what his family needed, because he saw that as his responsibility; a father's responsibility.

My husband is an angel sent from God and without him we would not be the strong family that we are. I will be eternally grateful to him for being in our lives. Our children feel the same.

Elaine

Have you ever had one of those moments when you first meet someone, where they make you feel so comfortable you could swear you've met them before? You both click, right into place, as if they've always been in your life. Well, this was how I felt the first time I met Elaine over twelve years ago.

Elaine first appeared in my life as a client when I was working in the first clinic we opened in Nairn. We shared a connection to Lagos, as she had spent some time living and working there. She was one of those people you just know are meant to be in your life.

Elaine is English but has been living in the Highlands for over 30 years. When I first met her, she had a high-powered, corporate job and came across as super-smart, but she was much more than that. She was incredibly funny and completely humble and, before her injury, had been part of the mountain rescue service.

For some reason I trusted her. I don't know why - I don't trust people very easily. I had always trusted people to be people, meaning human beings are capable of anything, but being in Elaine's company allowed me to be Kemi - the true Kemi that no one really sees or really knows.

Over the course of treating her on those winter's nights, I found myself opening up to her. I shocked myself the night I told her. She had been talking about her winter project - writing a novel – when my words fell out.

"I have a story you can write - you might not believe me though."

She was intrigued and so we set a date to meet up the following week. I told her my story while we sat in front of the big, blazing wood burner in her conservatory. I remember being very nervous about sharing my experiences of the Social Work Department and the courts, the shame associated with those events, and of what I had been accused. I was concerned that she wouldn't believe me, but ever since we arranged the meeting, there had been a part of me that knew I had to share my story with her.

She was shocked, but she believed me - and she believed in me - and with her kindness, agreed to help me by writing my story. It was perfect.

In the beginning, publishing was never on my mind. I had only wanted Elaine to write my story for when my children were older, so they would know the truth. We only met up a few times to discuss the book, but ultimately, life kept getting in the way of any progress, with Elaine always joking: "One of these winters, I will get your story done." We continued to meet up regardless and we would always talk a little about the book, but instead of a book being created, a friendship was.

It was during one of my morning walks with Craig and the dogs along the river in the forest - prompted by the *Black Trans Lives Matter* events I described at the beginning of this book - that I decided that I would start writing my story. And before a single word had been written, I knew Elaine would be the first person I would give it to. So, after I wrote the book, and after Craig had gone through it looking for corrections, I sent it off to Elaine for her honest opinion. This was her email reply:

What can I say? 'Wow' springs to mind, but it is a vast understatement. You are amazing, this is powerful and yes, it should be published. There is stuff that needs to be worked on to get it to that point (but only in small measure) and I would love to help you with that.

I am so glad that I failed miserably to get your story out sooner (like, it was only about 12 years ago that you asked me!!). My failure, along with recent events have enabled you to do this and no one could ever have written this on your behalf – the power, passion and sheer bravery shine through every word and I could never have done it justice. The very least I can do is work with you (which I would love to do if you are happy to have me).

Elaine would email me every day, subtly asking what at first appeared to be a random and irrelevant question regarding a chapter. Whenever I sat down to go back through the chapter to answer her question, I would open up - emotionally unravel – before being passionately compelled to rewrite whole sections at a time, including how I had felt and how I was affected - the good and the bad. The book more than doubled in size and suddenly went from being a document of evidence to a memoir of my life filled with all its emotions. Now that I have been unravelled and found true understanding of how my life has been, I can move forward in every part of it with my truth.

This book would not exist if it wasn't for Elaine. Without her belief and encouragement, I would never have done this. She has been with me, beside me, through each step of this book, just like how throughout the years she has always been there in our friendship.

Elaine thinks that by me re-sculpting her amazingly strong body I changed her life, but the truth is I don't have enough words to describe what her presence has done to help me shape my life. This has been a deeply cathartic experience for me and my whole family and I will carry Elaine in my heart forever. She is my mentor and life coach. She is my gate keeper; she held my story and kept it alive until I was ready to move forward and take full ownership of it. She helped me find my voice. Elaine is more than all these things to me; she is my sister. I knew that first night I drove away from her cottage that she would help me to heal. I told her my story and she held it for me until I was ready; well-healed.

I would like to share what Elaine gave to me on my 40th birthday - her introduction to 'Well-healed', my story.

We met

"Quite seriously," said Nan, "I think you should go and see her, she's amazing. She's fixed my back and after 20 years of pain, that's quite something."

I wasn't so sure; the saga of my knackered knee had been going on for nearly six years already and everyone I went to see after my disastrous key-hole operation told me the same story: "Don't do this . . . you can't do that . . . you'll have to slow down . . " I really didn't feel the need to go and hear someone else repeat the same old lines; all I wanted to do was get my life back and run again and I'd tried just about everything. However, my curiosity was aroused – who was this woman and what did she do?

"I'd heard loads of good reports about her," said Nan, "so I decided to give her a try and I'm really glad I did. You really should go Elaine; you'll love her she's half Nigerian."

Having just spent a few months working in Nigeria, I did have a soft spot for its people and their open-hearted, happy-go-lucky attitude, regardless of whether or not there was someone trying to do you out of your cash at the first opportunity!

Fast forward six months and many deliberations and procrastinations later.

It was one of those pitch-black, wet and miserable, early November evenings that seem to last for an eternity in the North of Scotland. I found myself walking into what had to be the tiniest 'sports clinic' I had ever visited. There was no one around, so I sat down in the waiting room, in front of the flickering Calor gas heater, taking in the musky smell of massage oil and scented candles. As I surveyed my surroundings, I could hear voices upstairs and was already beginning to get cold feet about the whole thing. Then the previous client came down the stairs, followed by the mysterious Nigerian lady. Sitting in front of this beautiful, almond-eyed woman, telling her the long and sorry saga of my knee was a strange experience. And I'll be very honest, when the broad Glaswegian accent came back at me, all I could think was that I'd made a very big mistake. Glaswegians are the world's best salespeople and here she was selling her services; telling me that I'd be able to run again and that everyone else had been wrong and she could basically work miracles. I almost walked out, but something made me stay. She was the first person who had said positive things in years . . . and that was whilst I still had my trousers on!

As the consultation progressed, I got more and more anxious; she dug her fingers in where no one else had dared to go and the pain was excruciating; what damage was she doing? Why did I come here? This was just terrible. She set to work on what had been described to me by a physiotherapist at the local sports clinic as a piece of bone that had fused itself to a tendon in the back of my knee; this was preventing me from kneeling down: "I'll get rid of that for you," said Kemi, "it's just scar tissue, give me a few minutes."

The consultation ended and she asked me to go back again a week later. I was still cynical as I made the appointment; good Glaswegian sales technique: get 'em bought in to a programme of treatment. I still felt as though I'd been duped as I parted with my £25 at the end of the 45-minute session (years later I realise what an absolute bargain that was!). "You'll feel tired and thirsty, and your urine will probably be quite deep in colour as your body flushes out all that rubbish," were her parting words.

I have to admit that as I walked down the street to my car, my knee felt unusually easy, but it wasn't until I got home that the full extent of the treatment became evident. On feeling the back of my knee where the lump of bone was fused to the tendon, I couldn't find it . . . it had gone. Gingerly, I tried to kneel down and did so without any pain or obstruction for the first time in over five years. I was hooked.

Over the next few days, I was tired and thirsty and guess what? Yes, I had darker than normal coloured urine – and that was without a glass of wine.

And mine isn't the only story like that. Her reputation has spread far and wide and she provides relief and hope to many people, with her unique brand of natural, organic, Nigerian-Glaswegian care and attention. I now treat both my legs to a 'Kemi' once a month and through her I have resumed hill-walking, managed the occasional run without pain and swelling and I'm really enjoying my active, outdoor life. We've become firm friends and she has also worked her magic on various parts of my husband's anatomy . . . and those of my incredibly active friends too.

It was whilst gritting my teeth over the months and in fact years – as Kemi moved muscles and tendons that I never knew I had – that I learned that this lady had a big story to tell. A huge story. Locally, we had already accepted her as some kind of witch doctor that healed everything, but nobody had any idea of the hardship that this woman had gone through to enable her to do just that – heal people. Heal people; protect her children; adore her husband; stay sane.

Kemi's is a monumental story of a woman's determination to provide the best possible life for those closest to her and to make a difference to other people's lives. Imagine my delight at being asked to tell this story for you. As Nan said, she's amazing.

From reading Elaine's intro, you get a very different view of me - certainly not one that suggests any evidence of the struggles I have detailed. I wanted to share the woman that people see every day. I feel it is important to share this with you to hopefully give you inspiration.

In my story, there is a lot of shame and fear and by reading my words, you will have shared my pain. I believe that all the pain and suffering in our lives provides an opportunity for growth and learning. I have come to understand my own pain and transformed it into a tool for helping others. This tool is what has helped me accompany them on their journey through their pain. This has been my dark night of the soul and it is what has made me truly successful in my helping others transform their lives.

We never know what is really going on in someone else's life. Owing to my work, the people in my life - clients and friends - see the part of me that has worked hard and achieved amazing success within my area of expertise. In the last 18 years I have never done a day's advertising, have always had a full diary of clientele and now a six-month waiting list. I have clients that travel to me from all over the UK, along with clients from all over the world who attend via Zoom.

My story is not who I am; I am who I am because of my story.

How far we've come

Writing has gone some way towards helping to heal the traumas I never believed could happen, along with some shameful wounds I hadn't realised I carried. It's allowed me to unburden, to process, to acknowledge. In recounting my life and its ever-present themes of unconscious, racial bias and racism, I have gained a deeper understanding of myself and of society. Throughout my life I have had to accept that existing in my brown skin was a problem - that I was a problem and that nothing would ever change. Society dictated so. Now however, highlighted by the global support of *Black Lives Matter,* I believe that everybody has an opportunity for change and to make things better in our world. Racism hasn't suddenly disappeared, nor will it, but for the first time in my life an awareness of its existence has emerged and I now have hope for us all as a society.

This awareness has encouraged white people to add their voices, very loudly, to this conversation. We are all learning, but for me and for any person of colour, this is a huge step forward. It doesn't matter how bad the situation looks or sounds - it doesn't even matter that some believe us and some strongly deny it - what matters are the voices that are now having the conversation. We will all learn if we talk together and this is how I believe true change comes about.

This is the reason I have shared my story. I wanted to share and inform on how racism has affected me and my family. With information we gain knowledge and with knowledge we can then enter the realm of acceptance. From here, we have a choice in how we go forward. There will be people who choose not to change, but I believe those people will be in the minority, as I truly believe most of us will choose to go forward in a better way.

It's been my experience that our biggest struggles tend to make us stronger. This conversation is going to be a struggle; however, no matter how uncomfortable it is to participate - for both people of colour and white people - we all must accept and work through the barrage of emotions that will undoubtedly arise to achieve change: anger to compassion; confusion to understanding; shame and blame to acceptance; all leading to change. It doesn't matter how bad some things appear, as long as we are seeing them. Again, awareness. If we can see it, it can be changed and made better.

The awareness of racism and unconscious, racial bias existing in our world has sent shockwaves reverberating throughout society and has created a movement of people determined to drive us forward to find our own new way together. We are finally looking at racism and we are finally gaining understanding. A ripple of change is occurring where previously there has been a struggle to gain acknowledgement.

As I began, I believe that unconscious, racial bias and racism are woven in the foundations of our society's tapestry, and while society has evolved, its institutions and out-dated beliefs have not. This is preventing us from being able to accept one another. As we come to realise and understand that our social structures are built on the beliefs and fears of our ancestors and their lack of understanding, we can move forward in our fight to rid ourselves of racism and unconscious, racial bias.

People of colour have always had race-related conversations, in the safety of our own groups and families. This is one of the ways we have survived. It is how we have had to raise our children - to endure - as we didn't believe change would be in our lifetime. However, white people are now having their own conversations too.

During the time of writing this book I've heard of more and more white people being part of unconscious, racial bias awareness groups, to investigate and better understand their own beliefs. Again, awareness. Unconscious, racial bias groups have popped up everywhere, allowing white people to look at their own privilege. They too need a safe space to be open and honest about their feelings and beliefs, to be able work through the undoubted feelings of shame that will arise. For some white people it may be difficult to look at and that's why these groups are so important.

This is an amazing first step forward and I believe it will help, but this alone will not generate enough change. White voices alone will not get us there. Only a person of colour knows how racism feels, so to truly move forward, people of colour need to be involved. White people, just like people of colour, cannot solely and independently decide how to end racism; both sides need to be present for this solution. We must come together to do this.

I understand that there will be a reluctance and a hesitation from some people of colour to talk to white people, to educate them about racism and all its forms. I get it; we are tired of struggling to be heard. However, right now, there is an audience of people – white people – wanting change, ready to listen and more importantly, ready to be educated. And who better to educate them than us: people of colour. So again, I do understand the reluctance and hesitation to educate, but right now - more than ever, people of colour – it is our responsibility to do everything possible to change the narrative for the next generation. To not want to be part of that is not okay. We all have to move through this and be part of this change together.

Once again, Nicola Sturgeon, First Minister of Scotland, is calling for an independent Scotland, saying that this is what the people want. Which people? Certainly not all the people. The people are divided. I would like to mention that I personally have never seen a person of colour being part of the pro-independence supporters. This division breeds racism in Scotland and has created a space for some people to be openly racist. It has driven the disconnection between white people and people of colour. Independence is all the Scottish government has spoken about for the past 10 years. They haven't focused on Scotland, just their own hatred of England and the English. If Scotland can't accept the English, how have people of colour got any chance? They don't. I know, I'm one of them.

I recently watched *Panorama's: I can't Breathe: Black and Dead in Custody*, an investigation into why black men in the UK are more likely than white men to have force used on them by police and to die in police custody. One of the cases followed Sheku Bayoh, a young black man who died while in police custody in Kirkcaldy, Scotland, in 2015.

The police were responding to calls of a black male, possibly intoxicated, erratically wandering the streets early on a Sunday morning carrying a knife. However, when the police arrived at the scene, Sheku no longer had a knife and was calmly walking away. Despite this, within 30 seconds the officers had used their batons and pepper spray, within 45 seconds Sheku lay pinned to the ground under six officers and within five minutes, while both his hands and legs were bound, he fell unconscious under their weight. Sheku was pronounced dead in hospital within 90 minutes of the police having arrived. He had 23 injuries, including a cracked rib and head wounds consistent with baton use.

At the time, both the police and the media accused Sheku of repeatedly stamping on a female officer, with written statements from several of the officers stating so. *The Scottish Sun* newspaper ran a full page spread titled, 'A petite female officer was punched, kicked and stamped on by a large man' – a quote attributed to a police union chief.

Two of the officers involved included the attack in their statements. PC Craig Walker recounted: "I had a clear view of him . . . he had his arms raised up at right angles to his body and brought his right foot down in a full-force stamp on to her lower back", while PC Ashley Tomlinson stated, "I thought he had killed her. He stomped on her back again".

PC Nicole Short, the alleged, attacked officer, failed to mention the stamping in her statement.

The officers' statements were littered with terminology such as: "I cannot emphasise the strength of this guy" and: "He was massive and is the biggest male that I have seen". Sheku Bayoh was 5ft 10in and weighed just under 13 stone. Two of the officers involved in the restraint were 6ft 4in, with one of them tipping the scales at 25 stone.

One of the officers even went as far as to use the derogatory term "coloured" in her statement and admitted because Sheku was black, she thought he could have been a terrorist: "I was also thinking at that point of the Lee Rigby incident in London, mainly due to the coloured male and the potential terrorist connotations."

Police Investigation and Review Commissioner (PIRC), the executive, non-departmental, public body of the Scottish Government that investigates complaints raised by the public against Police Scotland, launched an investigation into the circumstances surrounding Sheku's death. Sixteen months later, PIRC presented its findings to Lord Advocate, James Wolffe, Scotland's most senior prosecutor, for review.

In October 2018, the Lord Advocate came to the decision that no criminal, corporate or health and safety charges would be brought against the officers involved.

However, an eyewitness to the whole incident, Kevin Nelson, a white man, told *Panorama* that what he witnessed did not match the officers' versions of events. He saw Sheku trying to walk away from the officers before being sprayed with CS spray and that it was only then that Sheku retaliated by swinging a single punch, which knocked an officer to the ground. "He was running off . . . after the punch, there was no more attack on her at all." When asked about PC Walker's claims, Mr Nelson replied: "That never happened. I didn't see him stamping at all or, other than the punch, any raised arms."

Mr Nelson gave his account to PIRC two days after the incident. It was a further 30 days before the officers gave their accounts. Nobody from PIRC contacted Mr Nelson to investigate the discrepancies. After the Lord Advocate's decision not to prosecute, Mr Nelson decided to speak out about the officers: "They made the incident worse than it actually was just to justify what had happened and . . . that's not right."

Furthermore, CCTV and mobile phone footage of the incident later emerged – and it supports Mr Nelson's claims - which prompted Sheku's family to request a review of the Lord Advocate's decision. The Lord Advocate upheld his original decision stating there would be no criminal proceedings against the police.

Six months after the incident, the then Chief Constable Stephen House resigned after being criticised for visiting the officers involved in the restraint before meeting with Sheku's family. None of the officers has been disciplined; no criminal charges have ever been brought forward, while two of the officers have since retired early on medical grounds.

A public inquiry was opened on 30th November, 2020 to investigate the immediate circumstances leading to the death of Sheku, how the police dealt with the aftermath, the subsequent investigation into his death and whether race was a factor. The inquiry is expected to last a couple of years.

Panorama did an amazing job of highlighting awareness of unconscious, racial bias. *I Can't Breathe* was honestly terrifying and terrifyingly honest, but it showed how white people can have beliefs and bias about black people, especially if they haven't had any real interaction with people of colour.

Let's accept the officers' accounts to be their honest recollections and their true feelings surrounding the fatal incident. By their own admissions they believed Sheku to be a huge black man with monstrous super-strength and they felt immediately threatened upon arrival, despite Sheku no longer appearing erratic. Why? Because this is a real belief that some white people harbour – some without even realising they do. We need to mix more - share more; to educate. We need to get to know one another, or we won't ever learn. Laws alone are not enough.

I have always loved the Royal Family. As a little girl, I grew up with a fairy tale impression of them – and I am grateful for that. I got to enjoy being part of my Scottish gran's tradition of loving them and watching them whenever they were on TV. I especially enjoyed watching the weddings of the princesses, Diana Spencer and Sarah Ferguson. When I lived in London, I would often go to Buckingham Palace with my gran, while our house was always filled with all kinds of royal memorabilia, from commemorative cups and plates through to coins and everything else in between.

So, when it came time for me to start my own tradition with my own children, I remember watching William and Kate's wedding with Tola, feeling really excited. However, I can't even begin to describe the feelings of pride I felt – we felt – me, Joy and Tola, watching Harry and Meghan's wedding. We were so proud; we had our first brown princess in the Royal Family!

She represented so much for my family and any person of colour. It was a statement - a brown Princess in the Royal Family - and it was an opportunity to lead the way forward; an example for others to follow. I saw it as such an important moment, not just for the UK, but for the whole world. We had reached the moment of acceptance; we were finally ready. She was a beacon of light and brought hope in how far we had come, but it was an illusion; we weren't ready.

During the final stages of writing my book, Oprah's colossal interview, *Oprah with Meghan & Harry*, aired sending global tremors. The biggest shockwave centred around claims of racism within the Royal Family. Regarding their then unborn baby, Archie, the couple gave an insight into their experiences, confessing there were "concerns and conversations about how dark his skin might be when he's born".

Some described this as a shocking revelation. If you've made it this far in my book, you won't be surprised that I wasn't shocked - but nor was I angry; I was hopeful. Hopeful for yet another opportunity for conversation: a global discussion on racism. And thankfully, that's exactly what happened. The media went into a frenzy: TV, radio, the internet . . . everywhere. Everyone was talking about it - conversations that wouldn't normally occur - debates on whether the Royal Family could have racist views and unconscious, racial bias and if so, what did that mean for Britain as a whole.

Buckingham Palace's response on behalf of Her Majesty The Queen was: "The issues raised, particularly that of race, are concerning. While some recollections may vary, they are taken very seriously and will be addressed by the family privately."

I found it a shame that the statement fell short of publicly acknowledging and condemning racism, however my eyes were fixed on the change and not on the shame. I take this statement to show signs of change, as usually whenever an institution is accused of being racist, the response, more often than not, is a defiant denial. However, here there was no defiant denial, no refusal to accept the possibility of racism or unconscious, racial bias existing. There was an element of acceptance in acknowledging that no household or family is exempt from unconscious, racial bias.

I do not believe the Royal Family to be racist, but like everyone, I have no doubt they have been affected by the racism that is embedded in our whole social system. As far as I'm concerned, the Queen herself, regardless of the content of the story, has accepted that unconscious, racial bias could exist within the Family and has said that it will be looked at. I must believe people are capable of change - and trust them when they say they are open to change.

It was agony witnessing the media's racist coverage, their attempts to destroy Meghan because of the colour of her skin, especially when it appeared only people of colour could see it for what it was. I am so fed-up of hearing white people argue the media are not racist. Surprise! This behaviour is racist and every person of colour knows it. We've all shared the same experience - we've all received the same treatment. The UK media's stance is that they are not racist, but to me, they remind me of all the 'non-racists' I have come into contact with in my life; you know, the ones who aren't racist until their child brings home their new partner of colour.

Regardless of title, Meghan is the UK's first brown princess - she's the wife of a prince, but more than that, she is a gift. When they got married, we all believed we had changed so much as a society. We haven't; the UK wasn't ready for her. However, because of their marriage, the UK's unconscious, racial bias - the bias that most people were not aware existed, while others denied it - has been exposed. The awareness that this has brought is so valuable to our society because now that we can see it exists, we can change it. This was the gift.

I am truly sorry Meghan had to endure this treatment, but I am so grateful that she did. I believe our history books – our new history books – will signify a huge change for true equality in the UK because of our brown princess.

Epilogue

I woke up filled with excitement on that beautiful spring morning. I had finished writing my book and bar a few, last-minute alterations, I would be handing *Brown Girl in the Ring* over to Elaine the following day, for a final proofread. I felt so proud of myself for having managed to complete it.

During our morning walk through the forest with our little dog Merlin, Craig and I spoke about our desire – our intention – our need to get out of Scotland and return to the only place I've known to feel like home.

"We'll be gone by the summer Kem," Craig assured me as we made our way to the top of the world.

The 'top of the world', as we call it, is the highest part of the forest, elevated so high it offers spectacular views of the rolling fields scattered with sheep, the ever-flowing River Findhorn and its 'wadered' fishermen, and the array and abundance of trees that spread as far as your eyes can see. You really do feel like you're standing at the top of the world.

"I know, I can feel it," I replied excitedly while absorbing the breath-taking view, "but I will miss this place. I'm so glad that I will be leaving having finally found some form of peace with the land in which I was born."

"I'm just ready to go - the sooner the better," Craig said definitively. My husband, like my children, has always lived as a minority and desperately wants to experience living among people with whom he can identify and who recognise his culture.

"I don't think I'll ever come back to Scotland after we've gone," I said, surprising myself.

"I don't think you will - why would you want to?" Craig validated as he launched himself into the brambles to find Merlin's ball.

Friday 31st March 2021

I awoke to the familiar and comforting sounds of the resident woodpecker's drilling drumroll on the massive oak tree in my garden and the hypnotic rumbling of the neighbouring farmer's tractor as he tended to the field. Within five minutes and with two freshly brewed cups of coffee in hand, I climbed back into bed and gazed out over the lime-green fields to the line of pine trees that now surrounded and hid Darnaway Castle from my view.

I was already planning my day ahead: coffee in bed, forest walk with Craig and dogs, and then send my epilogue to Elaine for her final proofread before it goes off to the publisher, when the castle bells rang out their daily 9am alert; my signal to catch up on any emails and news updates. As I opened my phone and swiped to my widget page, a four-word headline screamed out at me causing me instant anxiety: Government Race Report Released. I quickly locked the screen refusing to start my day in fear and sat my phone back down on the bedside table. I needed my caffeine before I could even begin to look at the news feed.

"Thanks for the coffee," Craig said, kissing me while getting back into bed. *Beep.* "Who's that interrupting our coffee?" he teasingly joked.

As I looked at my phone, I could see an email from Elaine. Subject: Racism Report, followed by: "Have you seen this?"

"Kemi, there's a report out," Craig said, his eyes firmly fixed on his phone.

"I know – Elaine's just emailed - and I saw it was on my news feed," I replied, opening my phone to find out what was going on. The UK is not institutionally racist was as much as I could stomach reading.

"Kem, this is a joke!" Craig spat, while continuing to read the report aloud.

"Craig, I can't do this just now . . . it's too much."

I was sickened and shell-shocked; how could this be happening? I had literally just finished writing my piece on the Royal Family and within a day, here was the government trying to whitewash the existence of institutional racism.

"I thought we were further forward than this - this is very damaging," I said, massaging my neck, now seizing like it always did whenever I felt scared.

"Listen to this: the guy who wrote it is black . . . doesn't even believe in racial bias . . . and has publicly been homophobic!" Craig, clearly irritated, continued reading the findings.

"Craig, I need to take some time before I look at this properly," I said with determination. I could not bear to hear another word.

"Okay, sorry. I'm just so angry," he said, looking defeated as he closed his phone.

When I finally read some of the report that evening, I was left feeling unvalidated as a person of colour, consumed with anger and deflated with disappointment.

Five days after the release, I was still disappointed, but not surprised. At best, it highlights the ignorant disregard and disconnection the UK government has for people of colour and confirms they're too far removed to understand the existence of racism experienced everyday throughout every institution. At worst, they're gaslighting the situation, intentionally provoking a reaction of anger from people of colour in a bid to discredit support and understanding. Is it a coincidence the report was released while the government discusses giving police greater powers (Police, Crime, Sentencing and Courts Bill) in regard to public protesting? Under the amended bill, damage to memorials, (such as the toppling of slave trader Edward Colston's statue in Bristol during one of many anti-racism demonstrations throughout the UK following the death of George Floyd) could result in a ten-year custodial sentence.

I see this report to be nothing more than a distraction from what is important and what is really going on in our society. I feel there is a big movement to end racism in the UK - not from our government, but from the people. The power is in the people and the people will take us forward. I believe that if the people can change, so too can the government, but if this government doesn't change, I believe there are enough of us to change the government. The report is a distraction; I choose not to be distracted.

One thing we, people of colour, have learned through our struggles is that we are strong, and we can certainly endure. It is with this strength we can walk this new path – together, with white people. Their voices, mixed with ours, will be what is heard; only then. However, only we, people of colour, know what is needed to be equal, to feel equal; only we know what an acceptable society for us to live in feels like and that is why we must lead the direction.

"I have a dream that my four little children will one day live in a nation where they will not be judged by the color of their skin, but by the content of their character." Martin Luther King Jnr

We are now at the point in time that our ancestors - Martin Luther King, Rosa Parks, Nelson Mandela, to name but a few - have told us about; instilled hope in us about. We have now arrived at the time that we have all dreamed about: the time of change. We are taking a monumental step forward; the power has always been in the people. We change how we live; and we are doing it. My eyes are firmly fixed on the change I am seeing and I have belief that we all can move forward out of racism together. We are changing.

I believe my children will live in a better world.

Acknowledgements

I would like to acknowledge my chosen family, the people in my life whose unconditional love and belief in me has made it possible for me to believe in myself enough to write this book.

David and Sandra Stephens, I am deeply grateful to you for supporting me during a time in my life when I needed a mum and dad. You supported and believed in me in every way possible throughout one of the worst times in my life. You both surrounded me in unconditional love as parents should. Without you I do not think I would be here today.

William O'Connor, my first and most significant teacher; from you I have learned the most about who I am. You taught me how to understand myself and accept my life. You taught me that my learning was bigger and more important than any of the crises in my life. In friendship, you gave me acceptance and unconditional love and have never gone back on your promise of always being there.

To my girls, Chrisanthe Georgiou and Shirley Barr. You both came into my life at a point in time when I didn't know I needed girlfriends, but through your support during Joy's transition, you have shown me that the unexpected surprises can be the most valuable. You both have taught me that friendship is a safe place to be vulnerable and I look forward to our future memories and cocktails.

Tanja Wright, one of the strongest women I have ever known. Our friendship deepened during lockdown when you turned up as a PPE angel to help look after Joy. You were the first person to ask me if I was okay during the BLM protests. I was shocked and terrified at the same time, but because of the type of person you are, you taught me that it can be safe to talk about racism. Without the strength your friendship has given me, I would not have the courage to be able to speak openly and honestly about my experiences. I will be forever grateful.

Will Russell and Angie Alexandra, thank you both for sparing so much time, making a very difficult experience possible; for easing me with your support, love and friendship and for turning the fearful photo shoot into a fun-filled day out with friends.

Colin. You were one of the few people with whom I was desperate to share my book. More than a dear friend: a father-figure; someone I admire, respect and love. You were always there for me, offering support and advice, throughout the last nine years of my life. You knew nothing about my previous life, but have helped me understand what justice really means. I'm not sure why you showed me the care and kindness that you did, but you have helped me to believe in and value myself, and have taught me to say how I feel, in the now, before it's too late.

Sadly, Colin died a couple of weeks before my book went to the publisher. I will miss our walks and deep conversations.

Finally, to the team at New Generation Publishing, thank you all for your great service and for giving new writers like me the chance to have our work published. In a world where traditional publishing houses seem to favour celebrity authors over anyone else, the service you provide is invaluable to the writers of the future.

Printed in Great Britain
by Amazon